The Death Arts in Renaissance England

The first-ever critical anthology of the death arts in Renaissance England, this book draws together over seventy extracts and twenty illustrations to establish and analyse how people grappled with mortality in the sixteenth and seventeenth centuries. As well as providing a comprehensive resource of annotated and modernized excerpts, this engaging study includes commentary on authors and overall texts, discussions of how each excerpt is constitutive and expressive of the death arts, and suggestions for further reading. The extended Introduction considers death's intersections with print, gender, sex, and race, surveying the period's far-reaching preoccupation with, and anticipatory reflection upon, the cessation of life. For researchers, instructors, and students interested in medieval and early modern history and literature, the Reformation, memory studies, book history, and print culture, this indispensable resource provides at once an entry point into the field of early modern death studies and a springboard for further research.

WILLIAM E. ENGEL is the Nick B. Williams Professor of Literature at the University of the South, Sewanee. He is the author of five books on literary history, memory studies, and applied emblematics, including *Mapping Mortality* (University of Massachusetts Press, 1995) and *Death and Drama in Renaissance England* (Oxford University Press, 2002), and co-editor of *The Memory Arts in Renaissance England: A Critical Anthology* (Cambridge University Press, 2016). He is on the editorial board of *Renaissance Quarterly* and served two terms as the Renaissance Society of America's Discipline Representative for Emblems.

RORY LOUGHNANE is Reader in Early Modern Studies at the University of Kent. He is the author and editor of many books and play editions, including, for Cambridge University Press, *Late Shakespeare, 1608–1613* (2012), *The Memory Arts in Renaissance England: A Critical Anthology* (2016), and *Early Shakespeare, 1588–1594* (2020). He is a general editor of The Revels Plays series (Manchester University Press) and a series editor of *Elements in Shakespeare and Text* (Cambridge University Press).

GRANT WILLIAMS is Associate Professor of English at Carleton University, Canada. He has co-edited four collections: *Forgetting in Early Modern English Literature and Culture: Lethe's Legacies* (Routledge, 2004), *Ars reminiscendi: Memory and Culture in the Renaissance* (CRRS, 2009), *Taking Exception to the Law: Materializing Injustice in Early Modern English Literature* (University of Toronto Press, 2015), and *The Memory Arts in Renaissance England: A Critical Anthology* (Cambridge University Press, 2016). With Donald Beecher, he is co-editor of Henry Chettle's *Kind-Heart's Dream* and *Piers Plainness: Two Pamphlets from the Elizabethan Book Trade* (CRRS, 2021).

THE DEATH ARTS IN RENAISSANCE ENGLAND

A Critical Anthology

✥

Edited by

WILLIAM E. ENGEL
University of the South, Sewanee

RORY LOUGHNANE
University of Kent

GRANT WILLIAMS
Carleton University, Ottawa

CAMBRIDGE
UNIVERSITY PRESS

University Printing House, Cambridge CB2 8BS, United Kingdom

One Liberty Plaza, 20th Floor, New York, NY 10006, USA

477 Williamstown Road, Port Melbourne, VIC 3207, Australia

314–321, 3rd Floor, Plot 3, Splendor Forum, Jasola District Centre,
New Delhi – 110025, India

103 Penang Road, #05–06/07, Visioncrest Commercial, Singapore 238467

Cambridge University Press is part of the University of Cambridge.

It furthers the University's mission by disseminating knowledge in the pursuit of education, learning, and research at the highest international levels of excellence.

www.cambridge.org
Information on this title: www.cambridge.org/9781108479271
DOI: 10.1017/9781108782975

© William E. Engel, Rory Loughnane and Grant Williams 2022

This publication is in copyright. Subject to statutory exception and to the provisions of relevant collective licensing agreements, no reproduction of any part may take place without the written permission of Cambridge University Press.

First published 2022

Printed in the United Kingdom by TJ Books Limited, Padstow Cornwall

A catalogue record for this publication is available from the British Library.

Library of Congress Cataloging-in-Publication Data
NAMES: Engel, William E., 1957– author. | Loughnane, Rory, author. |
Williams, Grant, 1965– author.
TITLE: The death arts in Renaissance England : a critical anthology /
edited by William E. Engel, Rory Loughnane, Grant Williams.
DESCRIPTION: Cambridge ; New York, NY : Cambridge University Press, 2022.
IDENTIFIERS: LCCN 2021052126 (print) | LCCN 2021052127 (ebook) | ISBN
9781108479271 (hardback) | ISBN 9781108749565 (paperback) | ISBN
9781108782975 (ebook)
SUBJECTS: LCSH: Death–England–Early works to 1800. | Funeral rites and
ceremonies–England–Early works to 1800. |
Death–England–History–16th century. | Death–England–History–17th
century. | Funeral rites and ceremonies–England–History–16th century.
| Funeral rites and ceremonies–England–History–17th century. | Death
in literature. | English literature–Early modern, 1500-1700–History
and criticism.
CLASSIFICATION: LCC HQ1073.5.G7 D4187 2022 (print) | LCC HQ1073.5.G7
(ebook) | DDC 306.90942–dc23/eng/20211217
LC record available at https://lccn.loc.gov/2021052126
LC ebook record available at https://lccn.loc.gov/2021052127

ISBN 978-1-108-47927-1 Hardback

Cambridge University Press has no responsibility for the persistence or accuracy of URLs for external or third-party internet websites referred to in this publication and does not guarantee that any content on such websites is, or will remain, accurate or appropriate.

No creature under heaven may comfort me but thou, Lord God, the heavenly leech of man's soul which strikest and healest, which bringest a man nigh unto death and after restorest him to life again that he may thereby learn to know his own weakness and imbecility and the more fully to trust in thee.

> Katherine Parr, *Prayers Stirring the Mind unto Heavenly Meditations* (London: 1545; STC 4818), C6^{r-v}

This death is a gate and entrance unto eternal life; there, at the last, are we delivered from all wretchednesses, miseries, carefulness, disquietness, from all errors and juggling casts of the devil, neither shall we any more be defiled with the most stinking filthiness of sin, neither shall we be seduced and led away into heresies or errors, nor yet be thrown headlong into desperation.

> Thomas Becon, *The Solace of the Soul* (London: 1548; STC 1774), B5^{r-v}

The world is a sea, death is a hook, Christ is that fish in whose mouth was found a piece the price of our redemption; the tribute is paid and we are delivered.

> Peter Barker, *A Judicious and Painful Exposition upon the Ten Commandments* (London: 1624; STC 1425), O3^{r}

Towards winter I grew to eat very little, much less than I did before, so that I was exceeding lean, and, at last, nothing but skin and bones. A neighbouring gentlewoman, a very discreet person that had a great desire to see me came in at the back-door of the house unawares and found me in the kitchen, who, after she had seen me, said to Mrs. Wilson, 'She cannot live; she hath death in her face'. I would say still that every bit I did eat hastened my ruin, and that I had it with a dreadful curse; and what I ate increased the fire within me, which would at last burn me up, and I would now willingly live out of hell as long as I could.

> Hannah Allen, *A Narrative of God's Gracious Dealings* (London: 1683; Wing A1025), G6^{v}–G7^{r}

CONTENTS

List of figures	page x
Acknowledgements	xiii
A note on abbreviations	xv
A note on texts	xix

Introduction	1
The Legacy of the Death Arts	1
The Productive Ends of the Death Arts	5
The Visual Proliferation of the Death Arts	14
Representing the Death Arts	26
Gendering Death	27
Sexualizing Death	30
Racializing Death	36
Using this Anthology	43

PART I *Preparatory and Dying Arts*

Introduction to Part I		51
1.1	William Caxton, *To Know Well To Die* (1490)	55
1.2	Anonymous, *The Calendar of Shepherds* (1518)	58
1.3	Thomas Lupset, *The Way of Dying Well* (1534)	65
1.4	Katherine Parr, *The Lamentation of a Sinner* (1547)	69
1.5	Anne Locke, 'A Meditation of a Penitent Sinner' (1560)	72
1.6	John Bradford, *A Fruitful Treatise … against the Fear of Death* (1564)	76
1.7	John Fisher, *A Spiritual Consolation* (1578)	80
1.8	Robert Greene, *The Repentance of Robert Greene* (1592)	83
1.9	William Perkins, *A Salve For A Sick Man* (1595)	86
1.10	Dorothy Leigh, *The Mother's Blessing* (1616)	90
1.11	George Wither, Selected Works (1628, 1635)	93
1.12	Anonymous, 'The Unnatural Wife' (1628)	103
1.13	Jane Owen, *An Antidote against Purgatory* (1634)	109

I.14	Jeremy Taylor, *Holy Dying* (1651)	112
I.15	John Batchiler, *The Virgin's Pattern* (1661)	116
I.16	James Janeway, *A Token for Children* (1676)	120
I.17	Samuel Smith, 'A True Account of … Last Dying Speeches' (1690)	123

PART II Funereal and Commemorative Arts

Introduction to Part II		129
II.1	Edward Hall and Richard Grafton, *Chronicles* (1548)	133
II.2	Thomas Cranmer, 'The Order for the Burial of the Dead' (1549)	136
II.3	Church of England, *The Primer Set Forth at Large* (1559)	141
II.4	John Foxe, *Acts and Monuments* (1576)	145
II.5	William Allen, *The Glorious Martyrdom of Twelve Priests* (1582)	150
II.6	John Philips, *The Life and Death of Sir Philip Sidney* (1587)	153
II.7	Anne Dowriche, *The French History* (1589)	159
II.8	Mary Sidney, 'Doleful Lay of Clorinda' (1595)	163
II.9	Thomas Dekker, Selected Works (1603, 1604)	168
II.10	Martin Day, 'A Mirror of Modesty' (1621)	173
II.11	Lancelot Andrewes, 'A Sermon … the 5th of November, 1606' (1629)	178
II.12	Thomas Heywood, *The Phoenix of these Late Times* (1637)	181
II.13	Charles I, *Eikon Basilike* (1649)	185
II.14	Francis Beaumont, 'An Elegy on the Lady Markham' (1653)	188
II.15	Thomas Brooks, *A String of Pearls* (1657)	193
II.16	Katherine Philips, *Poems* (1669)	196
II.17	Mary Astell, 'An Essay upon Death' (1696)	201

PART III Knowing and Understanding Death

Introduction to Part III		207
III.1	Thomas Paynell, *The Despising of the World* (1532)	211
III.2	Thomas Elyot, *A Preservative against Death* (1545)	215
III.3	Elizabeth I, *A Godly Meditation* (1548)	218
III.4	Thomas Churchyard, *A Mirror for Magistrates* (1587)	222
III.5	Thomas Cogan, *The Haven of Health* (1588)	226
III.6	Jane Anger, *Protection for Women* (1589)	229
III.7	John Florio, *Montaigne's Essays* (1603)	233

III.8	Thomas Lodge, *The Works of Seneca* (1614)	237
III.9	Abraham Holland, *Navmachia* (1622)	240
III.10	Francis Bacon, 'Of Death' (1625)	245
III.11	Helkiah Crooke, *Mikrokosmographia* (1631)	249
III.12	Edmund Spenser, 'A View of the Present State of Ireland' (1633)	256
III.13	Alexander Ross, *A View of All Religions in the World* (1653)	259
III.14	John Graunt, *Natural and Political Observations* (1662)	263
III.15	Margaret Cavendish, *Philosophical Letters* (1664)	266
III.16	Thomas Creech, *Lucretius's Six Books* (1683)	270
III.17	Anne Conway, *Principles of the Most Ancient and Modern Philosophy* (1692)	274

PART IV *Death Arts in Literature*

	Introduction to Part IV	281
IV.1	Alexander Barclay, *The Ship of Fools* (1509)	285
IV.2	Anonymous, *The Summoning of Everyman* (1528)	291
IV.3	John Lydgate, *The Dance of Death* (1554)	295
IV.4	Henry Howard, 'Complaint of a Dying Lover' (1557)	303
IV.5	William Painter, 'A Strange Punishment' (1566)	307
IV.6	George Gascoigne, 'Gascoigne's Goodnight' (1573)	310
IV.7	Isabella Whitney, 'The Manner of her Will' (1573)	314
IV.8	Margaret Tyler, *The Mirror of Princely Deeds and Knighthood* (1578)	320
IV.9	Christopher Marlowe, Selected Works (1594, 1604)	323
IV.10	Samuel Rowlands, Selected Works (1606, 1614)	331
IV.11	Aemilia Lanyer, *Salve Deus Rex Judaeorum* (1611)	339
IV.12	Cyril Tourneur, Selected Works (1611, 1613)	343
IV.13	Elizabeth Cary, *The Tragedy of Mariam* (1613)	350
IV.14	Mary Wroth, *Urania* (1621)	354
IV.15	Anonymous, 'The Last Will and Testament of Philip Herbert' (1650)	357
IV.16	Andrew Marvell, 'The Nymph Complaining for the Death of her Fawn' (1681)	362
IV.17	Aphra Behn, *Oroonoko* (1688)	368

Index 373

FIGURES

0.1 Bellicose Death. Anonymous, *Allegory of Man* (England, *c.*1569), close-up. The Tate Britain. Used by permission and with licence, Tate Images *page* 16

0.2 *The Allegory of Man* (England, *c.*1569). The Tate Britain. Used by permission and with licence, Tate Images. 18

0.3 Rotten skull. Geoffrey Whitney, *A Choice of Emblems* (Leiden: 1586; STC 25438), f3^r. Image used courtesy of The Huntington Library 21

0.4 Striding Death. With motto: 'Bidt voor de sielen' (Pray for the souls [of the righteous]). Church tomb memorial wall plaque. Cathedral of St Bavo, Ghent, Belgium. Photo credit, William E. Engel 23

1.1 Allegorical deathbed scene. *To Know Well to Die* (London: William Caxton, 1490; STC 789), n.p. Image used courtesy of The Newberry Library 54

1.2 Death with coffin. *Calender of Shepherds* (London: Wynkyn de Worde, 1528; STC 22411), L4^v. Image used courtesy of The Newberry Library 62

1.3 Moor with horn. *Calender of Shepherds* (London: Wynkyn de Worde, 1528; STC 22411), U4^v. Image used courtesy of The Newberry Library 63

1.4 Infant leaning on a death's head. George Wither, *A Collection of Emblems* (London: 1635; STC 25899), G3^r. Image used courtesy of The Newberry Library 100

1.5 Owl on a death's head. George Wither, *A Collection of Emblems* (London: 1635; STC 25899), Aa1^v. Image used courtesy of The Newberry Library 101

1.6 Sepulchral death's head. Jeremy Taylor, *The Rule and Exercises of Holy Dying* (London: 1651; Wing T361A), frontispiece. Image used courtesy of The Newberry Library 114

LIST OF FIGURES

2.1	Burning of Anne Askew. John Foxe, *Acts and Monuments* (London: 1576; STC 11224), PPP3ᵛ. Image used courtesy of The Huntington Library	148
2.2	Funeral of Sidney. Thomas Lant, *The funeral of Sir Philip Sidney*, engraved by Theodore de Brij, 1587 (engraving). British Library, London, UK ©British Library Board. All Rights Reserved/Bridgeman Images	154
2.3	Architectural memorial design. Martin Day, *A Monument of Mortality* (London: 1621), title page. British Library, London, UK ©British Library Board. All Rights Reserved/Bridgeman Images	174
2.4	Charles I as penitent martyr. *Eikon Basilike* (n.p., 1649; Wing E299A), frontispiece. Private collection	184
2.5	Gisant effigy. Transi-tomb of Archbishop Henry Chichele (d.1443). Canterbury Cathedral. Photo credit, William E. Engel	190
3.1	Anatomical cadaver presenting its skin. *Mikrokosmographia* (London: 1631; STC 6063), title page. Image used courtesy of The Huntington Library	251
3.2	Animated skeleton with hourglass. *Mikrokosmographia* (London: 1631; STC 6063), B4ᵛ. Image used courtesy of The Huntington Library	252
3.3	Zodiacal map of human body. 'Homo Signorum'. Anonymous English almanac (*c.*1580). The Wellcome Collection, London (Wellcome Images/Wikimedia Commons)	254
4.1	Death summoning Fool. Alexander Barclay, *The Ship of Fools* (London: 1509; STC 3545), 177ᵛ. Image used courtesy of The Huntington Library	286
4.2	Message from the tomb. John Lydgate, 'The Daunce of Machabree' appended to *The Fall of Princes* (London: 1554; STC 3177), fol. CCxx5ʳ. Image used courtesy of The Newberry Library	297
4.3	Dance of Death. William Dugdale, *History of St. Paul's Cathedral* (London: 1658; STC 23341), Uuu1ᵛ. Image used courtesy of The Newberry Library	298
4.4	Dance of Death. John Lydgate, 'The Daunce of Machabree' appended to *The Fall of Princes* (London: 1554; STC 3177), fol. CCxxv. Image used courtesy of The Newberry Library	299

4.5   Death summons the Physician. Hans Holbein, *The Dance of Death* (Lyons: 1538). Image used courtesy of the New York Metropolitan Museum of Art (Creative Commons)   301

4.6   Coffined Overbury. Broadside of *Sir Thomas Overbury or The Poysoned Knights Complaint* (London: 1616(?); STC 21406). © of the Society of Antiquaries of London   336

ACKNOWLEDGEMENTS

Early modern authors greatly enjoyed the homophonic pun of 'death' and 'debt'. It is perhaps fitting then that we have accrued our own large share of dues in our studies of early modern mortality. We acknowledge gratefully all those who have responded generously to our queries about various parts of the book as it developed: Stephanie Batkie, Elisabeth Chaghafi, John Gatta, Adam Hawkins, Matthew Irvin, Mary Ellen Lamb, Scott Lucas, James Ross Macdonald, Willy Maley, Kirk Melnikoff, Scott Newstok, W. Brown Patterson, Philip Edward Phillips, Micheline White, and Matthew Woodcock. We would also like to thank Emily Hockley at Cambridge University Press for her superb guidance with, and support of, this project. So, too, we are grateful to the production team at the Press for expertly seeing the book through to publication.

Portions of the work have been discussed and presented at the following venues and international conferences: Carleton University English Department; Centre for Medieval and Early Modern Studies at the University of Kent; Eton College; International Conference of the Society for Emblem Studies (Université de Lorraine in Nancy, France, 2017); Renaissance Society of America (Toronto, 2019; New Orleans, 2018; Chicago, 2017; Boston, 2016); Shakespeare Association of America (Denver/virtual, 2020); and Sixteenth Century Society (Milwaukee, 2017; Albuquerque, 2018; St. Louis, 2019). Engel would like to thank The Office of the Dean at Sewanee, The University of the South, for granting a research leave 2020–2021; and Sewanee's Alderson-Tillinghast Fund for supplementing travel to archives abroad, 2018–2020. Loughnane was very grateful to receive a Francis Bacon Foundation Fellowship at The Huntington Library for research related to this project in the spring of 2020, which was, regrettably, disrupted by the global pandemic. He would like to thank Dympna Callaghan, William Engel, Catherine Richardson, Goran Stanivukovic, and Grant Williams for their advice upon, and support with, his application. Williams would like to thank Carleton University and SSHRC for a Development Grant, 2018, which facilitated related research at the British Library.

Research for this book was undertaken at the British Library, Canterbury Cathedral Library and Archives, The Folger Shakespeare Library, The

Huntington Library, Lambeth Palace Library, The Newberry Library, and The Warburg Institute; we wish to thank the librarians and research support staff at each institution for their invaluable input and assistance. We are especially grateful to Bill Sherman, and the staff at The Warburg Institute, for permitting us to host 'Memory and Mortality: An Interdisciplinary Symposium', 17 May 2019, and to all of the contributors, attendees, and correspondents who made it such a memorable and useful event.

A NOTE ON ABBREVIATIONS

The following abbreviated references are used:

Appleford, *Learning*	Amy Appleford, *Learning to Die in London, 1380–1540* (Philadelphia, PA: University of Pennsylvania Press, 2015).
Ariès, *Attitudes*	Philippe Ariès, *Western Attitudes Toward Death: From the Middle Ages to the Present*, trans. Patricia M. Ranum (Baltimore, MD and London: Johns Hopkins University Press, 1974).
Aristotle *CW*	*The Complete Works of Aristotle*, Jonathan Barnes (ed.), 2 vols. (Princeton, NJ: Princeton University Press, 1984).
Augustine *CG*	Augustine, *City of God, Volume IV: Books 12–15*, trans. Philip Levine, Loeb Classical Library (Cambridge, MA: Harvard University Press, 1966).
Beaty, *Craft*	Nancy Lee Beaty, *The Craft of Dying: A Study in the Literary Tradition of the Ars Moriendi in England* (New Haven, CT and London: Yale University Press, 1970).
Becker, *Death*	Lucinda M. Becker, *Death and the Early Modern Englishwoman* (Aldershot, UK; Burlington, VT: Ashgate, 2003).
Calabritto and Daly, *ED*	Monica Calabritto and Peter Daly (eds.), *Emblems of Death in the Early Modern Period* (Geneva: Droz, 2014).
Chaucer *WO*	*The Riverside Chaucer*, Larry D. Benson (ed.), 3rd ed. (New York: Houghton Mifflin, 1986).
Cicero *TD*	Cicero, *Tusculan Disputations*, trans. J. E. King, Loeb Classical Library (Cambridge, MA: Harvard University Press, 1927).

Cressy, *Birth*	David Cressy, *Birth, Marriage, and Death: Ritual, Religion, and the Life-Cycle in Tudor and Stuart England* (Oxford: Oxford University Press, 1997).
Donne *PO*	*John Donne's Poetry: A Norton Critical Edition*, Donald R. Dickson (ed.) (New York: Norton, 2007).
DPE	Morris Palmer Tilley, *A Dictionary of the Proverbs in England in the Sixteenth and Seventeenth Centuries: A Collection of the Proverbs Found in English Literature and the Dictionaries of the Period* (Ann Arbor, MI: University of Michigan Press, 1950).
Duffy, *Altars*	Eamon Duffy, *The Stripping of the Altars: Traditional Religion in England 1400–1580* (New Haven, CT and London: Yale University Press, 1992).
Engel, *Mortality*	William E. Engel, *Mapping Mortality* (Amherst, MA: University of Massachusetts Press, 1995).
Gittings, *Burial*	Clare Gittings, *Death, Burial and the Individual in Early Modern England* (London: Croom Helm, 1984).
Horace *EP*	Horace, *Satires, Epistles, The Art of Poetry*, trans. H. Rushton Fairclough, Loeb Classical Library (Cambridge, MA: Harvard University Press, 1926).
Horace *OD*	Horace, *Odes and Epodes*, trans. Niall Rudd (ed.), Loeb Classical Library (Cambridge, MA: Harvard University Press, 2004).
Houlbrooke, *Family*	Ralph Houlbrooke, *Death, Religion, and the Family in England, 1480–1750* (Oxford: Clarendon Press, 1998).
Langland *PP*	William Langland, *Piers Plowman: A Critical Edition of the B-Text*, A. V. C. Schmidt (ed.), 2nd ed. (London: J. M. Dent, 2000).
Llewellyn, *Art*	Nigel Llewellyn, *The Art of Death: Visual Culture in the English Death Ritual, c.1500–c.1800* (London: Reaktion, 1997).
MA	William Engel, Rory Loughnane, and Grant Williams (eds.), *The Memory Arts in Renaissance England: A Critical Anthology* (Cambridge: Cambridge University Press, 2016).
Marshall, *Beliefs*	Peter Marshall, *Beliefs and the Dead in Reformation England* (Oxford: Oxford University Press, 2002).

Neill, *Issues*	Michael Neill, *Issues of Death: Mortality and Identity in English Renaissance Tragedy* (Oxford: Clarendon Press, 1997).
OED	*Oxford English Dictionary*, www.oed.com
Ovid *MO*	Ovid, *Metamorphoses*, trans. Frank Justus Miller, Loeb Classical Library, 2 vols. (Cambridge, MA: Harvard University Press, 1976).
Phillippy, *Women*	Patricia Phillippy, *Women, Death and Literature in Post-Reformation England* (Cambridge: Cambridge University Press, 2002).
PL	Jacques-Paul Migne, *Patrologia Latina* (Paris: Garnier, 1844–1865).
Plato *CD*	*Collected Dialogues of Plato Including the Letters*, Edith Hamilton and Huntington Cairns (eds.) (New York: Pantheon, 1961).
Pliny *NH*	Pliny, *Natural History*, trans. H. Rackham et al., Loeb Classical Library, 10 vols. (Cambridge, MA: Harvard University Press, 1938–1962).
Seneca *EP*	Seneca, *Epistles*, trans. Richard M. Gummere, Loeb Classical Library, 3 vols. (Cambridge, MA: Harvard University Press, 1917–1925).
Spenser *FQ*	Edmund Spenser, *The Faerie Queene*, A. C. Hamilton et al. (eds.), 2nd ed. (Harlow, UK: Pearson Education, 2007).
STC	A. W. Pollard, G. R. Redgrave, P. R. Rider, K. F. Panzer, W. A. Jackson, and F. S. Ferguson (eds.), *A Short-Title Catalogue of Books Printed in England, Scotland, and Ireland and of English Books Printed Abroad, 1475–1640*, 3 vols. (London and Oxford: Bibliographical Society, 1986–1991).
Vinter, *Acts*	Maggie Vinter, *Last Acts: The Art of Dying on the Early Modern Stage* (New York: Fordham University Press, 2019).
Virgil *EGA*	Virgil, *Eclogues, Georgics, Aeneid: Books 1–6* and *Aeneid: Books 7–12*, trans. H. Rushton Fairclough, G. P. Goold (rev. ed.), Loeb Classical Library, 2 vols. (Cambridge, MA: Harvard University Press, 1916–1918).

Wear, *Medicine*	Andrew Wear, *Knowledge and Practice in Early Modern English Medicine, 1550–1680* (New York: Cambridge University Press, 2000).
Wing	D. G. Wing (ed.), *Short-Title Catalogue of Books Printed in England, Scotland, Ireland, Wales, and British America, and of English Books Printed in Other Countries 1641–1700*, 4 vols. (New York: Modern Language Association of America, 1994).

A NOTE ON TEXTS

All references to Shakespeare are taken from play and poem editions in *The New Oxford Shakespeare: Modern Critical Edition*, gen. ed. Gary Taylor, John Jowett, Terri Bourus, and Gabriel Egan (Oxford: Oxford University Press, 2016).

Unless otherwise noted, general references to the Bible are taken from the King James Version; however, when an entry includes biblical citations in the original margin notes, we reproduce them exactly as given by the author.

Abbreviations for the books of the Bible conform to *The SBL Handbook of Style*, 2nd ed. (Atlanta, GA: SBL Press, 2014).

Introduction

The Legacy of the Death Arts

> Prepare to die, out of this world of woe;
> Prepare to die, out of this sea of sin;
> Prepare to die, to haughty heaven to go;
> Prepare to die, the heavenly life to win;
> Prepare to die, to live within the sky;
> Prepare to die, I say, prepare to die.[1]

A Cambridge student, otherwise unidentified, exhorts his friend Dick to call to mind his own mortality and to prepare in all ways for his inevitable death. Titled 'Memento Mori', the poem, published in 1579, offers the same, familiar counsel about death that had been repeated since antiquity: 'remember death, and think upon the end'.[2] To 'remember death', the invocation of all *memento mori* traditions, works in two ways, and both are the duties of the living: first, the individual should remember that they too will die someday, and this act of remembrance will help call to mind those further actions that one might take to prepare for that moment; and second, the death of an individual should also be remembered and acted upon by their survivors. Remembrance is, then, individual and communal, operating both in anticipation of and subsequent to expiration. The Cambridge student's particular poem extends this duty as a poetic gesture of friendship, a concern for Dick's spiritual welfare as he nears death.

Contrariwise, Claudio, in *Measure for Measure*, confesses strong doubts about his approaching end:

> Ay, but to die, and go we know not where;
> To lie in cold obstruction, and to rot;
> This sensible warm motion to become

---

[1] Anonymous, 'Memento Mori' in *A poore knight his pallace of priuate pleasures Gallantly garnished, with goodly galleries of strang inuentio[n]s and prudently polished, with sundry pleasant posies, [et] other fine fancies of dainty deuices, and rare delightes* (London: 1597; STC 4283), I4ʳ.

[2] Ibid., I3ᵛ. The poem is addressed to his friend 'Richard Ra. lyinge *in his death bed*' (I3ʳ). For the familiar invocation to 'think upon the end', see Rory Loughnane, 'Studied Speech and *The Duchess of Malfi*: The Lost Arts of Rhetoric, Memory, and Death', *Sillages critiques*, 26 (2019).

> A kneaded clod, and the delighted spirit
> To bathe in fiery floods, or to reside
> In thrilling region of thick-ribbèd ice;
> To be imprisoned in the viewless winds,
> And blown with restless violence round about
> The pendent world; or to be worse than worst
> Of those that lawless and incertain thought
> Imagine howling—'tis too horrible!
> The weariest and most loathèd worldly life
> That age, ache, penury, and imprisonment
> Can lay on nature is a paradise
> To what we fear of death.[3]

Earthly existence, with all its assorted hardships and challenges, is, as Claudio notes, still better than the horrors a hell-bound afterlife affords.[4] Inverting traditional *contemptus mundi* tropes – those which Shakespeare's characters routinely deliver – Claudio here celebrates life's familiar miseries over death's unknown outcome.[5] His attitude evinces the uncertainties fostered by early modern religious disputes over what the afterlife would bring for the dead and how actions in this life affected the next. In Roman Catholic theology, the natural event of death sent the deceased's soul towards Heaven, Purgatory, or Hell (with an additional sub-state of Hell being 'Limbo of the Fathers' for those patriarchs of the Church who died before Jesus's coming). Mourners for the deceased prayed for their soul's spiritual health, helping the dead to eventually move from the intermediate state of Purgatory to Heaven. The jettisoning of Purgatory from Reformist teaching, owing to its absence from scripture, meant that lines of communication between the living and the dead were now broken, and that there was a new permanency to one's eternal destination.[6] But such permanency did not inspire all

---

[3] *Measure for Measure*, 3.1.116–131.
[4] For evocations of the *contemptus mundi* philosophical outlook in this period, see entries I.6 (Bradford), I.14 (Taylor), and II.14 (Beaumont).
[5] From Antonio in *Merchant of Venice* describing life as 'wretched' (4.1.263) to Macbeth's 'Life's but a walking shadow' (5.5.23) to Guiderius and Arviragus's plaintive song in *Cymbeline* ('Fear no more the heat o'th' sun / Nor the furious winter's rages'; 4.2.260–261), Shakespeare's works repeatedly invoke the idea that life is more to be endured than enjoyed.
[6] On the rejection of Purgatory in the reformed faith, and how it changed daily life in early modern England, see Gittings, *Burial*; Duffy, *Altars*; Cressy, *Birth*; Bruce Gordon and Peter Marshall (eds.), *The Place of the Dead: Death and Remembrance in Late Medieval and Early Modern Europe* (Cambridge: Cambridge University Press, 2000); and Marshall, *Beliefs*.

Protestants with confidence, since the elect, those predestined to join Christ in the bosom of Heaven, had no conclusive knowledge of whether or not they were saved.

The premeditative thoughts on the afterlife expressed by the Cambridge student and Claudio suggest not only the web of beliefs around spiritual death but also the extraordinary pressures of natural death in premodern England. As an event, death is a physical and existential terminus, the point at which the social and biological agent falls out of historical time, interrupting the everyday progress of civilization. In the period, lower life expectancy rates meant that death was a familiar if foreboding presence in people's lives.[7] Poverty, famine, disease, war, and violence afflicted English society in devastating ways, while living conditions, poor hygiene, few substantial medical advances, and ineffective public health services led to high mortality rates.[8] Urban-based populations across western Europe, which grew exponentially over the early modern period, fared worst in terms of average life expectancy.[9] Outbreaks of plague were especially devastating for these populations, as

---

[7] Average life expectancy rates in the premodern period would have differed in various environments. For example, Mary J. Dobson's study of early modern death in the south-east of England (Essex, Kent, and Sussex) observes a discrepancy between rates of mortality in lower marsh regions and upland regions:
> a baby born into [the lower-lying marsh region] in the seventeenth and eighteenth centuries might expect to live little more than twenty or thirty years. One in every three or four of all babies would die before its first birthday. [… In upland areas] a new-born baby might expect perhaps another forty or even fifty years of life and nine out of ten of all new-borns in the early modern era might survive beyond their first birthday.

Dobson, *Contours of Death and Disease in Early Modern England* (Cambridge: Cambridge University Press, 1997), p. 2.

[8] On England's changing population in this period, see E. A. Wrigley and R. S. Schofield, *The Population History of England 1541–1871* (Cambridge: Cambridge University Press, 1981).

[9] Research on London's changing population is especially instructive in this light for our study: P. E. Jones and A. V. Judges, 'London Population in the Late Seventeenth Century', *Economic History Review*, 6 (1935–1936), 45–63; Roger Finlay, *Population and Metropolis: The Demography of London, 1580–1650* (Cambridge: Cambridge University Press, 1981); Jeremy Boulton, *Neighbourhood and Society: A London Suburb in the Seventeenth Century* (Cambridge: Cambridge University Press, 1987); Vanessa Harding, 'The Population of London, 1550–1700: A Review of the Published Evidence', *London Journal*, 15 (1990), 111–28; and Peter Razzell and Christine Spence, 'The History of Infant, Child and Adult Mortality in London, 1550–1850', *London Journal*, 32 (2007), 271–92.

evidenced in London.[10] The germinal proto-capitalist economy increased income inequality between the tiers, lending itself to insufficient healthcare in a time of inadequate medical treatment.[11] Cumulatively, the effect was to draw people closer to death; mortality was not something that could be ignored but, paradoxically, lived with. Natural death, the cessation of an individual's time alive on this earth, was a fixture in the early modern mindset, a social preoccupation. Thus, the preacher Stephen Jerome advises the faithful to 'build the Ark before the flood come, prepare thy soul ere death come' for 'this is thy time, thy day, *tempus tuum*' but 'Death is God's day, *tempus suum*, and his time'.[12]

Although the anonymous poem and Shakespeare's dark comedy may be explained by the universality and ineluctability of a natural death, this study wants to shift the perspective on such *memento mori* pronouncements from 'the real' of the final terminus to the cultural production around mortality, what we call the death arts. The two printed texts do more than just echo the truism that we will all die; rather significantly, they contribute to the period's belief system, its zeitgeist, its symbolic order, its cultural imaginary, its historical record. Not to be confused with a terminus, a negation, or a loss, the death arts possess the vigour and energy that built up the early modern world and injected animation into everyday existence. Our chosen phrase, the 'death arts', while encompassing a plurality and heterogeneity of disciplines, activities, and techniques dedicated to mortality, foregrounds their artifice, thereby permitting us to conceive of the distinctive features and constructedness of Renaissance artefacts, whether textual, cognitive, or visual.

---

[10] Neil Cummins, Morgan Kelly, and Cormac Ó Gráda observe that
> the plagues of 1563, 1603, 1625, and 1665 were all of roughly equal relative magnitude, with burials running at 5.5 to 6 times the average level in the previous five years. Assuming a normal mortality rate of around 3.0–3.5 per cent, this implies that one-fifth of the city's population died each time, within the space of a few months.

See 'Living Standards and Plague in London, 1560–1665', *Economic History Review*, 69.1 (2016), 3–34, 4. See also Paul Slack, *The Impact of Plague in Tudor and Stuart England* (London: Routledge and Kegan Paul, 1985).

[11] For the relationship between income, life expectancy, and the state's welfare apparatus, see Paul Slack, *Poverty and Policy in Tudor and Stuart England* (London and New York: Longman, 1988). In England, and north-western Europe more broadly, life expectancy rates for the noble class exceeded those of the rest of Europe; see Neil Cummins, 'Lifespans of the European Elite, 800–1800', *The Journal of Economic History*, 77.2 (2017), 406–39.

[12] Stephen Jerome, *Moses his sight of Canaan with Simeon his dying-song. Directing how to liue holily and dye happily* (London: 1614; STC 14512), Dd7ᵛ.

Introduction

The Productive Ends of the Death Arts

The 'death arts' includes within its scope the *ars moriendi* while moving well beyond the traditional techniques of dying well. A strong historical reason for this expansion is that after the Reformation the *ars moriendi* became less rigorously ritualized and more loosely individualized with the Protestant turn to personal reading, meditation, and casuistry.[13] Even so, what we want to circumscribe by the death arts are the various and sundry artefacts, practices, images, and texts around dying, death, and the dead, stretching from contemplation and preparation, through expiration to funerals and commemoration – the full death-cycle, if you will. Their pluralization and wide reach during the early modern period must be attributed, at least in part, to the Protestant, Catholic, and humanist recruitment of the burgeoning printing press by which new and old genres overlapped, cross-pollinated, and proliferated: elegiac verse; theological and devotional works; psalters, primers, and prayer books; moral philosophy treatises; commonplace books; conduct manuals; repentance pamphlets; narrative poetry, romance, histories, and ballads, and so on.

The study's purpose is not to promote the ubiquity of a theme by rallying around textual sameness. Similar arguments have been made against – somewhat unfairly – scholars of rhetoric who find eloquence and oratorical patterns everywhere or 'symptomatic readings' that incessantly calculate the ideological valences of statements and texts. Even more pointedly, we do not want to confuse the death arts with just another great Western idea alongside justice, opinion, beauty, emotion, truth, and so forth.[14] They are not

---

[13] Ralph Houlbrooke affirms, 'The last act nevertheless bulked especially large in accounts of puritan lives. This was largely because the puritan way of dying assigned the individual's inner faith a particularly important role, and all but eliminated the supportive framework of liturgy and sacrament' ('The Puritan Death-bed, c.1560–c.1660', in *The Culture of English Puritanism, 1560–1700*, ed. Christopher Durston and Jacqueline Eales (New York: St. Martin's Press, 1996), p.122). On the differences between the Catholic and Protestant arts, see David W. Atkinson, 'The English *Ars Morendi*: Its Protestant Transformation', *Renaissance and Reformation / Renaissance et Réforme*, 6.1 (1982), 1–10.

[14] The clearest expression of such a scheme is 'The Synopticon', an index of the 102 great ideas to the sixty-book encyclopaedia set: Mortimer J. Adler, *The Great Books of the Western World*, 2nd ed. (Chicago, IL: Encyclopædia Britannica, 1990).

reducible to a transcendental signified that totalizes a cultural field of signs;[15] they, instead, testify to a vast array of signifiers diffused throughout that field, regardless of any privileged point of meaning. And so, our entries, far from fixating on the singularity of an arch concept or representation, accumulate lexical, idiomatic, and discursive copiousness, with which various writers spelled out their mortality.

It should be stated, however, that nowhere in the period do we find the literal combination of the two words as we use them in our title, and yet we stand behind the phrase's aptness in capturing succinctly and accurately the heterogeneity of the cultural work in question. Crucial to our thinking and curating is the period's understanding of 'art', which does not occupy the word's current semantic range.[16] Because the category 'ars' could broadly refer to any branch of study, sliding easily across modern disciplinary fissures as in Robert Hill's claim that 'it is the art of all arts, science of all sciences, to learn how to die',[17] the 'death arts' acknowledges the frequent sorties that established academic pursuits – whether they be the *studia humanitatis*, theology, law, natural history, medicine, and so on – make into issues of mortality.

Yet the early modern death arts, cutting an even wider swath, also encompass technical know-how and practical expertise, as William Caxton's translation of the *Tractatus artis bene moriendi*, the earliest of the printed versions in English, attests by its title 'the arte [and] crafte to knowe well to dye' and explains through its introductory sentences:

When it is so that what a man maketh or doeth, it is made to come to some end. And if the thing be good and well made, it must needs come to good end. Then by better and greater reason every man ought to intend in such wise to live in this world, in keeping the commandments of God, that he may come to a good end. (entry I.1)

---

[15] Jacques Derrida famously critiques the traditional great idea through the concept of the transcendental signified, which posits a metaphysical foundation to stabilize the signifying system (Derrida, *Of Grammatology*, trans. Gayatri Chakravorty Spivak (Baltimore, MD: Johns Hopkins University Press, 1976), p. 20).

[16] 'Any of various pursuits or occupations in which creative or imaginative skill is applied according to aesthetic principles; the various branches of creative activity, as painting, sculpture, music, literature, dance, drama, oratory, etc.' (*OED*). Beaty, *Craft*, p. 54, presupposes such an anachronistic notion of art by privileging the literariness of the *ars moriendi* treatises.

[17] Robert Hill, *Path-Way to Prayer and Pietie* (London: 1609; STC 13472.7), P7^r.

Behind the anonymous author's *ars moriendi* is Aristotle's definition of techne,[18] which signifies a 'productive form of knowledge', the skilfulness in doing and making something.[19] The treatise's passage particularly alludes to Aristotle's *Nicomachean Ethics*, whose opening posits that 'Every art and every inquiry, and similarly every action and choice, is thought to aim at some good; and for this reason the good has rightly been declared to be that at which all things aim'.[20] The art and craft of knowing how to die well, consistent with any other techne, seeks, after Aristotle, a good end, and, in a Christian era, presumably demands our greatest attention since it deals with the best end of all earthly ends. The death arts, then, operate on the basis of a premodern epistemology that unsettles contemporary expectations around mortality and its knowledge. The death arts did not just spin airy threads of intellectual speculation; they were good doing and good making – not only because they aimed heavenward with worshipful fervour but also because many were conducted under the auspices of the general category of techne, which strives for a practical and fulfilling telos. Our phrase accordingly circumscribes the skills and exercises that create habits, rituals, and artefacts around death, activities as diverse and multifaceted as hortatory sermonizing from the pulpit, performing Roman suicide on the stage, engraving woodcuts for a ballad, commemorating loved ones, drafting wills, mocking defunct enemies, and speechifying on the scaffold. What Maggie Vinter witnesses with active deaths on the early modern stage we register with the semantic alliance between art and artifice, which, allowing readers to move beyond the dead end of mourning, underscores the human agency and interpersonality inscribed within any early modern 'last act'.[21]

Our study's emphasis upon the cultural work occasioned by death invites renewed scholarly examination of a longstanding controversy associated

---

[18] We do not mean to imply that Aristotle used the term narrowly. For the techne's semantic richness in Aristotle as well as ancient philosophy, see Tom Angier, *Techné in Aristotle's Ethics: Crafting the Moral Life* (London: Bloomsbury, 2010).

[19] See Aristotle *CW*, *Metaphysics* 1046b3; 982a1; 1075a1–2; *Nicomachean Ethics* VI.4; *Topics* 157a10. Richard Whitford also introduces his *memento mori* instruction in terms of a techne. See Whitford, *A Daily Exercise and Experience of Death* (London: 1537; STC 25414), C4^{r-v}.

[20] Aristotle *CW*, *Nicomachean Ethics* 1094a1–2.

[21] Vinter makes a compelling argument that mourning and dying present two attitudes in the period. Whereas mourning emphasizes loss, dying suggests sociality and agency, and constitutes for her the object of study: the last 'act'. See Vinter, *Acts*, pp. 2–8.

with the investigations of Philippe Ariès, who contends that the alienated individual of contemporary society has lost touch with traditional communal attitudes toward dying and the dead.[22] Early modern social historians have tested out Ariès's claims specifically on the English historical record and drawn conclusions that complicate and revise, if not challenge, his sweeping generalizations about the historical barrier separating our mindset from that of the pre-modern past.[23] A lesser-known account provides us with a counterbalance to Ariès's received nostalgic narrative: Paul L. Landsberg suggests a progress model in which the dissolution of the feudal order led to a raised consciousness of one's own mortality disencumbered from the baggage of clan thinking.[24] Even though our study does not rally around either of Ariès's and Landsberg's narratives or, for that matter, the narratives of other cultural and intellectual historians examining attitudes toward death,[25] they compel us to acknowledge the importance of methodologically separating the two periods so that the integrity of Renaissance alterity is kept from collapsing into modernity. Indeed, death studies gives scholars valuable leverage with which to distinguish Renaissance

---

[22] See Philippe Ariès, *The Hour of Our Death: The Classic History of Western Attitudes toward Death over the Last One Thousand Years*, trans. Helen Weaver, 2nd ed. (New York: Vintage Books, 2008).

[23] Gittings, *Burial*, p. 18 n.5, pursues Ariès's correlation between emergent individuality and changing attitudes to death. But both Cressy, *Birth* and Houlbrooke, *Family* are sceptical of an overemphasis upon Ariès's thesis. Cressy's approach eschews 'a simple linear progression from medieval to modern' that looks for 'a growing sense of individualism', preferring to bring out in the evidence 'diversity and dialogue within a continuing contested conversation about religious and secular solemnities' (379). Houlbrooke disputes 'Ariès's belief that a sense of the irreplaceability of loved ones first became widespread in early modern times' because the evidence does not fully bear it out (380).

[24] Paul L. Landsberg, *The Experience of Death: The Moral Problem of Suicide*, trans. Cynthia Rowland (New York: Arno Press, 1977).

[25] For a representative selection of historians who posit a historical change in European attitudes toward death and the dead, see Johan Huizinga, *The Waning of the Middle Ages*, trans. Frederik Jan Hopman ([1924] Harmondsworth: Penguin, 1955); Michel Foucault, *The Birth of the Clinic*, trans. A. M. Sheridan Smith (New York: Vintage, 1975); Michel Vovelle, *La Mort et l'Occident de 1300 à nos jours* (Paris: Gallimard, 1983); Duffy, *Altars*; Arthur Imhof, *Lost Worlds: How our European Ancestors Coped with Everyday Life and Why Life Is So Hard Today*, trans. Thomas Robisheaux (Charlottesville, VA: University of Virginia Press, 1996); Appleford, *Learning*; Marshall, *Beliefs*; and Thomas W. Laqueur, *The Work of the Dead: A Cultural History of Mortal Remains* (Princeton, NJ: Princeton University Press, 2016).

mentalities, subjectivity, and epistemology from later Enlightenment developments, as well as from their medieval precursors.[26]

An attention to the death arts, we believe, combats the post-Enlightenment caricature of mortal reflection as arising from dank religious pessimism and rioting necromania. Modernity tends to overplay the grave as absence and annulment, where all human values come to an end. Perhaps that is why today we often call those preoccupied with the macabre 'morose' and 'morbid': it is a sickly disposition that dwells on value-negating death.[27] Nietzsche's call for a transvaluation of Christianity's life-denying exaltation of suffering, no doubt, launches the clearest, if not the most persuasive, philosophical attack on the culture of the *ars moriendi*.[28] This contemporary attitude, notwithstanding the expression of the painful feelings of losing a loved one, significantly distorts our view of early modern death, which was saturated with competing and complementary cultural values. It is no mystery that during the period death profited the religiously minded, but it also accrued epistemological, juridical, educational, and literary capital, disseminated widely across the social spectrum from the existential through the collective to the commonwealth, and manifested itself most discernibly by the products of the printing press. Its values were tallied, scaled, exchanged, and compounded with one another, circulating in an economy that aligned and misaligned the worldly marketplace with the marts of Heaven, Hell, and Purgatory. Our phrase the 'death arts', the organizational principle of the study, ventures to give the sweeping economy of death its scholarly due.

Our selected entries take stock of death's thriving economy by making visible the extensive symbolic latticework – not just verbal patterns and occupational patter embedded in writing, but speech acts, images, artefacts, and

---

[26] Exemplary in this regard is Neill, *Issues*, which traces through drama the crisis of identity precipitated by the period's changing attitudes to mortality. Also worth noting is Brian Cummings, *Mortal Thoughts: Religion, Secularity, and Identity in Early Modern Culture* (Oxford: Oxford University Press, 2013), which also investigates identity in the period but argues against scholarly accounts that secularize the Renaissance and the Reformation.

[27] Beaty, *Craft*, p. 46, blames medieval necromania and the abnormal insecurities of material existence for inducing churchmen to violently renounce the values of the present life as depicted in the *danse macabre*. Johan Huizinga also criticizes the 'whole vision' of late medieval death as macabre, which partly springs from a 'spasmodic reaction against excessive sensuality' and 'deep psychological strata of fear' (*The Waning of the Middle Ages*, pp. 142, 146).

[28] See *The Anti-Christ* for his critique, in Friedrich Wilhelm Nietzsche, *Twilight of the Idols; and, The Anti-Christ*, trans. R. J. Hollingdale (London: Penguin, 1990).

activities – that the death arts built around 'the real' of the corpse.[29] Stretching throughout the civic social sphere, such scaffolding can be seen to have far-reaching implications for the cognition of early modern individuals, when we consider the findings of distributive psychology and extended mind theory: thinking involves the collaboration between the brain and its environment so much so that culture installs into human ecosystems feedback mechanisms in order to offload cognitive functionality and extend people's minds.[30] Active mental externalism may marshal not only technological artefacts (paper and ink, prayer beads, and adding machines), but also, less intuitively speaking, language.[31] The same mental externalism applies widely to the cultural work performed by the death arts – but on a larger scale. The things they produced from material artefacts – for instance, brasses, transi-tombs, monuments, family heirlooms, portraits, and skull rings – to more rhetorical resources – such as prayers, sermons, wills, and elegies – resulted in the expansion of a vast and inescapable web of relations, which continually primed early modern minds to reflect upon their mortality. Gail Kern Paster's implementation of the extended mind theory to grasp images of the Renaissance skull proves illuminating here. Despite disagreeing with her assertion of a binary between distributed cognition and the *memento mori* tradition, we see her four readings of the death's head as actually affirming the dynamic mental activity sparked by artefacts and techniques devoted to meditating on mortality.[32]

---

[29] As Catherine Belsey asserts by way of Lacan's concept of the real, 'Death doesn't do fiction, but eliminates the body and the speaking subject, with all it thinks it knows. Death puts an end to the cultural game for each of us' (*Culture and the Real* (London and New York: Routledge, 2005), p.14).

[30] The extended mind hypothesis, first articulated by Andy Clark and David Chalmers, 'The Extended Mind', *Analysis*, 58.1 (1998), 7–19, postulates that cognition is not confined to flesh and bone but occurs through couplings between the subject's brain and its environment. Consider the cognitive artefact of the calculator, which allows the user to achieve epistemic actions not achievable without the device.

[31] As Clark and Chalmers propose,
Without language, we might be much more akin to discrete Cartesian "inner" minds, in which high-level cognition relies largely on internal resources. But the advent of language has allowed us to spread this burden into the world. Language, thus construed, is not a mirror of our inner states but a complement to them. It serves as a tool whose role is to extend cognition in ways that on-board devices cannot. Indeed, it may be that the intellectual explosion in recent evolutionary time is due as much to this linguistically-enabled extension of cognition as to any independent development in our inner cognitive resources. (ibid., 18)

[32] Gail Kern Paster, 'Thinking with Skulls in Holbein, *Hamlet*, Vesalius, and Fuller', *The Shakespearean International Yearbook* (London: Routledge, 2011), vol. 11, pp. 43, 58.

Case in point is Richard Whitford's musings on his daily exercise that illustrate the way in which contemplation enabled practitioners to mitigate their fears of dying. Whitford, a Bridgettine monk at Syon and friend of More and Erasmus, compares those who lack the 'exercise, use, and experience' to children and women who, watching a play, are terrified of the actor representing the devil because they have no clue how theatre works.[33] Repeated mental activity habituates the object of dread and accumulates practical knowledge so that negative emotion will no longer compel the person to 'flee and avoid' thoughts of death. But Whitford's treatise, much like other English *artes moriendi*, does not dispense with dread altogether.[34] His first form of exercise urges the reader to consider how comforted she will be when at the time of her passing she will have been properly prepared.[35] The reader makes an imaginative leap forward to her dying day so that she can look back on how she spent her life and thereby use the emotional impact of this retrospection as a means of motivating current meditational activity. Whitford's exercise is representative of a major cognitive strategy implemented by *memento mori* artefacts, images, and techniques: fear management. The practitioner's raw feelings of apprehension are diverted from incapacitating mentation to stimulating salutary contemplation.

Whitford's leap forward to the dying day also raises the strategic image of the deathbed, a major cognitive template for the death arts. During the fifteenth century, block books transmitted a shorter version of the *Tractatus artis bene moriendi* with woodcut illustrations of the *moriens* beset by mortals, devils, saints, and the crucified Christ.[36] This powerful deathbed image did not just receive treatment from graphic artists, such as Hieronymus Bosch in *The Seven Deadly Sins* and Hans Holbein in *The Dance of Death*; sixteenth-century *ars moriendi* treatises deployed it as a mnemonic locus for prompting readers to project themselves into the future so that they would generate imagined regret and guilt, which would thereby help them to focus, in the here and the now, their deathward thoughts. As Thomas Lupset enjoins, 'When you rise in the morning, determine so to pass the day following as though at night a grave should be your bed. Let every day be reckoned with

---

[33] Whitford, *Daily Exercise*, C7^{r-v}.
[34] Of course, the ideal disposition toward death is boldness and hardiness (ibid., D4^r). But to obtain that condition, one requires motivation.
[35] Ibid., D1^v–D2^r.
[36] *The Ars Moriendi (Editio Princeps, circa 1450): A Reproduction of the Copy in the British Museum*, ed. W. Harry Rylands (London: Holbein Society, 1881).

you as your last' (entry I.3).[37] These few examples of visualization only scratch the surface of a vast network of cognitive artefacts and techniques that continually primed and sculpted early modern minds to meditate upon mortality.

If the death arts fostered distinctive habits of thinking with the world, they also structured – not unrelatedly – a peculiar way of perceiving the world. What the Enlightenment gradually left behind in the multiple passages from superstition and magic to science, from feudalism to capitalism, and from religious uniformity to sectarianism and secularization was a phenomenological outlook on mortality, alien to the contemporary subject's *Weltanschauung*. At our specific historical vantage point, death is viewed from within and through the framework of a living biosphere. It occupies a brief moment at the end of an overall socio-biological life cycle, designating the limit, for some, and the threshold, for others, of material existence. The labour inherent to the death arts upsets this seemingly natural outlook by not confining itself to a final event. The oft quoted and annotated line from Ecclesiastes 7:1, 'the day of death [is better] than the day of one's birth', crystallizes how early modern clergymen reframed life through mortality on the grounds that, when born, we enter into, according to Psalm 84:6 (Coverdale Bible) and the Book of Common Prayer (entry II.2), a vale of misery.[38] The transvaluation of life into death and death into life meant that the moribund permeated existence from the cycle's very beginning; as Thomas Lupset observes, 'And though we be not dead this day, yet it is truth that this day we die, and daily sithen our first birth we have died, in as much that daily some part of our life hath been diminished, and ever as we have grown, so ever life hath decreased' (entry I.3).[39] Every day is one's death day so to speak, for in the words of Christopher Sutton, another English *ars moriendi* treatise writer, 'the old Saints and servants of God … lived in a continual farewell from the world'.[40] Indeed, before nodding off at night, one should, George Gascoigne's poem urges readers, contemplate how death is akin to sleep, since sleep itself

---

[37] Jane Owen's *An Antidote against Purgatory* (entry I.13) and Thomas Becon's *The Sick Man's Salve* (London, 1559–1560; STC 1756.5) structure their texts around the bed of a virtual *moriens*. For a critique of the drama of the deathbed scene, see Montaigne (entry III.7).

[38] See William Perkins, *A Salve For A Sick Man* (entry I.9); Christopher Sutton, *Disce Mori: Learn to Die* (London: 1600; STC 23474), J7^r–J7^v; George Strode, *The Anatomy of Mortality* (London: 1618; STC 23364), M8^v, N3^v.

[39] Both Wither (entry I.11) and Cogan (entry III.5) make similar pronouncements.

[40] Sutton, *Disce Mori*, D1^v–D2^r.

is a little death we experience after each day,[41] awaking to a new life the next morning (entry IV.6). John Donne, St Paul's eloquent preacher, summarizes this overall outlook with characteristic pith: 'In all our periods and transitions in this life, are so many passages from death to death.'[42]

The thanatological view of existence that subtends the death arts may be explained by the bipartite division (that of body and soul) – or the more eschatologically precise tripartite division of death: the natural (external or bodily), the spiritual (internal or ghostly), and the eternal (of both body and soul).[43] Under the two overlapping schemes, a natural death entails 'a separation not an annihilation'[44] of the soul and so, because spiritual and eternal deaths hold graver consequences for a person than the natural one does, 'Let not sin therefore reign in your mortal body, that ye should obey it in the lusts thereof'.[45] St Paul introduces the paradoxical transvaluation of life into death by urging believers to become dead to sin, to die with Christ, and to be raised with Him into everlasting life. Put simply, eternity emaciates and mortifies the temporal.

Early modern death was not a theme or attitude but a way of looking at the world, a structuring of diurnal experience. Every waking moment was potentially a 'final act' when the early modern individual had to perceive the latent moribund condition of persons and objects within his field of vision. Behind the *contemptus mundi* and the *vanitas* traditions lay a phenomenology, which probed beneath the fleshly surface of things to expose the underlying necrosis.

---

[41] See S. Viswanathan, 'Sleep and Death: The Twins in Shakespeare', *Comparative Drama*, 13.1 (1979), 50: 'The conception of Sleep and Death as siblings—i.e., as the two children of Night—goes back to Homer and Hesiod, and was revived in Renaissance mythography, as we see from the dictionaries, the iconological accounts of Pausanias and Cartari, and Renaissance iconographical practice.' See Job 3:11–13; Homer, *Iliad, Volume I: Books 1–12*, trans. A. T. Murray, rev. William F. Wyatt, Loeb Classical Library (Cambridge, MA: Harvard University Press, 1924), 11.243–47 and *Aeneid* in Virgil *EGA*, 10.745–46, 12.309–10).

[42] *Death's Duel, or, A Consolation to the Soul against the Dying Life* (London: 1632; STC 7031), B3ʳ.

[43] Caxton (entry I.1) and Whitford, *Daily Exercise*, C5ᵛ, follow, for example, the omnipresent bipartite scheme, while some later writers invoke the lesser-known tripartite division: see Strode, *Anatomy of Mortality*, B1ᵛ, and Thomas Tuke, *A Discourse of Death, Bodily, Ghostly, and Eternal* (London: 1613; STC 24307), B3ʳ. Samuel Otes, *An Explanation of the General Epistle of Saint Jude* (London: 1633; STC 18896), CC2ᵛ, credits Augustine with making the division. Bradford postulates a quadratic scheme (entry I.6).

[44] Tuke, *Discourse of Death*, B3ʳ.

[45] Rom 6:12.

The mortal world's appearances could not be trusted. Like gaudy raiments and smooth skin that provoke desire, their layers had to be stripped down to the lifeless bone in an act of allegorical divestiture. Edmund Spenser's *The Faerie Queene* enshrines this thanatological phenomenology, where the episode of the House of Pride,[46] for example, moves from glitter to grave dust, from the palace to the dungeon and the pit – one of many scenes in which the phenomenal world undergoes the mortification of allegory.[47] Conversely, bare images of death and decay, as we will see, invited the viewer to imaginatively enflesh and reanimate the relics, briefly revivifying the mort to apprehend fully the irony woven into the world's mortal fabric.

The Visual Proliferation of the Death Arts

The imagery associated with the death arts in early modern England has a rich and venerable legacy.[48] The main precedents can be traced by way of medieval religious iconography,[49] applied emblematics in the visual and plastic arts,[50] especially memorial structures,[51] inscriptions, and ekphrastic descriptions concerning the personification of Death. Two prominent late medieval texts will serve to introduce briefly how this universally familiar yet still disruptively uncanny figure in the Western cultural imagination took on

---

[46] Cf. *MA* VI.2 (Spenser) concerning specifically the procession of the Seven Deadly Sins (pp. 283–87).

[47] See Spenser *FQ*, 1.4–5. In *The Origin of German Tragic Drama*, Walter Benjamin, the German philosopher and social critic, reaches similar conclusions about baroque allegory. For a discussion of this topic, see Bainard Cowan, 'Walter Benjamin's Theory of Allegory', *New German Critique*, 22 (1981), 109–22.

[48] Llewellyn, *Art*; Vanessa Harding, *The Dead and the Living in Paris and London, 1500–1670* (Cambridge: Cambridge University Press, 2002); Daniela Rywiková, *Speculum Mortis: The Image of Death in Late Medieval Bohemian Painting* (Lanham, MD: Lexington Books, 2020).

[49] Emile Mâle, *Religious Art from the Twelfth to the Eighteenth Century* (Princeton, NJ: Princeton University Press, 1983), pp. 59–72; Jean Seznec, *The Survival of the Pagan Gods: The Mythological Tradition and Its Place in Renaissance Humanism and Art*, trans. Barbara Sessions (New York: Pantheon, 1953), pp. 113, 225, 291; Marina Vicelja, 'Religious Iconography', in *The Routledge Companion to Medieval Iconography*, Colum Hourihane (ed.) (London and New York: Routledge, 207), pp. 221–34, esp. pp. 230–31.

[50] Calabritto and Daly, *ED*.

[51] Erwin Panofsky, *Tomb Sculpture* (London: Henry N. Abrams, 1964); Christina Welch, 'Exploring Late-Medieval English *Memento Mori* Carved Cadaver Sculptures', in *Dealing With The Dead: Mortality and Community in Medieval and Early Modern Europe*, ed. Thea Tomaini (Leiden and Boston: Brill, 2018), pp. 331–65.

new visual resonance during the early years of English printing. First, and fairly typical of the way music, dance, and related kinetic forms of cultural expression intersected with performative representations of death,[52] we have the example of John Lydgate's *Danse Macabre*. This text, based on and inspired by vignettes Lydgate saw on a Parisian church cemetery mural, is a series of admonitory dialogues between Death and people of all social stations being summoned individually to join an ineluctable dance (entry IV.3; Figures 4.3 and 4.4). Our second example, Chaucer's 'Pardoner's Tale',[53] deftly draws on and adds a new twist to the visual trope known as *Le Dit des trois Morts et des trois Vifs* (the legend of the three dead and the three living) frequently included in Books of Hours and Primers.[54] Three corpses in various and indeterminant states of decomposition gravely stand and address three wayfarers, often depicted as young aristocrats out for a hunt.[55] They learn, within the context of this allegory, that they are in fact the quarry marked for death. Chaucer opens his version of this visually evocative theme in a tavern where three dissipated young men express anger over the recent passing of a carousing companion whose death they rashly plan to avenge if they can discover who took his life. The tapster warns the riotous youths to think better of trying to hunt down this thieving murderer (see Figure 0.1 ['Bellicose Death']).

> There came a privee[56] thief men clepeth[57] Death,
> That in this country all the people sleeth,[58]
> And with his spear he smoot[59] his heart in two,
> And went his way withouten words mo[re].
> He hath a thousand slain this pestilence.[60]
> And, master, ere ye come in his presence,
> Me thinketh that it were necessary
> For to be war[61] of swich[62] an adversary.[63]

---

[52] Elina Gertsman, *The Dance of Death in the Middle Ages* (Turnhout, BE: Brepols, 2010), pp. 69–75.
[53] *Canterbury Tales*, Chaucer *WO*, VI (C) 462–968.
[54] Cf. entry II.3 (Primer).
[55] An example of a later printed version of this early medieval pictorial subgenre of the *memento mori* tradition is the 1554 'Primer of Salisbury use' produced in Rouen for the English market (Canterbury Cathedral Library, H/L-3-6).
[56] 'stealthy' [57] 'call' [58] 'he slays' [59] 'struck with a firm blow' [60] 'time of plague'
[61] 'wary' [62] 'such'
[63] *Canterbury Tales* (London: William Caxton, 1483; STC 5083), gg3ᵛ; cf. entry I.1 (Caxton).

FIGURE O.I Bellicose Death. Anonymous, *Allegory of Man* (England, *c.*1569), close-up. The Tate Britain. Used by permission and with licence, Tate Images

Such descriptions of the figure of Death, based on imagery regularly seen on church walls and featured in Books of Hours among other places, are indicative of the many ways that death came to be recognized as being a part of one's life. Horace's dictum *ut pictura poesis* (as is painting so is poetry)[64] is especially pertinent when representations of mortal temporality are involved. The easily

---

[64] Horace *EP*, l.361, p. 480. Cf. Simonides of Keos (as recorded by Plutarch, *Moralia, Volume IV*, trans. Frank Cole Babbitt, Loeb Classical Library (Cambridge, MA: Harvard University Press, 1936), p. 501: '*Poema pictura loquens, pictura poema silens*' (poetry is a speaking picture, painting mute poetry)).

identified figure of Death, however, is open to a wide range of interpretations, from the overly literal to much more sophisticated or at least more involved allegorical displays, such as the anonymous late sixteenth-century English painting, *The Allegory of Man* (see Figure 0.2). This work, very much marked by and indebted to an earlier scriptural tradition, brings together many of the visual and verbal commonplaces of the period associated with death in art that, as will be discussed, show up in a variety of ways in the entries of this anthology. The viewer (or indeed the reader, for the textual component of this painting is instrumental to comprehending the compound meaning of the work as a whole) is presented with what amounts to a carefully partitioned art of memory in which the images no less than explanatory words are intended to be taken to heart, each reinforcing and intensifying the meaning of the other.[65] One sees at a glance that the everyman figure is positioned at the centre of a cosmic, theological, and existential drama.[66] Although he is encircled by a protective scroll ('temperance', 'good reason', 'chastity', 'alms deeds', 'and compassion', 'meekness', 'charity', 'patience'), he is beset on all sides by mortal threats. On his right, he is being assaulted by representations of worldly temptations and vice, namely four of the traditional seven deadly sins; the alluring lady's arrows are labelled 'gluttony', 'sloth', 'lechery', and the miser's 'covetousness'. On his left, the sinister side in all respects of the term, is bellicose Death whose banner is woven into, or rather constitutes, his shield: 'Behind thee I steal like a thief, thy temporal life to devour'; and just below Death, a satyr-like Devil is ready to release arrows labelled 'pride', 'wrath', and 'envy' – the other three deadly sins. The central scroll, brought down by a guardian angel, urges preparation, thereby duly summing up the composite import of the encompassing allegorical images with a paraphrase of Matthew 25:13: 'Be sober therefore and watch, for thou knowest neither the day nor the hour.' Viewers follow the man's gaze heavenward toward Christ the Redeemer beside whom is a scroll with the opening words of 2 Corinthians 12:9 in Latin, which can be translated 'my grace is sufficient for you'. At the base of this vertical axis moving from Christ to the angel to everyman, the moral of the whole tableau is proclaimed explicitly:

O man, thou wretched creature, how mayest thou delight in riches, beauty, strength, or other worldly things. Remember thine enemies which continually seek thee to destroy and bring thee to nothing but sin, shame, and fire everlasting. Therefore, fast,

---

[65] On the sequencing and positioning of memory images during the early modern period, following a pattern established and developed in classical and medieval rhetoric, see *MA* 'Introduction' (esp. pp. 4–9).
[66] Cf. entry IV.2 (*The Summoning of Everyman*).

watch, and pray continually with fervent desire unto Jesus the mighty captain who only is able to defend thee from their fiery assaults.

It is easy to see how such involved, programmatic paintings like this one lent themselves as subjects for a variety of printed works, especially broadsides

FIGURE 0.2 *The Allegory of Man* (England, c.1569). The Tate Britain. Used by permission and with licence, Tate Images

and emblem books, which circulated widely in England during the early modern period.[67]

As the works discussed so far have shown, representations of death start with – and depend on – the body undergoing decay. In funerary monuments this can take the form of a transi-tomb, like that of Henry Chichele, Archbishop of Canterbury (see Figure 2.5, with reference to entry II.14). Depicted on the bottom tier is what the corpse interred beneath the tomb is in the process of becoming, thus mocking in art the lifelike rendering of the person memorialized on the top tier. This double, indeed chiastic, view of what he looked like in life and what he looks like now in death instructs onlookers, by way of a compound *memento mori* and *vanitas* token, to consider their own end and make proper provisions. Moreover, insofar as Chichele commissioned and oversaw the design of the tomb himself, it functioned as a reminder of his own mortality while he preached in Canterbury Cathedral. Reminders of human vanity, mortal transience, and hopes for futurity show up in so many different ways, ranging from fairly conventional cultural commonplaces like those just mentioned to more curiously wrought forms of expressions, such as *vanitas* paintings showing a sitter's face reflected in the mirror as a skull.[68] More rudimentarily, Geoffrey Whitney's emblem of a skull beside a dry bone, entitled '*Ex maximo minimum*' (from the greatest to the least), is poetically glossed as being a site 'where lively once, God's image was expressed' but now merely is 'a relic meet in charnel house to lie' (see Figure 0.3). The skull, as a synecdoche of a skeletal human frame, was the quintessential *memento mori* symbol of the Renaissance – whether in funeral monuments or book frontispieces and title pages that graphically imitate – or cite – just such architectural and memorial designs (as with Figures 1.6, 2.3 and 4.6). From classical antiquity (the putative homeland of the Latin motto '*et in Arcadia, ego*'[69]) up through the time of the Church Fathers (most notably

---

[67] See *MA* V.10 (*Ashrea*); and, for detailed analysis of a page from a printed emblem book with a comparable image replete with descriptive banners and biblical injunctions, see Engel, *Mortality*, p. 36.

[68] Such as the celebrated sixteenth-century *vanitas* double portrait of a husband and wife by Jacopo Ligozzi (on the front their youthful faces and on the back richly attired rotten skulls); see Engel, *Mortality*, pp. 171–72.

[69] A favourite theme among Baroque painters, especially Nicolas Poussin and Giovanni Francesco Barbieri (Guercino), showed Arcadian shepherds coming upon a skull, accompanied by the motto which translates as 'I too lived in Arcadia', where the absent speaker is one now deceased; alternatively, these are the words spoken by Death indicating his presence even amid the most idyllic settings.

Jerome, as will be discussed further), the human skull served as a token to spur serious – even pious – contemplation about one's own transience and end. During the Renaissance it was liable to be repurposed in somewhat more ludic but no less serious ways, such as in Hans Holbein's paintings, most famously *The Ambassadors* (1533), with its image of a skull hidden in anamorphic perspective at the bottom so as to offer an almost subliminal *memento mori* message; and as in Holbein's frequently reprinted and much copied engravings from his *Dance of Death* (see Figure 4.5).[70] The death's head in effect functions as something of a tacit master trope of the early modern period, for the skull, with no voice of its own, is made to speak emblematically, as if from beyond the grave, about our own mortality.[71] It becomes a mirror in which we see ourselves as someday we shall be 'a relic meet in charnel house to lie'. The death's head in early modern England was an always timely 'remembrancer', found among other places in popular emblem books,[72] built environments, ballads and broadsides, and a wide range of literary and dramatic texts and contexts.[73] These familiar depictions of death, so fundamental to the traditional visual literacy of Renaissance England, circulated in a variety of new and compelling – even performatively self-reflective – ways by virtue of advances in print technology. For example, in The Dance of Death sequence in *The Book of Christian Prayers*,[74] among the typical border vignettes are animated skeletons halting the activities – and lives – of workers in the printing house, namely those people responsible for reproducing just such depictions of death's immemorial dance. Many of the pages include a bottom-page border ornament showing the transi-tomb motif particularized after the manner of prosopopeia (where a disembodied textual voice gnomically

[70] First appearing as *Les Simulachres & historiées faces de la Mort* (Lyon, 1538) with forty-one woodcuts, the last page identifies the brothers Melchior and Gaspar Trechsel as having been behind the publication of Holbein's engravings.

[71] William E. Engel, *Death and Drama in Renaissance England* (Oxford: Oxford University Press, 2002), p. 18.

[72] Tamara A. Goeglein, 'Early Modern English Emblems of Death', in Calabritto and Daly, *ED*, pp. 59–95; and, on the dynamism and fluidity of English emblematic iconography, see Michael Bath, John Manning, and Alan R. Young (eds.), *The Art of the Emblem: Essays in Honor of Karl Josef Höltgen* (New York: AMS, 1993).

[73] With special reference to the latter, see the 'Introduction' to *The Shakespearean Death Arts: Hamlet Among the Tombs*, ed. William E. Engel and Grant Williams (New York and London: Palgrave, 2022).

[74] See *MA* V.5 (Day).

Introduction

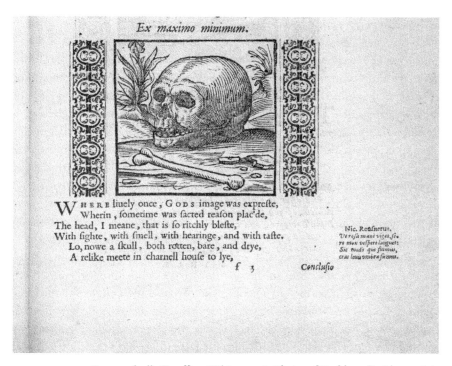

FIGURE 0.3 Rotten skull. Geoffrey Whitney, *A Choice of Emblems* (Leiden: 1586; STC 25438), f3ʳ. Image used courtesy of The Huntington Library

declares its identity): 'We printers wrote with Wisdom's pen: / She lives for aye,[75] we die as men.'[76]

The figure of Death as a skeletal cadaver striding upright and brandishing a 'deadly dart' – whether represented as spear or arrow (see Figure 0.4) – found its way into many pictorial and marmoreal works of the period. The same holds for a wide range of literary expressions of this commonplace in keeping with this visual precedent,[77] most notably Spenser's *The Faerie Queene*[78] and

---

[75] 'ever'
[76] As cited from a later version of *The Book of Christian Prayers* (London: Richard Day, 1608; STC 6432), Ll4ᵛ.
[77] See, for example, entries III.9 (Holland), IV.1 (Barclay), and IV.6 (Gascoigne).
[78] Spenser *FQ*, 2.11.21–22; the cadaverous Maleger, leader of the assault on Alma's House (an elaborate allegory of the human body) is thus described: 'Vpon his head he wore an Helmet light, / Made of a dead mans skull, that seemd a ghastly sight' (2.11.22.8–9).

Milton's *Paradise Lost*.[79] In the visual register of the period, whether inflected with primarily Catholic or Protestant theology and ideology, Death often appears as the necessary adjunct to and sometimes as a herald of Christ's ultimate triumph, consonant with God's divine plan and in fulfilment of the promise of mankind's hoped for redemption from sin and conducing to the four last things of Christian eschatology.[80] This aspect of Christian teleology is rehearsed with characteristic wit by John Donne's Holy Sonnet beginning 'Death, be not proud' and ending with the parting quip, 'Death, thou shalt die'.[81] And all of this allegorizing of Death takes place coincident with the rise of the new science and the development of increasingly sophisticated instruments for surgical procedures and the empirical study of anatomy. Many state-of-the-art medical books regularly included symbolically charged depictions of death, and even an hourglass (as discussed in entry III.11; see Figure 3.2), as well as other attributes associated with Father Time, thereby reminding readers of their temporary status in the world. The personification of Time (often situated in close proximity to Death, as is the case with the frontispiece of Helkiah Crooke's *Mikrokosmographia*, entry III.11; and also in the 'terrible battle between the two consumers of the whole world' presented allegorically by Samuel Rowlands, entry IV.10) has his telltale attribute of the reaping sickle or scythe which recalls the earlier tradition of Saturn, as Chronos, associated with the harvest – and also the devourer of all he brings forth into the world.[82] The

---

[79] Death shakes a 'dreadful dart' (John Milton, *Paradise Lost* in *Complete Poems and Major Prose*, ed. Merritt Y. Hughes (Indianapolis, IN: Bobbs-Merrill Educational Publishing, 1983), 2.672) that later is called by Sin a 'deadly arrow' (2.811); Milton seamlessly conflates these age-old allegorical attributes associated with Death personified, consistent with an inclusive and accumulative poetic practice that marks his epic throughout.

[80] As discussed by the Church Fathers and later commentators of the Latin Middle Ages, the *quattuor novissima* are Death, Final Judgement, Heaven, and Hell – the four last stages of the soul in life and the afterlife – a popular subject among Renaissance painters, such as Hieronymus Bosch, *The Seven Deadly Sins and the Four Last Things* (*c.*1500).

[81] Donne *PO*, pp. 139, l.14. With special reference to visual literacy and the death arts as regards Donne's 'pictures of the good death' and 'imagined dyings', see Arnold Stein, *The House of Death: Messages from the English Renaissance* (Baltimore, MD: Johns Hopkins University Press, 1986), chs. 3 and 7; see also Rebeca Helfer, 'Death and the Art of Memory in Donne', in *Memory and Mortality in Renaissance England*, ed. William E. Engel, Rory Loughnane, and Grant Williams (Cambridge: Cambridge University Press, at press), ch.1.

[82] A motif taken from Hesiod's *Theogony* (Hesiod, *Theogony, Works and Days, Testimonia*, trans. ed. Glenn W. Most, Loeb Classical Library (Cambridge, MA: Harvard University Press, 2018), 459), and reworked and transmitted by many classical authors, and chillingly depicted by, among others, Peter Paul Rubens, *Saturn Devouring his Son* (1638).

FIGURE 0.4 Striding Death. With motto: 'Bidt voor de sielen' (Pray for the souls [of the righteous]). Church tomb memorial wall plaque. Cathedral of St Bavo, Ghent, Belgium. Photo credit, William E. Engel

astrological influence of Saturn, considered the slowest of the planets, was deemed to be powerful; cold and dry Saturn therefore was associated with melancholy, old age, and death. As Erwin Panofsky observed, 'Death, like Saturn, was represented with a scythe or sickle from very early times' and 'it was from the image of Time that, about the last years of the fifteenth century, the presentations of Death began to borrow the characteristic hourglass, and sometimes even the wings'.[83]

---

[83] Erwin Panofsky, *Studies in Iconology: Humanistic Themes in the Art of the Renaissance* (1939; rpt. Boulder, CO: Westview Press, 1972), pp. 82–83.

As many of our entries will bear out, the hourglass, like the death's head, has a particularly potent symbolic role to play in the religious movements of the period. Traditionally a skull is among the attributes accompanying the figure of St Jerome in his retreat from the world to contemplate the truth of God's word and to translate it into Latin for others to read and take to heart. By the same token, a skull – said to be that of Adam, the first man who brought sin into the world – is often depicted at the base of the cross upon which Christ is crucified – the new man who redeems the sins of the world and who will conquer death.[84] Gazing upon such an ornament is the apparent rationale for John Skelton's ensuing musings on mortality and what we are to do in the face of such a recognition of our transience and inevitable future passing.[85] Skelton's tumbling verse reflection, moreover, mnemonically encapsulates and moves through the Canon of the Mass, with the poet as the celebrant who, in the course of the poem, is implicated as likewise requiring divine assistance.[86] Owing to the rushing rhythm of the incantatory rhymes, each section moves the reader through the phases of the service only to arrive exhausted and ready to take refuge in the Trinity. The envoy, 'Mirres vous y' ('see yourself therein'), urges readers to return to the title's main theme and engage in further self-reflection, but now from a double perspective: to see themselves mirrored in the dead man's head (that to which all must come) and also in the poem's mirroring of the mass (memorializing the hope for salvation). As with the Horatian tradition of *ut pictura poesis* mentioned earlier, the poem is a speaking picture while the skull tacitly provides the words in this case of the sermon.

The same multimodal impulse associated with visual literacy of the period marks George Wither's secular *Collection of Emblems* (entry I.11), insofar as he characterizes his poetic moralizations of pre-existing emblematic images as a 'puppet-play in pictures' and elsewhere as 'sculptures'.[87] Likewise using a visual image to leverage his poem's power to instigate contemplation of one's end, Henry Peacham presents a moral emblem with a picture of a death's

---

[84] Mâle, *Religious Art*, p. 114: 'In the language of religious art, the death's-head signifies Calvary.'
[85] See *MA* VI.1 (Skelton), esp. p. 281.
[86] Arthur F. Kinney, *John Skelton, Priest as Poet* (Chapel Hill, NC: University of North Carolina Press, 2011), ch. 3.
[87] *Collection of Emblems* (London: 1635; STC 25900d), A1ᵛ, A2ᵛ. Renaissance engravers usually signed themselves in their works as the sculptor, with reference to the printmaking technique that involves making incisions into a metal plate for retaining the ink that produces the resulting image.

head held by an outstretched hand issuing from a cloud. The motto is '*Nec metuas nec optes*' (Neither fear nor desire),[88] a sentiment echoed and glossed in the poem's closing couplet. The composite design visually and verbally clarifies an important aspect of the Renaissance humanist shared belief concerning the death's head as a classically derived (which is to say essentially pre-Christian) reminder to learn to die well.

> The Ethiopian Princes at their feasts,
> Did use amid their cates,[89] and costly cheer
> A dead man's head, to place before their guests,
> That it in mind might put them what they were:
>   And Phillip[90] daily caused one to say,
>   Oh King remember that thou art but clay.
>
> If pagans could bethink them of their end,
> And make such use of their mortality,
> With greater hope their course let Christians bend,
> Unto the haven of heavens felicity;
>   And so to live while here we draw this breath,
>   We have no cause to fear, or wish for death.

Emblems like this one by Peacham remind us to attend carefully to the multimodal heritage of the death arts in early modern England. Insofar as the many and various ways available for expressing mortal temporality mark nearly every medium of the period, one of the aims of our study is to highlight some of the more typical and telling instantiations of how people – and over a span of two hundred years – confronted death in the course of everyday life. Changing aspects of religious doctrine, as well as concomitant attitudes towards visual representation and built environments involving depictions of death can be traced through an English textual tradition augmented and accelerated by a thriving if state-regulated publishing industry.[91]

---

[88] Henry Peacham, *Minerva Britanna* (London: 1612; STC 19511), C4ʳ.
[89] 'dainty or choice food'
[90] Philip II, King of Macedon (reigned 359–36 BCE) and father of Alexander the Great, who conquered Greece.
[91] Cyndia Susan Clegg, *Press Censorship in Elizabethan England* (Cambridge: Cambridge University Press, 1997), pp. 3–29; Andrew Pettegree, 'Centre and Periphery in the European Book World', *Transactions of the Royal Historical Society*, sixth series (2008), vol. 18, pp. 101–28, esp. pp. 114–19; Kirk Melnikoff, *Elizabethan Publishing and the Makings of Literary Culture* (Toronto, ON: University of Toronto Press, 2017), pp. 3–26.

The steady and burgeoning traffic in printed materials assured there were an astonishingly large number of ways to represent and come to grips with death in Renaissance England.

Representing the Death Arts

The entries included in this anthology are collectively designed to enable readers to take stock of how death was shown to intersect with daily life in early modern England. We have sought to conceptualize more broadly how a range of concerns – from the psychological and deeply personal to the juridical and very public – is involved with spiritual as well as practical aspects of dying. We look at diverse genres and modes of expression, as well as tapping into a range of confessional frameworks, being mindful of the backlog of visual elements, mnemonic tropes and figures of thought, and also the various modes of meditative interiority that brought death within the general view of men, women, and children living and dying in Renaissance England.

Throughout this anthology we have sought to find representative entries of diverse forms of creative expression in the death arts that would have been easily, and with some regularity, recognized by early modern readers, viewers, and auditors.[92] As our remit is the mediation and circulation of ideas through *print*, we have not included examples drawn from manuscript-only primary sources (such a project would be of immense value, we think, not least in finding evidence of the death arts in personal diaries, correspondence, and coterie writing). One unavoidable consequence of focusing upon the production of the press is that the recovered voices tend to be white, male authors, a demographic that, for the most part, controlled the early modern publishing trade along with authorship networks.[93] The lower orders who fully inhabited oral traditions are then underrepresented by vehicles of literacy, which favour

---

[92] Regarding the latter, the actual audience of printed works was much larger than is reflected in book sales (let alone copies in circulation) owing to the multiplier factor; namely 'through public readings and commentaries, and so on' such that the 'number of people affected was far in excess of the number of copies printed, especially as the sale price fell in line with the reduction of production costs'; see Frédéric Barbier, *Guttenberg's Europe: The Book and the Invention of Western Modernity*, trans. Jean Birrell (Cambridge: Polity, 2016), p. 256.

[93] Still, women exerted significant influence in the mechanics and development of the publishing trade in early modern England (and in the mediation and editing of early modern writing since). See Valerie Wayne (ed.), *Women's Labour and the History of the Book in Early Modern England* (London: Bloomsbury, 2020).

Introduction

the views of the middle and upper classes. Folk beliefs, rituals, and lore about dying, death, and the dead are beyond this anthology's scope.[94] Death comes to all, but the early modern English death arts in print do not adequately articulate the full extent of the collective attitudes, understandings, hopes, and fears of England's heterogenous population. Nevertheless, despite the ideological constraints of the publishing record, issues of gender, sexuality, and race have strong implications for studying the death arts.

Gendering Death

The anthology tracks, to a certain degree, the involvement of women writers in the death arts through excerpting an abundance of genres, including prayer, elegy, mother's legacy, epistle, polemical pamphlet, religious and philosophical treatises, consolation, lyric, religious poetry, tragedy, and romance. Through our selection of passages, we have also attempted to foreground, at times, the complexities of gender relations around the cultural production of mortality. Several entries concentrate on women's writing about male death and men's writing about female death.[95] In the latter case, we include male memorializations to offer a sense of the patriarchal idealization of a woman's good dying and conversely the denigration of a woman's bad dying. Where possible, several excerpts have touched upon but only scratched the surface of the rich kinship relationships sustained and shaped by the death arts.[96] This area holds promise for future inquiry.[97] All in all, the death arts should be understood as collaborative enterprises rather than strictly solitary ventures – even solitary

---

[94] See Keith Thomas, *Religion and the Decline of Magic: Studies in Popular Beliefs in Sixteenth- and Seventeenth-Century England* (London: Weidenfeld and Nicolson, 1971) and Andy Wood, *The Memory of the People: Custom and Popular Senses of the Past in Early Modern England* (Cambridge: Cambridge University Press, 2013).

[95] See entry IV.11 (Lanyer), entry IV.17 (Behn), entry I.15 (Batchiler), and entry I.12 ('The Unnatural Wife').

[96] See entry I.10 (Leigh), entry I.12 ('The Unnatural Wife'), entry I.15 (Batchiler), entry I.16 (Janeway), entry II.8 (Sidney), and entry II.16 (Philips).

[97] For forays into this area, see Kathryn R. McPherson, '"My Deare Sister": Sainted Sisterhood in Early Modern England', in *Sibling Relations and Gender in the Early Modern World: Sisters, Brothers and Others*, ed. Naomi J. Miller and Naomi Yavneh (Aldershot, UK: Ashgate, 2006), pp. 182–94, and Carole Levin, 'Parents, Children, and Responses to Death in Dream Structures in Early Modern England', in *Gender and Early Modern Constructions of Childhood*, ed. Naomi J. Miller and Naomi Yavneh (Farnham, UK: Ashgate, 2011), pp. 39–49.

memento mori contemplation presupposes the artefacts, techniques, and emulation of others.[98] And thus, within each entry, our category 'about the author' regularly identifies collective and cooperative authorship.

That said, it has been more challenging to find a wide range of excerpts on the female experience of the death arts – especially in the sixteenth century – than it has been to locate a respective span of male passages. In the seventeenth century, for example, female poets account for a sizeable corpus of elegies,[99] but we have not come across a woman who has published an *ars moriendi* treatise. Anne Skelton's scriptural exegesis, *Comforts against the Fear of Death* (1641), excerpted in the epigraphs beginning Part I, is perhaps the closest approximation to the form. The primary reason for the narrow range of involvement stems from the fact that women 'faced tremendous obstacles in establishing themselves as public figures of any kind'.[100] Because of patriarchal domination (even during periods when the sovereign or regent was a woman) and the concomitant historical imposition of socio-religious norms, women were barred from the period's official institutions, such as politics, law, the military, the Church, medicine, and universities. Admonished to remain within the domestic sphere and set an example of docile piety, they did not have the same incentives, resources, or opportunities as men did to write for publication. Even when taking up the pen, they often confined themselves to particular genres, especially during the sixteenth century when many learned women, including Elizabeth Tudor, Anne Cooke, Anne Dowriche, Margaret Tyler, and Mary Sidney, gravitated to the less controversial path of translating works. As Margaret Ezell has argued, seventeenth-century manuscript culture better represents female authorship than does print.[101] Manuscripts enabled women to write for family members and friends without the impediments of

---

[98] A solid case for the study of collaborative authorship in gender studies has been made by Patricia Pender and Alexandra Day, 'Introduction' in *Gender, Authorship, and Early Modern Women's Collaboration*, ed. Patricia Pender (Cham, Switzerland: Palgrave Macmillan, 2017), pp. 1–19.

[99] For an introduction to this field, see Lauren Shohet, 'Women's Elegy: Early Modern', in *The Oxford Handbook of the Elegy*, ed. Karen Weisman (Oxford: Oxford University Press, 2010), pp. 433–41, and Anne K. Mellor, '"Anguish No Cessation Knows": Elegy and the British Woman Poet, 1660–1834', in ibid., pp. 442–62.

[100] Wendy Wall, *The Imprint of Gender: Authorship and Publication in the English Renaissance* (Ithaca, NY: Cornell University Press, 1993), pp. 279–80.

[101] For a study of how the print bias in scholarship has neglected women's literary involvement in manuscript culture, see Margaret J. M. Ezell, *Social Authorship and the Advent of Print* (Baltimore, MD: Johns Hopkins University Press, 2003), pp. 21–44.

social prohibition, thereby providing scholars with a fuller range of expression of female attitudes – including those on death – not hobbled by inhibitions and self-censorship.

None of this means, however, that early modern women occupied the sidelines of the public-orientated death arts. Unlicensed teaching of literacy,[102] medical treatment and midwifery,[103] family devotion, and religious instruction[104] were just some of the vital activities that women generally performed in a non-institutional and non-sanctioned capacity for their households and immediate communities. Despite the enforced Pauline interdiction against female preachers and teachers, Quakers, as well as Independents, such as Brownists, permitted women to sermonize during the Interregnum period. Along these lines, women gained a public voice through 'prophesying' too – the term used by William Perkins (see entry I.9) among others in the mid-sixteenth century to mean both preaching the Word in an assembly and also public prayer.[105] The print record thus obfuscates the deeply committed cultural and social engagement of early modern women with the entire death cycle: family members, female servants, and neighbouring women, whether or not paid, commonly attended the individual in his or her final sickness and dying;[106] before the late seventeenth-century saw the emergence of the professional undertaker, these aforementioned women, sometimes under the

---

[102] Kenneth Charlton and Margaret Spufford, 'Literacy, Society and Education', in *The Cambridge History of Early Modern English Literature*, ed. David Loewenstein and Janel Mueller (Cambridge: Cambridge University Press, 2003), p. 24. See also Michelle M. Dowd, *Women's Work in Early Modern English Literature and Culture* (New York: Palgrave Macmillan, 2009), esp. ch. 4 on 'Household Pedagogies: Female Educators and the Language of Legacy', pp. 133–72.

[103] Wear, *Medicine*, pp. 21–24.

[104] See Kenneth Charlton, 'Women and Education', in *A Companion to Early Modern Women's Writing*, ed. Anita Pacheco (Oxford: Blackwell, 2002), pp. 3–21, and Paula McQuade, *Catechisms and Women's Writing in Seventeenth-Century England* (Cambridge: Cambridge University Press, 2017).

[105] See Elaine Hobby, 'Prophecy', in Pacheco (ed.), *Companion*, pp. 264–81. See also Jeanne Shami, 'Women and Sermons', in *The Oxford Handbook of the Early Modern Sermon*, ed. Peter McCullough, Hugh Adlington, and Emma Rhatigan (Oxford: Oxford University Press, 2011), pp. 167–72. And yet the publication record of these sermons seems almost non-existent. Even Margaret Fell, an advocate for female preachers, 'did not publish any of her sermons among the many items that comprise her Works' (171). For the common usage of the word 'prophesying', see W. B. Patterson, *William Perkins and the Making of a Protestant England* (Oxford: Oxford University Press, 2014), pp. 117–19.

[106] Cressy, *Birth*, pp. 428–29.

direction of midwives, 'watched', washed, and prepared the body for burial, binding it in a winding sheet;[107] in a period when men constructed Protestant masculinity against the effeminacy of grief, women's communal mourning through immoderate lamentational practice preserved, deepened, and developed the emotional register around death;[108] old matrons, who presumably had a knowledge of their communities, collected invaluable data from gravesides for the bills of mortality written up by parish clerks;[109] and long after the funeral, women in affluent households could be curators and custodians of commemoration by passing on heirlooms and manuscript miscellanies that preserved the family's relational ties across generations.[110] An attentiveness toward the archive's gaps, innuendos, and in-between spaces can reveal and recover further female participation in the death arts.[111]

Sexualizing Death

The death arts, particularly manifested by literature's endless fascination with desire, prove fertile ground for exploring issues of early modern sexuality. Both the events of dying and orgasming are limit-experiences of selfhood, and their anticipation, either real or imaginary, triggers intense emotions charged with fear and anxiety. And yet, be that as it may, death, like sex, cannot be reduced to a single climactic act but also names an experience of the body, varied, local, and intimate.[112]

It is at the end of the fifteenth century that, according to Philippe Ariès, representations of death, as in the *danse macabre*, 'begin to take on an erotic meaning'.[113] While that may be so, eros and thanatos owe their entanglement

---

[107] Ibid. On the development of this profession, see Paul S. Fritz, 'The Undertaking Trade in England: Its Origins and Early Development, 1660–1830', *Eighteenth-Century Studies*, 28.2 (1994), 241–53.

[108] For the idea of 'immoderate' mourning ascribed to women, see Phillippy, *Women*, pp. 7, 24, 133–36, 166–67.

[109] See entry III.14 (Graunt).

[110] See Patricia Phillippy, *Shaping Remembrance from Shakespeare to Milton* (Cambridge: Cambridge University Press, 2018), pp. 59–90.

[111] See Phillippy, *Women*, for some of the most significant work on gender in the early modern cultures of memory and death. See also Becker, *Death*.

[112] We compare death's facticity here to Valerie Traub's basic fact of sex; see *Thinking Sex with the Early Moderns* (Philadelphia, PA: University of Pennsylvania Press, 2015), p. 4.

[113] Ariès, *Attitudes*, pp. 56–57. Karl S. Guthke observes the baroque as the first main period of death's eroticization too; see *The Gender of Death: A Cultural History in Art and Literature* (Cambridge: Cambridge University Press, 1999), p. 93.

to three distinctly medieval discourses, which had circulated for centuries: popular religion and theology grouped lust or lechery with the deadly sins;[114] medicine treated lovesickness as a disease whose outcome could prove fatal for sufferers;[115] and courtly love transferred the death-defying vow of homage and fealty from the feudal lord to the lady.[116] All three discourses exert their influence, for instance, on Chaucer's *Canterbury Tales*, especially 'The Knight's Tale'.[117] Whether pastoral/heroic – exemplified by Sidney's *Arcadia* – or chivalric – exemplified by Spenser's *The Faerie Queene*[118] – early modern romance continued to valorize the knight as a practitioner of a death-driven military art in the service of his mistress. Entries IV.8 (Tyler) and IV.14 (Wroth) strike this chord for the anthology, illustrating the way in which murderous violence is kindled by amorous passions and rationalized by the honour code.

Petrarchan poetry turns the outward threat inward, when the courtly lover without the distraction of a quest eats himself up with frustration and solicitude. Henry Howard's poem (entry IV.4), typical of the subgenre of the male lover's complaint,[119] also casts a sideways glance at lovesickness, the period's frequent diagnosis of the besotted lover, who wastes away mentally and physically. With respect to the disease, the French physician Du Laurens describes the sufferer as a walking corpse,[120] and Robert Burton, who finds no difference between the libidinal and death drives, prognosticates that 'Death is the common Catastrophe to such persons'.[121] The last-resort cure is to allow

---

[114] For early medieval campaigns against sex, see James A. Brundage, *Law, Sex, and Christian Society in Medieval Europe* (Chicago, IL and London: The University of Chicago Press, 1987), pp. 184–86.

[115] Jacques Ferrand, *A Treatise on Lovesickness*, ed. Donald A. Beecher and Massimo Ciavolella (Syracuse, NY: Syracuse University Press, 1990), pp. 62, 71, 82, 103.

[116] Roger Boase, *The Origin and Meaning of Courtly Love: A Critical Study of European Scholarship* (Manchester, UK: Manchester University Press, 1977), p. 89. Beecher and Ciavolella (eds.), 'Introduction', *A Treatise on Lovesickness*, p. 158.

[117] Chaucer *WO*, I (A) 859–3108.

[118] For an introduction to the types of romance, see Barbara Fuchs, *Romance* (New York and London: Routledge, 2004).

[119] Within love poetry, male as well as female speakers complain of their beloved's indifference and cruelty. The sonnet sequences *Astrophil and Stella* by Philip Sidney and *Delia* by Samuel Daniel frequently voice their speakers' sexual frustration.

[120] André Du Laurens, *A Discourse of the Preservation of the Sight: Of Melancholike Diseases; of Rheumes, and of Old Age* (London: 1599; STC 7304), R3ᵛ.

[121] Robert Burton, *The Anatomy of Melancholy*, 6 vols., ed. T. C. Faulkner, N. K. Kiessling, and R. L. Blair (Oxford: Clarendon Press, 1989–2000), vol. 3, pp. 174, 199.

the lovers to carnally enjoy one another.[122] For medical discourse, then, male sexuality was poised between the twin dangers of having too little sex and having too much. In the latter situation, the ejaculation of seed 'harmeth a man more, then if hee should bleed forty times as much'[123] because his body uses a great quantity of blood to distil a small amount of sperm. This medical axiom puts a more sinister spin on the pun of a little death (*petite mort*), with which erotic verse occasionally takes comic delight.[124] Orgasms were thought to gradually kill a sexually active man, and their potential lethality may explain why John Webster's *Duchess of Malfi* and John Marston's *Insatiate Countess* capitalize on staging widows with sharp sexual appetites, both protagonists being adopted from William Painter's collection of Italian and French novellas.[125] The widow's lust was proverbial in the period and, for tragedy, could stoke anxiety as well as salacious fantasy.[126] One cannot help but see the plays' execution of the two leading women as retribution for their threatening libidos. Another Painter novella translated from Marguerite de Navarre's *Heptaméron* and excerpted here (entry IV.5) presents an even stranger punishment of transgressive female sexuality. The common literary allegation in the period against women's excess or lack of concupiscence is finally flipped on its head by Jane Anger's exposure of a desperate and manipulative male lust (entry III.6).

The eroticization of death and the mortification of sex reach their apogees in early modern drama, which absorbs both romance and courtly poetry, but surpasses their feudal vision by depicting sexual scenarios from different epochs, societies, and classes.[127] For the theatre, there is something inescapably erotic about death (to 'die' could mean to orgasm, and dramatists repeatedly deploy this pun), attracting both the celibate and the initiate: not

---

[122] Ibid., p. 242.
[123] William Vaughan, *Natural and Artificial Directions for Health Derived from the Best Philosophers* (London: 1600; STC 24612), D7ᵛ–D8ʳ.
[124] See, for example, John Donne's 'Canonization' in Donne *PO*, pp. 77–78.
[125] For an analysis of how French novellas often depict women's sexuality as deadly, see Kathleen M. Llewellyn, 'Deadly Sex and Sexy Death in Early Modern French Literature', in Albrecht Classen (ed.), *Sexuality in the Middle Ages and Early Modern Times* (Berlin and New York: De Gruyter, 2008), pp. 811–35.
[126] Jennifer Panek, *Widows and Suitors in Early Modern English Comedy* (Cambridge: Cambridge University Press, 2004), pp. 1–4.
[127] For a theoretical introduction to theatre's longstanding relationship with the topic, see Karoline Gritzner (ed.), 'Introduction', in *Eroticism and Death in Theatre and Performance* (Hatfield: University of Hertfordshire Press, 2010), pp. 1–11.

infrequently do Elizabethan playwrights structure their action around the belief that losing one's life is preferable to relinquishing one's virginity, the unstated implication being that a maiden should save herself for the ultimate lover, so to speak;[128] playwrights were also known for setting trysts at tombs and graveyards, locations that emotionally compounded the thrill of fornication with flouting the taboos around the peaceful rest of the dead and the sacred inviolability of the grave – hence the repeated association of 'tomb' with womb.[129] Entry IV.12 from Tourneur's *The Atheist's Tragedy* illustrates such an assignation, although perhaps the most famous examples of tomb scenes are the finales of Shakespeare's *Romeo and Juliet* and *Antony and Cleopatra*. Both plays transfigure self-slaughter into an onanistic act in which each lover becomes both the object and subject of death. As well as demonstrating a glimmer of changing attitudes toward suicide,[130] this theatrical auto-eroticization rechannels the imagined ecstasy of the enraptured votary found throughout the period's religious poetry[131] and signals a sharp secular departure from the Catholic possibility of reuniting posthumously with one's beloved.[132] *The Revenger's Tragedy* by Thomas Middleton takes the charnel rendezvous to new heights, or rather new depths, when Vindice fabricates a female effigy with his beloved's skull in order to avenge himself on the lecherous Duke, who, expecting a warm body, unknowingly poisons himself from

---

[128] Theodore Spencer, *Death and Elizabethan Tragedy: A Study of Convention and Opinion in the Elizabethan Drama* (New York: Pageant Books, 1960), pp. 138–41.

[129] On this association, see, for example, Romeo's description of Juliet's tomb: 'Thou dètestable maw, thou womb of death' (*Romeo and Juliet*, 5.3.45). We do not mean to suggest that churchyards were barred from secular activities. On their use for commerce and leisure, see David Dymond, 'God's Disputed Acre', *Journal of Ecclesiastical History*, 50.3 (1999), 464–97.

[130] The Elizabethan and Stuart periods intensified a hostility toward the act until the Restoration decriminalized it. See Michael MacDonald and Terence R. Murphy, *Sleepless Souls: Suicide in Early Modern England* (Oxford: Clarendon Press, 1990).

[131] A sampling may be found in George Herbert's and Richard Crashaw's poetry. See Warren M. Liew, 'Reading the Erotic in George Herbert's Sacramental Poetics', *George Herbert Journal*, 31.1 (2007), 33–62; Alexander T. Wong, 'Mystic Excess: Extravagance and Indecorum in Richard Crashaw', *The Cambridge Quarterly*, 39.4 (2010), 350–69.

[132] Ramie Targoff's work traces the afterlife or lack thereof for lovers in the literature of the period; see Targoff, 'Burying Romeo and Juliet: Love after Death in the English Renaissance', in *Love after Death: Concepts of Posthumous Love in Medieval and Early Modern Europe*, ed. Bernhard Jussen and Ramie Targoff (Berlin: De Gruyter, 2014), pp. 147–66, and *Posthumous Love: Eros and the Afterlife in Renaissance England* (Chicago, IL: University of Chicago, 2014).

kissing the toxin-smeared mouth of the death-head.[133] The dark humour of necrophilia, likewise, punctuates Beaumont's elegiac blazon of Lady Markham (entry II.14).

It is easy to find violently sensational representations of the mortification of sex during the period. Propagated by biblical and Church prohibitions, and the long-lasting Tudor law that criminalized buggery with hanging,[134] moral panic encouraged the punishment of male same-sex relations in print, notably exemplified by the scene of regicide in Marlowe's *Edward II*, excerpted here (entry IV.9), and the pamphlet on the life and death of John Atherton, the Anglican bishop in the Church of Ireland, who was executed for sodomy.[135] Recent work in sexuality and queer studies, however, has chosen to investigate the latent and nuanced rather than the overt and heavy-handed. It recognizes the plurality, complexity, and indeterminacy of the erotic in an age before modern sexual categories and identities had come into their own.[136] Renaissance poets and playwrights who take their inspiration from Ovid's corpus, especially the *Metamorphoses* – that veritable encyclopaedia of all things thanatos and eros – accumulate a treasury of sensual tropes for verbalizing the affective experience of bodies and their loss.[137] In this respect, erotic epyllia exhibit an ornately embroidered death art. After the groundbreaking work of Alan Bray in the area of male friendship,[138] elegies mourning the demise of close companions may offer scholars further material for the study of sexuality and sexual difference. Our first excerpt from Katherine Philips's *Poems* (entry II.16), given the illuminating context of her literary circle, is as

---

[133] *The Revenger's Tragedy*, ed. MacDonald P. Jackson, in *Thomas Middleton: The Collected Works*, gen. ed. Gary Taylor and John Lavagnino (Oxford: Oxford University Press, 2007), 3.5.130–219.

[134] *The Statutes at Large, from the First Year of King Richard III to the Thirty-First Year of King Henry VIII Inclusive*, ed. Danby Pickering, 5 vols. (Cambridge: Cambridge University Press, 1763), vol. 4, p. 267.

[135] Nicholas Bernard, *The Penitent Death of a Woefull Sinner, Or, the Penitent Death of John Atherton Executed at Dublin the 5 of December 1640* (Dublin, 1641; Wing, B2017).

[136] Traub, *Thinking Sex*, pp. 10–11. See also James M. Bromley and Will Stockton, 'Introduction', in *Sex Before Sex: Figuring the Act in Early Modern England*, ed. James M. Bromley and Will Stockton (Minneapolis, MN: University of Minnesota Press, 2013), pp. 7 and 12.

[137] See *Ovid and Masculinity in English Renaissance Literature*, ed. John S. Garrison and Goran Stanivukovic (Montreal: McGill-Queen's University Press, 2020).

[138] Alan Bray, 'Homosexuality and the Signs of Male Friendship in Elizabethan England', in *Queering the Renaissance*, ed. Jonathan Goldberg (Durham, NC and London: Duke University Press, 1994), pp. 40–61.

much an elegiac encryption of abiding homoerotic passion as it is a commentary on tombs.[139] Again, the posthumous also opens our eyes to the sexualization of the death arts.[140] From an orthodox perspective, female and male fantasies of consummating an otherworldly marriage with Christ appear throughout religious verse, such as John Donne's Holy Sonnet 'Batter my Heart',[141] whose speaker begs for what moderns would call a sadomasochistic experience. From a more secular perspective, Shakespeare's *Sonnets*, which have a long critical history of yielding queer readings,[142] wrestles with the question of what it means to love a young man under the ever-darkening shadow of mortality.

Another factor that warrants mention is that the Grim Reaper was considered to be a sexual being. With the 'new iconography of the sixteenth century', Philippe Ariès claims, 'death raped the living', a characterization which Romeo would certainly not dispute.[143] The fear of further violation may have made the Virgin Queen oppose the embalming of her corpse, perhaps fearing, Patricia Phillippy speculates, for her chastity at the knife-wielding hands of her male embalmers. Elizabeth's wish was not unique among women in the period.[144] As Karl S. Guthke duly notes, however, sixteenth- and seventeenth-century death could be gendered female as well as male, some works like Holbein's *Dance of Death* and *Measure for Measure* presenting both.[145] Such gendered personifications give new meaning to the passivity of the gisant (a recumbent effigy) reclining on a bed-like sarcophagus and to deathbed depictions in which the *moriens* awaits death's coming.

[139] See Harriette Andreadis, 'Re-Configuring Early Modern Friendship: Katherine Philips and Homoerotic Desire', *Studies in English Literature, 1500–1900*, 46.3 (2006), 523–42 and Valerie Traub, '"Friendship so Curst": *Amor Impossibilis*, the Homoerotic Lament, and the Nature of Lesbian Desire', in *The Noble Flame of Katherine Philips: A Poetics of Culture, Politics, and Friendship*, ed. David L. Orvis and Ryan Singh Paul (University Park, PA: Penn State University Press, 2015), pp. 243–66.
[140] See Ramie Targoff's work, n.132.
[141] Donne *PO*, p. 140.
[142] For an introduction to this topic, see Bruce R. Smith, 'Shakespeare's Sonnets and the History of Sexuality: A Reception History', in *A Companion to Shakespeare's Works, Volume IV: The Poems, Problem Comedies, Late Plays*, ed. Richard Dutton and Jean E. Howard (Malden, MA and Oxford: Blackwell, 2003), pp. 1–26.
[143] Ariès, *Attitudes*, p. 56. *Romeo and Juliet*, 5.3.103–105.
[144] Phillippy, *Women*, pp. 54–57.
[145] Guthke, *Gender of Death*, pp. 99, 106, and 120. Guthke points out, though, that female death did not have an impact comparable to that of the male version. He also contends that the ambisexuality of death is based on the devil's ambisexuality, because both figures were at the time considered equivalent due to their close connection with sin (127).

Racializing Death

Any sustained investigation of the Renaissance death arts almost at once runs into the issue of race and the blatant racism that permeates early modern European thought.[146] To some extent this is the result of very ancient prejudices in the West that link blackness to evil and death,[147] such that, as Michael Neill has observed, 'blackness proves to be oddly like death'.[148] The connection is reinforced by the medieval vernacular name for the sporadic waves of virulent pestilence, 'the Black Death'[149] ('*Der schwarze Tod*' in German-speaking lands), owing to the dark-hued subcutaneous haemorrhaging that bruised and 'blackened' the bodies of those infected by the bacterium *Yersina pestis*.[150] Gangrene of the fingers, toes, and nose likewise were visible signs of

---

[146] Ayanna Thompson (ed.), *The Cambridge Companion to Shakespeare and Race* (Cambridge: Cambridge University Press, 2021); and, more specifically on the historical practices of generalization 'through which the personality of a singular individual becomes transcoded into the character of a collective totality of peoples, exemplifying processes of race-thinking and racialization', see Geraldine Heng, *The Invention of Race in the European Middle Ages* (Cambridge: Cambridge University Press, 2018), pp. 17–18. Also with particular relevance to our project, apropos of the ongoing need for 'expanding and theorizing the archive of race, seeking out new texts, questions, and vocabulary', see Peter Erickson and Kim F. Hall, '"A New Scholarly Song": Rereading Early Modern Race', in *Shakespeare Quarterly*, 67.1 (2016), 1–13, 7; Ayanna Thompson, *Passing Strange: Shakespeare, Race, and Contemporary America* (Oxford: Oxford University Press, 2013); K. J. P. Lowe, 'The Stereotyping of Black Africans in Renaissance Europe', in *Black Africans in Renaissance Europe*, ed. T. F. Earle and K. J. P. Lowe (Cambridge: Cambridge University Press, 2010), pp. 17–48; Imtiaz Habib, *Black Lives in the English Archives, 1500–1677* (London and New York: Routledge, 2008); and Jonathan Burton and Ania Loomba (eds.), *Race in Early Modern England: A Documentary Companion* (New York: Palgrave Macmillan, 2007).

[147] Cf. Kim F. Hall, *Things of Darkness: Economies of Race and Gender in Early Modern England* (Ithaca, NY and London: Cornell University Press, 1995), pp. 5–6, on 'the association of black people with the conflated imagery of blackness and death'.

[148] Neill, *Issues*, p. 147.

[149] Lars Walløe, 'Medieval and Modern Bubonic Plague: Some Clinical Continuities', *Medical History Supplement*, 27 (2008), 59–73. On the seasonal appearance in England of what probably was pneumonic plague, even more terrifying than the bubonic variety of the fourteenth-century Black Death, see J. R. Maddicott, 'Plague in Seventh-Century England', *Past and Present*, 156 (1997), 7–54, 22.

[150] Samuel K. Cohn, *The Black Death Transformed: Disease and Culture in Early Renaissance Europe* (London: Arnold, 2002); and see also Cohn's subsequent findings, 'Epidemiology of the Black Death and Successive Waves of Plague', *Medical History Supplement*, 27 (2008), 74–100.

the Black Death,[151] thus turning victims into living corpses that resembled allegorical depictions of Death (which were of course based on images of decaying human bodies). Throughout Mitteleuropa death personified was referred to as '*Der schwarze Mann*' ('the Black Man') and embodied the characteristics of an alien whose unwelcomed otherness betokened an eerie mirror image of what otherwise was familiar.[152] Death was the foreigner *par excellence* in the European popular imagination.[153] By the fifteenth century this construction of the dark, dangerous, and always suspect foreigner had become associated with the 'Moor', often expanded to 'Blackamoor',[154] which turned the already terrifying image of the 'oriental' infidel[155] into an avatar and harbinger of malignant forces in the world. And sometimes, as discussed in entry I.2 (*Calendar of Shepherds*), this stereotype was dialled down, domesticated, and contained as the racialized pitch-black subaltern and herald of Death (see Figure 1.3).

As is covered in more detail elsewhere in the Introduction with respect to visual literacy and the death arts, the 'Moor' was often depicted holding Death's main iconographic attribute, the dart or spear (see again Figures 0.1 and 0.4), a five-metre pole-weapon known colloquially in Elizabethan England

---

[151] For first-hand accounts translated and edited by Rosemary Horrox, see *The Black Death* (Manchester, UK: Manchester University Press, 1994).

[152] Engel, *Mortality*, pp. 77–87.

[153] A comparable argument can be made about the composite trope of 'The Wandering Jew' as a migratory yet ever-abiding figure, formalized by the pernicious medieval legends about Jews as 'Killers of Christ', 'Murderers of Children' linked to 'The Blood Libel', 'Poisoners of Wells', and 'Desecrators of the Host'; see Heiko Oberman, *The Roots of Antisemitism in the Age of Renaissance and Reformation* (Minneapolis, MN: Fortress Press, 1984); Léon Poliakov, *The History of Anti-Semitism* (Philadelphia, PA: University of Pennsylvania, 1974–1985); Klaus P. Fischer, *History of an Obsession: German Judeophobia* (London: Bloomsbury, 2001); Jeffrey Shoulson, *Fictions of Conversion: Jews, Christians, and Cultures of Change in Early Modern England* (Philadelphia, PA: University of Pennsylvania Press, 2013); and Magda Teter, *Blood Libel: On the Trail of an Antisemitic Myth* (Cambridge, MA: Harvard University Press, 2020). Cf. entry III.13 (Ross) on sixteenth-century understandings of Jewish mourning and burial customs.

[154] Engel, *Mortality*, pp. 72–73.

[155] On the 'Islamic Orient' as being 'viewed with distrust and loathing' notwithstanding English 'commercial, diplomatic, and social engagements with both Turks and Moors', and on contemporary critical efforts 'to correct "surface" readings of the cultural and historical significance of the Ottoman Empire as the West's bogey and demonized Other', see Walter S. H. Lim, 'Introduction: The English Renaissance, Orientalism, and the Idea of Asia—Framing the Issues', in *The English Renaissance, Orientalism, and the Idea of Asia*, ed. Debra Johanyak and Walter S. H. Lim (New York: Palgrave Macmillan, 2019), pp. 1–22, esp. pp. 4–5.

as a 'Moor's' pike[156] (because of its putative Moorish origin). And in lands closer to the Ottoman Empire, where there was always a threat of Turkish incursions into Christian Europe,[157] as is discussed in entry III.9 (Holland), the recurring character in the *Totentanz* ('Dance of Death'), a spry cadaver visiting people of all stations and leading them away from this life,[158] from time to time was depicted distinctively as a turbaned 'oriental' warrior.[159] Whether referred to as 'Moor' or Turk,[160] 'Blackamoor' or Saracen,[161] there is no mistaking the dark-skinned foreigner as an agent and simulacrum of death in the early European imagination.[162] While there was of course some historical precedent in the sixteenth century for fearing foreigners, especially in the Balkans and throughout the Mediterranean region, the image of the death-dealing 'Moor' persisted as a symbolic reminder, a stark *memento mori*, of the fragility and transience of life. The easy commerce between perceived reality and the symbolic register, signalling the concrete embodiment of abstract themes especially where issues of race are involved, at times marked, at times crossed, and at times melded zones of communally experienced tension and social anxieties associated with the recognition – and, indeed, the misrecognition – of cultural

---

[156] See, for example, Dromio of Syracuse's description in Shakespeare's *Comedy of Errors*: 'he that sets up his rest to do more exploits with his mace than a Moorish pike' (4.3.25).

[157] Noel Malcolm, *Useful Enemies: Islam and the Ottoman Empire in Western Political Thought, 1450–1750* (Oxford: Oxford University Press, 2019).

[158] Henri Stegemeier, *The Dance of Death in Folksong, with an Introduction on the History of the Dance of Death* (Chicago, IL: University of Chicago, 1939), pp. 22–23. See entry IV.3 (Lydgate).

[159] On 'Moors' dressed in the garb of a puissant 'oriental' potentate ('*Der Tod als Türke mit Turban*'), confronting the King in the Dance of Death, see Georg Carlen, 'Der Totentanz im Regierungsgebäude zu Luzern,' in *Todesreigen/Totentanz: Der Innerschweiz im Bannkreis barocker Todesvorstellungen* (Luzern, Switzerland: Raeber Verlag, 1996), pp. 112–13.

[160] With reference to the historicizing of terms such as 'Moor' and Turk', see Daniel J. Vitkus, 'Turning Turk in *Othello*: The Conversion and Damnation of the Moor', *Shakespeare Quarterly*, 48.2 (1997), 145–76, esp. 160.

[161] On the 'oriental' harbinger of death and the term 'Saracen' to denote North Africans in the white-European racialization of people referred to collectively as 'Moors', see Suzanne Conklin Akbari, *Idols in the East: European Representations of Islam and the Orient, 1100–1450* (Ithaca, NY: Cornell University Press, 2009), pp. 284–86.

[162] Emily C. Bartels, 'Making More of the Moor: Aaron, Othello, and Renaissance Refashioning of Race', *Shakespeare Quarterly*, 41 (1990), 432–54; and for further and extended analysis along these lines, see Emily C. Bartels, *Speaking of the Moor: From 'Alcazar' to 'Othello'* (Philadelphia, PA: University of Pennsylvania Press, 2009).

difference.[163] Thus, through fairly typical displays of displacement and transference, the anxieties traditionally felt about Death were transposed onto the 'Moor' and vice versa.

For a number of reasons, the term 'Moors' was generally applied to all Africans regardless of skin colour at least as earlier as the first century BCE,[164] a practice that continued, curiously, well into Shakespeare's day.[165] Moreover racial difference was mapped onto a scale of aesthetics and ethics which emphatically was not favourable to people of non-white complexion. From Helen of Troy to Queen Elizabeth with her white-face lead-based make-up,[166] statuesque

---

[163] See Neill, *Issues*, p. 145, on the 'Moor' – exemplarily Shakespeare's Othello – as 'alien territory to be subjected to the colonizer's all-mastering optic'; and on the larger issue at stake here: 'what precisely constituted the "nature" of foreign peoples was, of course, a fiercely contested one at a time when the modern ideology of "race" was only beginning to be hammered out on the anvil of European empire'. Also in this regard, see Ania Loomba, *Shakespeare, Race, and Colonialism* (Oxford: Oxford University Press, 2002), pp. 91–111; and on this play's construction of an idea of 'blackness and race that places severe constraints on black subjectivity', see Ian Smith, 'Othello's Black Handkerchief', *Shakespeare Quarterly*, 64.1 (2013), 1–25, esp. p. 3.

[164] Wayne B. Chandler, 'The Moor: Light of Europe's Dark Age', in *Golden Age of the Moors*, ed. Ivan Van Sertima (New Brunswick and London: Transaction, 1992), pp. 151–81: 'the Roman army entered West Africa where they encountered black Africans which they called "Maures" from the Greek adjective *mauros*, meaning dark or black' (151); and James E. Brunson and Runoko Rashidi, 'The Moors in Antiquity', in ibid., pp. 27–84: 'Black soldiers, specifically identified as Moors, were actively recruited by Rome and served tours of duty in Britain, France, Switzerland, Austria, Hungary, Poland, Romania' (47).

[165] Eldred Jones, *Othello's Countrymen: The African in English Renaissance Drama* (London: Oxford University Press for Fourah Bay College, 1965), p. 28; Anthony Gerard Barthelemy, *Black Face, Maligned Race: The Representations of Blacks in English Drama from Shakespeare to Southerne* (Baton Rouge, LA and London: Louisiana State University Press, 1987), pp. 7–17; Ruth Cowhig, 'Blacks in English Renaissance Drama and the Role of Shakespeare's *Othello*', in *The Black Presence in English Literature*, ed. David Dabydeen (Manchester, UK: Manchester University Press, 1985), pp. 1–25, esp. pp. 2–5; Roslyn L. Knutson, 'A Caliban in St. Mildred Poultry', in *Shakespeare and Cultural Traditions*, ed. Tetsuo Kishi, Roger Pringle, and Stanley Wells (Newark, NJ: University of Delaware Press, 1994), pp. 110–26, esp. p. 113; and Kim F. Hall, 'Troubling Doubles: Apes, Africans, and Blackface in *Mr. Moore's Revels*', in *Race, Ethnicity, and Power in the Renaissance*, ed. Joyce Green MacDonald (Cranbury, NJ: Fairleigh Dickinson University Press, 1996); Patricia Parker, *Shakespeare from the Margins: Language, Culture, Context* (Chicago, IL and London: University of Chicago Press, 1996), pp. 4–5, 275.

[166] On women's use of 'Venetian Ceruse' in the period, see Patricia Phillippy, *Painting Women: Cosmetics, Canvases, and Early Modern Culture* (Baltimore, MD: Johns Hopkins University Press, 2005); and Anna Riehl, *The Face of Queenship: Early Modern Representations of Elizabeth I* (New York: Palgrave Macmillan, 2010).

whiteness was the epitome of beauty; its nadir, the blackness of 'Moors'.[167] For example, in a sermon on 'The Devout Soul's Motto', Daniel Featley[168] makes the following comparison to illustrate the power of divine love on the soul: 'Surely though a deformed Black-a-moor look his eyes out upon the fairest beauty the world can present, he getteth no beauty by it, but seems the more ugly by standing in sight of so beautiful a creature.'[169] Racist comparisons along these lines were familiar enough in Stuart England to be featured in popular lyrics: 'The Grecian Helen was a Moor, / Compar'd to my dear Saint.'[170] The aesthetic issue of racialized notions of colour cannot be overcome even in Aphra Behn's *Oroonoko* (see entry IV.17), a work often considered one of the first abolitionist texts critical of colonial slavery.[171] In her description of the eponymous hero (whose slave name is Caesar, doubly ironic in that in the end he is betrayed by those whom he believes his friends), colour can never fully be redeemed in the Eurocentrically suffused mind's eye of the writer – and reader:

His nose was rising and Roman, instead of *African* and flat. His mouth, the finest shaped that could be seen; far from those great turned lips, which are so natural to the rest of the *Negroes*. The whole proportion and air of his face was so noble, and exactly formed, that, bating[172] his colour, there could be nothing in nature more beautiful, agreeable and handsome. (C3r)

Behn is at pains to make Oroonoko's outward features as accurate a reflection of his inner regality and dignity as is narratively possible given the long-inured canons of white-European ideal beauty. (As a seventeenth-century abolitionist who herself was positively disposed toward enslaved black people, even she cannot shake off her pan-European standards of 'the beautiful'.) But while the hero is being elevated by the idea of being worthy in moral terms because his physical appearance is similar to the European ideal, the writer and the reader cannot actually make him white, and his irreversible blackness marks him out as somehow destined for death. From the outset of his

---

[167] See Jean Michel Massing, 'From Greek Proverb to Soap Advert: Washing the Ethiopian', *Journal of the Warburg and Courtauld Institutes*, 58 (1995), 180–201.
[168] See *MA* V.6 (Featley) for another of his sermons that involves chromatic associations linked to moral behaviour.
[169] Daniel Featley, *Clavis Mystica* (London: 1636; STC 10730), p. 550.
[170] ' In Praise of his Mistress's Beauty', in *The Second Part of Wit and Drollery, or A Collection of Joviall Poems* (London: 1661; Wing S2295), D2ᵛ.
[171] Moira Ferguson, 'Oroonoko: Birth of a Paradigm', *New Literary History*, 23.2 (1992), 339–59, esp. pp. 339–40.
[172] 'with the exception of' (*archaic*)

Introduction 41

enslavement, Oroonoko in effect becomes a kinetic emblem of death, moving from episode to episode.[173] In this regard at least he is like the best of the classical stoics: striving to live nobly despite and by virtue of the deprivations and hardships he must endure, ever mindful of his mortality.

The same sort of racist prejudice involving complexion also informs Shakespeare's Lysander who, under the influence of a fairy love-potion, rebukes Hermia and declares his love for Helena: 'Who will not change a raven for a dove?'[174] Later, in his further railing against Hermia, his shunning of all things black comes to a head with the unmistakably racist epithets: 'Away, you Ethiope! … Out tawny Tartar, out!'[175] And while other terms for people of colour were current in the day, including (as with *Oroonoko*) 'Negroes',[176] there seems to remain a persistent will to ignorance where differentiating various races, cultures, and nations of the African and Asian continents are concerned. Notable exceptions, as discussed in entry III.13, are sixteenth-century proto-ethnographic efforts to understand (at least as far as long-engrained presumptions of white-European superiority allowed) the habits and customs of people in foreign lands where the English had or wanted to have trade relations, emissaries, and outposts.

Recalling the ancient prejudices, though, the word 'Moor' recurrently denotes anyone descended from Noah's son Cham.[177] Richard Eden's

---

[173] Cf. Lisa Hopkins, '"Black but Beautiful": *Othello* and the Cult of the Black Madonna', in *Marian Moments in Early Modern Drama*, ed. Regina Buccola and Lisa Hopkins (London and New York: Routledge, 2007), pp. 75–86, esp. p. 75: 'Death, then, is in our sights from the outset of *Othello* (and is fundamentally associated with blackness).'

[174] *A Midsummer Night's Dream*, 2.2.120.   [175] Ibid., 3.2.258, 265.

[176] Derived from the word for the colour black in Romance languages, the term 'Negro' circulated throughout western Europe during the Renaissance, usually to designate slaves; see F. O. Shyllon, *Black Slaves in Britain* (London: Oxford University Press, 1974), p. 1. However, around 1550, 'Sir Peter Negro' (also called 'Captain Negro') was sent against the Scots leading a band of soldiers from Spain, according to *Acts of the Privy Council*, n.s. 11, 1547–1550, ed. John Roche Dasent (London, 1902), pp. 16–17; see also Folarin Shyllon, 'Blacks in Britain: A Historical and Analytical Overview', in *Global Dimensions of the African Diaspora*, ed. Joseph E. Harris (Washington, DC: Howard University Press, 1982), pp. 170–94, esp. p. 171. And on 'Lucy Negro', who performed in The Gray's Inn Revels during Christmas 1594, see Edward Scobie, *Black Britannia: A History of Blacks in Britain* (Chicago, IL: Johnson Publishing Company, 1972), pp. 5–6.

[177] Gen 10:21; 1 Chr 5:40. George Best's *Discourse* (1578), from Richard Hakluyt's *The Principal Navigations*, transcribed and reprinted in James Walvin, *The Black Presence: A Documentary History of the Negro in England, 1555–1860* (London: Orbach & Chambers, 1971), pp. 34–37, recounts the legend that Cham sought to disinherit the offspring of his two brothers, and for this treachery 'God would a son should be born whose name was

compendious *Decades of the New World* (1555), for example, records that 'the people which now inhabit the regions of the coast of Guinea and the mid parts of Africa, as Libya the inner, and Nubia with divers other great and large regions about the same were in old time called Ethiopes and Nigrate, which we now call Moores, Moorens, or Negroes'.[178] And, as late as 1672, an anonymous pamphlet realigns death with people of colour in *A True Relation of the Inhumane and Unparalleled Actions, and Barbarous Murders of Negroes or Moors: committed on three English-men in Old Calabar in Guinny*.[179] As a collective noun, 'Moors' bears a striking similarity to the Anglicized Latin term for the character of Death, *Mors*; and the plural 'moorens', as often spelled 'morians', likewise is phonetically similar to the term used to refer to 'the dying person' in *ars moriendi* treatises, namely *moriens*.[180] In early modern English printed sources such as those discussed in this book then, the vocabulary of death and dying could all too easily slip into racist terminology.

***

Chus, who not only itself, but all his posterity after him should be so black and loathsome, that it might remain a spectacle of disobedience to all the world. And of this black and cursed Chus came all these black Moors which are in Africa' (37). The 'cause' of blackness, was 'the curse and natural infection of blood, and not the distemperature of the climate; which also may be proved by this example, that these black men are found in all parts of Africa, as well without the Tropics'. Whereas Cain was marked for having committed murder, the mark of blackness on the descendants of treacherous Cham is an enduring 'spectacle of disobedience to all the world'. Such a string of assumptions, commonplace during the English Renaissance, seem to be implicit in Iago's use of tropes of blackness connoting Othello's 'monstrous generativity'; see Janet Adelman, 'Iago's Alter Ego: Race as Projection in *Othello*', *Shakespeare Quarterly*, 48.2 (1997), 125–44, esp. p. 130.

[178] Richard Eden, *Decades of the New World* (London: 1555; STC 647), UUUU3ᵛ (original spelling of these racialized designations is retained here and in the following quotations to preserve the mid-sixteenth-century orthography). See also Thomas Hickock's translation of *The Voyage and Travail of M. Caesar Frederick, Merchant of Venice* (London: 1588; STC 10746), G2ʳ: 'The kingdom of Bengala in times past hath been as it were in the power of Moores'; and Andrew Boorde, *The Introduction of Knowledge* (London: 1562; STC 3385), M3ᵛ–M4ᵛ, which consistently spells the term as 'more': e.g., 'of the Mores which do dwell in Barbary'; 'a black More born in Barbary'; and 'the inhabitors be called the Mores, there be white mores and black mores'.

[179] *A True Relation* (London: 1672; Wing T2970).

[180] See entry I.1 (Caxton), A2ᵛ. For further glossing of *'moriens'*, see Phoebe S. Spinrad, *The Summons of Death on the Medieval and Renaissance English Stage* (Columbus, OH: Ohio State University Press, 1987), p. 31; Mary Catharine O'Connor, *The Art of Dying Well: The Development of the Ars Moriendi* (New York: Columbia University Press, 1942), p. 49. And, on the homophonic 'morians', see John Lydgate, *The Life and Death of Hector* (London: 1614; STC 5581.5), K2ᵛ: 'For as I find the Moores or Morians / On Iuban long

This study does not aspire to say the final word on the death arts. Their dispersal throughout manifold discourses, genres, mental habits, practices, rituals, and artefacts attests to the vanity of trying to codify them with a master canon or to bound them in a discrete and coherent area of social relationships, state institutions, or knowledge formation. The anthology attempts to disentangle a selection of death arts from a variety of the period's printed texts and visual imagery in order to demonstrate how they contributed to the cultural production of Renaissance England and were woven into the warp and weft of people's existence – the artifice of everyday life.

Using this Anthology

The following anthology of entries is divided into four parts: 'Preparatory and Dying Arts'; 'Funereal and Commemorative Arts'; 'Knowing and Understanding Death'; and 'Death Arts in Literature'. Each part is prefaced by a set of epigraphs to prompt further exploration of relevant literature and a short introductory essay to explain its concept and to introduce the entries. Each entry in each part is arranged by chronological order of publication (not composition). The entries can be read sequentially, but we have included cross-references both to other entries in this anthology (for example, 'See entry IV.7 (Whitney)') and to entries in our companion anthology *The Memory Arts in Renaissance England* (for example, 'See *MA* entry I.7 (Willis), pp. 73–84') to encourage readers to find their own pathway through both anthologies. Each entry includes short sections about the author, about the overall text from which the excerpt is drawn, and about the entry's connection to the death arts. In a few cases, we have allocated to a single author more than one entry from multiple works, and so the second passage may correspond more readily to another category; for instance, Samuel Rowlands has a literary and a non-literary excerpt.

The spelling and punctuation for each excerpt has been thoroughly modernized, as have the titles in our citations of any work from the period. Under the headings of Textual Notes, we include a short version title of the excerpted

ador'd and worshipped'; Thomas Heywood, *The Fair Maid of the West, Part II* (London: 1631; STC 13320), D1ᵛ: 'the same morian intreated me lie with him'; and Edward Fairfax's translation of Tasso's *Gerusalemme Liberata* entitled *Godfrey of Bulloigne: Or the Recovery of Jerusalem* (London: 1600; STC 23698): 'the Turks and Morians armed be' – this same spelling is used as late as the 1686 edition (B1ʳ).

work in original spelling, with relevant publication details; the same applies to quotations from an early text when we have deemed it important to preserve the orthography. Catalogue and signature numbers are included for ease of reference to the original excerpted text. Where and when possible, we have consulted texts in person (see our 'Acknowledgements' above), but otherwise we have drawn upon online resources such as *Early English Books Online* and *Literature Online* to establish our copy text. Square bracketed material in excerpts indicates editorial interpolations or ellipses.

The first two parts cover, roughly, expressions of the death arts *before* and *after* the moment of death. The first part includes, for example, instructional treatises about dying well, penitential writing in advance of death, accounts of people dying, and philosophical and theological assertions about the afterlife. Shifting the perspective to what follows for the living after the death of others, the second part includes, for example, historical and hagiographical writing, descriptions of liturgical practice, and elegiac writing of various forms. The third part is concerned with how death came to be understood and interpreted in humanist as well as pre- and post-Reformation English thinking, covering a range of authors including influential thinkers such as Thomas Elyot, Francis Bacon, and Margaret Cavendish. The final section includes excerpts from some of the most fruitful and imaginative literary engagements with the death arts; here we have attempted to include overlooked authors (for example, Margaret Tyler and Samuel Rowlands) alongside canonical authors (for example, Christopher Marlowe and Aphra Behn). The excerpts we have chosen represent, we think, a broad spectrum of the early modern English death arts, but it is a selection and not the final say. There are some obvious *loci classici* we have excluded, most often because of their ease of access elsewhere (for example, a representative selection of entries by Shakespeare or Milton, or John Donne's Holy Sonnet X ('Death be not proud')) or because we thought their general expression of the death arts was covered adequately elsewhere.

Given the pressing ubiquity of death in the world and as expressed in early modern English print culture, a few words about the organization of the anthology of excerpts are in order. Dividing the book into four parts with seventeen entries each was not arbitrary, and warrants comment both by way of explanation and also to give a foretaste of some of the entries. Of the many ways we considered setting up the book, we decided finally to let the categories 'suggest themselves' as we reviewed the several hundred initially collected. Like metal spurs to magnets, the entries began to move toward four topical nodes (resulting in the four divisions just specified above).

Early philosophers found harmony in numbers, and the number four has a special place in Western thought and literature for symbolic no less than mystical reasons.[181] Heraclitus saw the cosmos as a theatre for the strife of opposites held together in a kind of tense unity (apostrophized later as divine love by Boethius in *The Consolation of Philosophy*[182]). Empedocles posited as first principles the four elements: fire, air, water, and earth – four 'roots of the universe'. There is something very satisfying about the number four, at once signalling continuity and stability, and, to a certain extent, completion. For Pythagoras, four is associated with justice, wholeness, and completion (when a circle is drawn along a line that connects the two centres, a perfect shape of a square exists within the circle). Accordingly, there are four cardinal points of direction, poetically described by Homer in terms of the four winds (Boreas, Eurus, Notos, Zephyrus), alluded to in passing by Andrew Marvell (entry IV.16); even as there are four seasons corresponding to the four ages of man (see entry I.2 (*Calendar of Shepherds*)), as allegorized by Hesiod and Ovid. Anne Conway relates that 'time is divided into four parts, according to the age of a man living in this world, which is infancy, youth, manhood, and old age, even until death; so that all things which are bounded with time are subject unto death and corruption, or are changed into another species of things' (entry III.17). Correlating the stages of life with the qualities of heat, cold, moisture, and dryness, in Galenic medical tradition, the four elements correspond to the four humours, as discussed in Thomas Cogan's *Haven of Health* (entry III.5). More concretely, as already noted, four points determine a square, and upon this base a stable structure might be erected. Spenser's House of Temperance (an emblem of the well-regulated body in harmony with the soul) thus is perfectly proportioned – 'o worke diuine ... a quadrate was the base'.[183] Architecturally speaking, four columns provide the greatest stability of a structure, as with the funeral 'monument' supported by the four treatises organizing Martin Day's book (entry II.10): 'A Wakening for Worldlings', 'Meditations of Consolation', 'Comfortable Considerations', and 'A Mirror of Modesty' – and illustrated as such (see Figure 2.3 in that entry). Mary Wroth's *Urania* is organized into four books, if for other

---

[181] S. K. Heninger, Jr, *Touches of Sweet Harmony: Pythagorean Cosmology and Renaissance Poetics* (San Marino, CA: The Huntington Library, 1974), pp. 71–145.
[182] Boethius, *Theological Tractates, The Consolation of Philosophy*, trans. H. F. Stewart, E. K. Rand, and S. J. Tester, Loeb Classical Library (Cambridge, MA: Harvard University Press, 1973), 2.m.8, pp. 226–27.
[183] Spenser *FQ*, 2.9.22. Cf. *MA* VI.2.

reasons, and is also represented architecturally on the title page of her romance. Margaret Cavendish's *Philosophical Letters* (entry III.15) likewise falls into four sections. The same is true for George Wither's *Collection of Emblems*, to which he adds a lottery encouraging readers to revisit various emblems (entry I.11). And there are four sections to Jane Owen's *Antidote against Purgatory* exhorting wealthy English recusants to open their purses for the cause (entry I.13). Four also figures significantly with regard to thematic and symbolic precedents involving the social rituals of consolation and burial, such as with Thomas Becon's *The Sick Man's Salve* (1561) structured as a deathbed scene in which four companions prepare their dying friend for his death; and four is the customary number of knights for properly mourning a fellow knight.[184] The number four lends itself conveniently for discussions of death; for example, John Bradford identifies four kinds of death – natural, spiritual, temporal, and eternal (entry I.6). As translated by the eleven-year-old Elizabeth Tudor, future Queen of England (entry III.3), a female narrator addresses Christ from a four-fold point of view – as mother, daughter, sister, and wife – following Marguerite de Navarre's mourning of her infant son in *Miroir de l'âme pécheresse* (1531). Four also is the number of layers of the skin, metaphorized by Helkiah Crooke as 'the case, rather the coffin or winding-sheet wherein nature hath wrapped this living body of death' (entry III.11). Penultimately, the New Testament specifies four horsemen of the Apocalypse (Revelations 6:2–8) representing conquest, war, famine, and the last, the 'Pale Rider', is Death, in his train Hell personified, maw wide open to receive the newly dead. And finally (as discussed earlier in this Introduction), there are 'The Four Last Things' in Christian eschatology, the *quattuor novissima*: Death, Final Judgement, Heaven, and Hell. While the four parts of this book do not correspond identically to this last or any of the other examples just mentioned, the ample precedents for associating the number four with death make it an apt organizing principle for the sixty-eight entries.

Moreover, we have allotted seventeen entries to each of the four parts because, as it happens, seventeen was considered the number of death in the Renaissance.[185] The Roman numeral XVII, by an anagrammatic shift

---

[184] Ronald Strickland, 'Pageantry and Poetry as Discourse: The Production of Subjectivity in Sir Philip Sidney's Funeral', *ELH*, 58.1 (1990), 19–36.

[185] Each section of the *Memory Arts* anthology consists of ten entries, since the 'decade' (ten things to be recalled, and hence ten images to be placed against the larger background mnemonic) was deemed the appropriate number for constructing a useful artificial memory scheme; on the setting up of ten mnemonic 'places', see *MA* I.7 (Willis), esp. pp. 82–83.

Introduction

(a favourite intellectual pastime among classical grammarians, Talmudic exegetes, and humanist luminaries alike), results in VIXI, which is the Latin word meaning 'I have lived'[186] (implying that one is dead). As an idiom, *vixi* implies simply 'my life is over' in response to some catastrophic event or a failure to carry out an important plan. In some parts of southern Europe, especially around the Mediterranean, the number seventeen still is considered the unluckiest number because, after all, it is the number given to death.[187] According to Euclid's *Elements* and Boethius's *On Arithmetic*, seventeen is a very special number owing to its unique qualities,[188] which in some esoteric traditions has led to attributions of mystical signification.[189] Taking such matters into account, it seemed fitting then that we should have seventeen entries per part in a book on the early modern death arts.

---

[186] *Vixi* is the first-person singular perfect active indicative of *vivo*, from the verb *vivere* (to live).

[187] We can confirm anecdotally the following: as late as 2005 Alitalia airplanes did not number the seventeenth row; some modern Italian (and Brazilian) hotels do not have a seventeenth floor indicated on elevator buttons, neither do they have a Room 17, the number of death (akin to the North American and northern European superstition about thirteen).

[188] Mathematicians for millennia have marvelled that seventeen is the sum of the first four prime numbers (and it is the only prime number made up of four consecutive primes); as the seventh prime, it has special status in the heptameral tradition (the seven days of God's creation of the world – and rest – in Genesis; later commentators balance this chiastically against the last seven days in the Book of Revelation).

[189] Following principally Iamblichus (*c*.242–*c*.325), the Syrian Neoplatonist who edited Plotinus' works and was the author of among other texts (and fragments), *The Theology of Arithmetic* (see Vittorio De Falco (ed.), *Iamblichi theologoumena arithmeticae* (Leipzig, Germany: Teubner, 1922)).

PART I
Preparatory and Dying Arts

¶ *The complaint to the Dying Creature to Dread, saying thus*:
Ah Dread, where be ye? Is there no help and succour with you to speak for me when I shall come to my judgement?

¶ *The answer of Dread*:
No, certainly for when you were set in pleasance and delectation of the world, reason put in your mind that you died not well, and I, Dread, was with you at all times and in every place and failed not to speak unto you and to put you in mind of the shame of this world and dread of damnation and of the peril that would follow as well here as elsewhere rehearsing unto you the punishments that our Lord ordained for sin ….

> Anonymous, *The Dying Creature* (London: 1506; STC 6033.5), A3^v

I walked out, but suddenly a friend of mine me met
And said 'if you regard your health, out of this lane you get
And shift you to some better air, for fear to be infect:
With noisome smell and savours ill, I wish on that respect,
And have regard unto your health, or else perhaps you may
So make a die and then adieu, your woeful friends may say'.
I thanked him for his carefulness, and this for answer gave:
'I'll neither shun, nor seek for death, yet oft the same I crave,
By reason at my luckless life, believe me this is true'.
'In that' (said he) 'you do amiss', then bade he me adieu.

> Isabella Whitney, 'The Author to the Reader', in *A Sweet Nosegay* (London: 1573; STC 25440), A6^r

Memento mori must be every man's motto: a point that as the scripture enjoins, so the saints have practised, and the heathens have approved this principle, that *Tota hominis vita, mortis meditatio*, the whole life of a man ought to be the meditation of death.

Stephen Jerome, *Moses His sight of Canaan* (London: 1614; STC 14512), Dd7^v

[T]herefore, O my soul, seeing there is no escaping death, thy only way is to prepare for [it to] get the sting of it taken away, so shall it not hurt thee, nor be terrible to thee; no cause then to fear Death for it shall be but a messenger sent from God, thy father, to fetch thee home to Him, and free thee from all sins.

Anne Skelton, *Comforts against the Fear of Death* (London: 1649; Wing S23932a), A6^{r-v}

Introduction to Part I

One of the most important trends in early print was the proliferation of writings about death. While death as subject matter featured abundantly across genre and form, the early modern period also saw the publication of a large number of bespoke studies about preparations for death, or, more precisely, instructions for how to die well. Over fifty manuals or treatises about dying well were published between 1590 and 1700, only several of which are excerpted in this anthology. Some representative titles will offer a flavour of their content: Thomas Lupset's *The Way of Dying Well* (1534; see entry I.3); Anonymous, *The Manner to Die Well* (1578); John More's *A Lively Anatomy of Death* (1592); Christopher Sutton's *Disce Mori* [or] *Learn to Die* (1600); George Strode's *The Anatomy of Mortality* (1632); and Jeremy Taylor's *Holy Dying* (1651; see entry I.14). Such studies were influenced by the Continental phenomenon of the *ars moriendi* (the art of dying), a set of instructional manuals in how best to prepare for death that circulated widely in the fifteenth and early sixteenth centuries.[1]

These Christian treatises drew, of course, upon a much longer philosophical concern with living well and thereby dying well that can be traced back to Socrates' famous lament: 'Ordinary people seem not to realize that those who really apply themselves in the right way to philosophy are directly and of their own accord preparing themselves for dying and death.'[2] Such a desire for readiness for death, and how it intertwines with a virtuous life, finds some comparison with Aristotle's conception of *eudaimonia* (or happiness leading to virtue) and Cicero's 'let us obey joyfully and thankfully [in death] and consider that we are being set free from prison and loosed from our chains'.[3] The cognate *memento mori* tradition, the invocation to remember one's mortality as a prompt to prepare for death, also finds roots in antiquity, and is most clearly articulated in the Stoic philosophy of Seneca. With reason leading to virtuous thought and action in this tradition, death – and its

---

[1] These circulated in two versions: the *Tractatus* or *Speculum, artis bene moriendi*, attributed to an anonymous Dominican friar (possibly undertaken at the request of the Council of Constance); and the shorter *Craft of Dying*, which is based upon the second chapter of the longer work (see William Caxton's version, entry I.1).
[2] *Phaedo* in Plato *CD*, 64a.   [3] Cicero *TD*, 1.49.

accompanying loss of reason – was something to be feared; paradoxically, however, a life filled with fear of death 'will never do anything worthy of a man who is alive'.[4] Thus, preparation for death was key for Seneca, helping the individual negate their fear of death and enabling them to live a virtuous life. Mortality was something to be always kept in mind, something to be contemplated daily as the days, hours, and minutes moved ceaselessly towards the individual's final end.[5]

In early Christian teaching, the afterlife held at first two paths: Heaven or Hell. Purgatory, the middle path by which the departed could eventually reach Heaven (through the expiation of their sin by suffering, aided by prayers of intercession from those left behind) only became Church doctrine in western Europe by the twelfth century. It was this middle path, which offered hope for those in sin, that was central to the wars of religion and religious reformations of the late medieval and early modern period. Good preparation for death in the Roman Catholic belief system, as prescribed in the early *ars moriendi* manuals noted above, circled around the belief that it was never too late to repent for a life badly led, and that virtuous action in this life directly impacted upon the individual's destination in the afterlife. Within such a set of beliefs, an individual's final moments were especially significant: the eternal fate of one's soul was dependent upon its state as it departs the body natural (see entry IV.2 *The Summoning of Everyman* for a dramatic representation of dying well). The leaders of the Protestant Reformation denounced and rejected the idea of Purgatory as a superstitious relic without scriptural basis; for followers of Jean Calvin, only some, the elect, were now thought predestined for Heaven while the remainder were doomed for Hell. In the reformed faith of the English state religion, established through Henry VIII's Act of Supremacy (1534) but only fully outlined doctrinally, and in terms of liturgical practice, in the decades that followed (see entry II.2 on 'The Order for the Burial of the Dead'), what occurred at the moment of death was central to continuing disputes. The tidal shifts between the austere Protestantism of Edward VI, the Counter-Reformation of Mary I, and the

---

[4] Seneca, *De Tranquillitate Animi*, in *Moral Essays*, trans. John W. Basore, Loeb Classical Library (Cambridge, MA: Harvard University Press, 1932), vol. 2, 11.6.
[5] Cf. 'every day a little of our life is taken from us; even when we are growing, our life is on the wane. We lose our childhood, then our boyhood, and then our youth. Counting even yesterday, all past time is lost time; the very day which we are now spending is shared between ourselves and death' (Seneca *EP*, 1.24.20).

more moderate Protestantism of Elizabeth I, meant that, for people of all ranks in English society, preparations for death were tied up with broader existential questions about what death entailed. The imperative to remember to die well, perpetuated by the authors of instructional manuals, as well as preachers, philosophers, and poets, meant that old Church thinking about the *ars moriendi* enjoyed a second life in post-Reformation England. Our entries in Part I exemplify the evolution of this tradition.

54 PREPARATORY AND DYING ARTS

FIGURE 1.1 Allegorical deathbed scene. *To Know Well to Die* (London: William Caxton, 1490; STC 789), n.p. Image used courtesy of The Newberry Library

I.1

WILLIAM CAXTON

To Know Well To Die (1490)

About the author

William Caxton (1415x24–1492), while an apprentice to a prosperous London silk merchant in the Low Countries, was drawn to the lucrative possibilities of the new industry of printing. He established a press in Bruges where he was part of the household of Margaret of York (sister of Edward IV and wife of Charles the Bold, Duke of Burgundy), who encouraged him to publish stories from Homer, thus making his *Recuyell of the Histories of Troy* the first book printed in English. Other translations followed upon his return to Westminster around 1476, when he set up the first press in England and produced over a hundred books including Ovid's *Metamorphoses*, Chaucer's complete works, *The Golden Legend*, *Aesop's Fables*, and *Le Morte d'Arthur*.

About the text

Like many of Caxton's books, *To Know Well To Die* was his own translation of a French text from a work originally written in Latin. As it happens, he was working on it in the months leading up to his own death. Manuscripts of his source survive in two distinct versions, one long and the other short. Caxton had a keen eye for identifying what kinds of book would prove marketable (about a hundred editions were printed in Europe before his English version), and he correctly speculated that this popular Continental work of domestic piety would attract a wide readership in England.[1]

The arts of death

Caxton's *To Know Well To Die* is a continuation of the medieval *ars moriendi* devotional practice designed to bring consolation and pragmatic instruction to the dying person (the *moriens*) and attending family. The long version is

---

[1] Later English *ars moriendi* texts in the main follow Caxton's successful model; see entries I.3 (Lupset) and I.14 (Taylor).

attributed to an anonymous Dominican friar: the first four of its six chapters give hope to the *moriens* by keeping him from temptation, reminding him of Christ's love, and urging him to imitate Christ; the final two chapters advise family and friends about deathbed protocol, and supply suitable prayers for the occasion. The short version (from which our excerpt is drawn) is the second chapter of the longer one which concerns the five temptations to be resisted while dying. These temptations and their mitigating 'inspirations' are depicted in ten illustrations that frequently accompany *ars moriendi* block books, showing five scenes of demons assailing the *moriens* and five of angels coming to his aid (see Figure 1.1). Bridging the confessional divide of Catholicism and Protestantism, the *ars moriendi* predates printing and persists as a literary genre well into the eighteenth century.

Textual notes

[T]*he arte [and] crafte to knowe well to dye* (Westminster, 1490; STC 789), A1^r–A2^r.

To Know Well To Die

When it is so that what a man maketh or doeth, it is made to come to some end. And if the thing be good and well made, it must needs come to good end. Then by better and greater reason every man ought to intend in such wise to live in this world, in keeping the commandments of God, that he may come to a good end. And that out of this world full of wretchedness and tribulations he may go to heaven, unto God and His saints, into joy perdurable.[2] But now in these days, few there be that advise them of their end so much as they ought to do. Though they be sick, ancient, or old, and to them cometh this folly by a foolish hope that every man, in what estate he be, hath an hope to live long. And, therefore, hath this present treatise been made, composed in short terms for to teach every man well to die whilst he hath understanding, health, and reason, to the end that it is needful to him to be the better warned, informed, and taught. The which treatise is divided into six parts, of which the first treateth of the praising of death and how one ought to die gladly. The second treateth of the temptations that they have which be or lie in the article of death. The third treatise is of the questions

---

[2] 'everlasting'

that ought be made to them then. The fourth containeth a manner of instructions and of teaching that ought to be made to them. The fifth, of the remembrance that God hath won and suffered for us. The sixth and last treateth of certain orisons and devout prayers that they ought to say if they may; or else ought to be said before them, by some that be assistant or present.

Of the allowing or praising of the death and how one gladly ought for to die.

As then the bodily death is the most fearful thing of all other things, so yet is the death of the soul of as much more terrible and reproachable as the soul is more noble and more precious than the body. And the death of sinners is right cursed and evil, but the death of just and true people is precious before God, for the dead men be well happy that die in our Lord. To this purpose, sayeth Plato, 'the continual remembrance of the death is sovereign wisdom'.[3] Also for truth the bodily death of good people always is none other thing but the issue, or going out, of prison and of exile, and discharging of a right grievous burden, that is to wit of the body; finishing of all things, and end of all maladies and sicknesses, and also of all other strifes mortal. It is the voiding of this present wretchedness; it is consumption of all evils, and the breaking of all the bonds of this cursed and evil world. It is the payment of the debt of nature, return into the country, and entry into joy and glory. Therefore, sayeth the wiseman[4] 'that the day of thy death is better than the day of thy birth'.[5] But this word ought to be understood for them that be good only. […]

For well to die is gladly to die; and to conne[6] die is to have in all times his heart ready and apparelled to[7] things heavenly and supernal. And that at every hour, when the death shall come to the person, that he be found ready; and that he receive it without any contradiction but also joyfully as he should abide the coming of his good friend. To this purpose, sayeth the philosopher,[8] 'That natural reason well counselled judgeth that the good death ought better to be chosen than the evil life, and that one ought sooner to choose thy bodily death than do anything against the weal of virtue'.[9] Thus then it

---

[3] *Phaedo* in Plato *CD*, 67d–e
[4] Solomon, king of Israel (reigned 970–31 BCE), renowned for his learning, discernment, and wise judgements
[5] Eccl 7.1 (Vulgate); cf. entry I.9 (Perkins)   [6] 'know how to' (from OE. *cunnan*)
[7] 'prepared for'   [8] Aristotle
[9] Aristotle *CW*, *Nicomachean Ethics* 1115a, 6–10; a classical theme echoed by Cicero, *On Duties*, trans. Walter Miller, Loeb Classical Library (Cambridge, MA: Harvard University Press, 1913), 1.13.

appeareth of the praising of the death; and that every good person and religious ought to desire departing of the body and soul for to be with our Lord Jesus Christ, and for to leave this present world for the better to live in the world to come.

Suggested further reading
Appleford, *Learning*.
Beaty, *Craft*.
William Blades, *The Life and Typography of William Caxton*, 2 vols. (Cambridge: Cambridge University Press, 2014).

I.2

ANONYMOUS

The Calendar of Shepherds (1518)

About the author

The work of several contributors drawing on a range of French manuscript sources, *Le Compost et kalendrier des bergiers* (Paris, 1493) was first printed by Guyot Marchant who had enjoyed considerable success with *La Danse Macabre* (1485), some images from which were reused in the *Kalendrier*. A Scots-English translation by Alexander Barclay was published by Antoine Vérard (Paris, 1503); three years later, Richard Pynson printed a corrected English version with the French woodcuts. Wynkyn de Worde brought out a rival English version (London, 1508) translated by Robert Copland[1] to whom 'the Horner' poem is attributed (included below in the excerpts). Julian Notary's 1518 edition however, based on Copland's translation, became the standard text for subsequent English printings as it deftly brings together and augments the earlier versions.[2]

---

[1] Cf. *MA* I.3 on Copland's other translation activities.
[2] See Joseph J. Gwara, 'Wynkyn de Worde, Richard Pynson, and *The Kalender of Shepherdes*: A Case Study in Cast-Off Copy and Textual Transmission', *The Papers of the Bibliographical Society of America*, 112.3 (2018), 293–356: 'The early Tudor printers competed aggressively to issue revised editions of *The Kalender of Shepherdes* at regular intervals, copying and updating each other's books every two or three years' (295).

About the text

While capitalizing on the fashion of pastoral themes and characters associated with living a simpler life in harmony with nature, this book offers a range of contemporary views on medicine (especially phlebotomy and physiognomy), nutrition, and astronomy; it maps planetary influences onto the body and links the annual calendar to a person's life, each month being equated to six years of the biblically prescribed lifespan of 'three score and ten' (Ps 90:10). A heavily illustrated compendium of useful information, it contains a perpetual calendar, phases of the moon, folk wisdom, and proverbs; sacred concerns include the ten commandments, Lord's Prayer and Creed, meditations for a range of spiritual needs, the seven deadly sins, and exhortations to reform one's life followed by descriptions and vivid images of tortures in Hell.

The arts of death

There is a distinct overlap between the *Calendar of Shepherds* and *Dance of Death* in imagery and content. Some of the same woodcuts appear in both works, and each offers practical advice about how to live well so as to make proper provision for death. Our excerpt consists of three sections where this *memento mori* message is delivered in terms of 'the saying of a dead man', 'the song of death' (Figure 1.2),[3] and a five-stanza rhyme royal poem – showing a 'Blackamoor'[4] blowing his horn of warning while holding Death's dart[5] (Figure 1.3) – admonishing readers to 'cease of their sins at the sounding of a dreadable[6] horn'.[7] The visual trope of the domesticated and subservient 'Blackamoor' as a herald and harbinger, in this case of death, has a long

---

[3] This same image is used, among other places, on the 1530 title page of *The Summoning of Everyman* (entry IV.2).

[4] The word 'blakemor' as a way to refer generally to people of African descent appears as early as the thirteenth century, a term also used in heraldic blazoning. See the Introduction for a more detailed account of the problematic racialized linking of blackness to death in early modern European thought and literature.

[5] Cf. entry IV.6 (Gascoigne); see Figure 0.1.

[6] 'worthy of dread'; fearful expectation or anticipation of some horrific outcome warranting awe and great care; cf. Shakespeare (*Hamlet* 3.1.79), 'the dread of something after death'

[7] Cf. John Gower, *Confessio Amantis* (London: 1493; STC 12142), fol. xxii^v, an inset tale concerning one for whom the 'trump of death' has sounded, being advised to show proper humility and penance so the king will be inclined toward clemency and countermand the order of execution

history in the European popular imagination,[8] stemming in part from the homophonic correspondence of 'Moors' and *mors* (the Latin noun for death).[9]

Textual notes

The kalender of shepardes (London: 1518; STC 22410), M4ʳ–M4ᵛ; (London: 1528; STC 22411), L4ᵛ–L5ʳ, U4ʳ–X1ʳ.

The Saying of a Dead Man

Man look and see
Take heed of me
How thou shalt be
When thou art dead,
Dry as a tree
Worms shall eat thee
Thy great beauty
Shall be like lead.

The time hath been
In my youth green
That I was clean
Of body as ye are,
But for mine eyen[10]
Now two holes bene[11]
Of me is seen
But bones all bare.

Now entend[12]
For to amend.

---

[8] e.g., Abraham Cowley, *Cutter of Coleman Street* (London 1663; Wing C6669), 4.6.48: 'He's Dead long since, and gone to the Blackamore's below.' See Introduction, 'Racializing Death'.

[9] This perennial theme is elaborated further (also with reference to 'morris' dancing) by William E. Engel, 'Death Slips onto the Renaissance Stage', in *Acts and Texts: Performance and Ritual in the Middle Ages and the Renaissance*, ed. Laurie Postlewate and Wim Hüsken (Amsterdam: Rodopi, 2007), pp. 269–302, esp. pp. 269–71.

[10] 'my eyes'

[11] 'are'; also owing to phonic similarity, a possible pun on the Anglo-Saxon derived word for bone, *bein*

[12] 'attend'; 'direct attention to'

[13] 'impure'; 'unclean'   [14] 'liking', 'delight'

O mortal creatures, sailing in the waves of misery
Avail the sail of your conscience unpure[13]
Flee from the perils of this unsteadfast weary
Drive to the haven of charity most sure
And cast the anchor of true confession
Fastened with the great cable of contrition clean
Wind up thy merchandise of whole satisfaction
Which of true customers shall be over seen
And brought to the warehouse of perfection
As perfect merchants of God by election
    […]

The song of death to all Christian people

(See Figure 1.2.)

Though my picture be not to your pleasance[14]
And if you think that it be dreadable
Take it worth[15] for surely in substance
The light of it may to you be profitable
There is no way also more doubtable
Therefore learn to know yourself and see
Look how I am and thus shall thou be
And take heed of thy self, in adventure rede I[16]
For Adam's apple we all must die.
[…]

    How every man and woman ought to cease of their sins
    at the sounding of a dreadable horn
    (See Figure 1.3)

---

[15] 'as something valuable'; 'worthy matter'
[16] 'be advised by me about your risky journey'

FIGURE 1.2 Death with coffin. *Calender of Shepherds* (London: Wynkyn de Worde, 1528; STC 22411), L4ᵛ. Image used courtesy of The Newberry Library

The Calendar of Shepherds (1518) 63

FIGURE 1.3 Moor with horn. *Calender of Shepherds* (London: Wynkyn de Worde, 1528; STC 22411), U4ᵛ. Image used courtesy of The Newberry Library

> Ho, ho, you blind folk, darked in the cloud
> Of ignorant fume,[17] thick and mystical
> Take heed of my horn, tooting all aloud

[17] 'noxious vapour'

With boisterous sounds, and blasts boreal[18]
Giving you warning, of the Judgement final
The which daily is ready, to give sentence
On perverse people, replete with negligence.

Ho, ho, betime, or that it be too late
Cease while ye have space and portunate[19]
Leave your follies, or death make you checkmate
Cease your ignorant incredulity
Cleanse your thoughts of immundicity[20]
Cease of your pecunial pensement[21]
The which defileth your entendement.[22]

Ho, ho, people, infected with negligence
Cease your sins, and manifold cruelties
Dread God your maker, and his righteous sentence
Cease your blindness of worldly vanities
Lest he you smite with endless infirmities
Cease your coveting, gluttony, and pride
And cease your superfluous garments wide.

Cease of your oaths, cease of your swearing,
Cease of your pomp, cease of your vainglory,
Cease of your hate, cease of your blaspheming,
Cease of your malice, cease of your envy,
Cease of your wrath, cease of your lechery,
Cease of your fraud, cease your deception,
Cease of your tongues making detraction.

    Flee faint falsehood, fickle, foul, and fell
    Flee fatal flatterers, full of fairness
    Flee fair feigning, fables and favel[23]

---

[18] 'cold', 'bracing' (ME. *boriall*, north wind) [19] 'opportunity'
[20] 'immundite things'; 'impurities' [21] 'thoughts of financial gain'
[22] 'right understanding'
[23] 'flattery'. Favel is among the personified vices encountered on the allegorical ship of state in John Skelton, *Bouge of Court* (London: 1499; STC 22597).

> Flee folks' fellowship frequenting falseness
> Flee frantic facers, fulfilled of forwardness
> Flee fools' fallacies, flee fond fantasies
> Flee from fresh fablers, feigning flatteries.
>
> Thus endeth the horner.

Suggested further reading

Martha W. Driver, 'When Is a Miscellany Not Miscellaneous? Making Sense of the *Kalender of Shepherds*', *The Yearbook of English Studies*, 33 (2003), 199–214.

Phebe Jensen, *Astrology, Almanacs, and the Early Modern English Calendar* (Abingdon and New York: Routledge, 2021), pp. 74–93.

Kathleen E. Kennedy, 'Moors and Moorishness in Late Medieval England', *Studies in the Age of Chaucer*, 42 (2020), 213–51.

K. J. P. Lowe, 'The Stereotyping of Black Africans in Renaissance Europe', in *Black Africans in Renaissance Europe*, ed. T. F. Earle and K. J. P. Lowe (Cambridge: Cambridge University Press, 2010), pp. 17–48.

1.3

THOMAS LUPSET

The Way of Dying Well (1534)

About the author

Thomas Lupset (*c*.1495–1530) was a humanist scholar and ecclesiastic, who was associated by education, career, and friendship with many of the leading figures of the Northern Renaissance. He was educated in the household of John Colet, leading to further tutelage under William Lily, probably at the newly founded St Paul's School, before proceeding to university at Cambridge. By 1513, at age eighteen or so, he was assisting Desiderius Erasmus on his new Latin edition of the New Testament. Lupset travelled widely, receiving further instruction from Niccolò Leonico Tomeo at the University of Padua. This was also where he first came into contact with Reginald Pole, an emerging senior figure in the English Church, who would have a great influence upon Lupset's career.

About the text

Lupset writes *The Way of Dying Well*, his final extant work, in the winter of 1529–1530, completing it 'at Paris the [10th] day of January'. Lupset would die within the year from tuberculosis. His treatise about dying well was printed posthumously by Thomas Berthelet, the royal printer. Lupset's treatise is best understood in the context of the religious upheaval of the 1520s and 1530s: it is a work of counsel with a sharp political edge. It was one of several works about death published in the politically charged period before the break with Rome: compare with Thomas More's *Dialogue of Comfort* (1534), Richard Whitford's *Daily Exercise of Death* (1534), and an anonymous translation of Erasmus's *De praeparatione ad mortum* (completed in 1534, commissioned by Thomas Boleyn; translated and published as *Preparation to Death* in 1538). Amy Appleford notes that these works' 'common call to readers to face death with fortitude, confidence, and joy is fiercely focused on the political present'.[1]

The arts of death

The counsel offered in Lupset's work is addressed to John Walker, a servingman to Pole. It begins with a pointed comparison between the deaths of two men: Canius, a Roman nobleman put to death by Caligula, who calmly accepted his death and thereby 'showed himself to be in spirit as far above all kings' violent power'; and Francis Philip, a traitor executed at Tyburn in 1524, who, 'quaking and trembling' could 'scant … speak one word' upon the scaffold, and thereby 'died so cowardly'. With such a template for dying well or otherwise in mind, Lupset insists that death is something not to be feared if the individual has lived a good life. His humanist counsel, based upon a Senecan model of the moral essay,[2] is specifically directed towards men in service. Nancy Lee Beaty notes that in Lupset's study, the 'old wine of ecclesiastical tradition, now stale, was combined with the rather heady vintage of ancient death-literature, and poured into the new bottle of the classical moral essay'.[3] Our selected excerpts include Lupset's most pragmatic advice for servingmen about how to live and die well: be in 'continual remembrance' of your mortality; avoid idleness, in both a spiritual and practical sense; subordinate yourself to a virtuous master who will appreciate your virtuous actions;

---

[1] Appleford, *Learning*, p. 189.
[2] See entry III.8 (Lodge) for an exemplary moral essay by Seneca, 'On the shortness of life'.
[3] Beaty, *Craft*, p. 54.

say psalms and pray to God 'ever continually' to be 'ever well minded' and thereby also a perfect servant to your master.

Textual notes

A compendious and a very fruteful treatyse, teachynge the waye of dyenge well (London: 1534; STC 16934), E5^{r}–E8^{v}.

The Way of Dying Well

In my mind, nothing shall further us more to a glad death than shall an ordinate[4] life: that is, to live in a just and a due manner after one rule and one form, ever awake in a quick remembrance of death as though every hour were our last space of endurance in this world. When you rise in the morning, determine so to pass the day following as though at night a grave should be your bed. Let every day be reckoned with you as your last. […] This is the thing that Christ would have us do, when he so often warneth and admonisheth us to take heed and to look about us because neither the day nor the hour of our calling is certain to us. Therefore, it is our part, of a time so much uncertain to make a time sure, certain, and present, that we never be taken unawares. By the which means we shall gladly suffer death saying it is a thing so long before prepared. For why should it be a strange thing to reckon every day to be the last? I see not but that thing that happeneth and chanceth to some of us, might come to any of us, and likewise all might have that that a few hath. There is no cause to deny, but as well this day you or I might die, as we see this day some other deed. And though we be not dead this day, yet it is truth that this day we die, and daily sithen[5] our first birth we have died, in as much that daily some part of our life hath been diminished, and ever as we have grown, so ever life hath decreased. We were babies, we were children, we were boys, we were young men, all these ages be lost, and 'til yesterday all time past is gone and lost. This same-self day that we now live is divided and parted with death. Still without ceasing we approach to death by the expense and waste of life. Thus dying we always be, though death be not always upon us. Conceive, then, this ordinate life in your mind and bestow your time whilst you have the time.

---

[4] 'observant of order'; 'moderate'; 'temperate'   [5] 'since'

[Lupset digresses to praise John Walker's master, Reginald Pole, saying that Walker can lack for nothing and therefore might be tempted to be idle. Lupset describes idleness as 'the grave of living men'.]

It is not now my purpose to show what you should do that you might not only fly idleness, but also be well occupied. [...] If you see that death is not to be feared, and that by continual remembrance of death you shall prepare yourself to die gladly with a good will, the which you cannot do unless you be in hope of the everlasting life. And this hope requireth some trust in the cleanse of a good conscience, the which ever followeth a gracious intent of living well. So that if you live well, you shall die well. And of the way to live well you cannot miss if you arm your mind to be strong against all suddenness of death. Pray ever continually without ceasing you must. But what is this continual prayer I would you learned? For of prayer it is but one final portion: the saying of psalms or asking with words of God his grace. The very prayer is to be ever well minded, to be ever in charity, to have ever the honour of good in remembrance, to suffer no rancour, no ire, no wrath, no malice, no sin to abide in your delight, but to be in a continual good thought, the which you may keep whether you sleep or wake, whether you eat or drink, whether you feast or fast, whether you rest or labour, and never peradventure you can pray better than when you must give yourself to serve your master, to whom the course of your life is due. (And bounden specially when God hath given you such a master, whom your service cannot please without you be studious to please God.) For well you see, that without virtue your service were to your master an unsavoury thing. But, as I have said, it is not now my purpose to appoint you the way of living well: if you have heard enough to die well, I have for my part now said enough, and shortly by the same you shall of yourself without farther help find the way to live well.

Suggested further reading
Appleford, *Learning*, esp. pp. 205–18.
Beaty, *Craft*, esp. ch. 2.

I.4

KATHERINE PARR

The Lamentation of a Sinner (1547)

About the author

Katherine Parr (1512–1548), twice widowed and twenty years younger than Henry VIII when they married in 1543, was permitted an active role in governance. She served as Henry's regent in 1544 during his last campaign in France, the triumphant if costly Siege of Boulogne. Her household became the hub of reformed religion at court by virtue of her hosting readings of the latest English translations of the Bible and debates about the Reformation with her husband in the company of friends and theologians. Although Parr's first book most likely was a translation of John Fisher's *Psalms and Prayers* (1544), an important piece of wartime propaganda, she has the distinction of being the first woman to publish under her own name in England with *Prayers or Meditations* (1545), a selection of vernacular texts for private devotion drawn from an unobjectionable spiritual manual, *The Imitation of Christ* by Thomas à Kempis. Parr was circumspect enough never to have been linked to the presumed heresy of Anne Askew.[1]

About the text

The publication of *Lamentation* was deferred prudently until after Henry's death. It is structured as a conversion narrative recounting Parr's own religious journey. Despite several references to her identity, the form and tone of the work are sufficiently universal that readers easily can see their own experience mirrored in it. The tripartite sequence begins with confession (albeit relentlessly self-abasing in a way not usually associated with aristocratic authors of the day) and repentance; moves next to conversion and Parr's recognition of God's truth expressed through the reformed Church; and finally, addresses prophesy with special reference to death and the Final Judgement. The text thus concludes with a timely warning that if readers do not embrace reformed soteriology then they will be condemned to hellfire. Stridently

---

[1] See entry II.4 (Foxe).

anti-Roman Catholic throughout, Parr advocates 'scripture alone' (A2^v) and 'justification by faith' (B7^v), exhorting those who would attain salvation to confess their sins by looking within themselves rather than outward to 'this saint or that martyr' (G6^r).

The arts of death

Lamentation of a Sinner focuses intently on the end of one's mortal life as a prompt to discover how to gain eternal life. Parr writes of the 'maze of death', using a term that is freighted with the implications of its earlier meaning of 'delusion'.[2] In this sense, then, death becomes a false illusion that keeps people desperately clutching at 'visible idols and images made of men's hands' (A5^r). Such things 'obfuscate and darken the great benefit of Christ's passion' (A6^v) and reinforce a fearful prospect of dying without the intercession of papally sanctioned ceremonies and 'indulgences' promising remission from sin. Instead, 'the blood of Christ' alone is 'sufficient' to cleanse the faithful of sin, 'as he hath appointed by his word' (A5^v). Everything thus hinges on the dead body of Christ, rather than on 'such riffraff as the bishop of Rome hath planted in his tyranny' (A5^v). Penitent Christians therefore should be convinced by God's holy word (by which is meant the scriptures in an approved English translation such as Henry's 'Great Bible' of 1539) and the 'book of the crucifix'.[3] The latter is for Parr a powerful devotional mnemonic image drawn from the Gospels (a metaphor for Christ's ultimate sacrifice) that gives new and special Protestant meaning to the *Christus mortuus*[4] and *memento mori* traditions.

Textual notes

The lamentacion of a sinner (London: 1547; STC 4827), B1^v–B4^r, C2^r–C4^r.

[2] OE. *mæs* connotes 'bewilderment', from *amasian*, 'to confound'.
[3] Cf. *MA* IV.7, Thomas Fuller's expression of how Christ's crucified body, memorialized through the Eucharist, 'teaches thee an art of memory' (p. 212) by means of which one can apprehend the true significance of his sacrifice.
[4] *Christus mortuus* (meditating on the dead body of Christ), as part of larger devotional practice of reflecting on Christ's humanity, received exemplary expression in medieval Christianity by Anselm of Canterbury (d.1109) in his *Meditations and Prayers*. Martin Luther, familiar with Anselm's work as well as with Bernard of Clairvaux's references to the 'sacred heart' and 'divine *viscera*', likewise pursued this intimate form of spiritual exercise in his *Meditation on the Passion of our Lord* (1519), a work which may well have come to Parr's attention.

The Lamentation of a Sinner

Behold, Lord, how I come to thee, a sinner, sick, and grievously wounded. I ask not bread, but the crumbs that fall from the children's table. Cast me not out of thy sight, although I deserve to be cast into hell fire.

If I should look upon my sins, and not upon thy mercy, I should despair; for in myself I find nothing to save me, but a dunghill of wickedness to condemn me. If I should hope by my own strength and power to come out of this maze of iniquity and wickedness wherein I have walked so long, I should be deceived. For I am so ignorant, blind, weak, and feeble that I cannot bring myself out of the entangled and wayward maze, but the more I seek means and ways to wind myself out, the more I am wrapped and tangled therein. Sooth,[5] I perceive my striving therein to be hindrance; my travail to be labour spent in going back. It is the hand of the Lord that can and will bring me out of this endless maze of death; for without I be[6] prevented by the grace of the Lord, I cannot ask forgiveness nor be repentant or sorry for them. [...] Saint Paul sayeth we be justified by the faith in Christ, and not by the deeds of the law.[7] For if rightwiseness[8] come by the law, then Christ died in vain.[9] Saint Paul meaneth not here a dead human, historical faith, got by human industry, but a supernatural lively faith which worketh by charity, as he himself plainly expresseth.[10] [...] Therefore, to learn to know truly our own sins is to study the book of the crucifix, by continual conversation in faith, and to have perfect and plentiful charity, is to learn first by faith the charity that is in God towards us.

We may see also in Christ upon the cross how great the pains of hell and how blessed the joys of heaven be and what a sharp, painful thing it shall be to them that from that sweet, happy, and glorious joy, Christ, shall be deprived. Then this crucifix is the book[11] wherein God hath included all things, and hath most compendiously written therein all truth profitable and necessary for our salvation. Therefore let us endeavour ourselves to study this book, that we (being lightened with the spirit of God) may give him thanks for so great a benefit.[12] If we look further in this book, we shall see Christ's great victory upon the cross, which was so noble and mighty. [...] And in this one battle, he overcame forever all his enemies. There was never so glorious a spoil. Neither a more rich and noble than Christ was upon the cross, which

---

[5] 'truly' [6] 'except that I am' [7] Rom 3:20 [8] 'righteousness' (from OE. *rihtwīs*)
[9] Gal 2.21 [10] Marginal note: 'Gal. 5.' [11] Marginal note: '1 Cor. 2.'
[12] Marginal note: 'Christ's victory.'

delivered all his elect from such a sharp, miserable captivity. He had in this battle many stripes,[13] yea, and lost his life, but his victory was so much the greater. [...] Christ hath not only overcome sin, but rather he hath killed the same, in as much as he hath sacrificed for it himself, with the most holy sacrifice and oblation of his precious body in suffering most bitter and cruel death.

[13] i.e., marks on the flesh from scourging

Suggested further reading
Kimberly Anne Coles, *Religion, Reform, and Women's Writing in Early Modern England* (Cambridge: Cambridge University Press, 2008), ch. 2, esp. pp. 45–62.
Janel Mueller, 'A Tudor Queen Finds Voice: Katherine Parr's *Lamentation of a Sinner*', in *The Historical Renaissance: New Essays on Tudor and Stuart Literature and Culture*, ed. Heather Dubrow and Richard Strier (Chicago, IL: University of Chicago Press, 1988), pp. 15–47.
Micheline White, 'Katherine Parr and Royal Religious Complaint: Complaining For and About Henry VIII', in *Early Modern Women's Complaint: Gender, Form, and Politics*, ed. Sarah Ross and Rosalind Smith (Cham, Switzerland: Palgrave Macmillan, 2020), pp. 47–66.

1.5

ANNE LOCKE

'A Meditation of a Penitent Sinner' (1560)

About the author

Anne Locke (*c*.1530–1590x1607) was a poet, translator, and reformist activist. She was a friend and confidant to the leading Scottish reformer, John Knox (*c*.1514–1572).

About the text

In 1557, Locke joined Knox in Geneva, the Swiss city of the French theologian Jean Calvin (1509–1564) and the centre of staunch European reformist thought. While there she undertook an English translation of Calvin's sermons 'upon the songe of Ezechias made after he had been sicke, and afflicted by the hand of God' (that is, Hezekiah's song of praise from Isaiah 38[1]). After the translation follows a sequence of twenty-six sonnets. The translator of the sermons is identified as 'A. L.' – a set of initials recognizable to London's Protestant community – but the sonnets are attributed more cryptically: 'this meditation … was delivered me by my friend with whom I knew I might be so bold to use and publish it as pleased me'. This anonymous 'friend' is most likely a fiction by Locke to disguise her authorship, though the attribution to her pen is not entirely secure. The sonnet sequence is the first published in English. It borrows its form from Thomas Wyatt and structure from Henry Howard.[2]

The arts of death

The sonnets offer a paraphrase reading of Psalm 51. In this familiar psalm about penitence, David seeks God's mercy and forgiveness for sins committed in his adultery with Bathsheba and machinations ensuring Uriah's death. This poetic paraphrase of twenty-one sonnets (typically one sonnet is given for each verse) is prefaced by five sonnets, excerpted here, which seek to express the 'passioned mind of the penitent sinner'. These prefatory sonnets, which are not based upon another text, reflect more broadly upon the conditions of penitence and grace, expressed from the perspective of a sinner craving God's mercy. The speaker, whose imagined death is near, laments their 'distained life' and human wretchedness. They recognize their imminent damnation should no 'grant of grace and pardon' come. Juxtaposing a horrific vision of 'everlasting night' with hopeful pleas for mercy – the meditation on Psalm 51 that follows provides a means to beg for mercy – the speaker outlines memorably for the reader the fears that must accompany the onset of physical death.

Textual notes

Sermons of Iohn Caluin, vpon the songe that Ezechias made after he had bene sicke and afflicted by the hand of God, conteyned in the 38. chapiter of Esay. Translated out of Frenche into Englishe (London: 1560; STC 4450), H2[r]–H3[v].

---

[1] Hezekiah's song was part of 'The Order for the Burial of the Dead' and primers. See entry II.2 (Cranmer) and entry II.3 (Church of England).
[2] See entry IV.4 (Howard).

'A Meditation of a Penitent Sinner'

The heinous guilt of my forsaken ghost
So threats, alas, unto my feebled sprite[3]
Deserved death, and (that me grieveth most)
Still stand so fixed before my dazzled sight
The loathsome filth of my distained[4] life,
The mighty wrath of mine offended Lord,
My Lord whose wrath is sharper than the knife,
And deeper wounds than double-edged sword,
That as the dimmed and foredulled[5] eyen,[6]
Full fraught with tears and more and more oppressed
With growing streams of the distilled brine
Sent from the furnace of a grateful breast,
Cannot enjoy the comfort of the light,
Nor find the way wherein to walk aright.

So I, blind wretch, whom God's enflamed ire
With piercing stroke hath thrown unto the ground,
Amid my sins still grovelling in the mire,
Find not the way that other[s] oft have found,
Whom cheerful glimpse of God's abounding grace
Hath oft relieved and oft with shining light
Hath brought to joy out of the ugly place,
Where I in dark of everlasting night
Bewail my woeful and unhappy case,
And fret[7] my dying soul with gnawing pain.
Yet blind, alas, I grope about for grace.
While blind for grace I grope about in vain,
My fainting breath I gather up and strain,
Mercy, mercy, to cry and cry again.

But mercy while I sound with shrieking cry
For grant of grace and pardon while I pray,
Even then despair before my ruthful[8] eye

---

[3] 'spirit'   [4] 'sullied'; 'dishonoured'; 'defiled'   [5] 'made dull'; 'stupefied' (*obsolete*)
[6] 'eyes'   [7] 'gnaw'; 'consume'; 'wear away' (*obsolete*)   [8] 'lamentable'

Spreads forth my sin and shame, and seems to say
In vain thou brayest forth thy bootless[9] noise
To him for mercy, O refused wight,[10]
That hears not the forsaken sinner's voice.
Thy reprobate and fore-ordained sprite,
Fore-damned vessel of his heavy wrath,
(As self-witness of thy beknowing heart,
And secret guilt of thine own conscience sayeth)
Of his sweet promises can claim no part:
But thee, caitiff,[11] deserved curse doth draw
To Hell, by justice, for offended law.

This horror when my trembling soul doth hear,
When marks and tokens of the reprobate,
My growing sins, of grace my senseless cheer
Enforce the proof of everlasting hate,
That I conceive the Heaven's King to bear
Against my sinful and forsaken ghost:
As in the throat of Hell, I quake for fear,
And then in present peril to be lost
(Although by conscience wanteth to reply,
But with remorse enforcing mine offence,
Doth argue vain my not availing cry)
With woeful sighs and bitter penitence
To him from whom the endless mercy flows
I cry for mercy to relieve my woes.

And then not daring with presuming eye
Once to behold the angry Heaven's face,
From troubled sprite I send confused cry,
To crave the crumbs of all sufficing grace.
With faltering knee I, falling to the ground,
Bending my yielding hands to heaven's throne,
Pour forth my piteous plaint[12] with woeful sound,
With smoking sighs, and oft-repeated groan,

---

[9] 'useless' [10] 'person' (usually implying some pity or commiseration for them)
[11] 'prisoner'; 'wretch' [12] 'expression of sorrow'

> Before the Lord, the Lord, whom sinner I,
> I cursed wretch, I have offended so,
> That dreading, in his wreakful[13] wrath to die,
> And damned down to depth of Hell to go,
> Thus, tossed with pangs and passions of despair,
> Thus, crave I mercy with repentant cheer.

[13] 'vengeful'

Suggested further reading

Patrick Collinson, 'The Role of Women in the English Reformation Illustrated by the Life and Friendships of Anne Locke', *Studies in Church History*, 2 (1965), 258–72.

Kel Morin-Parsons, '"Thus Crave I Mercy": The Preface of Anne Lock', in *Other Voices, Other Views: Expanding the Canon in English Renaissance Studies*, ed. Helen Ostovich, Mary V. Silcox, and Graham Roebuck (Cranbury, NJ: Associated University Presses, 1999), pp. 271–89.

1.6

JOHN BRADFORD

A Fruitful Treatise ... against the Fear of Death (1564)

About the author

John Bradford (1510?–1555) was an evangelical preacher, imprisoned at the King's Bench Prison in Southwark for holding heretical nonconformist religious views during the reign of Mary I. While imprisoned he wrote a series of influential Protestant treatises, emerging as a leading figure in contemporary Anglican reformist thought. Burned at the stake for heresy at Smithfield[1] in the summer of 1555, he was celebrated as a martyr in John Foxe's *Acts and Monuments*.[2] Bradford's 'good death' was acclaimed by Foxe: 'Bradford took a faggot [i.e., from the woodpile to burn him] in his hand, and kissed it, and so likewise the stake', welcoming his death.

[1] Close to London's centre, the Elms, Smithfield, was an open space, used for tournaments, markets, and public executions.

[2] See entry II.4 (Foxe).

About the text

Writing while imprisoned and facing execution, Bradford first observes that, through 'man's judgement', he has been 'never so near' to death's 'door'. Bradford explains that there are four kinds of death – natural, spiritual, temporal, and eternal – and that the focus of his consolation will be upon the first kind, natural or physical death. He defines spiritual death as when though 'the body [is] living the soul is dead', because of sinful behaviour. Temporal death is 'a death where through the body and the affections thereof are mortified, that the spirit may live'; meaning to put to death whatever is earthly and to 'set your mind on things above' (Col 3.3–5, which Bradford cites). Eternal death is, of course, Hell. Bradford notes the oddity that people seem to fear natural death most:

> the judgement of the world is not to be approved, for it careth less for spiritual death than for natural death; it esteemeth less eternal death than temporal death, or else would men leave sin, which procureth both the one and other [meaning, spiritual and eternal deaths] and [would choose] temporally to die, that by natural death they might enter into the full fruition of eternal life, which none can enjoy nor enter into that here will not temporally die, that is, mortify their affections and crucify their lusts and concupiscences. (A3^{r-v})

The arts of death

Railing against the pleasures to be pursued futilely in life's activities and commodities, Bradford supplies a Protestant version of well-worn *contemptus mundi* themes and tropes, and advises readers to instead recognize life's brevity and their own temporality. In one blunt passage, Bradford contrasts the brief pleasures of sexual intercourse with the pains of its pursuit in courtship, or the 'sting of conscience' if the act is unlawfully forced (that is, through rape). Rejecting the brief, inconstant, and intermittent pleasures to be found in life, he sets out the multiple hardships of misery and disease that assault the human body. Next, he considers the temptations and vices of this life, and how often people are made prey to various kinds of evil. Within these contexts of fleeting pleasures, disease, and vice, Bradford concludes that rather than fearing natural death it should be welcomed, for life is a thing to be loathed.

Textual notes

A frutefull treatise and ful of heauenly consolation against the feare of death (London: 1564; STC 3481), A5^r–A8^r. Preserved copies of the earlier 1560 edition are incomplete.

A Fruitful Treatise ... against the Fear of Death

First, consider the pleasures of this life: what they be, how long they last, how painful we come by them, what they leave behind them, and thou shalt even in them see nothing but vanity.[3] As, for example, how long lasteth the pleasure that man hath in the act of generation? How painfully do men behave themselves before they attain it? How doth it leave behind it a certain loathsomeness and fullness? I will speak nothing of the sting of conscience, if it be come by unlawfully. Who, well-seeing this, and forecasting it aforehand, would not forego the pleasures willingly as far as need will permit and suffer? If, then, in this one, whereunto nature is most prone, and hath most pleasure in, it be thus, alas, how can we but think so of other pleasures?

Put the case that the pleasures of this life were permanent during this life, yet in that this life itself is nothing in comparison, and, therefore, is full well compared to a candle light which is soon blown out, to a flower which fadeth away, to a smoke, to a shadow, to a sleep, to a running water, to a day, to an hour, to a moment, and to vanity itself.[4] Who would esteem these pleasures and commodities which last so little a while? Before they be begun, they are gone and passed away. How much of our time spend we in sleeping, in eating, in drinking, and in talking? Infancy is not perceived; youth is shortly overblown; middle age is nothing; old age is not long; and, therefore, as I said, this life, through the considerations of the pleasures and commodities of it, should little move us to love it, but rather to loathe it. God, open our eyes to see these things, and to weigh them accordingly.

Secondly, consider the miseries of this life, that if so be the pleasures and commodities in it should move us to love it yet that miseries might countervail and make us to take it as we should do; I mean, rather to desire to be

---

[3] Marginal note: 'This life is not to be loved in respect of the pleasures thereof, being nothing else but vanity.'

[4] Marginal note: 'What this life is, mark here, and learn.' These are all based on biblical allusions; for example, life is a flower (Isa 40:7), smoke (Ps 102:3), shadow (Job 8:9), etc.

loosed and dismissed hence, than otherwise. Look upon your bodies and see in how many perils and dangers you are: your eyes are in danger of blindness and blearedness; your ears in danger of deafness; your mouth and tongue of cankers, toothache, and dumbness; your head in danger of rheums[5] and megrims;[6] your throat in danger of hoarseness; your hands in danger of gouts and palseys,[7] etc.[8] But who is able to express the number of diseases, whereto man's body is in danger, seeing that some have written that more than 3,000 diseases may happen unto man? I speak nothing of the hurt that may come to our bodies by prisons, venomous beasts, water, fire, horses, men, etc.[9]

Again, look upon your soul: see how many vices you are in danger of, as heresy, hypocrisy, idolatry, covetousness, idleness, security, envy, ambition, pride, etc. How many temptations may you fall into? But this shall you better see by looking on your old falls, folly, and temptations, and by looking on other men's faults: for no man hath done anything so evil, but you may do the same. Moreover, look upon your name, and see how it is in danger to slanders and false reports. Look upon your goods, see what danger they are in for thieves, for fire, etc. Look upon your wife, children, parents, brethren, sisters, kinsfolks, servants, friends, and neighbours, and behold how they also are in danger, both soul, body, name, and goods as you are.[10] Look upon the commonweal and country, look upon the church, upon the ministers and magistrates, and see what great dangers they are in; so that if you love them, you cannot but for the evil which may come to them, be heavy and sad. You know it is not in your power nor in the power of any man to hinder all evil that may come. How many perils is infancy in danger of? What danger is youth subject unto? Man's state is full of cares; age is full of diseases and sores. If thou be rich, thy care is the greater; if thou be in honour, thy perils are the more; if thou be poor, thou art the more in danger to oppression. But, alas, what tongue is able to express the miserableness of this life? The which considered, should make us little to love it.

---

[5] 'watery or mucous secretions' (*OED*)
[6] 'migraine'; 'dizziness' (vertigo); 'low spirits', 'depression'   [7] 'tremors'
[8] Marginal note: 'This life is more to be loathed for the miseries, than loved for the pleasures thereof. The miseries of this life concerning the body.'
[9] Marginal note: 'The miseries of this life concerning the soul. By looking on our old faults and temptations, and other men's faults we may see what danger we are always ready to fall into.'
[10] Marginal note: 'Great and weighty causes for us to be sad and heavy, and little to joy in the pleasures of this life.'

Suggested further reading
Seymour Byman, 'Guilt and Martyrdom: The Case of John Bradford', *The Harvard Theological Review*, 68.3–4 (1975), 305–31.
Richard Wunderli and Gerald Broce, 'The Final Moment before Death in Early Modern England', *The Sixteenth Century Journal*, 20.2 (1989), 259–75.

1.7

JOHN FISHER

A Spiritual Consolation (1578)

About the author

John Fisher (*c.*1469–1535), bishop of Rochester, was a leading scholar at Cambridge University, a favourite of Lady Margaret Beaufort (the mother of Henry VII), and a distinguished and prominent Catholic theologian. His outspoken opposition to Henry VIII's divorce from Catherine of Aragon, and refusal to acknowledge Henry as the 'Supreme Head of the Church of England', sealed his fate: he was beheaded at the Tower of London on 22 June 1535. He was instantly heralded across Europe as a martyr of the Catholic Counter-Reformation.

About the text

Fisher was imprisoned in the Tower from April 1534, and, resisting all pressure to acknowledge the King's actions through the Oath of Succession, would have been aware of his imminent fate. Here he writes to his sister, Elizabeth, a Dominican nun in Dartford, Kent, to offer guidance and consolation in the form of a spiritual meditation. The work was probably never intended for publication.

The arts of death

Fisher advises that Elizabeth should imagine her final moments before death, since consideration of this will help her to attend more devoutly to 'a good and virtuous life'. In Fisher's continuation of the death arts in the Catholic vein, he sets out three guidelines for the meditation: first, that his sister should 'devise in [her] mind, all the conditions of a man or woman suddenly taken and ravished by death'; second, that she should undertake this meditation alone and in private; and, third, that she must preface the meditation with a prayer to God to beseech his help with this. The meditation then adopts some familiar *contemptus mundi* themes, contrasting fleeting secular pleasures with everlasting spiritual life ('O corruptible body, O stinking carrion, O rotten earth to whom I have served'), and expounding upon Heaven's joys and Hell's terrors. Fisher emphasizes how meditating upon and preparing for a good death, keeping natural death at the forefront of one's mind, can enable one to live a good life.[1] Fisher's advice may be seen as a double art; that is, offering both a template for his own preparations for death, and a legacy for his sister.

Textual notes

A spirituall consolation, written by Iohn Fyssher Bishoppe of Rochester, to hys sister Elizabeth, at suche tyme as hee was prisoner in the Tower of London (London: 1578; STC 10899), A2^r–A4^r; B4^r–C1^v.

A Spiritual Consolation

Sister Elizabeth, nothing doth more help effectually to get a good and a virtuous life, than if a soul, when it is dull and unlusty without devotion, neither disposed to prayer nor to any other good work, may be stirred or quickened again by fruitful meditation. I have, therefore, devised unto you this meditation that followeth. Praying you, for my sake and for the weal of your own soul, to read it at such times as you shall feel yourself most heavy and slothful to do any good work. It is a manner of lamentation and sorrowful complaining made in the person of one that was hastily prevented by death (as, I assure you, every creature may be), none other surety we have, living in this world here.

[…]

Alas, alas, I am unworthily taken, all suddenly death hath assailed me, the pains of his stroke be so sore and grievous that I may not long endure them; my last home, I perceive well, is come. I must now leave this mortal body. I must now depart hence out of this world never to return again into it. But whither I shall go, or where I shall become, or what lodging I shall have this night, or in what company I shall fall, or in what country I shall be received, or in what manner I shall be entreated, God knoweth for I know not. What if

---

[1] Cf. these adapted themes and tropes in the Protestant faith in Bradford (entry I.6).

I shall be damned in the perpetual prison of Hell, where be pains endless and without number? Grievous it shall be to them that be damned forever, for they shall be as men in most extreme pains of death, ever wishing and desiring death, and yet never shall they die. It should be now unto me much weary, one year continually to lie upon a bed were it never so soft; how weary then shall it be to lie in the most painful fire so many thousand of years without number? And to be in that most horrible company of devils most terrible to behold, full of malice and cruelty? O wretched and miserable creature that I am, I might so have lived and so ordered my life by the help and grace of my Lord Christ Jesu, that this hour might have been unto me much joyous and greatly desired. Many blessed and holy Saints were full joyous and desirous of this hour, for they knew well that by death their souls should be translated into a new life: to the life of all joy and endless pleasure, from the straits and bondage of this corruptible body, into a very liberty and true freedom among the company of heaven, from the miseries and grievances of this wretched world to be above with God in comfort inestimable that cannot be spoken nay thought. They were assured of the promises of Almighty God which had so promised to all them that be his faithful servants. And sure I am that if I had truly and faithfully served him unto this hour, my soul had been partner of these promises. But unhappy and ungracious creature that I am, I have been negligent in his service, and therefore now my heart doth waste in sorrows seeing the nighness of death and considering my great sloth and negligence.

[...]

Therefore, first and before all things prepare for this, delay not in any wise, for if you do, you shall be deceived as I am now. I read of many, I have heard of many, I have known many that were disappointed as I am now. And ever I thought and said and intended, that I would make sure and not be deceived by the sudden coming of death. Yet nevertheless I am now deceived, and am taken sleeping, unprepared, and that when I least weened of his coming, and even when I reckoned myself to be in most health, and when I was most busy, and in the midst of my matters. Therefore, delay not you any farther, nor put your trust overmuch in your friends: trust yourself while ye have space and liberty, and do for yourself now while you may. I would advise you to do that thing that I by the grace of my Lord God would put in execution if his pleasure were to send me longer life. Recount yourself as dead and think that your souls were in prison of Purgatory, and that there they must abide till that the ransom for them be truly paid, either by long sufferance of pain there, or else by suffrages done here in earth by some of your special friends. Be you your own friend, do you these suffrages for your own soul, whether they be prayers or alms, deeds, or any other penitential painfulness. If you will not effectually and heartily do these things for your own soul, look you never that others will do them for you, and in doing them in your own persons, they shall be more available to you a thousandfold than if they were done by any other: if you follow this counsel and do thereafter, you be gracious and blessed, and if you do not, you shall doubtless repent your follies but too late.

Suggested further reading
Klaus P. Jankofsky, 'Public Executions in England in the Late Middle Ages: The Indignity and Dignity of Death', *OMEGA—Journal of Death and Dying*, 10.1 (1980), 43–57.
Paul Strauss, *In Hope of Heaven: English Recusant Prison Writings of the Sixteenth Century* (New York and Bern: Peter Lang, 1995).

1.8

ROBERT GREENE

The Repentance of Robert Greene (1592)

About the author

Robert Greene (1558–1592), the first infamous print author in English, composed six stage plays and over thirty prose titles from romances and satires to cony-catching pamphlets. He gained notoriety for his dissolute behaviour and ignominious end, which the cheap-print industry commercialized with a spate of repentance pamphlets, including Henry Chettle's forged *Greene's Groatsworth of Wit, Bought with a Million of Repentance*.

About the text

Though several scholars regard *The Repentance* as a fictional account penned by Chettle or someone else, John Jowett has made a thorough case for it being mostly written by Greene and only edited for the press by Chettle. This short pamphlet, more sober and less playful than *Groatsworth*, consists primarily of two main sections: 'The Repentance of Robert Greene, Master of Arts' followed by 'The Life and Death of Robert Greene, Master of Arts'. The excerpt comes near the beginning of the first section just after Greene has confessed to living the life of a reprobate scornful of believers and mired in excessive debauchery.

The arts of death

The excerpt dramatizes not only the infidel's mindset toward the death arts but also the turning point of Greene's moral decline, when during a terrible illness he consults Edmund Bunny's *A Book of Christian Exercise, Appertaining to Resolution*, particularly Chapter IX 'Of the Pains Appointed for Sin after this Life'. A translation of a treatise by the Jesuit Robert Parsons, Bunny's guide to dying slightly modified the Catholic text for Protestant consumption, and, having gone through multiple editions from the 1580s onwards, attested to the need for re-engaging with the *ars moriendi*'s affective dimension, which Calvinism had discouraged.

Lori Humphrey Newcomb has observed that Greene's conversion scene breaks with the Elizabethan faith in the spoken word as the chief means of conveying the divine truth's power to change hearts. Later in the second section, Greene mentions how a hellfire sermon he heard at Norwich deeply moved him, but his new outlook could not withstand the jests of his mates; what does leave a lasting impression upon him is none other than reading a popular print work – a suitable activity for proselytizing in the age of a robust pamphlet industry and, as Newcomb claims, for the growing Protestant acceptance of the printed word to impart divine revelation. Along with Greene's various commercialized deathbed repentances, the medium of conversion depicted in the excerpt bears witness to the printing press and trade as an engine of the death arts.

Textual notes

The repentance of Robert Greene Maister of Artes. Wherein by himselfe is laid open his loose life, with the manner of his death (London: 1592; STC 12306), B1^v–B2^v.

The Repentance of Robert Greene

Consuetudo peccandi tollit sensum peccati;[1] my daily custom in sin had clean taken away the feeling of my sin, for I was so given to these vices aforesaid, that I counted them rather venial scapes[2] and faults of nature than any great and grievous offences. Neither did I care for death, but held it only as the end of life. For coming one day into Aldersgate street to a well-willer's[3] house of mine, he with other of his friends persuaded me to leave my bad course of life, which at length would bring me to utter destruction, whereupon I scoffingly made them this answer: 'Tush, what better is he that dies in his bed than he that ends his life at Tyburn?[4] All owe God a death.[5] If I may have my desire while I live, I am satisfied; let me shift[6] after death as I may'. My friends, hearing these words, greatly grieved at my graceless resolution, made this reply: 'If you fear not death in this world, nor the pains of the body in this life, yet doubt the second death, and the loss of your soul, which without hearty repentance must rest in hell fire forever and ever'. 'Hell', quoth I, 'what talk you of hell to me? I know if I once come there, I shall have the company of better men than myself. I shall also meet with some mad knaves in that place, and so long as I shall not sit there alone, my care is the less. But you are mad folks', quoth I, 'for if I feared the judges of the bench no more than I dread the judgements of God, I would before I slept dive into one carle's[7] bags or other, and make merry with the shells[8] I found in them so long as they would last'. And though some in this company were friars of mine own fraternity[9] to whom I spake the words, yet were they so amazed at my profane speeches, that they wished themselves forth[10] of my company. Whereby appeareth that my continual delight was in sin, and that I made myself drunk with the dregs of mischief. But being departed thence unto my lodging, and now grown to the full, I was checked by the mighty hand of God, for sickness (the messenger of death) attached[11] me, and told me my time was but short, and that I had not long to live, whereupon I was vexed in mind, and grew very

---

[1] Translation follows in text. [2] 'thoughtless transgression' or 'escape from moral restraint'
[3] 'a person who desires the well-being of another'
[4] London's permanent gallows, located outside the city
[5] To 'owe God a debt' was a commonplace in the period, expressed memorably by the Scottish captain, Jamey, in *Henry V*: 'Ay owe Got a death, and I'll pay't as valorously as I may' (3.3.48–49). For further reading on this subject, see Jonathan Baldo, 'Spiritual Accountancy in the Age of Shakespeare' in *Memory and Mortality in Renaissance England*, ed. William E. Engel, Rory Loughnane, and Grant Williams (Cambridge: Cambridge University Press, 2022).
[6] 'let me look after myself'
[7] A 'carle' is a common name for a countryman or similar fellow of low birth.   [8] 'coins'
[9] 'close compatriots'   [10] 'out'   [11] 'to seize hold of' as by a disease or death

heavy. As thus I sat solemnly thinking of my end, and feeling myself wax sicker and sicker, I fell into a great passion, and was wonderfully perplexed, yet no way discovered my agony, but sat still calling to mind the lewdness of my former life. At what time suddenly taking the book of *Resolution*[12] in my hand, I light upon a chapter therein, which discovered unto me the miserable state of the reprobate,[13] what hell was, what the worm of conscience was, what torments there was appointed for the damned souls, what unspeakable miseries, what unquenchable flames, what intolerable agonies, what incomprehensible griefs; that there was nothing but fear, horror, vexation of mind, deprivation from the sight and favour of God, weeping and gnashing of teeth, and that all those tortures were not termined[14] or dated within any compass[15] of years, but everlasting world without end; concluding all in this of the Psalms: *ab inferis nulla est redemptio*.[16]

---

[12] Edmund Bunny, *A Book of Christian Exercise* (London: 1584; STC 19355).
[13] 'a person predestined by God to eternal damnation'
[14] 'decided' or 'determined'   [15] 'within due limits'
[16] 'From hell there is no redemption'; this line derives from the Office of the Dead, a prayer cycle for departed souls that consists of scripture, prayers, and psalms. Hence, Greene refers to it as Psalms. See entry II.2 (Cranmer).

Suggested further reading
John Jowett, 'Johannes Factotum: Henry Chettle and "Greene's Groatsworth of Wit"', *The Papers of the Bibliographical Society of America*, 87 (1993), 453–86.
Lori Humphrey Newcomb, 'A Looking Glass for Readers: Cheap Print and the Senses of Repentance', in *Writing Robert Greene: Essays on England's First Notorious Professional Writer*, ed. Edward Gieskes and Kirk Melnikoff (Aldershot, UK; Burlington, VT: Ashgate, 2008), pp. 133–56.

I.9

WILLIAM PERKINS

A Salve For A Sick Man (1595)

About the author

William Perkins (1558–1602), Cambridge don, theologian, and pastor, was a prolific apologist for the established Elizabethan Church. He wrote forty-eight texts, about half published posthumously. His works on 'practical divinity' concern the nature of salvation, define the crucial role of preaching, and stress the need for following a moral way of life. In England his writings outsold Calvin, Bèze, and Bullinger combined,[1] three of the main Continental Reformation thinkers to whom Perkins refers when discussing 'election to eternal life' and 'the mystery of predestination'.

About the text

Beginning with Ecclesiastes 7:1 ('the day of death is better than the day that one is born')[2] and using a catechistic question-and-answer format that anticipates objections to the points of doctrine presented by giving biblical precedents for learning how to die well, Perkins explains that a sick person's obligations are threefold: duties owed to God, to oneself, and to one's neighbour. He ties this back into a simplified explanation of the thorny reformist theological notion of supralapsarianism (the logical sequence of God's decrees), specifically that God controls, knows, and has foreordained when and how sickness occurs and the day of one's death. Instead of teaching resignation or fatalism,[3] Perkins sees this as another opportunity to rejoice in God's created order and 'glorify God in all things', most notably in the 'special providence' of sickness and death that everyone daily must confront.

The arts of death

Perkins's *ars moriendi* is more than just a manual to prepare for death in hope of dying well.[4] As with his earlier writings on conscience, this treatise focuses on navigating everyday life ever cognisant of the prospect of eternal life. The subtitle designates three types of people that the book 'may serve for spiritual instruction': '1. Mariners when they go to sea. 2. Soldiers when they go to battle. 3. Women when they travail of child.' Far from being a random sampling of possible readers, this list reflects Perkins's communitarian aims of safeguarding England's integrity and perpetuating the Protestant Elizabethan state, namely those risking their lives to sustain economic security and prosperity; those making the ultimate sacrifice for Queen and country; and those whose

---

[1] *A Legacy of Preaching, Volume One*, ed. Benjamin K. Forrest, Kevin L. King, and Dwayne Milioni (Grand Rapids, MI: Zondervan, 2018), p. 375.
[2] Bishops' Bible (1568); for a comparable treatment of this same verse, see entry I.1 (Caxton).
[3] Consistent with Perkins's *Antidicsonus* (London: 1584; STC 19064); see *MA*, p. 37.
[4] Cf. entry I.14 (Taylor).

lives are put in peril to bring forth the next generation. Consistent with Perkins's lifelong advocacy of social justice, he maintains that anyone's death diminishes the nation and should be considered both 'a private and a public loss' (G5^v).

Textual notes

A salve for a sicke man, or, A treatise containing the nature, differences, and kindes of death as also the right manner of dying well (Cambridge, 1595; STC 19742), A4^r–A6^r, G5^r–G5^v.

A Salve For A Sick Man

The kinds of death are two, as the kinds of life are, bodily and spiritual. Bodily death is nothing else but the separation of the soul from the body, as bodily life is the conjunction of body and soul: and this death is called the first, because in respect of time it goes before the second. Spiritual death is the separation of the whole man both in body and soul, from the gracious fellowship of God. Of these twain, the first is but an entrance to death, and the second is the accomplishment of it. For as the soul is the life of the body, so God is the life of the soul, and his spirit is the soul of our souls, and the want of fellowship with him brings nothing but the endless and unspeakable horrors and pangs of death. […] Death is the wages of sin (Rom 6:23), it is an enemy of Christ (1 Cor 15), and the curse of the law. Hence it seems to follow, that in and by death, men receive their wages and payment for their sins; that the day of death is the doleful day in which the enemy prevails against us; that he which dieth is cursed.

Answer. We must distinguish of death; it must be considered two ways: first, as it is by itself in his own nature; secondly, as it is altered and changed by Christ. Now death by itself considered, is indeed the wages of sin, and enemy of Christ and of all his members, and the curse of the law, yea the very suburbs and the gates of Hell; yet in the second respect, it is not so. For by the virtue of the death of Christ, it ceaseth to be a plague or punishment, and of a curse it is made a blessing, and is become unto us a passage or mid-way between this life and eternal life, and as it were a little wicket or door whereby we pass out of this world and enter into heaven. And in this respect the saying of Solomon is most true.[5] For in the day of birth, men are born and brought

---

[5] Eccl 7.1: 'the day of death is better than the day that one is born'; it is the proof text of this section of his treatise.

forth into the vale of misery, but afterward when they go hence, having death altered unto them by the death of Christ, they enter into eternal joy and happiness with all the saints of God forever.

[…]

And thus much of the first point of doctrine, namely that there is a certain way whereby a man may die well; now I come to the second. Whereas therefore Solomon sayeth that the day of death is better than the day of birth,[6] we are further taught that such as truly believe themselves to be the children of God, are not to fear death overmuch. I say overmuch because they must partly fear it, and partly not. Fear it they must for two causes: the first, because death is the destruction of human nature in a man's own self and others; and in this respect Christ feared it without sin; and we must not fear it otherwise than we fear sickness, and poverty, and famine, with other sorrows of body and mind, which God will not have us to despise or lightly regard, but to feel with some pain, because they are corrections and punishments for sin. And he doth therefore lay upon us pains and torments, that they may be feared and eschewed; and that by eschewing them we might further learn to eschew the cause of them, which is sin; and by experience in feeling of pain, acknowledge that God is a judge and enemy of sin, and is exceeding angry with it. The second cause of the fear of death is the loss of the Church or commonwealth, when we or others are deprived of them which were indeed or might have been an help, stay, and comfort to either of them, and whose death hath procured some public or private loss.

Again, we are not to fear death, but to be glad of it, and that for many causes.

[6] Eccl 7.1

Suggested further reading
David W. Atkinson, 'The English *ars moriendi*: Its Protestant Transformation', *Renaissance and Reformation*, 6.1 (1982), 1–10.

W. B. Patterson, *William Perkins and the Making of a Protestant England* (Oxford: Oxford University Press, 2014).

Louis B. Wright, 'William Perkins: Elizabethan Apostle of "Practical Divinity"', *Huntington Library Quarterly*, 3.2 (1940), 171–96.

1.10

DOROTHY LEIGH

The Mother's Blessing (1616)

About the author

Dorothy Leigh (*née* Kempe) (d. in or before 1616) leaves next to no record. She may have been the daughter to a William Kempe or a Robert Kempe, and may have been married to Ralph Leigh, who served under the Earl of Essex at Cádiz. We know with more assurance the names of her three sons, to whom her work's second dedication is addressed.

About the text

Leigh's text belongs to a subgenre of conduct books, identified as the mother's legacy. The subgenre presents a maternal voice that, stirred by an approaching death – whether or not an immediate threat – gives religious guidance to the imminently bereaved children. Although Leigh's overt purpose is to enjoin her sons to feed their souls with godly wisdom, her counsel, by virtue of going into print, addresses and seeks out a far larger audience than her progeny. In each of the forty-five chapters, Leigh sermonizes on a separate topic dear to early modern reformers, such as the necessity of private prayer, the observance of public worship on the sabbath, the choice of godly wives, and religious instruction for one's children and servants. With its twenty-three printings subsequent to its initial publication, *The Mother's Blessing* achieved a remarkable seventeenth-century popularity, being launched to the ranks of a best-seller among female-authored texts.

The arts of death

The text lucidly exhibits the early modern woman's multiple roles in the *ars moriendi*, a chief responsibility of which was to compose a last will and testament. For the wife and mother, death is family business, not just an individual consideration, since Leigh conscientiously stewards the affairs of both her deceased husband and her predeceased children. In the first excerpt, Leigh states her concern with carrying out her husband's will to ensure that their sons are well instructed in Christian piety and devotion. Her own legacy, then, is very much a matter of discharging her duty to the head of the household. From a chapter entirely devoted to issues of the *ars moriendi*, the second excerpt demonstrates her solicitude over her sons' proper attitude toward and preparation for death. Finally, the overall text suggests the way in which pronouncing 'last words' gave Leigh a rhetorical platform from which she could speak with authority in a male-dominated culture that prescribed silence for women. Scholars have thus unpacked the text's political strategy of using the maternal voice sanctified by the deathbed to confer on its author the licence to enter and be heard in the public sphere.

Textual notes

The mothers blessing. Or The godly counsaile of a gentle-woman not long since deceased, left behind her for her children … (London: 1616; STC 15402), A6^r–A7^v, B7^v–B9^v.

The Mother's Blessing

To my beloved sons, George, John, and William Leigh, all things pertaining to life and godliness

My children,

God having taken your father out of this vale of tears[1] to his everlasting mercy in Christ, myself not only knowing what a care he had in his life time, that you should be brought up godlily, but also at his death being charged in his will by the love and duty which I bear him, to see you well instructed and brought up in knowledge, I could not choose but seek (according as I was by duty bound) to fulfil his will in all things, desiring no greater comfort in the world, than to see you grow in godliness, that so you might meet your Father in heaven, where I am sure he is, myself being a witness of his faith in Christ. And seeing myself going out of the world, and you but coming in, I know not how to perform this duty so well, as to leave you these few lines, which will show you as well the great desire your father had both of your spiritual and temporal good, as the care I had to fulfil his will in this, knowing it was the last duty I

---

[1] Ps 84:6 (Bishops' Bible)

should perform unto him. But when I had written these things unto you and had (as I thought) something fulfilled your father's request, yet I could not see to what purpose it should tend, unless it were sent abroad to you, for, should it be left with the eldest, it is likely the youngest should have but little part in it. Wherefore setting aside all fear, I have adventured to show my imperfections to the view of the world, not regarding what censure shall for this be laid upon me, so that herein I may show myself a loving mother and a dutiful wife, and thus I leave you to the protection of him that made you, and rest till death,

Your fearful, faithful, and careful mother, D. L.

[…]

Chapter 7. The fifth cause is not to fear death

The fifth cause is to desire you never to fear death, for the fear of death hath made many to deny the known truth, and so have brought a heavy judgement of God upon themselves. A great reason why you should not fear death is because you can by no means shun it. You must needs endure it, and therefore it is meet that you should be always prepared for it and never fear it. *He that will save his life*,[2] sayeth Christ, *shall lose it, and he that will lose his life for my sake and the Gospels, shall find it*. Do not fear the pains of death, in what shape soever he come, for perhaps thou shalt have more pains upon thy bed and be worse provided to bear them, by reason of some grievous sickness, than thou art like to feel, when God shall call thee forth to witness his truth. The only way not to fear death is always to be provided[3] to die. And that thou mayest always be provided to die, thou must be continually strengthening thy faith with the promises of the Gospel; as, *He that liveth*[4] *and believeth shall not die, and, though he were dead, yet*[5] *shall he live. Meditate in the laws of the Lord day and night* (as the Psalmist sayeth) and then thou shalt be fit to bring forth fruit in due season. Then thou shalt be fit to serve God, thy king and country, both in thy life and in thy death, and always shalt show thyself a good member of Jesus Christ, a faithful subject to thy prince, and always fit to govern in the Christian commonwealth, and then thou mayest faithfully and truly say:[6] *Whether I live or die, I am the Lord's*. But without continual meditation of the word this cannot be done. And this was one of the chief causes why I writ unto you, to tell you that you must meditate in the word of God, for many read it and are never the

---

[2] Marginal note: 'Math. 16. 26.' Leigh actually refers to Matt 16:25.
[3] 'to make preparation or provision beforehand' [4] Marginal note: 'John. 11. 25–26.'
[5] Marginal note: 'Psal. 1. 2.' [6] Marginal note: 'Rom. 14. 8.'

better for want of meditation. If ye hear the word and read it, without meditating thereon, it doth the soul no more good than meat and drink doth the body, being seen and felt, and never fed upon, for as the body will die although it see meat, even so will the soul, for all the hearing and reading of the word, if that ye do not meditate upon it and gather faith and strengthen it, and get hold of Christ; which if ye do, Christ will bring you to the kingdom of his Father, to which you can come by no means but by faith in him.

Suggested further reading
Jennifer Louise Heller, *The Mother's Legacy in Early Modern England* (Farnham, UK: Ashgate, 2011).
Edith Snook, *Women, Reading, and the Cultural Politics of Early Modern England* (Aldershot, UK: Ashgate, 2005), pp. 57–82.

I.11

GEORGE WITHER

Selected Works (1628, 1635)

About the author

George Wither (1588–1667), Puritan poet and pamphleteer, supported the Parliamentarians. John Aubrey records that John Denham appealed for Wither's life when he was captured, quipping that 'whilst G.W. lived he should not be the worst poet in England'. After two years at Magdalen College, Oxford, Wither studied law in London where he published a verse satire, *Abuses Stript and Whipt* (1613), for which he was imprisoned. He then tried his hand at less incendiary work, and his much-praised eclogue *The Shepherd's Hunting* (1615) was anthologized well into the nineteenth century. Wither's remaining publications included more satires (for which he was again imprisoned), *Juvenilia* (1622), and poems on religious themes – most notably *Hymns and Songs of the Church* (1623), the first hymnbook in English not based entirely on the Psalms.

About the text

Drawing on his experiences during the London plague of 1625, Wither published an admonitory poem in eight cantos, *Britain's Remembrancer* (1628).[1] A 'remembrancer', properly speaking, was a minor official attached to the Exchequer, variously termed 'memorator' or 'rememorator', who compiled 'memorandum rolls' to remind concerned parties about pending business. Wither's register declares 'the mischiefs present' and offers 'a prediction of judgements to come if repentance prevent not'. In the selection excerpted here from canto II, Wither makes much of Charles's first Parliament (assembled June 1625, prior to his coronation), set against the backdrop of a plague in London so virulent that the second session had to be convened at Oxford. Wither concurs with those in Parliament who complained about the king's marriage contract with the Roman Catholic Henrietta Maria of France that included, in his estimation, unacceptable concessions to English Catholics.

The arts of death

Wither assumes the role of a 'remembrancer' in this verse plague tract, giving a moralized account of the chaotic time of pestilence that hampered the opening years of Charles I's reign. He uses the term in the same sense as Bishop Joseph Hall who reflected on how all things in the world, if properly beheld, are 'Death's Remembrancers'.[2] Wither's account of the capital city overrun by disease and contagion – and the abject fear among the living of impending death – conveys many of the commonplaces of this genre in the service of delivering chastening warnings about the breakdown of the government and church offices, as well as the devastating rupture of familial and social bonds.

Textual notes

Britain's Remembrancer containing a narration of the plague lately past (London: 1628; STC 25899), D10^r–D10^v, F7^r--F7^v.

---

[1] See entry II.9 (Dekker) for a treatment of the plague at the beginning of James I's reign, 1603–1604.
[2] Joseph Hall, *Susurrium cum Deo. Soliloquies* (London: 1559; Wing H421), H5^r.

Britain's Remembrancer

>When, as you heard before, the Court of Heaven
Commission[3] to the Pestilence had given
To scourge our sins, and signed her direction
She took up all her boxes of infections,
Her carbuncles,[4] her sores, her spots, her blains,[5]
And every other thing which appertains
To her contagious practices; and all
Her followers she did about her call;
Appoint them to their places, and their times,
Direct them to the persons, and the crimes
They should correct, and how they should advance
Her main designment[6] in each circumstance.
>>Then, on she marched; not as doth a foe
Proclaiming war, before he strikes the blow;
But like an enemy, who doth surprise
Upon the first advantage he espies.
For, passing through the streets of many a town
Disguised like a fever, she, unknown,
>>>Stole into London, and did lurk about
The well-filled suburbs; spreading there, no doubt,
Infection unperceived, in many a place
Before the blear-eyed[7] searchers knew her face;
And since they knew her, they have bribed been
A thousand times, to let her pass unseen.
>>>>But at the length, she was discovered at
A Frenchman's house[8] without the Bishopsgate.[9]
To intimate, perhaps, that such as be

---

[3] This alludes to the 'Court of High Commission', an ecclesiastical court set up by the crown to enforce laws of the Reformation settlement. The court was controversial because it was seen as an instrument of repression against those not acknowledging the authority of the Church of England. It was thus abolished in 1641 as one of Charles I's concessions to Parliament.
[4] 'boil cluster'   [5] 'inflammatory swelling'; 'sores'   [6] 'plan'
[7] 'tired eyes'; 'fatigued eyes from waking and watching'
[8] a possible allusion to one of the many followers of Henrietta Maria, recently come from France
[9] ward named after one of the original eight gates of London; a site of coach inns for travellers heading out of town

Our spiritual watchmen should the more foresee
That they with discipline made strong the ward,
Which God appointed hath for them to guard;
And chiefly, at this present, to have care,
Lest now, while we and France united are
In bodily commerce, they bring unto us
Those plagues which may eternally undo us.
For, such like pestilences soon begin,
And, ere we be aware will enter in,
Unless our bishops, both betimes and late,
Be diligent and watchful at their gate.
     As soon as ere the women-spies descried
This foe about the city to reside,
There was a loud all-arm.[10] The countrymen
Began to wish themselves at home again.
The citizens were gen'lly appalled;
     The senators themselves to counsel called;
And all (who might advise in such a case)
Assembled in their common meeting place;
Where, what discretion publicly was used;
What was admitted of, and what refused;
What policies, and stratagems invented;
That mischiefs,[11] coming on, might be prevented,
I cannot say: For I had never wit,
Nor wealth enough, to sit in counsel, yet.

[…]

For with a doubled, and redoubled stroke
The plague went on; and, in (among us) broke
With such unequalled fury, and such rage;
As Britain never felt in any age.
With some at every turning she did meet.
Of every alley, every lane and street
She got possession: and we had no way,

---

[10] 'alarm'; 'a warning cry' (call 'to arms')   [11] 'nefarious schemes'

Or passage, but she there, in ambush, lay.
Through nooks, and corners, she pursued the chase,
There was no barring her from any place:
For in the public fields in wait she laid;
And into private gardens was conveyed.
Sometime, she did among our garments hide;
And, so, disperse among us (unespied[12])
Her strong infections. Otherwhile (unseen)
A servant, friend, or child betrayed hath been,
To bring it home; and men were fearful grown
To tarry, or converse, among their own.
Friends fled each other, kinsmen stood aloof;
The son, to come within his father's roof
Presumed not; the mother was constrained
To let her child depart unentertained.
The love, betwixt the husband, and the wife,
Was oft neglected, for the love of life;
And many a one their promise falsified,
Who vowed, that naught but death should them divide.
Some, to frequent the markets were afraid;
And some to feed on what was thence purveyed.
For on young pigs such purple spots were seen,
As marks of death on plague-sick men have been;
And it appeared that our suburb-hogs
Were little better, then our cats and dogs.
      Men knew not whither they might safely come,
Nor where to make appointments, nor with whom.
Nay, many shunned God's-house, and much did fear
So far to trust him, as to meet him there.
In brief, the plague did such destruction threat,
And fears, and perils were become so great,
That most men's hearts did fail; and they to flight
Betook themselves, with all the speed they might:
Not only they, who private persons were,
  But, such as did the public titles bear.

---

[12] 'unnoticed', 'undetected'

Suggested further reading

Andrew McRae, 'Remembering 1625: George Wither's *Britain's Remembrancer* and the Condition of Early Caroline England', *English Literary Renaissance*, 46.3 (2016), 433–55.

Kira L. S. Newman, '"Shutt Up": Bubonic Plague and Quarantine in Early Modern England', *Journal of Social History*, 45.3 (2012), 809–34.

Rebecca Totaro, *The Plague Epic in Early Modern England: Heroic Measures, 1603–1721* (New York: Routledge, 2012), pp. 171–226.

About the text

Wither's main contribution to *A Collection of Emblems* (1635) consists in his straightforward verse commentaries on 200 emblems printed from plates originally engraved by Crispijn van de Passe for Gabriel Rollenhagen's two-volume *Nucleus emblematum selectissimorum* (1611–1613). Wither divides his collection into four books and adds a 'lottery' at the end of each book,[13] a single verse speaking directly to readers about the lot that came their way, with reference to each specific emblem. To facilitate this recreation, a pattern for a cut-out spinner is included at the end, thereby enhancing the reader's engagement with the text, whether alone or in sociable groups. 'For my meaning is not, that any should use it as an oracle, which could signify, infallibly, it is divinely allotted; but, to serve only for a moral pastime' (A2ᵛ).

The arts of death

Out of 200 already existing emblems to which Wither contributed his own distinctive moralizing poems, 10 explicitly show a death's head or skeleton,[14] and another 30 admonish readers to use their brief time on earth in wholesome endeavours – and yet all of them, in one way or another, urge readers to consider each emblem as a goad to self-improvement. Although Wither had no say about the images, he did exercise considerable liberty with his explanatory poems. In the two representative excerpts included here, he engages key aspects of the visual lexicon associated with the death arts and elaborates on the conditions of mortal temporality. Each emblem is introduced with a

---

[13] No lotteries appear in Rollenhagen's work; a precedent can be found, however, in a Jesuit emblem book by Jean David, *Veridicus Christianus* (Antwerp, 1601).

[14] See *MA* VI.7 for a comparable emblem by Francis Quarles with the scriptural motto: 'Who shall deliver me from the body of this Death?'

rhymed couplet (a feature not found in Rollenhagen's original format), followed by a circular image encompassed by a Latin motto, which provides the point of departure for his poetic ingenuity. A few of Wither's heading couplets will serve to indicate how prominently the death arts figure into his overall project: 'By knowledge only, life we gain, / All other things to death pertain' (B1^r); 'This rag of death, which thou shalt see, / Consider it; and pious be' (B4^v); 'Death is no loss, but rather, gain; / For we by dying, life attain' (D3^r); 'Death, is unable to divide / Their hearts, whose hands true-love hath tied' (P3^r); and, in a description of ageing he writes that stomach aches and other maladies, 'The harbingers of death, sometime, begin / To take up your whole body, for their inn' (Cc1^v). He even uses his own image prefacing the volume as an occasion for meditating on morality (A3^v–A4^r)[15]:

> When I behold my picture, and perceive,
> How vain it is, our portraiture to leave
> In lines, and shadows (which make shows, today,
> Of that which will, tomorrow, fade away).
> […]
> Our everlasting substance lies unseen,
> Behind the foldings of a carnal screen,
> Which is but vapors thickened into blood,
> (By due concoction of our daily food)
> And still supplied, out of other creatures,
> To keep us living, by their wasted natures
> Renewing, and decaying, every day,
> Until that veil must be removed away.

Textual notes

A Collection of Emblemes, Ancient and Moderne, Quickened With Metricall Illustrations, Both Morall and Divine … and disposed into lotteries (London: 1635; STC 25900d), G3^r, Aa1^v (see respectively Figure 1.4 and Figure 1.5)

---

[15] This ploy was not lost on Edward Collier who included it in his *Still Life with a Volume of Wither's 'Emblemes'* (1696) among other images associated with the *vanitas* tradition such as musical instruments, wine, and jewels emblematic of the fleeting pleasures of life; a skull and hourglass symbolizing the inevitability of death; and a Latin inscription at the top left corner from Eccl 1:2, 'Vanity of vanities, all is vanity'; Tate Britain (ref. N05916).

A Collection of Emblems

As soon, as we to be, begun;
We did begin, to be undone.

FIGURE 1.4 Infant leaning on a death's head. George Wither, *A Collection of Emblems* (London: 1635; STC 25899), G3ʳ. Image used courtesy of The Newberry Library

When some, in former ages, had a meaning
An emblem of mortality to make,
They formed an infant, on a death's head leaning,
And, round about, encircled with a snake.[16]
The child so pictured, was to signify,
That, from our very birth, our dying springs:
The snake, her tail devouring, doth imply
The revolution, of all earthly things.

[16] the 'ouroboros' symbol, associated with eternity in the Hermetic humanist tradition

For, whatsoever hath beginning, here,
Begins, immediately, to vary from
The same it was; and, doth at last appear
What very few did think it should become.
The solid stone, doth molder[17] into earth,
That earth, ere long, to water, rarifies;[18]
That water, gives an airy vapour birth,
And, thence, a fiery comet doth arise:
That, moves, until itself it so impair,
That from a burning-meteor, back again,
It sinketh down, and thickens into air;
That air, becomes a cloud; then, drops of rain:
Those drops, descending on a rocky ground,
There, settle into earth, which more and more,
Doth harden, still; so, running out the round,
It grows to be the stone it was before.
Thus, all things wheel about; and, each beginning,
Made entrance to its own destruction, hath.
The life of nature, ent'reth[19] in with sinning;
And, is forever, waited on by death:

FIGURE 1.5 Owl on a death's head. George Wither, *A Collection of Emblems* (London: 1635; STC 25899), Aa1[v]. Image used courtesy of The Newberry Library

[17] 'decay'; 'slowly disintegrate'   [18] 'makes more refined'
[19] 'enters'; 'from its initial appearance'

The life of grace, is formed by death to sin;
And, there, doth life-eternal straight begin.

Whilst thou dost, here, enjoy thy breath,
Continue mindful of thy death.

When thou beholdest on this burying-stone,
The melancholy night-bird,[20] sitting on
The fleshless ruins of a rotten skull,[21]
(Whose face, perhaps, hath been more beautiful,
Then thine is now) take up a serious thought;
And, do as thou art by the motto taught.
Remember Death: and, mind, I thee beseech,
How soon, these fowls may at thy window screech;
Or, call thee (as the common people deem)
To dwell in graves, and sepulchres, by them,
Where nothing else, but bats, and owls, appear;
Or, goblins, formed by fancies, and, by fear.
If thou shalt be advised, to meditate
Thy latter end, before it be too late,
(And, whilst thy friends, thy strength, and wits may bee
In likely case, to help and comfort thee)
There may be courses taken, to divert
Those frights, which, else, would terrify thy heart,
When death draws near; and help thee pluck away
That sting, of his, which would thy soul dismay.
But, if thou madly ramble onward, still,
Till thou art sinking down that darksome-hill,
Which borders on the grave (and dost begin
To see the shades of terror, and of sin

---

[20] 'owl'; sacred to Athena (Minerva in the Roman pantheon), goddess of wisdom and prudence

[21] See Introduction with reference to Geoffrey Whitney's emblem entitled '*Ex maximo minimum*' (from the greatest to the least): 'Lo, now a skull, both rotten, bare, and dry, / A relic meet in charnel house to lie' (f3ʳ).

To fly across thy conscience) 'twill be hard
To learn this lesson; or, to be prepared
For that sad parting; which, will forced bee,
Between this much beloved world, and thee.
Consider this, therefore, while time thou hast,
And, put not off this business, till the last.

Suggested further reading
Miranda Anderson, 'Mirroring Mentalities in George Wither's *A Collection of Emblemes*', *Emblematica*, 20 (2013), 63–80.
Calabritto and Daly, *ED*
Pierre Le Duff, '"Emblemes, Ancient and Moderne": George Wither's *Collection of Emblemes*', *Revue de la Société d'études anglo-américaines des XVIIe et XVIIIe siècles*, 76 (2019), https://doi.org/10.4000/1718.2894.

I.12

ANONYMOUS

'The Unnatural Wife' (1628)

About the text

The English broadside ballad gained cultural currency during the rise of the sixteenth-century printing press. Along with the pamphlet, it became the dominant cheap print vehicle, capitalizing upon sensational topics such as religious controversies, bawdy drinking songs, wonders and divine portents, plagues, military conflicts, and notorious crimes. Its frequent combination with a woodcut illustration enabled common folk to see themselves reflected in both verbal and visual media, thus helping to establish a proto-public sphere before the advent of the newspaper. Street ballads regularly omitted the author's name as in the case of 'The Unnatural Wife', included here in its entirety. It is an example of 'a good night ballad', which supposedly communicates the dying confession of a murderer on the eve of execution. Alice Davis, the unnatural wife in question, slew her husband with a kitchen knife, when he demanded a shilling from her. Though records attest that Alice entered a plea of pregnancy in an attempt to escape the death penalty, she was executed for 'petty treason'. Statute law regarded the murder of a husband as a kind of treason against the sovereign and the state, and consequently Alice was not hanged but burned at the stake after the manner of a convicted traitor. Alice's case inspired at least one other ballad, 'A Warning for all Desperate Women' (London: 1628; STC 6367).

The arts of death

The shame of being remembered in a murder ballad clashes strikingly with the wish for a blessed passing. 'O to think', laments the eponymous 'insatiate countess' of Marston's play, 'whilst we are singing the last hymn, and ready to be turned off, some new tune is inventing by some metre-monger, to a scurvy ballad of our death!'[1] For their time, early modern murder ballads promulgated an inverted *ars moriendi*. Whereas the traditional art instructed believers in the preparation for a good death, the murder ballad warned readers, as does the repentant Alice in her final stanza, to avoid the doubly fatal path taken by the condemned: her fiery punishment for her crime may be the prologue of a second, ultimate immolation at the Last Judgement. Alice's pitiful confession of how she was caught up in a juridical-disciplinary regime starting with the constable and ending with the judge also internalizes the institutional imperatives of the civic order. According to Stuart Kane, this ballad turns her domestic, private malefaction into a public spectacle for the buying audience. The way in which it reveals the elaborate surveillance machinery operating around mariticide – first the crime and then the punishment – suggests that, in this case, the death arts belong less to the individual woman than to the omniscient state.

Textual notes

The unnatural wife: or, the lamentable murther, of one goodman Davis, Locke-Smith in Tutle-streete, who was stabbed to death by his wife, on the 29 of June,

---

[1] John Marston et al., *The Insatiate Countess*, ed. Giorgio Melchiori (Manchester, UK: Manchester University Press, 1984), 5.2.60 ff.

1628. For which fact, she was arraigned, condemned, and adjudged to be burnt to death in Smithfield, the 12 July 1628 (London: 1628; STC 6366).

'The Unnatural Wife'

To the Tune of Bragandary[2]

If woeful objects may excite
    the mind to ruth and pity,
Then here is one will thee affright
    in Westminster's fair city.
A strange inhuman murder there,
To God and man as doth appear:
    oh murder,
    most inhumane,
To spill my husband's blood.

But God that rules the host of heaven
    did give me o'er to sin,
And to vild[3] wrath my mind was given,
    which long I lived in;
But now too late I do repent,
And for the same my heart doth rent:
    [chorus][4]

Let all cursed wives by me take heed,
    how they do, do the like,
Cause not thy husband for to bleed,
    nor lift thy hand to strike;
Lest like to me, you burn in fire,
Because of cruel rage and ire:
    [chorus]

---

[2] A tune, which would have been familiar to many buyers, was always included with a ballad's title.
[3] 'vile'
[4] The chorus is the last three typographic lines of the first stanza: 'oh murder, / most inhumane, / To spill my husband's blood'.

A locksmith late in Westminster
    my husband was by trade,
And well he lived by his art,
    though oft I him upbraid;
And often times would chide and brawl,
And many ill names would him call.
    [chorus]

The second part. To the same tune.

I and my husband forth had been
    at supper at that time,
When as I did commit that sin,
    which was a bloody crime;
And coming home he then did crave,
A shilling of me for to have.
    [chorus]

I vow'd he should no money get,
    and I my vow did keep,
Which then did cause him for to fret,
    but now it makes me weep;
And then in striving for the same,
I drew my knife unto my shame:
    [chorus]

Most desperately I stabbed him then,
    with this my fatal knife,
Which is a warning to women,
    to take their husband's life;
Then out of doors I straight did run,
And said that I was quite undone.
    [chorus]

My husband I did say was slain,
    amongst my neighbours there,
And to my house they strait way came,
    being possessed with fear,

And then they found him on the floor,
    Stark dead all welt'ring in the gore.[5]
        [chorus]

Life fain I would have fetched again,
    but now it was too late,
I did repent I him had slain,
    in this my heavy state;
The constable did bear me then
Unto a justice with his men.
        [chorus]

Then justice[6] me to Newgate[7] sent,
    until the sessions[8] came,
For this same foul and bloody fact,
    to answer for the same;
When at the bar I did appear,
The jury found me guilty there.
        [chorus]

The judge gave sentence thus on me,
    that back I should return
To Newgate, and then at a stake,
    my bones and flesh should burn
To ashes, in the wind to fly,
Upon the earth, and in the sky.
        [chorus]

Upon the twelfth of July now,
    I on a hurdle[9] placed't,
Unto my execution drawn,
    by weeping eyes I past;
And there in Smithfield[10] at a stake,

---

[5] i.e., to lie prostrate in one's blood   [6] 'a judge or magistrate'
[7] London prison; see entry I.17 (Smith).   [8] 'the sitting of a judge to hold a judicial trial'
[9] a kind of frame or sledge upon which traitors were pulled through the streets on their way to execution
[10] See entry I.6 (Bradford).

My latest breath I there did take.
    [chorus]

And being chained to the stake,
    both reeds and faggots then
Close to my body there was set,
    with pitch, tar, and rozin,[11]
Then to the heavenly Lord I prayed,
That he would be my strength and aid.
    [chorus]

Let me a warning be to wives
    that are of hasty kind,
Lord grant that all may mend their lives,
    and bear my death in mind,
And let me be the last I pray,
That ere may die by such like way.
    oh Father
    for thy Son's sake,
Forgive my sins for aye.

[11] 'resin', a flammable material

Suggested further reading

Simone Chess, '"And I my vowe did keepe": Oath Making, Subjectivity, and Husband Murder in "Murderous Wife" Ballads', in *Ballads and Broadsides in Britain, 1500–1800*, ed. Patricia Fumerton and Anita Guerrini with the assistance of Kris McAbee (Aldershot, UK; Burlington, VT: Ashgate, 2010), pp. 131–47.

Stuart A. Kane, 'Wives with Knives: Early Modern Murder Ballads and the Transgressive Commodity', *Criticism*, 38.2 (1996), 219–37.

1.13

JANE OWEN

An Antidote against Purgatory (1634)

About the author

Jane Owen (*fl.* 1617–1625), an English recusant, hailed from Godstow, Oxfordshire, according to the title page of her only existing work. Little is known about her, other than the fact that she was, in all likelihood, a descendant of George Owen (1499–1558), the longstanding royal physician who acquired Godstow Abbey as his principal residence. During Jane's lifetime, George's descendants were noted for their recusancy at Godstow and on the Continent.

About the text

Owen's treatise is basically a fundraising salvo for the Catholic community forced underground by England's laws. The treatise's four sections lay out a transparent agenda of exhorting wealthy English recusants to open their purses. The first section, explicitly committed to evoking fear, translates a chapter from Cardinal Bellarmine's *The Mourning of the Dove* (1617) that graphically depicts the pains endured by Purgatory dwellers. The second section explains how the title's antidote, that is, charitable acts or 'alms-deeds', can mitigate such afterlife suffering. For this reason, Owen apparently directed the printer (*5^r–*5^v) to insert in the footers of facing pages the verse from Matthew 5:26 in the Vulgate: at each leaf's turn, the reader will be able to meditate upon the ominous words 'Thou shalt not go out from thence, till thou repay the last farthing'.[1] The third section builds a persuasive case for actively working toward avoiding or mitigating Purgatory's afflictions, and, finally, the fourth raises the specific good works to be practised; for example, donating funds to maintain the education of poor young English scholars overseas will save them from entering the ungodly Protestant universities of their homeland and, when they return from the Continent, will allow them to keep the Catholic religion alive in England (I3^v–I7^v). Since the treatise may have been published at St Omer in the Spanish Netherlands, Owen's call for

---

[1] translated from the Douay–Rheims Bible

alms-deeds may have been made on behalf of St Omer's Jesuit College, which educated English recusant men, and on behalf of Mary Ward's Institute of the Blessed Mary, a convent which, established by the Yorkshire woman, set up schools for English recusant girls. The treatise's affiliation with Flanders suggests that Owen may have conveyed donations herself to the needy English Catholics abroad.

The arts of death

Owen's treatise indicates not only the doctrinal force that Purgatory still exerted on English Catholics but also the dated nature of that vision – a vision at odds, according to Dorothy Latz's analysis, with newer attitudes promoted by the Council of Trent, whose edict discouraged preaching and instruction from promulgating medieval superstitions about Purgatory as a place of torture. In the excerpt, which comes from the treatise's third section, Owen wants to rouse schismatic Christians from spiritual lethargy by contemplating their final moments as an ultimate vantage point for self-reflection upon their current behaviour. She invites them to imagine themselves on their deathbed – a pre-eminent mnemonic locus freighted with anxiety, truth, and authority – where they will have a final colloquy with their souls on how they conducted their lives.

Textual notes

Antidote against purgatory. Or discourse, wherein is shewed that good-workes, and almes-deeds, performed in the name of Christ, are a chiefe meanes for the preuenting, or migatating the torments of purgatory ([Saint-Omer], 1634; STC 18984), F8^v–F9^v, G1^r–G2^r; G3^r.

An Antidote against Purgatory

Well then, my poor and dear Catholic, who for many years through thy wicked dissimulation in matters of religion hast most highly offended God. Imagine thyself that at this very instant thou wert lying upon thy deathbed: (that bed, I say, which the Prophet calleth, *lectum doloris*, (Psalm 40)[2] the bed of grief) worn away with pain and sickness and not expecting to escape but

---

[2] Ps 40:4 (Vulgate)

looking every minute for thy last dissolution. How would thy judgement be altered? and wouldst thou not thus, in all likelihood, reason and dispute with thy own soul? 'True it is, I thank God, of his most infinite and boundless mercy, that as a straying sheep I am at length brought into Christ's sheepfold, and I hope to die (through the benefit of our Saviour's passion, and of the holy Sacraments) his servant, and in state of grace, and finally to enjoy the interminable joys of heaven. But alas, though the guilt of eternal damnation, incurred by my long former schismatical life and by my many other infinite sins, as I hope through God's infinite mercy, be remitted; yet temporal punishment due for all my former said sins in most inexplicable torments of purgatory doth expect me.

'My poor soul must continue in those burning flames (how many years, his divine Majesty only knoweth) for the expiating of my said sins, before I can arrive to heaven. When I was in health, enjoying my temporal state in all fullness, how easily with a voluntary relinquishing of a reasonable part thereof to pious and religious uses, could I have avoided, at least mitigated, these now imminent and unavoidable torments? Good God! where then were my wits? The very ploughman provides for the time of winter; yea the ant, to the which we are sent by God's word (Proverbs 6)[3] to be instructed, hoards grains of corn for his after sustenance. And have I so negligently carried myself, as to lay up beforehand no provision against this tempestuous and rugged future storm? O beast, that I was! Sweet Jesus, how far distant were my former course of life and daily actions from ever thinking of this unavoidable danger?

[…]

O that I had been so happy, as to have followed the wholesome advice, given to me by way of presage in a little treatise, entitled *An Antidote against Purgatory*. I then did read it, but with a certain curiosity, as thinking it nothing to belong to me. But, alas, I now find it to be a true Sybil[4] or prophet of my future calamitous state.

Well then, seeing my own hourglass is almost run out, let me turn my speech to you, dear Catholics, in my health my chiefest familiars and with whom I did most consociate[5] in my former pleasures. There is no difference between you and me, but the time present and the time to come. You all must once be forced to this bed of sorrow and be brought to your last sickness. To

---

[3] Prov 6:6–8 (Vulgate)
[4] one of a group of ancient women thought to have the abilities of prophecy and divination
[5] 'associate together'

you then, and to all others, who are negligent in providing against this day, I do direct this my charitable admonition. You are yet in health and perhaps as improvident in laying up spiritual riches against this fearful day, as myself have been. O change your course, while there is time. Let my present state preach to you and suffer these my last dying words to give life to your future actions; since they preach feelingly whose pulpit is their deathbed'.

[…]

To these and the like disconsolate and tragical lamentations in the inward reflex of thy soul, my dear Catholic, shalt thou in thy last sickness be driven, if thou seek not to prevent the danger in time. Therefore, remember that he is truly wise who laboureth to be such in his health, as he wisheth to be found in God's sight at the hour of his death.

Suggested further reading
Stephen Greenblatt, *Hamlet in Purgatory* (Princeton, NJ: Princeton University Press, 2001), pp. 25–26, 71–72.
Dorothy L. Latz (ed.), 'Introductory Note', 'Jane Owen' in *The Early Modern Englishwoman: A Facsimile Library of Essential Works* (Aldershot, UK: Ashgate, 2000), part 2, vol. 9.

1.14

JEREMY TAYLOR

Holy Dying (1651)

About the author

Jeremy Taylor (15 August 1613–13 August 1667) received his BA and MA from Gonville and Caius College, Cambridge, and was advanced by William Laud, Archbishop of Canterbury. He preached at Lambeth and was appointed Chaplain in Ordinary to Charles I. Owing to Laud's trial and eventual execution by the House of Commons toward the end of the First English Civil War (1644–1645), Taylor understandably came under suspicion and several times was imprisoned. He travelled to Wales where he served as chaplain to and was protected by Richard Vaughan, Earl of Carbery. After the Restoration, Taylor was made Bishop of Down and Connor in Ireland. He is remembered in the Church of England's calendar of saints on 13 August.

About the text

Written as a follow-up to *The Rule and Exercises of Holy Living* (1650), Taylor's *Holy Dying* (1651) reads as a consolation for his patron, Lord Vaughan, upon the death of his wife (Taylor's own wife died, incidentally, after the publication of the first volume). The first half of *Holy Dying* gives practical suggestions for cleansing and building up the soul in preparation for the attainment of Heaven; the second half is a memorial sermon. Taylor's periodic sentences imitate at the grammatical level what the larger work concerns, namely, last things. Taylor favours, and his prose fully realizes, the rhetorical possibilities inherent in the Ciceronian grand style which emphasizes the main idea by placing it at the end, after a concatenation of subordinate, often meandering, clauses and other modifying terms and suggestive parallel images. Readers thus find themselves experientially adrift in the flow of the sentence, discovering along the way new insights and contingent considerations about the larger theme until, at last, with the period, coming to a satisfying place of rest – and hence reflection.

The arts of death

Taylor's book stands prominently at the end of a long line of English works steeped in the late medieval *ars moriendi* (see Figure 1.6). It blends the conventional consolation form with familiar and perennial tropes associated with *contemptus mundi*, *vanitas*, and *memento mori* to instruct readers in the 'means and instruments' of preparing for a 'blessed death'. In the style of a sermon, he discloses (as the subtitle puts it) 'the remedies against the evils and temptations proper to the state of sicknesses, together with prayers and acts of virtue to be used by sick and dying persons, or by others standing in their attendance'. Each chapter has discussions of moral instruction and theology, usually with summary sections couched in terms of 'the consideration reduced to practice', and provides model prayers to help readers frame their own supplications to God whose aid is fundamental to the achievement of one's spiritual aims in the face of death.

Textual notes

The rule and exercises of holy dying (London: 1651; Wing T361A), B1^v–B2^r, B5^v–B6^r.

FIGURE 1.6 Sepulchral death's head. Jeremy Taylor, *The Rule and Exercises of Holy Dying* (London: 1651; Wing T361A), frontispiece. Image used courtesy of The Newberry Library

Holy Dying

So is every man: he is born in vanity and sin; he comes into the world like morning mushrooms, soon thrusting up their heads into the air and conversing with their kindred of the same production, and as soon they turn into dust and forgetfulness; some of them without any other interest in the affairs of the world, but that they made their parents a little glad, and very sorrowful: others ride longer in the storm; it may be until seven years of vanity be expired, and then peradventure the sun shines hot upon their heads and they fall into the shades below, into the cover of death, and darkness of the grave to hide them. But if the bubble stands the shock of a bigger drop, and outlives the chances of a child, of a careless nurse, of drowning in a pail of water, of being overlaid by a sleepy servant, or such little accidents, then the young man dances like a bubble, empty and gay, and shines like a dove's neck or the image of a rainbow, which hath no substance, and whose very imagery and colours are phantastical; and so he dances out the gaiety of his youth, and is all the while in a storm, and endures, only because he is not knocked on the head by a drop of bigger rain, or crushed by the pressure of a load of indigested meat, or quenched by the disorder of an ill placed humour: and to preserve a man alive in the midst of so many chances, and hostilities, is as great a miracle as to create him; to preserve him from rushing into nothing and at first to draw him up from nothing were equally the issues of an almighty power.

[...]

It is a mighty change that is made by the death of every person, and it is visible to us who are alive. Reckon but from the spritefulness of youth, and the fair cheeks and full eyes of childhood, from the vigorousness, and strong flexure of the joints of five and twenty, to the hollowness and dead paleness, to the loathsomeness and horror of a three days' burial, and we shall perceive the distance to be very great, and very strange. But so have I seen a rose newly springing from the clefts of its hood,[1] and at first it was fair as the morning, and full with the dew of heaven, as a lamb's fleece; but when a ruder breath had forced open its virgin modesty, and dismantled its too youthful and unripe retirements, it began to put on darkness, and to decline to softness, and the symptoms of a sickly age; it bowed the head, and broke its stalk, and at night having lost some of its leaves, and all its beauty, it fell into the portion

---

[1] the prominent and pliant topmost part of a flowering plant

of weeds and outworn faces. The same is the portion of every man, and every woman; the heritage of worms and serpents, rottenness and cold dishonour, and our beauty so changed that our acquaintance quickly knew us not, and that change mingled with so much horror, or else meets so with our fears and weak discoursings, that they who six hours ago tended upon us, either with charitable or ambitious services cannot without some regret stay in the room alone where the body lies stripped of its life and honour. I have read of a fair young German gentleman who living often refused to be pictured, but put off the importunity of his friends' desire by giving way that after a few days' burial they might send a painter to his vault and, if they saw cause for it, draw the image of his death unto the life. They did so, and found his face half eaten, and his midriff and back bone full of serpents, and so he stands pictured among his armed ancestors. So does the fairest beauty change, and it will be as bad with you and me; and then, what servants shall we have to wait upon us in the grave, what friends to visit us, what officious people to cleanse away the moist and unwholesome cloud reflected upon our faces from the sides of the weeping vaults, which are the longest weepers for our funeral.

Suggested further reading
Benjamin Guyer, *The Beauty of Holiness: The Caroline Divines and Their Writings* (London: Canterbury Press, 2012), esp. ch. 6.
Gerard H. Cox III, 'A Re-Evaluation of Jeremy Taylor's *Holy Living* and *Holy Dying*', *Neuphilologische Mitteilungen*, 73.4 (1972), 836–48.
Jeremy Taylor, *Holy Living and Holy Dying*, ed. P. G. Stanwood, 2 vols. (Oxford: Clarendon Press, 1989), introduction.

1.15

JOHN BATCHILER

The Virgin's Pattern (1661)

About the author

John Batchiler (1615–1674) received his BA and MA from Emmanuel College, Cambridge. He served as chaplain in the Parliamentarian army, during which time he was appointed one of twelve licensers who authorized the publication of divinity works. With the Restoration, he added his name to the ranks of clergymen ejected from the Church of England and is remembered as a Protestant dissenter by Edmund Calamy's early-eighteenth-century *Nonconformist Memorial*. Shortly after his ejection, he worked at the girls' school that his father-in-law, Robert Perwich, ran out of his home in Hackney.

About the text

This octavo book eulogizes John Batchiler's sister-in-law, Susanna Perwich, the most talented and brightest pupil of the 800 girls who passed through the Hackney school. The title page identifies Susanna as 'Mrs.', though she was most assuredly not wed – the honorific could prefix the name of an unmarried lady or girl in the period. Not only did she possess the typical parts of good breeding such as needlework, accountancy, housewifery, and cookery, but she was also a 'delicious' and admirable singer, a gifted and accomplished musician on the bass viol and lute, and an incomparably skilful dancer in English country and French forms. The turning point in her life came when her gentleman suitor intent on making a match suddenly died, inducing her to recommit herself to God. Composing both a prose and a lengthier verse biography, Batchiler holds up her strict devotional regimen as a rare pattern for others to emulate. That is ostensibly why he dedicated the book to the young ladies and gentlewomen of the girls' schools in and about London. But commemorating Susanna also gave Batchiler a platform for defending these schools against accusations of morally corrupting their charges and promoted the educational efficacy of the Hackney school where he worked. Batchiler does not fail to advertise the names of Susanna's individual masters whose expert tutelage made possible the blossoming of her numerous accomplishments.

The arts of death

Susanna died at twenty-five years old, in 'the flower of her age', after having caught a chill from sleeping in wet linens during a visit to London. Eleven of the prose biography's forty-two pages describe her drawn-out death. The great attention Batchiler places on the event suggests that Susanna's passing was the climax of her ongoing communion with God and the crowning achievement of her life, shedding light on the Restoration's idealization of maidenhood. The excerpt demonstrates the enduring power of the 'good death' in the *ars moriendi*, not just for Protestant dissenters but even for the wider educated public. Though owning very little, Susanna expresses a dying wish to leave both a material and spiritual legacy: her friends are to receive her personal belongings and her directions for a godly life.

Textual notes

The virgins pattern, in the exemplary life and lamented death of Mrs. Susanna Perwich, daughter of Mr. Robert Perwich, who departed this life … July 3, 1661 (London: 1661; Wing B1076), C7^r–C7^v, D2^r--D2^v.

The Virgin's Pattern

At last as she was saying that she had nothing to leave them[1] in memorial of her, presently her father told her he gave her free liberty to dispose of whatever she had; at which she was very much pleased and thanking of him, distributed to every one according to her own mind; her several rings to be worn distinctly, as she directed, by her father, mother, and sisters; two of her rings she put upon her fingers, taking them off again, gave them to be kept for her two brothers beyond sea,[2] as a token to them from her dying hand; all her clothes, her watch, and a certain piece of plate marked with her own name, she gave to one sister; all her works and instruments of music to be divided betwixt three other sisters; her books also she disposed of; and as a legacy to all gentlewomen of the school, she commended her dying desires[3] and requests to them that they would not spend their time in reading of vain books but instead thereof, to betake themselves to the best book of all, the Bible, and such other choice books, as might do their souls most good; as also that they would be constant in the use of private prayer that they would be careful to sanctify the Lord's Day, and not waste those precious hours in over-curious dressings; and that they would behave themselves reverently at the public ordinances,[4] it having been a great offence to her formerly when any have done the contrary.

[…]

---

[1] Marginal note: 'With her father's leave gives all she had to several friends.'
[2] Marginal note: 'Distributes her rings, clothes, works, books, and instruments.'
[3] Marginal note: 'Her legacy to the gentlewomen of the school.'
[4] 'instituted worship, as opposed to private devotion'

On the Monday morning, she often muttered out very softly, these words, 'two days[5] and an half more, and then I shall be at rest', which she repeated two or three times; and accordingly from that very time, she did live two days and an half, to wit, till[6] Wednesday noon following, and then began to draw on apace towards her last breath.

Indeed, her pains now seemed to leave her, or her strength rather, being able no more to struggle; and so lying in a kind of quiet sleep at last panting for breath a short space in a small silent groan gave up her precious soul into the hands of God, whose angels carrying it away to heaven (as we have comfortable ground of hope to believe) left us all in bitter mourning and wailing over her dead body.

When she was laid out in the chamber where she died, dressed in her night[7] clothes, one would have thought she had been in a kind of smiling slumber; and now the gentlewomen, with the rest of the family, and some neighbours coming to see her and give her their last salute, it would have broken one's heart to have heard and seen many cries, tears, and lamentations that the room was filled with.

---

[5] Marginal note: 'She foretells the hour of her own death.'
[6] Marginal note: 'And dies at the same hour.'
[7] Marginal note: 'The great lamentation at her laying out.'

Suggested further reading

Felicity James, 'Writing Female Biography: Mary Hays and the Life Writing of Religious Dissent', in *Women's Life Writing, 1700–1850: Gender, Genre, Authorship*, ed. Daniel Cook and Amy Culley (Basingstoke, UK and New York: Palgrave Macmillan, 2012), pp. 117–32.

Amanda Eubanks Winkler, *Music, Dance, and Drama in Early Modern English Schools* (Cambridge: Cambridge University Press, 2020), ch. 4.

1.16

JAMES JANEWAY
A Token for Children (1676)

About the author

James Janeway (1636–1674) was a popular nonconformist minister, who came from a family of preachers. According to Edmund Calamy's *Nonconformist Memorial*, he established a meeting at Rotherhithe, in south-east London, attracting such a great following that the Church of England's high party sought to have him shot on two occasions. His evangelistic publications were as well sold as his meetings were attended.

About the text

Divided into two parts and preceded by a short introduction to educators, the 1676 edition gathers together thirteen examples of the lives of pious children. With the examples, Janeway hopes to proselytize the young, for he does not pull any punches when posing his blunt rhetorical questions to parents and teachers: 'Are the souls of your children of no value? Are you willing that they should be brands of hell?' (part 1, A3ʳ). The first part's preface, which follows the introduction, is fittingly addressed to juvenile readers who will receive spiritual edification from, in the words of the subtitle, 'holy and exemplary lives and joyful deaths'. Well into the eighteenth century, Janeway's little book became an essential literary vehicle, an evangelistic companion to Bunyan's *Pilgrim's Progress*, by which the more Puritan-leaning of English and American families captivated the moral imagination of their young charges. The excerpt, extracted from the finale to the volume's concluding example, gives an account of the rapturous death of the son of a Dutch merchant, the eleven-year-old John Harvy, who died from the 1665 plague.

The arts of death

What is noteworthy about Janeway's text is that it collects and fetishizes the last words of expiring children, embracing fully this oft-neglected age group within the Protestant practices of the *ars moriendi*. As Janeway reassures readers in the introduction to educators, his sources are based upon eye and ear witnesses of 'experienced solid Christians', and 'several passages are taken verbatim in writing from [children's] dying lips' (part 1, A5^r–A5^v). The recorded last words, transcending everyday communication, belong to the 'language of Canaan',[1] an expression Janeway applies to the speech of the precocious Anne Lake in the ninth example (part 2, A12^v). The other deathbed children similarly discourse with scriptural authority and divine inspiration so much so that the pedagogical relationship between parent and progeny turns upside down. In the excerpt, the bible-quoting John Harvy, a wise old soul, spends his final moments instructing, nay passionately adjuring, his disconsolate mother to conduct herself as a pious Christian before the Almighty. The Protestant death arts were not as overtly scripted as the traditional *ars moriendi*, but, nonetheless, radiated as much, if not more, emotional and intellectual intensity as the former.

Textual notes

A token for children being an exact account of the conversion, holy and exemplary lives and joyful deaths of several young children (London: 1676; Wing J478), part 2, D9^v–D12^r.

A Token for Children

40. His mother looking upon his brother, shaked her head, at which he asked, if his brother were marked.[2] She answered, 'Yes, child'. He asked again, whether he were marked. She answered nothing. 'Well', says he, 'I know I shall be marked; I pray let me have Mr. Baxter's book,[3] that I may read a little more of Eternity before I go into it'. His mother told him that he was not able to read. He said that he was, 'However, then pray by me, and for me'. His mother answered that she was so full of grief that she could not pray now, but she desired to hear him pray his last prayer.

---

[1] 'Grammar teacheth to speake well, but not the language of Canaan, that is, the holy language of God, as prayer doth,' says William Burton, *An exposition of the lords prayer* (London: 1594; STC 4174), A6^r.

[2] 'marked': 'to choose or destine for death by God, Death, or the Devil'; see *Richard III*, 1.3.292. It may also allude to the mark placed on a building inhabited by plague victims.

[3] 'He was (next to the Bible) most taken with reading of Reverend Mr. Baxter's works, especially his *Saints' Everlasting Rest*' (part 2, D9^v).

41. His mother asked him whether he were willing to die and leave her. He answered, 'Yes, I am willing to leave you, and go to my heavenly Father'. His mother answered, 'Child, if thou hadst but an assurance of God's love I should not be so much troubled'.

42. He answered and said to his mother, 'I am assured, dear mother, that my sins are forgiven, and that I shall go to heaven', for, said he, 'Here stood an angel by me that told me I should quickly be in glory'.

43. At this, his mother burst forth into tears. 'O, mother', said he, 'did you but know what joy I feel, you would not weep, but rejoice. I tell you I am so full of comfort that I can't tell you how I am. O, mother, I shall presently have my head in my Father's bosom, and shall be there, where the *four and twenty elders cast down their crowns and sing hallelujah, glory and praise, to him that sits upon the throne: and unto the Lamb forever.*'[4]

44. Upon this, his speech began to fail him, but his soul seemed still to be taken up with glory, and nothing now grieved him but the sorrow that he saw his mother to be in for his death. A little to divert his mother, he asked her what she had to supper, but presently in a kind of divine rapture, he cried out, 'O what a sweet supper have I making ready for me in glory'.[5]

45. But seeing all this did rather increase than allay his mother's grief, he was more troubled and asked her what she meant thus to offend God: 'know you not, that it is the hand of the Almighty. *Humble yourself under the mighty hand of God,*[6] lay yourself in the dust, and kiss the rod of God, and let me see you do it in token of your submission to the will of God, and bow before him'.[7] Upon which, raising up himself a little, he gave a lowly bow and spake no more, but went cheerfully and triumphantly to rest in the bosom of Jesus.

Hallelujah.

FINIS.

---

[4] reference to Rev 4:10 [5] Rev 19:9 [6] 1 Pet 5:6
[7] 'all they that go down to the dust shall bow before him' (Ps 22:29)

Suggested further reading

Ralph Houlbrooke, 'Children's Deaths in the Seventeenth Century', in *Childhood in Question: Children, Parents and the State*, ed. Stephen Hussey and Anthony Fletcher (Manchester, UK: Manchester University Press, 1999), pp. 37–56.

1.17

SAMUEL SMITH

'A True Account of … Last Dying Speeches' (1690)

About the author

Samuel Smith (1620–1698), son of a London grocer, earned both BA and MA at St John's College, Oxford. He lost his rectorship at the parish church of St Benet Gracechurch, when he refused to take the oath prescribed by the 1662 Act of Uniformity. In 1676, London's court of aldermen appointed him the Ordinary – that is, chaplain – of Newgate, an ecclesiastical living attached to the city's largest and most infamous prison.

About the text

Late in the seventeenth century, there arose a new type of reportage on last dying speeches, which had long been propagated by ballads and criminal biographies. As it came to be entitled, with slight variations, 'The Ordinary's Account of the Behaviour, Confession, and Dying Words … of the Malefactors executed at Tyburn …' was a companion to 'The Proceedings of the Old Bailey', the publication of London's central criminal court, located beside Newgate Prison. The account officially recorded the Ordinary's ministrations to the condemned, especially his attempt to bring them to repentance through spiritual counsel, before they were carted three miles to Tyburn, where the principal gallows of London stood. This regular serial publication, first started by Samuel Smith in the 1670s, became one of the actual duties of Newgate's Ordinary. It had a popularity that did not wane until the mid-eighteenth century.

The arts of death

The serialized account commercialized the *ars moriendi* on an altogether new level. It permitted readers a voyeuristic glimpse of the final intimate scene where the chaplain ministered to the individual prior to his or her passing. But what distinguished the situation from the earlier deathbed vigil was that the Ordinary enforced upon the criminal a 'good death' so as to elicit, during the confession, sensational stories ripe for saleable copy. For example, later that same year, Smith published an account of the Golden Farmer, a notorious robber and murderer, but, despite his repeated, nay desperate, cajoling to disburden his conscience, Smith could not prevail upon him to confess the lucratively lurid details of his wicked life (*A True Account* [London, 1690; Wing S4206B]). Smith's hypocritical self-righteousness at the expense of those whose suffering he exploited for profit, ironically enough, earned him printed parodic elegies when he died.[1] As suggested by the excerpt's treatment of Catholics, the office of the Ordinary was a bully pulpit at Newgate, on the Scaffold, and in print, ideologically managing and controlling the condemned prisoners during the juridical stages post-sentencing so that they would not impeach church and state authority at their execution – a public spectacle that attracted large crowds.

Textual notes

A true account of the behaviour, confession, and last dying speeches of the seven criminals that were executed at Tyburn, on Friday the ninth of May, 1690 (London: 1690; Wing T2351A), Brs.

'A True Account of … Last Dying Speeches'

On the Lord's day[2] the Ordinary preached twice on the 3rd verse of the 147th Psalm, viz., 'He heals the broken in heart, and binds up their wounds'. Whence was observed that sin makes deep and deadly wounds in all the soul's faculties, especially in the conscience. It is a spreading and a deceitful, destructive wound, because most men suffer it to rank and fester.

Then were laid down the recital of such sins which do most wound the conscience and grieve the Spirit of God; and for what reasons sinners must be sensible of their sinful state, before they will apply themselves to Christ for healing and renewing grace.

On Monday the Ordinary inquired how their hearts were affected. They did one by one give some account that they were sensible of their sin and misery. To which was replied that there are many deceitful pretences on which

---

[1] See for example, *Elegy occasioned by the death of the Reverend Mr. Samuel Smith late ordinary of Newgate* (London: 1698; Wing E353) and *The Works of Mr. Thomas Brown*, ed. J. Drake, 3rd ed., 4 vols. (1715), vol. 4, pp. 41–45.

[2] Sunday, the day of rest and worship

most men build their hopes of future happiness. Therefore, I[3] stated the whole method of salvation as clearly as I could to their mean understandings, and found that, as they obtained more knowledge, they grew more sensible of their sinful state, and more fit for the healing comforts of Gospel promises.

On Tuesday I required an account, whether they did clearly apprehend the requisite indispensable qualifications for salvation. But finding that they did not, I stated the nature of evangelical contrition, or true brokenness of heart for and from sin, how this differs from mere legal attrition[4] in the convictions only of conscience without any change of corrupt nature. Also, I stated what are the impediments of healing and renewing grace and urged on them many arguments to come to Christ for the binding up and healing their wounds in conscience. I laid down the characters[5] of true faith and repentance that they might not be deceived with false hopes of heaven. After much discourse with them severally, they were dismissed with prayer, and the singing of a Penitential Psalm.[6] I visited them every day till their execution, and most days twice.

[…]

Now remains somewhat to be spoken as to the other three condemned prisoners, viz., John Williams, James Chambers, and William Column, who all appeared at the time of their execution to be Papists, though visited often by the Ordinary. Williams spoke particularly, saying that he died a Papist and was always true to the interest of the late King James,[7] denying the fact for which he was condemned. The other two said little, but continued praying to themselves, by turning their faces from the other four before mentioned. Yet one thing may be noted, whilst the Ordinary was praying with the other four, Column seemed to attend devoutly, which Williams and Chambers checked him for.

Afterwards the Penitential Psalm being sung, they were all turned off.[8]

Let every true hearted and unprejudiced Protestant, of what rank and quality soever, see now what kind of instruments, and dubbed utensils, the late King James has to work withal, no better than housebreakers, and

---

[3] In his accounts, Smith's narration routinely shifts from third person to first person.
[4] i.e., repentance motivated by fear of punishment and inferior to true contrition
[5] 'tokens and signs'
[6] The Penitential Psalms are the seven psalms numbered 6, 32, 38, 51, 102, 130, and 143.
[7] James II, the Catholic King deposed by the Protestants William and James's daughter Mary in 1689
[8] 'hanged'

common thieves, who have been fairly convicted by our English laws: yea, such laws that King James himself must needs have made use of, for the conviction of such cruel miscreants as these were, if he had been seated in the royal throne (which God forbid). These, and such like, are the men that, even when the ropes are about their necks, and just ready to be turned off, they will spit their venom against the face of the government, and if it were possible stone to death all the spectators. Yea, the very civil officers who are ordered by law to attend their execution were affronted, the prisoners dying (as it were) like mad men, putting a bold face upon't, as if there were no heaven to condemn, nor no hell to torment, trusting only to the deluding vanities of a vain hoped-for purgatory. Which the laborious and never wearied Jesuits, and untired Popish priests do always buzz in their ignorant ears, till they have them so fast that they can never be unlinked, from the cunning devices, and devilish stratagems of that Whore of Babylon[9] who has always been striving to make the nations drunk with the blood of her fornications, by joining their Gog and Magogs[10] together to undo, yea, (and if it were possible) to deceive the very elect,[11] which such silly earthworms as those will not be sensible of till they come to feel the dreadful effects of it (in another world) to their final and everlasting destruction and misery, from which dismal sentence they can never be redeemed.

This is the whole account which I can give of this session, though I visited them every day till their execution.

Dated this 9th of May, 1690.   Samuel Smith
Ordinary.

---

[9] a disparaging name for the Roman Catholic Church (Rev 17:5)
[10] apocalyptic enemies of the Church (Rev 20:8), typologically drawn from the prophesied destruction of Israel in Ezek 38
[11] i.e., those chosen to go to Heaven

Suggested further reading

Peter Linebaugh, 'The Ordinary of Newgate and his Account', in *Crime in England, 1550–1800*, ed. J. S. Cockburn (London: Methuen, 1977), pp. 246–69.

Andrea McKenzie, *Tyburn's Martyrs: Execution in England, 1675–1775* (London: Bloomsbury, 2007).

PART II
Funereal and Commemorative Arts

ə̀

Thou drawest near unto them that seek thee to hear their prayers; yea, thou art their shield and protection in all their necessities. As for the proud workers of iniquity, thou seest them afar off, thou beholdest them with a fierce look, to their confusion, to destroy and root out their memorial out of the everlasting beatitude.

> Anne Wheathill, *A Handful of Wholesome (though Homely) Herbs Gathered out of the Goodly Garden of God's Most Holy Word* (London: 1584; STC 25329), N7^v–N8^r

Neither doth *Corin* full of worth and wit,
That finished dead *Musaeus* gracious song,
With grace as great, and words, and verse as fit;
Chide meagre death for doing virtue wrong:
He doth not seek with songs to deck her hearse,
Nor make her name live in his lively verse.

> Henry Chettle, *England's Mourning Garment Worn Were by Plain Shepherds, in Memory of their Sacred Mistress, Elizabeth* (London: 1603; STC 5122), D2^r

Death is a divider, and so is doom, two shall be in the field, the one shall be taken, and the other shall be refused.

> William Leigh, *The Dreadful Day Dolorous to the Wicked* (London: 1610; STC 15423.5), F1^v

… the Lord brought me into the shadow of death time after time, laying me on my sick bed, and pale death still looking me in the face with dreadful terrors and amazement; yea to the very pit's brink of hell (in my own apprehensions) which is the worst of deaths; yea, through a land where no man passeth, or dwells, having none to condole my misery, none being acquainted with it, or me ….

> Anne Venn, *A Wise Virgins Lamp Burning … Written by her own Hand, and Found in her Closet after her Death* (London: 1658; Wing V190), U3^v

Introduction to Part II

By covering the post-mortem period of the death arts, this section of the anthology complements the first with its focus on the pre-mortem. There is an important distinction, as Peter Marshall notes, between death and the dead, since the latter constituted 'an elaborate cultural construction and a complex social presence' not confined to the 'ever growing army of corpses'.[1] The entries accordingly fall within the timespan, starting with the advent of the ceremonial burial and continuing with the remembrance of the deceased.

Prior to Protestantism taking root in England, the clergy and laity said intercessory prayers whereby they sought to decrease the time spent by loved ones in Purgatory's punishing fires. This work of intercession was most significantly conducted through masses not only held at the funeral but also performed afterwards for memorializing the dead. Testators commissioned masses on the anniversary of their death (obits), after a month (Trentals and 'month's mind'), after a week, or daily thereafter, the last usually provided for by an endowment called a chantry.[2] The practices of bell-ringing, candle-burning, and alms-giving would support the commemorative service, as they did the burial service.[3] Less affluent testators and benefactors could pay money to be inscribed on the parish bede-roll, so that their names read out by the priest at least once a year in full or in abbreviated form weekly would prompt parishioners to pray for them.[4]

The early modern funereal and commemorative arts underwent irrevocable change during England's protracted Reformation, when the Church, deeming Purgatory to be fraudulent and superstitious, prohibited the observance of intercessory rituals for alleviating the torment of purgatorial souls. 'Of all the medieval activities held to assist the soul after death', Eamon Duffy asserts, 'the relief of the poor was the only one permitted and indeed actively encouraged by the Protestant authorities after 1547'.[5] Despite arguably 'redefining the boundaries of the human community' by terminating the living's

---

[1] Marshall, *Beliefs*, pp. 1–2.
[2] On anniversaries, see Clive Burgess, 'A Service for the Dead: The Form and Function of the Anniversary in Late Medieval Bristol', *Transactions of the Bristol and Gloucestershire Archaeological Society*, 105 (1987), 183–212. See also Alan Kreider, *English Chantries: The Road to Dissolution* (Cambridge, MA: Harvard University Press, 1979).
[3] Burgess, 'Service for the Dead', p. 184.
[4] Marshall, *Beliefs*, pp. 24–25; Duffy, *Altars*, pp. 334–37.   [5] Ibid., p. 505.

communication with those who passed on, Protestantism, nonetheless, did not fully abandon the dead.[6] Post-mortem commemoration increasingly manifested itself through epitaphs, funeral elegies, and funeral sermons: as Scott Newstok argues, the post-Reformation epitaph acquired a larger textual footprint, going beyond an inscription on tombs to appearing throughout a range of genres and discourses,[7] and, from the end of the sixteenth century and well into the seventeenth century, presses continued to turn out a growing number of elegiac poems and funeral sermons.[8] Epitaphs and funeral sermons were especially cautious in steering clear of Catholic memorial practice: whereas inscriptions on brasses and tombs had once solicited prayers on behalf of the defunct, they now memorialized earthly achievements and pious lives, while intensifying the 'affective language of loss and bereavement';[9] so as not to tempt their auditors into sinful superstition, preachers focused their energy on explicating doctrine before briefly praising the dead's virtues.[10]

No matter how dominant religious culture was, chronicles, histories, and proto-biographies contributed to, we must not forget, the gradual secularization of remembering the dead and their deaths during the period. The heraldic death arts, gaining social prominence with the rise of sixteenth-century antiquarianism and the influence of the College of Arms, had no bearing on the Christian afterlife and yet supplied other options for well-to-do gentility.[11] The designs of portraits, funerals, and tombs were planned and often realized by professional heralds for those who desired to be memorialized with tokens of status based upon their worldly pedigree.[12] The testators wanted to leave a memorial legacy of and for their inter-generational family. Conversely,

---

[6] Ibid., p. 8.
[7] Scott L. Newstok, *Quoting Death in Early Modern England: The Poetics of Epitaphs Beyond the Tomb* (Basingstoke, UK: Palgrave Macmillan, 2009), pp. 16–17, 28.
[8] On funeral sermons, Cressy, *Birth*, pp. 408–09, p. 572 n.39, and Houlbrooke, *Family*, pp. 295–330. On funeral elegies, see Dennis Kay, *Melodious Tears: The English Funeral Elegy from Spenser to Milton* (Oxford: Clarendon Press, 1990), and Lorna Clymer, 'The Funeral Elegy in Early Modern Britain', in *The Oxford Handbook of the Elegy*, ed. Karen Weisman (Oxford: Oxford University Press, 2010), pp. 170–86.
[9] Marshall, *Beliefs*, p. 271.
[10] Frederic B. Tromly, '"According to sounde religion": The Elizabethan Controversy over the Funeral Sermon', *The Journal of Medieval and Renaissance Studies*, 13.2 (1983), 302.
[11] See MA IV.10 (Dugdale) on heraldry's relationship to memory.
[12] On these three, see Robert Tittler, *Portraits, Painters, and Publics in Provincial England 1540–1640* (Oxford: Oxford University Press, 2013), pp. 102–24; Gittings, *Burial*, pp. 166–87; and Llewellyn, *Art*, p. 72.

broadside and pamphlet literature appealing to an incipient public sphere carved out an ever-widening space for remembering humble folk, whether they be criminals, eccentric individuals, or the unnamed masses. Plague pamphleteers, anticipating the role later assumed by newspapers, mourned the loss of poor Londoners consigned to burial in unmarked graves.[13] A further point towards the limits of commemoration might be said to appear in our time frame with the emergence of demographical record-keeping, in which the dead along with the living have been reduced to silent numbers, ushering in the conditions of what Foucault has called 'biopower'.[14]

Whether or not the period's funereal and commemorative arts turned decisively toward the secular and the individualistic, they did allow more latitude for the expression of the mourner's affect and the mourned's status, piety, and earthly achievement. And here we might register the chief difference between Catholic and Protestant modes of memorializing the dead. Before the Reformation, the elaborate network of rituals of remembering was not so much directed to the past as to the present moment, as when one says, 'I am thinking of you'. In contrast, Reformed commemoration, akin to modern practices, thought of the dead as what they once were on the earth, locking them in a pluperfect domain, the imagined past. English Protestants took to heart Augustine's oft-quoted dictum that funereal rituals 'are not for the bare commendation of the dead, but for the instruction and consolation of them that are alive'.[15]

---

[13] See II.9 (Dekker).
[14] See III.14 (Graunt). Michel Foucault, *Security, Territory, Population: Lectures at the Collège de France*, ed. Michel Senellart, trans. Graham Burchell (Basingstoke, UK: Palgrave Macmillan, 2007), pp. 1–4.
[15] On the popularity of the saying, see Marshall, *Beliefs*, p. 52. Qtd. in Robert Hill, *Path-Way to Prayer and Pietie* (London, 1609; STC 13472.7), U2ᵛ. The passage comes from Augustine, 'The Care to be Taken for the Dead [*De cura pro mortuis gerenda*]', trans. John A. Lacy, in *Treatises on Marriage and Other Subjects*, ed. Roy J. Deferrari (Washington, DC: Catholic University of America Press, 1955), p. 355.

II.1

EDWARD HALL AND RICHARD GRAFTON
Chronicles (1548)

About the authors

Edward Hall (1497–1547), historian, lawyer, and Member of Parliament in the House of Commons, secured a series of political appointments and commissions, working closely with Thomas Cromwell and overseeing Anne Askew's 1545 confession at Ludgate Prison.[1] Hall's death in 1547 meant that his *Chronicles* were completed by Richard Grafton (1506/07–1573), a prominent stationer involved with the publication of Reformist materials. In April 1540 Grafton was employed as the printer (with Edward Whitchurch) of the Great Bible, its completion and publication overseen by his patron Thomas Cromwell.

About the text

Hall's grand scheme for the *Chronicles* covers the history of the Wars of the Roses until the reign of Henry VIII. He left behind draft materials for the later years of Henry's reign which Grafton edited, and, presumably, added to. Our excerpt focuses on the execution of Thomas Cromwell, a man personally acquainted with both Hall and Grafton. Cromwell (b. in or before 1485, d.1540) rose from humble beginnings to become the trusted chief minister to Henry VIII. Over the 1530s he wielded extraordinary influence over matters of state, advancing the English Reformation and break from Rome, arranging the annulment of Henry's marriage to Catherine of Aragon and his new marriage to Anne Boleyn, overseeing the falls of Cardinal Wolsey,[2] Sir Thomas More,[3] and Boleyn, and the dissolution of the monasteries. Henry's displeasure in his marriage to Anne of Cleves, orchestrated by Cromwell, contributed to his downfall, but so too did Cromwell's alienation of powerful opponents, including Bishop Stephen Gardiner and Thomas Howard, Duke of Norfolk (uncle to Boleyn, and to another later executed queen, Catherine Howard).

---

[1] Cf. entries I.4 (Parr) and II.4 (Foxe).   [2] See entry III.4 (Churchyard).
[3] See *MA* V.1, for an example of Thomas More's spiritual writing designed to personalize the imagery of death.

Sudden reversals in fortune were not unknown in the Henrician court, but Cromwell's fall was still shocking. In April 1540 he was made Earl of Essex by Henry and appointed to the role of Lord Great Chamberlain; three months later he was beheaded at the Tower of London. Cromwell was arrested and imprisoned over trumped-up charges, and accused of high treason, heresy, extortion, and embezzlement.

The arts of death

The description of Cromwell's arrest, imprisonment, and execution in *Chronicles* offers a carefully balanced account of the minister's varying reputation among churchmen, politicians, and the laity. Cromwell's scaffold speech, which was reported in several early accounts, sees the minister acknowledging his sin, accepting his fate, and begging for the forgiveness, but not pardon, of his king. Before this public proclamation, Cromwell had in fact sought mercy from Henry but none was forthcoming; his severed head was later thrust on a spike on London Bridge, the fate of traitors. Henry would later repent his actions. The excerpt offers an exemplary account of early English historical writing, a form of secular commemorative writing, with the historian weighing objective description with subjective opinion. Here, notably, Hall (or, perhaps, Grafton) condemns the crass or sloppy work of the 'ragged and butcherly' executioner, which Cromwell 'patiently' endured. Future readers should not doubt, the historical account insists, that Cromwell died well.

Textual notes

The vnion of the two noble and illustre famelies of Lancastre [and] *Yorke, … and so successiuely proceadyng to the reigne of the high and prudent prince kyng Henry the eight, the vndubitate flower and very heire of both the sayd linage* (London: 1548; STC 12722), fol. CCxlii [r-v], SSS2[r-v].

Chronicles

The 9th day of July, Thomas Lord Cromwell, late made Earl of Essex, as before you have heard, being in the council chamber, was suddenly apprehended and committed to the Tower of London; the which many lamented, but more rejoiced, and specially such as either had been religious men or favoured religious persons; for they banqueted and triumphed together that night, many wishing that that day had been seven year before, and some, fearing lest he should escape although he were imprisoned, could not be merry; other[s], who knew nothing but truth by him, both lamented him and heartily prayed for him. But this is true, that, of certain of the clergy he was detestably hated; and specially such as had borne swing,[4] and by his means was put from it for indeed he was a man, that in all his doings, seemed not to favour any kind of Popery, nor could not abide the snuffing pride of some prelates, which undoubtedly whatsoever else was the cause of his death, did shorten his life, and procured the end that he was brought unto: which was that the 19th day of the said month, he was attainted by Parliament, and never came to his answer, which law many reported, he was the causer of the making thereof, but the truth thereof I know not. The articles for which he died appeareth in the record, where his attainder is written, which are too long to be here rehearsed, but to conclude he was there attainted of heresy and high treason. And the 28th day of July was brought to the scaffold on the Tower Hill, where he said these words following:

'I am come hither to die, and not to purge myself, as may happen, some think that I will, for if I should so do, I were a very wretch and miser: I am, by the law, condemned to die, and thank my lord God that hath appointed me this death for mine offence. For sithence[5] the time that I have had years of discretion, I have lived a sinner, and offended my Lord God, for the which I ask him heartily forgiveness. And it is not unknown to many of you, that I have been a great traveller in this world, and being but of a base degree was called to high estate, and sithence the time I came thereunto, I have offended my prince, for the which I ask him heartily forgiveness, and beseech you all to pray to God with me, that he will forgive me. O Father, forgive me. O Son, forgive me. O Holy Ghost, forgive me. O three persons in one God, forgive me. And now I pray you that be here, to bear me record, I die in the Catholic faith,[6] not doubting in any article of my faith, no nor doubting in any sacrament of the Church. Many hath slandered me and reported that I have been a bearer of such as hath maintained evil opinions, which is untrue, but I confess that like as God by his Holy Spirit doth instruct us in the truth, so the Devil is ready to seduce us, and I have been seduced.

---

[4] 'had full sway or control'   [5] 'since'
[6] This is not an admission of Roman Catholic faith but rather a mainstream Protestant expression of devotion to 'the Church'.

But bear me witness that I die in the Catholic faith of the Holy Church. And I heartily desire you to pray for the King's grace, that he may long live with you in health and prosperity. And after him that his son, prince Edward, that goodly imp, may long reign over you. And, once again, I desire you to pray for me that so long as life remaineth in this flesh I waver nothing in my faith'.

And then made he his prayer, which was long, but not so long as both Godly and learned, and after committed his soul into the hands of God, and so patiently suffered the stroke of the axe by a ragged and butcherly miser, which very ungoodly performed the office.

Suggested further reading
G. R. Elton, 'Thomas Cromwell's Decline and Fall', *The Cambridge Historical Journal*, 10.2 (1951), 150–85.
Diarmaid MacCulloch, *Thomas Cromwell, A Life* (London: Allen Lane, 2018).

11.2

THOMAS CRANMER

'The Order for the Burial of the Dead' (1549)

About the author

Thomas Cranmer (1489–1556), Archbishop of Canterbury, was a leading Reformist theologian in the court of Henry VIII and Edward VI. After throwing his support behind the 'Nine Days' Queen', Lady Jane Grey, he found disfavour with the Catholic Mary I and was put on trial for treason and then also heresy. He was burnt at the stake in Oxford – burning was the punishment for heresy – famously renouncing any written recantations of faith he had made while imprisoned by holding his writing hand in the flames and saying 'This hand hath offended'.

About the text

Cranmer was the prime mover behind *The Book of the Common Prayer and Administration of the Sacraments, and other Rites and Ceremonies of the Church after the Use of the Church of England,* in which 'The Order for the Burial of the Dead' appears. Cranmer worked with a committee to produce the book; he had particular responsibilities for translating and editing parts of the Latin service. He also adopted materials from German Church orders. As its title sets out, this was the first complete English prayer book and provided a Reformed liturgy for the state religion. It supplied instructions and guidelines for the daily offices of Matins (morning) and Evensong, identified the introit psalms, collects, epistles to be used during weekly services and holy days, outlined the order for Communion and the litany, and described the practices and prayers to be used for services for Baptism, Confirmation, Matrimony, Visitation of the Sick, and Burial (excerpted here). Following these are instructions for the Purification of Women (a blessing given to women after childbirth) and Ash Wednesday. A revised version of the Book of Common Prayer was issued in 1552, which omitted the introit psalms and made significant changes to the communion and burial service.

The arts of death

With the jettisoning of Purgatory in the reformed faith, there was no longer any need for the living to perform intercessory and supplicatory services for the dead (e.g., obits, trentals, month-minds, and chantry prayers). The burial service itself was similarly stripped back. It no longer began in the home and there was no procession to the church; rather, the priest first encounters the 'corpse' at the entrance to the church and proceeds thereafter to the prepared grave. Without the possibility of any communion between the living and the dead, funerals were more stark affairs, marking the burial of the bodily remains and reminding the bereaved of the transience and misery of terrestrial life.[1] The 1549 text, excerpted here, includes petitions and supplications for the dead which later were excised in the 1552 text.

Textual notes

The booke of the common prayer and administracion of the sacramentes, and other rites and ceremonies of the Churche: after the vse of the Churche of England (London: 1549; STC 16270a), fol. cxxvi–cli.

---

[1] Cf. *MA* IV.5, John Weever's *Ancient Funeral Monuments* (1631), which expands upon the history of medieval English burial rites, funeral architecture, and sepulchres, with special reference to epitaphs and inscriptions.

'The Order for the Burial of the Dead'

The priest, meeting the corpse at the church-stile, shall say, or else the priests and clerks shall sing, and so go either into the church, or towards the grave:

'I am the resurrection and the life, sayeth the Lord, he that believeth in me, yea though he were dead,[2] yet shall he live. And whosoever liveth and believeth in me, shall not die forever. I know that my redeemer liveth, and that I shall rise out of the earth in the last day,[3] and shall be covered again with my skin, and shall see God in my flesh: yea, and I, myself, shall behold him, not with other but with these same eyes. We brought nothing into this world,[4] neither may we carry anything out of this world. The Lord giveth, and the Lord taketh away. Even as it pleaseth the Lord, so cometh things to pass: blessed be the name of the Lord'.

When they come at the grave, whiles the corpse is made ready to be laid into the earth, the priest shall say, or else the priest and clerks shall sing:

'Man that is born of a woman,[5] hath but a short time to live and is full of misery: he cometh up and is cut down like a flower, he flyeth as it were a shadow, and never continueth in one stay. In the middest of life we be in death, of whom may we seek for succour but of thee, O Lord, which for our sins justly art moved: yet O Lord God most holy, O Lord most mighty, O holy and most merciful saviour, deliver us not into the bitter pains of eternal death. Thou knowest, Lord, the secrets of our hearts, shut not up thy merciful eyes to our prayers: But spare us Lord most holy, O God most mighty, O holy and merciful saviour, thou most worthy judge eternal, suffer us not at our last hour for any pains of death, to fall from thee'.

Then the priest, casting earth upon the corpse, shall say:

'I commend thy soul to God the father almighty, and thy body to the ground, earth to earth, ashes to ashes, dust to dust, in sure and certain hope of resurrection to eternal life, through our Lord Jesus Christ, who shall change our vile body, that it may be like to his glorious body, according to the mighty working whereby he is able to subdue all things to himself'.

Then shall be said or [sung]:[6]

'I heard a voice from heaven, saying unto me "Right blessed are the dead which die in the Lord. Even so", sayeth the spirit, "that they rest from their labours"'.

---

[2] Marginal note: 'John 11.'   [3] Marginal note: 'Job 19.'
[4] Marginal note: '1 Timothy 6; Job 1.'   [5] Marginal note: 'Job 9.'
[6] Reads 'song' in text.

'The Order for the Burial of the Dead' (1549)

'Let us pray. We commend into thy hands of mercy, most merciful father, the soul of this our brother departed, [name]. And his body we commit to the earth, beseeching thine infinite goodness, to give us grace to live in thy fear and love, and to die in thy favour: that when the judgement shall come which thou hast committed to thy well-beloved son, both this our brother, and we, may be found acceptable in thy sight, and receive that blessing, which thy well-beloved son shall then pronounce to all that love and fear thee, saying: "Come, ye blessed children of my father: Receive the kingdom prepared for you before the beginning of the world". Grant this, merciful father, for the honour of Jesu Christ, our only saviour, mediator, and advocate. Amen'.

This prayer shall also be added.

'Almighty God, we give thee hearty thanks for this thy servant, whom thou hast delivered from the miseries of this wretched world, from the body of death and all temptation. And, as we trust, hast brought his soul, which he committed into thy holy hands, into sure consolation and rest: Grant we beseech thee, that at the Day of Judgement, his soul and all the souls of thy elect, departed out of this life, may with us and we with them, fully receive thy promises, and be made perfite[7] altogether, through the glorious resurrection of thy son Jesus Christ our Lord'.

These psalms with other suffrages following, are to be said in the church, either before or after the burial of the corpse.

[Psalms 116, 139, 146, followed by a lesson taken from 1 Corinthians 15 (verse 20 to the end)]

The lesson ended, then shall the priest say:

> Lord have mercy upon us.
> Christ have mercy upon us.
> Lord have mercy upon us.
>> Our father which art in heaven, etc.[8]
>> And lead us not into temptation.

Answer.
But deliver us from evil. Amen.
Priest.
Enter not, O Lord, into judgement with thy servant.
Answer.
For in thy sight no living creature shall be justified.

---

[7] 'perfect'; 'spiritually immaculate'   [8] i.e., The Lord's Prayer is said.

> *Priest.*
> From the gates of Hell.
> *Answer.*
> Deliver their souls, O Lord.
> *Priest.*
> I believe to see the goodness of the Lord.
> *Answer.*
> In the land of the living.
> *Priest.*
> O Lord, graciously hear my prayer.
> *Answer.*
> And let my cry come unto thee.

Let us pray. O Lord, with whom do live the spirits of them that be dead: and in whom the souls of them that be elected, after they be delivered from the burden of the flesh, be in joy and felicity: Grant unto this thy servant, that the sins which he committed in this world be not imputed unto him, but that he, escaping the gates of hell, and pains of eternal darkness, may ever dwell in the region of light, with Abraham, Isaac, and Jacob, in the place where is no weeping, sorrow, nor heaviness: and when that dreadful day of the general resurrection shall come, make him to rise also with the just and righteous, and receive this body again to glory, then made pure and incorruptible: set him on the right hand of thy son Jesus Christ, among thy holy and elect, that then he may hear with them these most sweet and comfortable words: come to me ye blessed of my father, possess the kingdom which hath been prepared for you from the beginning of the world: grant this, we beseech thee, O Merciful Father, through Jesus Christ our mediator and redeemer. Amen.

Suggested further reading
Gordon Jeanes, 'Cranmer and Common Prayer', in *The Oxford Guide to The Book of Common Prayer: A Worldwide Survey*, ed. Charles Hefling and Cynthia Shattuck (Oxford: Oxford University Press, 2006), pp. 21–38.
Diarmaid MacCulloch, *Thomas Cranmer: A Life* (New Haven, CT: Yale University Press, 1996).

11.3

CHURCH OF ENGLAND

The Primer Set Forth at Large (1559)

About the author

Primers have a complicated, overgrown bibliographical and liturgical family tree – their authorship no less so. Because a primer is essentially a private prayer book based upon the public worship service, its author is originally the medieval Catholic Church. Widely observed throughout England prior to the Reformation, the Sarum Rite (first developed at Salisbury Cathedral during the eleventh century), a variant on the Roman liturgy, formed the pith of the devotional content of many English primers. The Elizabethan primer excerpted here is a reissue of the 1551 Edwardian revision (STC 16053) of the King's Primer, authorized by Henry VIII in 1545. The Henrician King's Primer, published in response to the proliferation of translated prayer books, was printed near the end of his reign and died out quickly under Elizabeth. The frequently printed primer of her reign is the Edwardian one, based on Cranmer's Book of Common Prayer.

About the text

'Primer' is the English word for a book of hours, probably because it was the 'first' book by which schoolboys received instruction in reading. The book of hours became famous for containing the Little Office of the Blessed Virgin Mary, a devotion that had evolved from the Divine Office – the Church's public liturgy as contained in the breviary. The book's name refers to the eight canonical hours, the times during the day when the Divine Office appointed prayers to be said. It was chiefly designed to be a lay person's breviary for private use in church or at home, gaining widespread acceptance with the rise of the Marian cult in the late medieval period. Its secondary use was by religious guilds or confraternities, which supported their members not only in life but also in death by ensuring a proper funeral along with saying the requisite prayers. Next to the Little Office, the primer's most important element, then, was the Office of the Dead, with which readers could follow the service and intercede on behalf of those who passed into Purgatory. Illuminated books of hours were used throughout the Continent but, because they were expensive to copy out by hand, only the wealthy could afford to own them. The age of mechanical reproduction expanded the market of such Latin prayer books, which were printed with or without woodcuts and were also in numerous cases translated into English. Primers became a staple of the stationers' trade, and later William Seres enjoyed the privilege of printing them under Elizabeth.

The arts of death

The excerpts below belong to the 'Dirige', the traditional title for the Office of the Dead. The Latin heading derives from the first antiphon (Ps 5:8) in the morning office of the dead and was used to identify this particular office (matins), eventually coming to designate the entire prayer cycle for the dead (vespers, matins, and the Requiem Mass). As with the other offices, the dirige contains prayers, antiphons, collects, and scriptural lessons. Included here is a requiem prayer, a collect, a lesson from Job with an antiphon, and Hezekiah's song. The dirige did not just remember the dead but, according to Catholic doctrine, enabled the devout to intercede on behalf of those languishing in Purgatory. Consider the comic banquet scene from Marlowe's *Doctor Faustus*.[1] When a Cardinal interprets the mayhem caused by the invisible Faustus as the supernatural unrest of a revenant 'newly crept out of Purgatory', the Pope orders his friars to 'prepare a dir[i]ge to [al]lay the fury of this ghost'.[2] The prayers of the living, along with alms-giving and fasting, constituted expiatory acts of 'satisfaction' – part of the sacrament of penance – which could alleviate the dead's torments. Even though by 1559 the Book of Common Prayer had stripped the official public liturgy of its intercessory prayers in the burial service, Elizabethan primers still left personal devotional scope to remember and pray for the dead. The dirige's citation of biblical passages from Job, David, and Hezekiah provided the laity with what were thought to be representative sentiments of those suffering in Purgatory. In reciting these verses spoken by voices of pain, despair, penitence, and hope, the devout ritualistically forged strong imaginative identifications with the dead – identifications that the return of the Reformation to Elizabethan England did not eliminate.

---

[1] *The Tragical History of Doctor Faustus* (London: 1604; STC 17429), D2^r. See entry IV.9 (Marlowe).

[2] Cf. *MA* VI.12 for a more serious dramatic treatment of a ghost (that of Hamlet's father) returning to the world of the living and 'making necessarily vague references to a purgatorial origin' (p. 328).

Textual notes

[*The primer set furth at large, with many godly and deuoute prayers*] (London: 1559; STC 16087), M1ᵛ–M2ʳ, N1ᵛ–N2ʳ, N4ʳ–O1ʳ.

The Dirige³

[…]
Lord, give thy people eternal rest.
And light perpetual shine on them.
From the gates of Hell,
Lord, deliver their souls.
I trust to see the goodness of the Lord,
In the land of life.
Lord, hear my prayer,
And let my cry come to thee.

Let us pray.

O God, whose nature and property is ever to have mercy and to forgive, receive our humble petition and, though we be tied and bound with the chain of our sins, yet let the pitifulness of thy great mercy loose us, for the honour of Jesu Christ's sake our mediator and advocate. Amen.

We beseech thee, O Lord, to show upon us thine exceeding great mercy, which no tongue can worthily express, and that it may please thee to deliver us from all our sins, and also from the pains that we have for them deserved. Grant this, O Lord, through our mediator and advocate Jesu Christ. Amen.

[…]

*The First Lesson. Job x.*⁴

Thine hands hath made me, and fashioned me altogether round about, and wilt thou destroy me suddenly? O remember that thou madest me of the mould of the earth, and shalt bring me into dust again; hast thou not put me together as it were milk, and hardened me to crudds⁵ like cheese? Thou hast covered me with skin and flesh, and joined me together with bones and sinews. Thou hast granted me life and mercy, and the diligent heed that thou takest on me hath preserved my spirit.

---

³ literally, 'direct' (imperative) ⁴ Job 10:8–12 ⁵ 'curds'

The Anthem.[6]

I know that my redeemer liveth, and that I the last day shall rise from the earth, and shall be clad again with mine own skin, and in mine own flesh I shall see God, whom I myself shall see, and mine eyes shall look upon and none other; this hope is laid up in my bosom.

[...]

Ego dixi.[7] *Psal. Esaie. xxxviii.*[8]
Thanks for the recovery of health.

I said, in the midst of my days, I shall go to the gates of Hell.

I desired the residue of my years, I said, I shall not see the Lord God in the land of the living.

I shall see man no more, nor him that dwelleth in rest.

My time is taken from me, and folden up, as the shepherd's tent.

My life is cut off like a weaver's web; when I yet began, he cut me down; from morning until the night thou wilt make an end of me; I was in hope until morning but as a lion so he bruises all my bones.

From morning until night, though wilt make an end of me, as a young swallow so shall I chatter and shall mourn as a dove.

Mine eyen[9] dazzled with looking on high.

Lord I suffer force; answer for me what shall I say? Or what shall he answer me, since I have done it?

I shall remember all my years unto thee with bitterness of my heart.

Lord if life be thus, and the life of my spirit be after such sort, thou shalt correct me, and quicken me. Lo in peace my sorrow is most bitter.

But thou hast delivered my soul that it should not perish. Thou hast cast behind thy back all my sins.

For neither Hell shall knowledge thee, nor death shall praise thee; they that descend into the pit shall not look for thy verity.

He that is living, the living person, shall knowledge the like as I do now; the father to the children shall declare thy truth.

Preserve me, O Lord, and we shall sing our Psalms in the Lord's house all the days of our life.

---

[6] 'antiphon': a short chant or piece of plainsong recited before and after a psalm or canticle; Job 19:25–27
[7] literally, 'I said'   [8] 'Psalm', that is, the Song of Hezekiah; Isa 38:10–20   [9] 'eyes'

Suggested further reading
Duffy, *Altars*, pp. 209–98.
Susan M. Felch, 'A Brief History of English Private Prayer Books', in *Elizabeth Tyrwhit's Morning and Evening Prayers* (Aldershot, UK; Burlington, VT: Ashgate, 2008), pp. 19–32.
Micheline White, 'Dismantling Catholic Primers and Reforming Private Prayer: Anne Lock, Hezekiah's Song and Psalm 50/51', in *Private and Domestic Devotion in Early Modern Britain*, ed. Alec Ryrie and Jessica Martin (Aldershot, UK; Burlington, VT: Ashgate, 2012), pp. 93–114.

II.4

JOHN FOXE

Acts and Monuments (1576)

About the author

This entry can be said to have at least three authors. Anne Askew (1521–16 July 1546), who twice left her Lincolnshire Catholic husband to go to London to speak freely among Protestants as a 'gospeller' or preacher, kept a record of her detention and torture.[1] John Bale (1495–1563), Reformation controversialist and biographer, was the first to commemorate Askew's martyrdom by publishing her examinations (1546–1547).[2] John Foxe (1516/17–1587) left his post at Oxford and, fearing for his life with the accession of Queen Mary, fled to the Continent where, in Strasbourg in 1554, he published a history of Christian persecutions in Latin that laid the foundation for *Acts and Monuments*. Three folio pages plus a stock image of a public burning are devoted to Askew in Foxe's *Book of Martyrs* (as it popularly was known), a signal publishing event of the English Reformation going through four editions during Foxe's lifetime and that of his collaborator, the pre-eminent Protestant printer, John Day.[3]

---

[1] See entry II.1 (Hall and Grafton). [2] STC 848; STC 850
[3] See *MA* V.5 on John Day's career, especially his extended legacy through books reprinted by his son, Richard.

About the text

Our excerpt comes from the third edition of Foxe's *Book of Martyrs* (1576),[4] 'newly recognised and enlarged by the author', which covers the two examinations of Askew and (as preserved and 'elucidated' by John Bale) her first-person narrative. It is in equal parts documentary reflection, spiritual autobiography, and polemic for the reformist cause. Recent scholarship treats it as a contested textual site among Anglo-Catholics, Tudor court conservatives, and Protestant reformers. Irrespective of controversies over printed versions of Askew's writings, as John King observed, Askew initially ran afoul of English clerical and secular authorities because she violated prohibitions on public Bible reading at Lincoln Cathedral, which in itself was not a capital offence. It was her non-adherence to the Six Articles Acts (1539)[5] – resulting in her being questioned by the Bishop of London, Chancellor, and the King's secretaries (who wanted her to implicate others, especially women at court[6]) – that carried the death penalty (Figure 2.1).

The arts of death

This excerpt presents martyrdom as moral steadfastness in the face of impending death.[7] Contrary to the Catholic hagiographic impulse to venerate objects and relics associated with a saint's supreme sacrifice, Foxe eschews superstition and miracles to focus on historical events associated with bearing witness to true Christian faith. Askew's state-sponsored inquisition and public burning were not unusual for the period; what is noteworthy is the rich textual tradition and literary afterlife of this forensically astute Englishwoman. Absent of signs and wonders, Foxe's account of Askew's faith in 'scripture alone', that led her to reject the 'Real Presence', made her a model for everyday Protestants to put death in its proper perspective.

---

[4] See *MA* V.2 (Foxe), esp. pp. 235–38, on the 1563 preface concerning how the *Book of Martyrs* marks 'the point at which the textually oriented memorializing of English Protestantism sublates the commemorative function of the saint's life'.

[5] Spurred by Henry VIII's renewed desire for religious conformity, six key questions of church doctrine were discussed in Parliament and Convocation in his presence. The denial of transubstantiation was the only one of the six articles punished by burning.

[6] Cf. entry I.4 (Parr).   [7] Cf. entry II.13 (Charles I).

Textual notes

[...] *actes [and] monumentes* (London: 1576; STC 11224), PPP3ᵛ–PPP4ʳ (signature and page numbering extremely irregular throughout).

Acts and Monuments

I, Anne Askew of good memory, although my merciful father hath given me the bread of adversity and[8] the water of trouble: yet not so much as my sins have deserved: confess myself here a sinner before the throne of his heavenly majesty, desiring his forgiveness and mercy. [...] But this is the heresy which they report me to hold that after the priest hath spoken the[9] words of consecration, there remaineth bread still. They both say, and also teach it for a necessary article of faith, that after those words be once spoken, there remaineth no bread, but even the self-same body that hung upon the cross on good Friday, both flesh, blood, and bone. To this belief of theirs, say I nay. For then were our common creed false, which sayeth that he sitteth on the right hand of God the father almighty, and from thence shall come to judge the quick and dead. Lo, this is the heresy that I hold, and for it must suffer the death. But as touching the holy and blessed supper of the Lord, I believe it to be a most necessary remembrance of his glorious sufferings and death. [...] There be some do say that I deny the Eucharist or sacrament of thanksgiving but those people do untruly report of me.[10] For I both say and believe it, that if it were ordered like as Christ instituted it and left it, a most singular comfort it were unto us all.[11] But as concerning your mass, as it is now used in our days, I do say and believe it to be the most abominable idol that is in the world. For my God will not be eaten with teeth, neither yet dieth he again. And upon these words that I have now spoken, will I suffer death. [...]

By me, Anne Askew.

After that she, being born of such stock and kindred, that she might have lived in great wealth and prosperity, if she would rather have followed the world, then Christ, now had been so tormented, that she could neither live long in so great distress, neither yet by her adversaries be suffered to die in

---

[8] Marginal note: 'The confession of Anne Askew, going to her execution.'
[9] Marginal note: 'The matter and cause that Anne Askew suffered death.'
[10] Marginal note: 'Anne Askew falsely reported to deny the Holy Eucharist.'
[11] Marginal note: 'The Mass an abominable idol.'

FIGURE 2.1 Burning of Anne Askew. John Foxe, *Acts and Monuments* (London: 1576; STC 11224), PPP3ᵛ. Image used courtesy of The Huntington Library

secret[12] the day of her execution being appointed, she was brought into Smithfield[13] in a chair[14] because she could not go on her feet, by means of her great torments. When she was brought unto the stake, she was tied by the middle with a chain, that held up her body. When all things were thus prepared to the fire, Doctor Shaxton[15] who was then appointed to preach[16] began his sermon. Anne Askew hearing, and answering again unto him, where he said well, confirmed the same: where he said amiss, there said she he misseth, and speaketh without the book.[17]

---

[12] Marginal note: 'Anne Askew brought unto the stake.'
[13] place of execution, close to central London
[14] Marginal note: 'Anne Askew lamed upon the rack.'
[15] Nicholas Shaxton (c.1485–1556), a bishop opposing the Six Articles in Parliament, resigned his commission for which he was imprisoned though later pardoned. This fact explains why he was chosen to seek Askew's recantation.
[16] Marginal note: 'Shaxton preached at Anne Askew's burning.'
[17] 'deviating from scripture'

The sermon being finished, the martyrs standing there tied at three several stakes ready to their martyrdom, began their prayers. The multitude and concourse of the people was exceeding, the place where they stood being railed about, to keep out the press.[18] Upon the bench under St. Bartholomew Church sat Wriothesley,[19] Chancellor of England, the old Duke of Northfolk, the old Earl of Bedford, the Lord Mayor with divers other more. Before the fire should be set unto them, one of the bench[20] hearing that they had gunpowder[21] about them, and being afraid lest the faggots[22] by strength of the gunpowder would come flying about their ears, began to be afraid, but the Earl of Bedford declaring unto him how the gunpowder was not laid under the faggots, but only about their bodies, to ride them out of their pain which having vent, there was no danger to them of the faggots, so diminished that fear. Then Wriothesley, Lord Chancellor, sent to Anne Askew letters, offering to her the king's pardon if she would recant.[23] Who refusing once to look upon them, made this answer again: that she came not thither to deny her lord and master. Then were the letters likewise offered unto the others, who in like manner following the constancy of the woman, denied not only to receive them, but also to look upon them. Whereupon the Lord Mayor commanding fire to be put unto them, cried with a loud voice, *fiat justitia*.[24]

And thus the good Anne Askew with these blessed martyrs, being troubled so many manner of ways, and having passed through so many torments, having now ended the long course of her agonies, being compassed in with flames of fire, as a blessed sacrifice unto God, she slept in the Lord, anno domini 1546, leaving behind her a singular example of Christian constancy for all men to follow.

[18] 'people packed in tightly'   [19] i.e., Thomas Wriothesley, 1st Earl of Southampton
[20] a metonym for judges of a particular court
[21] a mercy sometimes allowed pyre victims for speedier death
[22] 'bundles of sticks'   [23] Marginal note: 'Anne Askew refuseth the king's pardon.'
[24] Marginal note: '*justitia injusta*' [unjust justice]; 'let justice be done'; the first part of the legal injunction *Fiat justitia ruat coelum* [Let justice be done, though the heavens should fall].

Suggested further reading
Thomas S. Freeman and Sarah E. Wall, 'Racking the Body, Shaping the Text: The Account of Anne Askew in Foxe's Book of Martyrs', *Renaissance Quarterly*, 54.4 (2001), 1165–96.
John N. King, 'How Anne Askew Read the Bible', *Reformation*, 25.1 (2020), 47–68.
Patricia Pender, 'Reading Bale Reading Anne Askew: Contested Collaboration in *The Examinations*', *Huntington Library Quarterly*, 73.3 (2010), 507–22.

II.5

WILLIAM ALLEN

The Glorious Martyrdom of Twelve Priests (1582)

About the author

William Allen (1532–1594) was a leading English Roman Catholic who rose to prominence during the reign of Mary I; upon the accession of Elizabeth I, and England's return to Protestantism, Allen refused to swear the Oath of Supremacy to the new queen and fled England for the Continent in 1561. He was a key figure in setting up the English seminary in Douai and the English College in Rome, training schools for English missionary priests.

About the text

Allen's account of the martyrdom of twelve English priests, including notable figures such as Edmund Campion, is an important work of Counter-Reformation propaganda. It was intended for a wide Catholic readership, translated into Latin and Italian, and details in often horrifying ways the pains and suffering of these priests' scenes of execution. The executions followed a similar routine, with the priests, who were imprisoned in appalling conditions at either the Tower of London or Newgate Prison, paraded through the centre of London and brought to the gallows at Tyburn. There, the priests were offered the opportunity to be saved if they would only renounce the Pope and their faith. Unwaveringly, they rejected this, as seen in our excerpt with the executions of Laurence Richardson and Thomas Cottam. The priests were then hanged (until either dead or nearly so) and quartered; their decapitated heads were later set on London Bridge as a warning for all traitors. Allen draws upon eyewitness accounts for his descriptions – confusingly, they are written from his perspective though he was not present – noting how each priest met his fate, and any conversations and speeches that were overheard.

The arts of death

The high theatricality of these execution proceedings is evident throughout Allen's account. Set high on a cart, visible to the baying crowd, the priests were offered the opportunity to be saved. Each person plays their role in the proceedings: the accused, the accusers, the attending authorities, the executioner, and so on. The notorious torturer Richard Topcliffe is present in our excerpt, as is Bull, the hangman of Newgate. The most important person, the Queen, is, of course, absent, though those enacting the execution operate on Elizabeth I's authority, and it is to her that the accused address most of their speeches. Latin clashes with English, as the priests refuse to say their prayers in the vernacular, while any speeches protesting innocence or declarations of support for the Queen are met with distrust. Capital punishment as a public spectacle affirms the cruel yet abundant power of the state; Allen's account records and commemorates for posterity the priests' miserable final moments.

Textual notes

A briefe historie of the glorious martyrdom of XII. reuerend priests, executed vvithin these tweluemonethes for confession and defence of the Catholike faith (Rheims, 1582; STC 369.5), B6ᵛ–B8ʳ.

The Glorious Martyrdom of Twelve Priests

After that, whilst they were talking with M. Richardson, M. Cottam took Bull the Hangman by the sleeve and said to him,[1] 'God forgive thee and make thee his servant, take heed in time, and call for grace, and no doubt but God will hear thee; take example by the executioner of Saint Paul, who, during the time of his execution, a little drop of blood falling from Saint Paul upon his garment, white like milk, did afterward call him to remembrance of himself, and so became penitent for his sins and became a good man, whose example I pray God thou mayest follow, and I pray God give thee of his grace'.[2] The minister of Saint Andrew's said, 'what, did milk fall from his breast?' Cottam: 'No, blood fell from his neck or head, in likeness of milk'.[3] Minister of Saint Andrew's: 'What? do you say he was saved by that blood which fell upon him?' Cottam: 'No'.
 [...]

---

[1] Marginal note: 'A very zealous and charitable act.'
[2] This apocryphal account of Paul's execution first appears in the second-century non-canonical writings. See Richard I. Pervo, *The Acts of Paul: A New Translation with Introduction and Commentary* (Cambridge: The Lutterworth Press, 2014), II.5.
[3] Marginal note: 'The wrangling of a minister.'

Then the rope being put about both their necks and fastened to the post, the sheriff said, 'Now, Richardson, if thou wilt confess thy faults and renounce the Pope, the Queen will extend her mercy towards thee, and thou shalt be carried back again'. Richardson answered, 'I thank her majesty for her mercy, but I must not confess an untruth or renounce my faith'. All this while M. Cottam was in prayer, and uttering of divers good sentences, saying, 'All that we here sustain is for saving of our souls', and therewithal lifting up his eyes to heaven, said: 'O Lord thou knowest our innocency'. Then he was willed to confess his treasons. 'O Lord', said he, 'how willingly would I confess if I did know anything that did charge me, and if we had been guilty of any such thing,[4] surely one or other of us either by racking or death would have confessed it, or else we had been such people as never were heard of. And I protest before God that before my coming into England I was armed to go into India, and if I might be set at liberty, I would never rest but on the journey towards that country'. With that the sheriff said, 'The Queen will be merciful to thee if thou wilt thyself'. He answered, 'I thank her grace'; saying farther, 'do with me what you think good', and therewithal the sheriff commanded that the rope should be loosed from the post, and he removed down from the cart.

Then M. Richardson was willed once again to confess and ask pardon of the Queen. He answered that he never offended her to his knowledge. Then Topcliffe said, 'The like mercy was never showed to any offender, and if you were in any other commonwealth you should be torn in pieces with horses'.[5] Then he was willed to pray. He prayed, desiring all Catholics to pray with him. He said his Paternoster, his Ave, and his Creed, and when the cart passed, 'Lord, receive my soul, Lord Jesu, receive my soul'. And even as the cart passed away, M. Cottam said, 'O good Lawrence, pray for me. Lord Jesus, receive thy soul', which he repeated several times.

All this time M. Cottam was with the sheriff and the rest of the ministers upon the ground, having the rope still about his neck. I could not well hear what persuasions the sheriff and the ministers had with him. But I do conjecture that if he would renounce his faith, he should have his pardon. For I heard him well utter these words, 'I will not swerve a jot from my faith[6] for

---

[4] Marginal note: 'A most notorious evidence of all their innocency. In the most barbaroust place whereof he had found better entertainment than here at home. How gladly they would have had any one of them, to confess the pretended fault.'

[5] Marginal note: 'That were strange.'   [6] Marginal note: 'A notable constancy.'

anything; yea, if I had ten thousand lives I would rather lose them all than forsake the Catholic faith in any point'. And with that he was lifted up into the cart again. And the sheriff said withal, 'Dispatch him, since he is so stubborn'.

Then he was turned backward to look upon M. Richardson who was then in quartering, which he did, saying, 'Lord Jesus, have mercy upon them; Lord, have mercy upon them. O Lord, give me grace to endure to the end. Lord give me constancy to the end', which saying he uttered almost for all the time that M. Richardson was in quartering, saving once he said, 'Thy soul pray for me' and at the last said, 'O Lord, what a spectacle hast thou made unto me?' The which he repeated twice or thrice, and then the head of M. Richardson was holden up by the executioner,[7] who said, as the manner is, 'God save the Queen'. To which M. Cottam said, 'I beseech God to save her and bless her and withal my heart I wish her prosperity as my liege and sovereign Queen and chief governess'.

[7] Marginal note: 'INNOCENCIE.'

Suggested further reading

Peter Marshall, *Heretics and Believers: A History of the English Reformation* (New Haven, CT: Yale University Press, 2007), chs. 15–17.

Lucy E. C. Wooding, *Rethinking Catholicism in Reformation England* (Oxford: Clarendon Press, 2000).

11.6

JOHN PHILIPS

The Life and Death of Sir Philip Sidney (1587)

About the Author

John Philips (*fl.* 1570–1591) was a Cambridge-educated author of a puritanical bent who wrote a series of extended elegiac verses and epitaphs, along with anti-Catholic and religious tracts.

FIGURE 2.2 Funeral of Sidney. Thomas Lant, *The funeral of Sir Philip Sidney*, engraved by Theodore de Brij, 1587 (engraving). British Library, London, UK ©British Library Board. All Rights Reserved/Bridgeman Images

The Life and Death of Sir Philip Sidney (1587)

About the text

Sir Philip Sidney died on 17 October 1586, at the age of thirty-one, having suffered a fatal battlefield injury in an exchange with Spanish forces outside Zutphen in the Netherlands. The early death of this court favourite and esteemed embodiment of scholarly learning and nobility (though he was not in fact born a titled nobleman) produced an extraordinary outpouring of grief in England.[1] His long-delayed funeral took place on 16 February 1587. Philips writes his poem from the perspective of Sidney, an approach he borrows from the *Mirror for Magistrates*' copybook.[2] The poem, consisting of seven-line rhyme royal stanzas, first gives an account of Sidney's life, achievements, and death, before describing in fine detail the soldier-scholar's elaborate ceremonial funeral. The poem becomes as much a social history of a great Elizabethan civic occasion as an expression of mourning. It is dedicated to the Earl of Essex, who was, notably, a one-time rival to Sidney, and someone whose role in the funeral procession Philips emphasizes.

The arts of death

Sidney's funeral was extravagant even by the standards of the day; indeed, part of the reason it was so long delayed was to raise funds for the event. Philips's poem emphasizes the grief occasioned by Sidney's early death, while outlining how the protocols of Sidney's funeral ceremony display the stratified social order. While united in grief, mourners are demarcated by social class and military grade. Yet as Philips lists the sets of mourners, from

---

[1] See entry II.8 (Sidney) for an elegy written from the perspective of his sister. See also Fulke Greville's *The Life of the Renowned Sr Philip Sidney* (London: 1651; Wing B4899) which recounts, in excruciating detail, the slow and painful death of Sidney, resulting from a failure of medical expertise. Recognizing that the attending surgeons cannot save him, Sidney seems to sense his approaching death through a change in how he smells: 'he one morning lifting up the clothes for change and ease of his body, smelt some extraordinary noisome savour about him, differing from oils and salves, as he conceived, and, either out of natural delicacy, or at least care not to offend others, grew a little troubled with it […] Shortly after, when the surgeons came to dress him, he acquainted them with these piercing intelligences between him and his mortality. Which, though they opposed by authority of books, paralleling of accidents, and other artificial probabilities, yet moved they no alteration in this man, who judged too truly of his own estate and from more certain grounds than the vanity of opinion in erring artificers could possibly pierce into' (L6ᵛ). We are grateful to Willy Maley for drawing our attention to this passage.

[2] See entry III.4 (Churchyard).

members of the aristocratic ruling class, to representatives from the Low Countries (Flanders), to those of the citizen class and middling sort, he is keen to demonstrate that those of each group contributed meaningfully to the ceremony; Sidney was beloved equally by the 'Prince and peers' and the citizens of London (see Figure 2.2, an excerpt from Thomas Lant's series of engravings of the funeral procession). At the centre of this spectacle is Sidney's unseen corpse, wrapped within a winding sheet and enclosed within a coffin. Switching between a bird's-eye view of the proceedings ('Throughout the streets, no sign of mirth was shown') and Sidney's bodily remains ('Thus from my grave I bid you all adieu'), Philips is at pains to demonstrate that the social decorum of the ceremony is apiece with Sidney's natural and tranquil transition to heaven ('My body earth, my soul the heavens hath won').

Textual notes

THE Life and Death of Sir Phillip Sidney, late Lord gouernour of FLVSHING: His funerals Solemnized in Paules Churche where he lyeth interred; with the whole order of the mournfull shewe, as they marched thorowe the citie of London, on Thursday the 16 of February, 1587 (London: 1587; STC 19871), 3ʳ–4ᵛ.

The Life and Death of Sir Philip Sidney

First to the poor I clad in weeds of woe,[3]
Whose blubbered eyes did show their inward grief,
The yeomen's looks their heavy cheer did show,
And of their care I was their causer chief,
The gentles all languished without relief,
They left their silks to think upon my wrack,
And wailful wise were clothed all in black.

The drum and fife rang forth my wailful knell,
A woeful march the knights and captains past,
The ensigns wrapped foretold all was not well,
To see my days by direful death defaced,
My standard brave far out of order placed,

---

[3] Black mourning garments were bought for the poor at the fore of the procession.

Trailed on the ground, in grievous doleful wise,
Made rich and poor, with plains to pierce the skies.

My barbed staves[4] appointed for the field,
Whereon I erst encountered with my foe,
Contrary kind enforced were to yield,
And for my want a course of care did show,
My warlike lance, of me beloved so,
In pieces burst, and all to shivers torn,
Gave all estates occasion meet to mourn.

Before my corpse, six heralds[5] passed on,
The first my spurs with pensive tacks did bear.
The second he my want for to bemourn,
Supported sure the gauntlets I did wear,
The third my sword and shield upright did rear,
The fourth in hand my crest and colours had,
The fifth and six, with vizards wan and sad.

My coat of arms did bear in equal wise,
Next came my corpse, by worthy chieftains borne,
Whose joys were sacked, the tears fell from their eyes,
Their mazed[6] minds with care were all forlorn,
The standers-by for Sidney's want did mourn,
Their tender hearts did grieve that I was gone,
Throughout the streets, no sign of mirth was shown.

Next to my corpse to weep my sudden fall,
My brother dear in weeds of woe was dight,[7]
On horseback then my peers to sorrow thrall,
With watered eyes bewailed a marshal knight,
And after them in order rode aright,

---

[4] 'pole weapons'
[5] As Ronald Strickland notes, 'There were six assistants to the chief mourner, the number prescribed for the funerals of barons, rather than four, the customary number for the funeral of a knight' (30).
[6] 'stupefied', 'dazed'   [7] 'dressed'

My loving lords with care and grief oppressed,
And everywhere to mourn my foes were pressed.

Then mounted well next them in open show,
Of Flanders[8] did, the courteous states succeed,
Their grief was great, their stomachs fraught with woe,
This did my want, of woe a well spring breed.
But as of Prince and peers I was beloved indeed.
So London left me not forgotten quite
But gave to me the thing that was my right.

For next the states in gowns of violet fair
Lord Mayor did with senators most grave
On horseback make to mourn me their repair,
But God hath that that he unto me gave,
Though I be dead, my Christ my soul will save,
He is and was the pillar of my trust,
I know at last that rise again I must.

Next these my friends in order passed on,
The gentle crew of grocers[9] comely clad.
These, these my friends, their loving friend did moan,
They for their friend to mourn occasion had,
Next these the drums and fifes with sounds right sad,
My passing bell and knell with care did ring,
Thus to the grave with dole they did me bring.

[8] a delegation of representatives from the Low Countries
[9] i.e., members of the Company of Grocers

Suggested further reading

Sander Bos, Marianne Lange, and Jeanine Six, 'Sidney's Funeral Portrayed', in *Sir Philip Sidney: 1586 and the Creation of a Legend*, ed. Jan Van Dorsten, Dominic Baker-Smith, and Arthur F. Kinney (Leiden: E. J. Brill, 1986).
John Buxton, 'The Mourning for Sidney', *Renaissance Studies*, 3.1 (1989), 46–56.
Susan Harlan, *Memories of War in Early Modern England: Armor and Militant Nostalgia in Marlowe, Sidney, and Shakespeare* (New York: Palgrave Macmillan, 2016).
Ronald Strickland, 'Pageantry and Poetry as Discourse: The Production of Subjectivity in Sir Philip Sidney's Funeral', *ELH*, 58.1 (1990), 19–36.

11.7

ANNE DOWRICHE

The French History (1589)

About the author

Anne Dowriche (d. in or after 1613) was a poet and historian. Born into a wealthy family, she received a good education. *The French History*, her only published work, is an accomplished and creative mélange of historical documentation, narrative history, and imaginative poetic engagement.

About the text

Dowriche's poem in three parts covers separate notable incidents from the French Wars of Religion (see the extended title in the Textual notes), of which our excerpt comes from her treatment of the St Bartholomew's Day Massacre. Dedicating it to her brother, Pearse Edgcombe, a prominent MP, Dowriche notes the pleasure she has taken in researching and writing the poem. Her principal sources were Jean de Serres's *Three Partes of the Commentaries ... of the Ciuill warres of Fraunce* translated by Thomas Tymme (London: 1574; STC 22242) and François Hotman's *A true and plaine report of the Furious outrages of Fraunce* (London: 1573; STC 13847). Our excerpt – which features an oration on the night before the Massacre by Catherine de' Medici to her son, King Charles IX, and to others – borrows liberally from Simon Patericke's English translation of Innocent Gentillet's *Contre-Machiavel* (1576), published later (London: 1602; STC 11743); Dowriche must have had access to the work in manuscript.

The arts of death

The St Bartholomew's Day Massacre, culminating in the deaths of 2,000 to 3,000 people in Paris alone, and a further 4,000 to 7,000 in the provinces, was one of the most notorious episodes of the Counter-Reformation in Europe. As part of the settlement to The Peace of St Germain (1570), ending the Third War of Religion in France, Charles IX arranged for a controversial marriage between his sister Marguerite de Valois and Henri de Navarre (hailing from a notable Huguenot family). Despite Pope Gregory XIII's refusal to grant a dispensation for the inter-confessional marriage, they were married on 18 August 1572 at Notre Dame Cathedral. Tensions between Catholics and Protestants rose to fever pitch in Paris, and the attempted assassination of a leading Huguenot, Admiral de Coligny, a few days after the wedding proved the spark for the violence to follow. Huguenots demanded retribution. On the evening of 23 August, Catherine de' Medici met her son and other counsellors, and made a decision to eliminate a small number of Huguenot leaders in the city. That night the city walls were shut and the King's Swiss Guard put the plan into action; what followed over the coming week was a hunt for Huguenots, leading to a vast number of deaths. Catherine was widely held responsible across Europe, with Elizabeth I condemning the Massacre. Our excerpt shows how Dowriche, a committed Protestant, depicts Catherine as a villainous arch-Machiavellian, downplaying her agency as a woman while manipulating others to her ends; murder is promoted by Catherine, paradoxically and ironically, as a political art that can soon save further lives.

Textual notes

The French historie That is; a lamentable discourse of three of the chiefe, and most famous bloodie broiles that haue happened in France for the Gospell of Iesus Christ. Namelie; 1 The outrage called the winning of S. Iames his Streete, 1557. 2 The constant martirdome of Anna Burgæus one of the K. Councell, 1559. 3 The bloodie marriage of Margaret sister to Charles the 9. anno 1572 (London: 1589; STC 7159), G3^r–G4^r.

The French History

But here the prologue ends, and here begins the play,[1]
For bloody minds resolved quite to use no more delay.
The mother queen[2] appears now first upon the stage,
Where, like a devilish sorceress with words demure and sage,
The King she calls aside with other trusty mates
Into a close and secret place, with whom she now debates

---

[1] Deploying frequent theatrical language, Dowriche's poem anticipates Marlowe's famous depiction in *The Massacre at Paris* (1592).
[2] Catherine de' Medici

The great desire she had to quit them all from care,
In planting long a bloody plot which now she must declare.
'O happy light', quoth she, 'O thrice most happy day,
Which thus hath thrust into our hands our long-desired prey.
We have them all in hold, we have the chiefest fast,
And those for whom we waited long we have them all at last.
Why should we longer stay? What can we farther crave?
What are not all things come to pass which we do long to have?
Doth not our mightiest foe lie wounded in his bed,
Not able now to help himself, which others long hath led?
The Captains captive are, the King of Navarre[3] sure.
The Prince of Condé,[4] with the rest that mischief did procure
Are close within our walls; we have them in a trap.
Good fortune, lo, hath brought them all and laid them in our lap.
By force or flight to save their lives it is too late,
If we, to cut off future fear and cause of all debate,
Do take the proffered time, which time is only now,
And wisdom matched with policy our dealings doth allow.
We need not fear the spot of any cruel fame,[5]
So long as we may feel some ease or profit by the same.
For wisdom doth allow the prince to play the fox,[6]
And lion-like to rage, but hates the plainness of an ox.
What though ye do forswear?[7] What though ye break your faith?
What though ye promise life, and yet repay it with their death?[8]
Is this so great a fault? Nay, nay, no fault at all,

---

[3] Henri de Navarre, later King Henry IV of France (reigned 1589–1610; assassinated by a zealous Catholic)
[4] cousin to Henri de Navarre, Henri I of Bourbon; another leading Huguenot
[5] Over the following passage, Dowriche borrows directly from Gentillet's *Contre-Machiavel*. In a marginal note, keyed to the translation, she writes, 'The queen mother was a good scholar of that devil of Florence, Machiavel, of whom she learned many bad lessons, as this: "That a prince must not care to be accounted cruel, so that any profit come by it".'
[6] Marginal note: 'A prince must imitate the nature of a fox and a lion: a fox to allure and deceive; a lion to devour without mercy, when occasion is offered.'
[7] Marginal note: 'That a prince may not doubt to forswear, to deceive and to dissemble.'
[8] Condemning Catherine's active manipulation, Dowriche adds in the margin: 'This is a wholesome school-mistress for a young King.'

For this we learn we ought to do if such occasions fall.
Our masters do persuade a king to cog and lie,[9]
And never keep his faith,[10] whereas his danger grows thereby.
Cut off therefore the head of this infectious sore,
So may you well assure yourselves this bile will rise no more.
The captains being slain, the soldiers will be faint,
So shall we quickly on the rest perform our whole intent.
Pluck up therefore your sprites and play your manly parts,
Let neither fear nor faith prevail to daunt your warlike hearts.
What shame is this that I, a woman by my kind,
Need thus to speak, or pass you men in valour of the mind?
For here I do protest, if I had been a man,
I had myself before this time this murder long began.
Why do you doubting stand, and wherefore do you stay?
If that you love your peace or life, procure no more delay.
We have them in our hands, within our castle gates,
Within the walls of Paris town the masters and their mates.
This is the only time this matter to dispatch,
But being fled, these birds are not so easy for to catch.
The town of Paris will most gladly give consent,
And threescore thousand fighting men provide for this intent.
So shall we quickly see the end of all our strife,
And in a moment shall dispatch these rebels of their life.
But if we stand in fear, and let them 'scape our hand,
They will procure in time to come great trouble in our land;
For if the Admiral[11] his strength receive again,
Can any doubt but that he will be mindful of his pain?
It is a simple thing for princes to believe
That new goodwill an ancient hate from galled hearts can drive.
Therefore, if we permit these rebels to retire,
We soon shall see by wars again our country set on fire.
This is a woman's mind, and thus I think it best
Now let us likewise hear, I pray thee, sentence of the rest'.

---

[9] Marginal note: 'That a prudent prince is not to keep faith, where any ill may grow by it.'
[10] Dowriche adds in the margin: 'These be the pillars, and this the fruit of Popish [i.e., Roman Catholic] religion.'
[11] i.e., Admiral de Coligny

Suggested further reading
Randall Martin, 'Anne Dowriche's *The French History*, Christopher Marlowe, and Machiavellian Agency', *Studies in English Literature, 1500–1900*, 39.1 (1999), 69–87.
Megan Matchinske, 'Moral, Method, and History in Anne Dowriche's *The French History*', *ELR*, 34.2 (2004), 176–200.

11.8

MARY SIDNEY

'Doleful Lay of Clorinda' (1595)

About the author

Mary Sidney (27 October 1561–25 September 1621), Countess of Pembroke after her marriage to Henry Herbert, was among the first women in England renowned for her poetry. She is listed in John Bodenham's *Garden of the Muses* (1610) as one of the pre-eminent writers of the age. A patron of the arts, she also translated many Continental works, including Robert Garnier's *Mark Antony* (among the first English dramas in blank verse) and Petrarch's 'Triumph of Death'. She also produced a metrical version of the Psalms with her brother, Philip; and, after his death in 1586 (see entry II.6), was instrumental in editing and publishing his unfinished pastoral romance, *Arcadia*, the sonnet sequence *Astrophil and Stella*, and his *Defence of Poetry*.[1]

About the text

The 'Doleful Lay' was published as part of Edmund Spenser's 'Astrophel' within his collection of seven pastoral elegies, some by 'diverse hands', 'upon the death of … Sir Philip Sidney', *Colin Clout's Come Home Again* (1595).[2]

---

[1] See *MA* II.5 (Sidney), for an excerpt from this work about poetry's capacity to impress itself upon one's mind.
[2] The printing of the untitled poem conventionally referred to as the 'Doleful Lay of Clorinda' is separated from the rest of 'Astrophel' with a page break (F4ᵛ); a printer's ornamental 'flowers design' is placed conspicuously in the middle of the blank half-page, indicating that something distinctive and discrete begins on the facing page.

While some prominent Sidney scholars consider Mary Sidney the author,[3] the definitive attribution remains unresolved.[4] At all events, Astrophel was the well-known pastoral analogue of Philip Sidney and so Clorinda, by extension, is Mary Sidney. The lay is introduced in the final stanza of Spenser's 'Astrophel': 'But first his sister that Clorinda hight,[5] / The gentlest shepherdess that lives this day: / And most resembling both in shape and spright / Her brother dear, began this doleful lay. / Which least I mar the sweetness of the verse, / In sort[6] as she it sung, I will rehearse' (F4^v).

The arts of death

The 'Doleful Lay' continues the pastoral conceit of Spenser's larger collective work in which it is situated, and 'Clorinda' uses standard elegiac tropes to mourn the death of her brother, including trying to identify to whom her 'complaint' should be addressed. Transposed to this bucolic setting, and as dictated by the genre, there is an apotheosis. The shepherdess projects an image of her departed brother ensconced blissfully in a celestial paradise and reflects finally on those left below whose labour must now be to live with his loss, honour his memory, and find meaning – if not solace – in mourning.

Textual notes

Colin Clouts come home againe (London: 1595; STC 23077), G1^r–G2^v.

'Doleful Lay of Clorinda'

> Ay me, to whom shall I my case complain,
> That may compassion my impatient grief?
> Or where shall I unfold my inward pain,

---

[3] G. F. Waller, *Mary Sidney, Countess of Pembroke: A Critical Study of Her Writings and Literary Milieu* (Salzburg, Austria: Salzburg University Press, 1979), pp. 89–92; Betty Travitsky, *The Paradise of Women: Writings by Englishwomen of the Renaissance* (New York: Columbia University Press, 1989), p. 21; and Margaret P. Hannay, *Philip's Phoenix* (Oxford: Oxford University Press, 1990), pp. 63–68.

[4] Helen Hackett, 'Courtly Writing by Women', in *Women and Literature in Britain, 1500–1700*, ed. Helen Wilcox (Cambridge: Cambridge University Press, 1998), pp. 169–89, 180; and Gavin Alexander, *Writing after Sidney* (Oxford: Oxford University Press, 2010), pp. 69, 83.

[5] 'is named'   [6] 'to paraphrase'

That my enriven[7] heart may find relief?
>Shall I unto the heavenly pow'rs it show,
>Or unto earthly men that dwell below?

To heavens? Ah, they, alas, the authors were,
And workers of my unremedied woe:
For they foresee what to us happens here,
And they foresaw, yet suffered this be so.
>From them comes good, from them comes also ill,
>That which they made, who can them warn to spill.

To men? Ah, they, alas, like wretched be,
And subject to the heavens' ordinance:
Bound to abide whatever they decree.
Their best redress is their best sufferance.
>How then can they, like wretched, comfort me,
>The which no less need comforted to be?

Then to myself will I my sorrow mourn,
Sith none alive like sorrowful remains:
And to myself my plaints shall back return,
To pay their usury with doubled pains.
>The woods, the hills, the rivers shall resound
>The mournful accent of my sorrow's ground.

Woods, hills, and rivers now are desolate,
Sith he is gone the which them all did grace:
And all the fields do wail their widow state,
Sith death their fairest flow'r did late deface.
>The fairest flow'r in field that ever grew,
>Was Astrophel; that was, we all may rue.

What cruel hand of cursed foe unknown,
Hath cropped the stalk which bore so fair a flow'r?
Untimely cropped, before it well were grown,
And clean defaced[8] in untimely hour.

---

[7] 'ripped'   [8] 'obliterated'

> Great loss to all that ever him did see,
> Great loss to all, but greatest loss to me.

[…]
Death, the devourer of all the world's delight,
Hath robbed you and reft[9] from me my joy:
Both you and me and all the world he quite
Hath robbed of joyance, and left sad annoy.
> Joy of the world, and shepherds' pride was he,
> Shepherds' hope never like again to see.

O Death, that hast us of such riches reft,[10]
Tell us at least, what hast thou with it done?
What is become of him whose flow'r here left
Is but the shadow of his likeness gone:
> Scarce like the shadow of that which he was,
> Naught like, but that he like a shade did pass.

But that immortal spirit, which was decked
With all the dowries of celestial grace:
By sovereign choice from th'heavenly choirs select,
And lineally derived from angels' race,
> Oh, what is now of it become, aread.[11]
> Ay me, can so divine a thing be dead?

Ah no: it is not dead, ne[12] can it die,
But lives for aye, in blissful Paradise:
Where like a new-born babe it soft doth lie,
In bed of lilies wrapped in tender wise,
> And compassed all about with roses sweet,
> And dainty violets from head to feet.

There thousand birds all of celestial brood,
To him do sweetly carol day and night:
And with strange notes, of him well understood,
Lull him asleep in angel-like delight;

---

[9] 'take away'   [10] 'robbed'   [11] 'declare'   [12] 'neither'

      Whilst in sweet dream to him presented be
      Immortal beauties, which no eye may see.

But he them sees and takes exceeding pleasure
Of their divine aspects, appearing plain,
And kindling love in him above all measure,
Sweet love still joyous, never feeling pain.
      For what so goodly form he there doth see,
      He may enjoy from jealous rancor free.

There liveth he in everlasting bliss,
Sweet spirit never fearing more to die:
Ne dreading harm from any foes of his,
Ne fearing savage beasts' more cruelty.
      Whilst we here, wretches, wail his private lack,
      And with vain vows do often call him back.

But live thou there still happy, happy spirit,
And give us leave thee here thus to lament:
Not thee that dost thy heaven's joy inherit,
But our own selves that here in dole are drent.[13]
      Thus do we weep and wail, and wear our eyes,
      Mourning in others, our own miseries.

[13] 'drenched'

Suggested further reading
Elisabeth Chaghafi, '"Astrophel" and Spenser's 1595 Quarto', *Explorations in Renaissance Culture*, 41.2 (2015), 419–77.
Pamela Coren, 'Edmund Spenser, Mary Sidney, and the *Doleful Lay*', *Studies in English Literature*, 42.1 (2002), 25–41.

11.9

THOMAS DEKKER

Selected Works (1603, 1604)

About the author

Thomas Dekker (*c*.1572–1632), dramatist and pamphleteer, helped to chronicle the life and times of early modern Londoners. Perhaps best known today for his fantastical comic play about social mobility, *The Shoemaker's Holiday* (1600), Dekker was a prominent figure within London's literary scene at the turn of the seventeenth century and worked in collaboration with such authors as Ben Jonson and Thomas Middleton.

About the text

Here we excerpt from two of Dekker's pamphlets, written while the theatres were shut in London due to the outbreak of a virulent plague in 1603–1604.[1] More than 30,000 perished, the worst epidemic in many generations. That this plague coincided with the months following the death of Elizabeth I (d.24 March 1603), monarch since 1558, and the new reign of James VI of Scotland on the English throne (as James I), left little doubt and much concern that this outbreak was connected to the unfolding political developments. One of James's first actions as King was to reissue realm-wide 'Orders' (first issued in 1583), with strict instructions on how to contain the plague; for example, if a person became infected, their entire household was to be closed off for six weeks, admitting no visitors and only allowing other householders to leave under strict conditions. The first pamphlet excerpted here is *The Wonderful Year* (1603); Dekker's title takes 'wonder' in its literal sense, though there is doubtless some irony intended also. The pamphlet report consists of three principal parts: a sorrowful description of the death of, and funeral proceedings for, Elizabeth; an expression of hope at James's accession, tempered by the renewed grief caused by the onset of plague; and, in a remarkable section, at which our excerpt begins, a detailed description of the horrors of plague in early modern London.

---

[1] See entry I.11 (Wither) for a treatment of the plague in 1625 at the beginning of Charles I's reign.

The arts of death

Bubonic plague was a matter of ongoing concern for the citizens of early modern London and other large urban sites. The origins and spread of the disease or 'pestilence' were little understood, but its effects were felt throughout society. Dekker's pamphlet reveals both its nightmarish effect on the populace and the helplessness that they felt. In an extended metaphor, Plague is later personified as the 'Muster-Master and Marshall of the Field', fighting for Death, leading an army whose junior commanders are 'Burning Fevers, Boils, Blains, and Carbuncles', and who devastate all that cross their path. In our passage, overturning a common poetic conceit, Dekker rejects the Muses and calls instead for only 'Sorrow' and 'Truth' to guide his narrative; this is not a time for art with any 'counterfeit shadowing', he claims (while loading up the various extended metaphors, vivid personifications, and witty ascriptions), but rather clear expression that only delineates the battle between life and death he describes. Dekker's is, rather, an art of depicting the horrors of mass death, especially of the commoners.

Textual notes

The wonderfull yeare. Wherein is shewed the picture of London lying sicke of the Plague (London: 1603; STC 6535), C3^r–C4^r.

The Wonderful Year

A stiff and freezing horror sucks up the rivers of my blood. My hair stands on end with the panting of my brains. Mine eyeballs are ready to start out, being beaten with the billows of my tears. Out of my weeping pen does the ink mournfully and more bitterly than gall drop on the pale-faced paper, even when I do but think how the bowels of my sick country have been torn. Apollo,[2] therefore, and you bewitching silver-tongued Muses, get you gone! Invocate none of your names. Sorrow and Truth, sit you on each side of me, whilst I am delivered of this deadly burden. Prompt me that I may utter ruthful and passionate condolement. Arm my trembling

---

[2] The nine Muses, inspiring all activities in arts, literature, and music are led by Apollo; see *MA* II.10 (Ross), esp. p. 139, on the mythographic origins of these daughters of Jupiter and Mnemosyne.

hand, that it may boldly rip up and anatomize the ulcerous body of this anthropophagized[3] plague. Lend me art, without any counterfeit shadowing, to paint and delineate to the life the whole story of this mortal and pestiferous battle. And you, the ghosts of those more by many than 40,000, that with the virulent poison of infection have been driven out of your earthly dwellings; you desolate hand-wringing widows, that beat your bosoms over your departing husbands; you woefully distracted mothers that with dishevelled hair fallen into swoons, whilst you lie kissing the insensible cold lips of your breathless infants; you outcast and down-trodden orphans, that shall many a year hence remember more freshly to mourn, when your mourning garments shall look old and be forgotten; and you, the *genii*[4] of all those emptied families, whose habitations are now among the antipodes; join all your hands together, and with your bodies cast a ring about me. Let me behold your ghastly visages, that my paper may receive their true pictures. Echo forth your groans through the hollow trunk of my pen, and rain down your gummy tears into mine ink, that even marble bosoms may be shaken with terror, and hearts of adamant melt into compassion.

What an unmatchable torment were it for a man to be barred up every night in a vast silent charnel-house? Hung, to make it more hideous, with lamps dimly and slowly burning, in hollow and glimmering corners; where all the pavement should, instead of green rushes, be strewed with blasted rosemary, withered hyacinths, fatal cypress and ewe, thickly mingled with heaps of dead men's bones; the bare ribs of a father that begat him, lying there; here the chapless[5] hollow skull of a mother that bore him; round about him a thousand corpses, some standing bolt upright in their knotted winding sheets: others half-mouldered in rotten coffins, that should suddenly yawn wide open, filling his nostrils with noisome stench, and his eyes with the sight of nothing but crawling worms. And to keep such a poor wretch waking, he should hear no noise but of toads croaking, screech-owls howling, mandrakes shrieking; were not this an infernal prison? Would not the strongest-hearted man, beset with such a ghastly horror, look wild? and run mad? and die?

---

[3] Marginal note: 'Anthropophagi are Scythians that feed on men's flesh.' The additional pun here is on anthropomorphization, by which Dekker attributes human-like qualities to the plague.
[4] 'spirits'   [5] 'without a lower jaw' (or 'chap')

And even such a formidable shape did the diseased city appear in. For he that darest, in the dead hour of gloomy midnight, have been so valiant as to have walked through the still and melancholy streets, what think you should have been his music? Surely the loud groans of raving sick men, the struggling pangs of souls departing; in every house grief striking up an alarum, servants crying out for masters, wives for husbands, parents for children, children for their mothers. Here he should have met some franticly running to knock up sextons;[6] there, others fearfully sweating with coffins, to steal forth dead bodies, lest the fatal handwriting of death should seal up their doors. And to make this dismal consort more full, round about him bells heavily tolling in one place, and ringing out in another. The dreadfulness of such an hour is unutterable.

About the text

News from Gravesend: Sent to Nobody (1604), an anonymously published pamphlet now attributed to Dekker and the poet-dramatist Thomas Middleton (1580–1627), treats of not only the widespread pestilence and suffering but also how the epidemic reveals the social disparity between the wealthy and poor. In particular, it complains of the flight of the wealthy from the city to the countryside, leaving behind only the poor to endure or perish. The pamphlet's long dedicatory epistle is addressed to one 'Sir Nicholas Nemo, alias Nobody' and signed off by 'Somebody'; in a delicious irony, it praises the gentleman 'Nobody', for staying in the city (see entry III.14 [Graunt]). *News from Gravesend* is even darker in tone and more socially radical than *The Wonderful Year*, as the co-authors (though primarily Dekker) theorize about the causes of plague. They first settle on the idea that it is a 'miasma', an airborne contagion, but then disregard this because they do not see plague's handiwork in the rivers, trees, or seas. Rather, they suspect the pestilence is the product of man's own vice, and, in a bold move, lay the blame on the iniquity of the ruling classes (peers, courtiers, churchmen, lawyers, and so on); that London has survived the worst excesses of the plague, without the support or intervention of the wealthy who have fled, suggests the self-sufficiency of those poorer citizens who did not leave.

---

[6] 'gravediggers'

The arts of death

Our excerpt derives from the very final passage of the pamphlet. It follows on from earlier subsections on 'the cause of the plague', 'the horror of the plague' and 'the cure of the plague', to conclude with a sobering and largely unironic discussion of the plague's 'necessity' to restore some economic and social balance in a city suffering from the effects of over-population and an upper class who contribute no labour. From this perspective, and drawing upon both scriptural allusion and contemporary medical practice, the plague is remarkably described as not an illness but a 'purge to cleanse the city'; in other words, it works like a Galenic remedy, a medical and therapeutic evacuant for tempering the humoral balance of the civic order.

Textual notes

Newes from Graues-end sent to nobody (London: 1604; STC 12199), F4$^{\text{r-v}}$.

The Necessity of a Plague

Yet to mix comfortable words,
Though this be horrid, it affords
Sober gladness and wise joys,
Since desperate mixtures it destroys.
For if our thoughts sit truly trying
The just necessity of dying
How needful, though how dreadful, are
Purple plagues or crimson war.
We would conclude, still urging pity:
A plague's the purge to cleanse a city.
Who amongst millions can deny
(In rough prose or smooth poesy)
Of evils, 'tis the lighter brood,
A dearth of people, than of food!
And who knows not, our land ran o'er
With people, and was only poor
In having too, too many living,
And wanting living, rather giving
Themselves to waste, deface and spoil,
Than to increase, by virtuous toil,

The bankrupt bosom of our realm
Which naked births did overwhelm.
This begets famine and bleak dearth,
When fruits of wombs pass fruits of earth;
Then famine's only physic, and
The med'cine for a riotous land
Is such a plague. So it may please
Mercy's distributer to appease
His speckled anger, and now hide
Th'old rod of plagues, no more to chide
And lash our shoulders and sick veins
With carbuncles, and shooting blains:
Make us the happiest amongst men,
Immortal by our prophes'ing pen,
That this last line may truly reign:
The plague's ceased; heaven is friends again.

Suggested further reading

Robert Maslen, 'Introduction' to *News from Gravesend: Sent to Nobody*, in *Thomas Middleton: The Collected Works*, gen. ed. Gary Taylor and John Lavagnino (Oxford: Oxford University Press, 2007).

Kathleen Miller, *The Literary Culture of Plague in Early Modern England* (London: Palgrave Macmillan, 2016).

Rebecca Totaro and Ernest B. Gilman (eds.), *Representing the Plague in Early Modern England* (New York: Routledge, 2011).

11.10

MARTIN DAY

'A Mirror of Modesty' (1621)

About the author

Martin Day (15??–1629) was educated at Cambridge and Oxford universities, receiving his Doctor of Divinity from the latter. Besides holding the rectorships of St Faiths in London and Stoke near Launceston in Cornwall, Day was Chaplain in Ordinary to James I – one of forty-eight chaplains who

FIGURE 2.3 Architectural memorial design. Martin Day, *A Monument of Mortality* (London: 1621), title page. British Library, London, UK ©British Library Board. All Rights Reserved/Bridgeman Images

served the royal household by presiding over the Eucharist and preaching sermons. Two collections of his sermons were published posthumously.

About the text

'A Mirror of Modesty' was issued during Day's lifetime in a book entitled *A Monument of Mortality*. *A Monument* is a curious octavo volume, for it pursues an extended *memento mori* rumination upon the implications of an impending death for all mortals, while also commemorating Anna Bill – the recently deceased daughter of Thomas Mountford, Vicar of St Martins-in-the-Field and wife of the octavo's printer, John Bill. The preface makes no mention of Anna even though it describes the volume's architectural fabric in terms of a monument, alluding to its engraved title page that depicts a sarcophagus with a recumbent effigy of a woman, presumably Anna, underneath a stone canopy supported by four columns (see Figure 2.3). Two books hold up two of the columns and two hold up the sarcophagus, each of the four representing one of the treatises: 'A Wakening for Worldlings', 'Meditations of Consolation', 'Comfortable Considerations', and 'A Mirror of Modesty'. Entitled 'Peplum Modestiae, the Veil of Modesty', the fifth section, not identified in the preface, contains a series of verses written by Anna's loved ones, including her father, commending her virtues and blessing her memory. It seems that the printer-husband built his wife's bookish monument upon the bulk of Day's treatises.

The arts of death

'A Mirror of Modesty', organized around 1 Peter 3:3–4, enjoins wives to adorn their hearts with a meek and a quiet spirit rather than adorning their bodies with plaited hair, gold jewellery, and fine apparel. The verses are notorious for codifying a stumbling block to womankind that the Church Fathers would later love to condemn. Day remarks at a few points that his treatise serves to memorialize Anna Bill. But he treads cautiously in praising her memory, betraying Protestant anxieties over appearing to approve Catholic masses and prayers for the dead. Perhaps, this anxiety motivates him to compose 'The Sacred Use of Christian Funerals', the coda of 'A Mirror of Modesty', from which the two excerpts are taken. After stressing that obsequies do not assist the dead or add to their felicity, Day develops an argument that the living owe a debt of gratitude to remembering the deceased, while the deceased's worthy life can be 'set forth as a pattern and example' (F3ʳ) to many. The justification of memorialization finished, Day then transitions to recognizing Anna's rare virtue, as though he had to explain his practice of funereal remembrance before he could actually perform it. The second excerpt, the last paragraph of 'A Mirror of Modesty', discloses Day's reason for focusing on the verses from 1 Peter. Anna Bill made this passage her personal touchstone – a mirror for self-reflection – and so, by reflecting upon it with Day, readers are able to observe the Christian funeral's sacred use of remembering her person without risking any taint of papal ritual.

Textual notes

A monument of mortalitie (London: 1621; STC 6427.5), E8ᵛ–F1ᵛ, F3ʳ⁻ᵛ.

'A Mirror of Modesty'

And last of all, that we tender unto the deceased such honour, as the quality of the person, and his life did justly deserve at our hands, and his funeral make due and payable at that time and place to his surviving memory. And we cannot well conceive how the engaged posterity should be free from the aspersion of ingratitude, if by just commendations they redeem not from oblivious captivity, the virtuous and memorable actions of men and women famous in their generations and even to the ages succeeding, venerable. And it may seem no small degree of stupidity,[1] neither to feel our present loss when our near friends, the delight of our eyes, shall be taken from us, nor fear any future danger, when the chariot of Israel, and the horsemen[2] shall be smitten, and the righteous taken away from the evil to come; nor foresee an advantage of gain and commodity that may arise unto us by the wholesome examples of their life, which dying they bequeath us, as a fragrant legacy; not together with the body to be raked up in the dust; but as a revenue[3] for our use to be raised from the sepulchre, *tanquam mel de petra*,[4] as honey to

---

[1] 'lack of feeling or interest'
[2] 'And Elisha saw it, and he cried, My father, my father, the chariot of Israel, and the horsemen thereof' (2 Kgs 2:12).
[3] 'the return or profit from any land, property, or other source of income'
[4] 'like honey from the rock'. Reference to Ps 81:16. In ancient times, it was thought the best honey came from deep clefts.

Sampson out of the lion's carcass.[5] And I cannot judge them guilty of less than immanity,[6] who, instead of rendering unto these their deserved praises, do by envious detractions sully their good names and by the strong breath of foul aspersions, arising from the rankness of their own breasts, maliciously taint their odoriferous balm, and their remembrance, which is like the composition of the perfume that is made by art of the apothecary,[7] sweet as honey in all mouths, and as music at a banquet of wine.[8]

[…]

Amongst the many precepts and examples, with which she[9] was well acquainted, it seemed to those with whom she most conversed that she never set any so much before her eyes, as this text of scripture: *Let the hidden man*[10] *of the heart be uncorrupt, with a meek and quiet spirit, which is before God a thing much set by.*[11] By this scripture (as by a glass) she attired herself, which is therefore fitly chosen for the ground and basis of her monument after death. It was the hidden man of the heart, which in this mirror she ever much regarded, which doth therefore so reflect upon her memory, that being now hidden, she is not without regard. She was graciously blest with a meek and quiet spirit, which is before God a thing much set by; and this is an argument, that as her remembrance is now with us, so her soul in the sight of God shall be forever much set by, with the holy women, which trusted in God, and even after this manner in times past did attire themselves.

[5] Judg 14:8 [6] 'beastly cruelty'
[7] 'And thou shalt make it a perfume, a confection after the art of the apothecary, tempered together, pure and holy' (Exod 30:35).
[8] a course of wine – often with sweetmeats and fruit – served as either part of a meal or a separate entertainment
[9] Anna Bill   [10] Marginal note: '1. Pet. 3.4.'   [11] 'set by': 'to esteem highly'

Suggested further reading
Daniel W. Doerksen, *Conforming to the Word: Herbert, Donne, and the English Church before Laud* (Lewisburg, PA; London: Bucknell UP; Associated UP, 1997), p. 54.
Russell West-Pavlov, *Bodies and their Spaces: System, Crisis and Transformation in Early Modern Theatre* (Amsterdam: Rodopi, 2006), pp. 146, 211.

11.11

LANCELOT ANDREWES
'A Sermon ... the 5th of November, 1606' (1629)

About the author

Lancelot Andrewes (1555–1626), Bishop of Winchester, was the foremost preacher at the court of James I. He was appointed as royal almoner in 1605, a role traditionally reserved for the monarch's favourite preacher. Andrewes gained recognition and was widely celebrated for his series of annual sermons before King James: at Easter, Whitsunday, Christmas, and on the anniversary of two infamous failed attempts on James's life, the Gowrie Conspiracy (5 August 1600) and the Gunpowder Plot (5 November 1605).

About the text

Our excerpt derives from the opening of Andrewes's sermon on the first anniversary of the Gunpowder Plot, preached before James at Whitehall on 5 November 1606. A year earlier a group of Catholic insurgents plotted to blow up the House of Lords during the State Opening of Parliament; in doing so, they sought to assassinate James, Queen Anne, and Prince Henry, hoping that the fallout to this would provide opportunities for Catholics to regain control of the state government. In the summer months, as they waited for the long-delayed Parliament to open, the conspirators hid explosives in the undercroft beneath the House of Lords. The plot was discovered just in time – an anonymous letter alluding to the plot alerted authorities – and the plotters were arrested. Guy Fawkes, the person entrusted to set off the explosives, was found in the undercroft the evening before Parliament was to open. The conspirators were captured, tortured, tried, and executed by hanging, drawing, and quartering. The Catholic conspiracy was condemned, leading to stricter governmental restrictions on recusancy and widespread anti-Catholic sentiment, while, propagandistically, James, and his sermon-writers, interpreted the late discovery as a form of divine intervention. In early 1606 the Observance of 5th November Parliamentary Act was passed, requiring ministers to commemorate and celebrate the King's 'deliverance' through services.

The arts of death

The sermon expands upon Psalm 118: 23–24, which, unsurprisingly given the occasion, celebrates God's audacious powers of intervention. Andrewes relates 'the Lord's doing' to events that transpired a year earlier. The sermon in part justifies the annual celebration of this potential 'day of all our deaths', while meditating upon why it is important to keep such solemn memories fresh. Andrewes himself would have been present at the opening of Parliament and his evocation of violent death here is personal and affecting; he later describes 'the baskets of heads' and 'pieces of rent [i.e., torn apart] bodies' that would have been taken from the wreckage. In being saved from death, Andrewes argues they may live to praise God and his 'marvellous deed'. In Andrewes's reading, the day itself, that is the memory of the day, should never die, for such a failure of remembrance would be to forget 'a day of God's making'. Andrewes would play his role in such acts of commemoration, delivering a new Gunpowder Plot sermon each anniversary over the following years.

Textual notes

XCVI. sermons by the Right Honorable and Reverend Father in God, Lancelot Andrewes, late Lord Bishop of Winchester. Published by His Majesties speciall command (London: 1629; STC 606), I3^{r-v}.

'A Sermon … the 5th of November, 1606'

A Domino factum est istud, et est mirabile in oculis nostris.
Haec est dies quam fecit Dominus; exultemus et laetemur in ea.

This is the Lord's doing, and it is marvellous in our eyes.
This is the day which the Lord hath made; let us rejoice and be glad in it.

To entitle this time to this text, or to show it pertinent to the present occasion, will ask no long process. This day of ours, this fifth of November, a day of God's making; that which was done upon it, was the Lord's doing. Christ's own application, which is the best, may well be applied here: 'This day is this Scripture fulfilled in our ears'.[1] For, if ever there were

---

[1] Luke 4:21

a deed done, or a day made by God, in our days; this day, and the deed of this day was it: if ever He gave cause of marvelling (as in the first); of rejoicing (as in the second verse), to any land; to us this day, He gave both. If ever saved, prospered, blessed any; this day, He saved, prospered, and, as we say, fairly blessed us.

The day, we all know, was meant to be the day of all our deaths; and we, and many were appointed, as sheep to the slaughter; nay, worse than so. There was a thing doing on it, if it had been done, we all had been undone. And, the very same day, we all know the day, wherein that appointment was disappointed by God, and we all saved, that we might 'not die but live, and declare the praise of the Lord':[2] the Lord, of whose doing, that marvellous deed was, of whose making this joyful day is that we celebrate.

This merciful and gracious Lord (sayeth David, Psalm 111, verse 5) 'hath so done His marvellous works, that they ought to be had, and kept in remembrance'. Of keeping in remembrance, many ways there be: among the rest, this is one, of making days; set solemn days to preserve memorable acts, that they be not eaten out, by them, but ever revived, with the return of the year, and kept still fresh in continual memory. God himself taught us this way. In remembrance of the great delivery from the destroying angel, He himself ordained the day of the Passover yearly to be kept. The Church, by Him taught, took the same way. In remembrance of the disappointing of Haman's bloody lots, they likewise appointed the days of Purim[3] yearly to be kept. The like memorable mercy did He vouchsafe us: the destroyer passed over our dwellings this day: it is our Passover. Haman and his fellows had set the dice on us, and we by this time had been all in pieces: it is our Purim day.

We have, therefore, well done and upon good warrant to tread in the same steps, and by law to provide that this day should not die, nor the memorial thereof perish, from ourselves, or from our seed; but be consecrated to perpetual memory, by a yearly acknowledgement to be made of it, throughout all generations. In accomplishment of which order, we are all now here in the presence of God, on this day, that He first, by His act of doing hath made; and we, secondly, by our act of decreeing, have made before Him, his holy Angels, and men, to confess this His goodness, and ourselves eternally

---

[2] Ps 118:7

[3] The Jewish holiday of Purim (meaning 'lots') celebrates and commemorates the saving of the Jews from Haman, an official who planned to kill all Jews as recounted in the biblical Book of Esther.

bound to Him for it. And, being to confess it, with what words of scripture can we better or fitter do it than those we have read out of this Psalm? Sure, I could think of none fitter, but even thus to say, *A domino factum*, etc.[4]

[4] i.e., '*A domino factum est illud, et est mirabile in oculis nostris*' (Ps 118:23: 'This was the Lord's doing, and it is marvellous in our eyes' (*Geneva Bible*)).

Suggested further reading
Lori Anne Ferrell, *Government by Polemic: James I, the King's Preachers, and the Rhetorics of Conformity* (Stanford, CA: Stanford University Press, 1998), ch. 3.
Peter McCullough (ed.), *Lancelot Andrewes: Selected Sermons and Lectures* (Oxford: Oxford University Press, 2005).

11.12

THOMAS HEYWOOD

The Phoenix of these Late Times (1637)

About the author

Thomas Heywood (1573–1641), chiefly known as a prolific playwright, had a writing career that spanned almost half a century. He tried his hand at an astonishing range of poetic and prose genres, translating classical texts, including Ovid's *Ars Amatoria* (*The Art of Love*), and composing defences of womankind and the acting trade. His biography of Henry Welby emerges from his career's final phase, when he seems to have been scraping together a living as a journalistic pamphleteer.

About the text

Two years earlier, Heywood had published a broadside biography with an engraved picture, 'The Wonder of This Age'. That earlier account sensationalizes an apparent Methuselah, 'Old Parr', who had seen at least 152 years. *The Phoenix* adopts a similar marketing strategy but possesses a much more complicated format. The quarto, excerpted here, consists of a frontispiece portrait of Welby; dedicatory verses to the volume by J. B. and the playwright

Shackerley Marmion; a description of the gentleman; a main section on Welby's life; commendatory verses on the virtuous Welby by the miscellanist Thomas Brewer and the 'Water Poet' John Taylor; and, finally, a funeral elegy by Heywood. In the second edition of *The Phoenix*, Heywood claims to have known Welby before he became a recluse. Not only were the pair countrymen, hailing from Lincolnshire, but Heywood also counted him a familiar acquaintance, recalling some of his witty sayings (E3^v–E4^r).

The arts of death

Shaken up by his brother's failed attempt to murder him, Welby retired to a house near Cripplegate, where he committed himself to the regimen of an ascetic, a veritable desert father just a doorstep away from London's frenetic temptations and distractions. Private devotion to the *ars moriendi* has made 'this gentleman' a Christian paragon worthy of public remembrance; indeed, what is most noteworthy about the pamphlet's verbal and visual description of Welby, a fairly well-off member of the gentry, is the absence of any heraldic markers of social status for memorializing him. His description is even more remarkable when we consider that he was a Protestant celebrated by a Protestant author for a Protestant readership. The monastic residues in his asceticism do not detract from his wonder. Welby's seclusion illustrates a principle integral to many of the death arts: the Christian paradox that life should be a death so that death will bring life. Disengaging one's body from the sensory and transitory world prepares one for spiritual existence. The phoenix, a longstanding symbol and emblem of Christ's resurrection, elaborates upon this paradox: shedding one's mortal skin opens up a gateway to eternity for those who have cast behind them short-sighted earthly values and desires. Heywood evokes the phoenix's sacrificial logic in its perfumed nest cum funeral bier, which sublimates the rotting stench of a corpse into an incense offering to God. In other words, God smells the difference between a good and a bad death.

Textual notes

The excerpts are taken from the longer of the two 1637 editions: *The phoenix of these late times: or the life of Mr. Henry Welby, Esq.; who lived at his house in Grub-street forty foure yeares, and in that space, was never seene by any, aged 84* (London: 1637; STC 25226.5), A1^r–A2^r, E4^{r-v}.

The Phoenix of these Late Times

This gentleman, Master Henry Welby, was forty years of age before he took this solitary life, being eighty-four years old when he died. Those that knew him and were conversant with him in his former time do report that he was of a middle stature, a brown complexion, and of a pleasant cheerful countenance. His hair, by reason no Barber came near him for the space of so many years, was much overgrown, so that he at his death appeared rather like an hermit of the wilderness than the inhabitant of a city. His habit was plain and without ornament, of a sad[1] coloured cloth, only to defend him from the cold, in which there could be nothing found, either to express the least imagination of pride or vainglory. The expense of his time was study, the use he made of it, meditation. Those hours he retired from reading, he spent in prayer. He bought all books whatsoever, which came forth, only making use of the best; such as broached controversy, he laid by, as aiming at the peace of his own conscience. What should I say? He died living that he might live dying; his life was a perpetual death that his death might bring him to an eternal life; who accounted himself no better than a glow-worm[2] here on Earth, that he might hereafter shine a most glorious saint in heaven.

[...]

I cannot reckon up the least of infirmities in this nature done by him, and therefore I leave them to the favourable consideration of the charitable and understanding reader, thus concluding, he may not improperly be called a phoenix. For as in his life he might be termed a bird of paradise,[3] so in his death he might be compared to that Arabian Monady,[4] who having lived fourscore and four years, half in the world, and half from the world, built his own funeral nest or pile, composed of the terebinth[5] and cinnamon,[6] interwoven with onyx and galbanum,[7] with the sweet and odoriferous smells of

---

[1] 'dark, deep, sombre' [2] a term of contempt in the period
[3] a type of bird belonging to the family *Paradiseidæ*
[4] Heywood's epithet for the phoenix, 'monad' meaning 'number one and unity' since there was supposedly only one such bird in existence (Pliny *NH*, 10.2)
[5] resin from tree of that name, used for aromatic and medicinal purposes
[6] spice from tree of that name, used for one of the ingredients in the perfumed oil anointing the tabernacle and its vessels (Exod 30:23)
[7] 'Onyx' or, rather, onycha, and 'galbanum' refer to ingredients used in the incense offering burned at the holy place's golden altar (Exod 30:34).

myrrh, aloes, and cassia;[8] and so made his deathbed an altar, and his godly zeal kindling those sweet spices, sent up his soul in an acceptable incense, to that blessed and sacred throne, where a contrite heart and humble spirit were never despised.[9]

[8] 'Myrrh, aloes, and cassia' are used to make an unguent with which to perfume garments (Ps 45:8).
[9] Ps 51:17: 'The sacrifices of God are a broken spirit: a broken and a contrite heart, O God, thou wilt not despise.'

Suggested further reading
David Souden, 'Welby, Henry (d. 1636), recluse', *Oxford Dictionary of National Biography* (Oxford: Oxford University Press, 2004).

FIGURE 2.4 Charles I as penitent martyr. *Eikon Basilike* (n.p., 1649; Wing E299A), frontispiece. Private collection

11.13

CHARLES I
Eikon Basilike (1649)

About the author

The putative author is Charles I (1600–1649), according to William Levett, groom of the bedchamber, who accompanied the king during his imprisonment on the Isle of Wight where he witnessed him writing it. The first serious questioning of authorship came nine months after its publication: John Milton, commissioned by the Council of State to write in defence of the Commonwealth, published *Eikonoklastes* with the aim of, as the Greek title announces, shattering the King's image. After the Restoration, John Gauden, Bishop of Exeter, to bolster his petition for advancement to the see of Winchester, asserted to Edward Hyde, Earl of Clarendon, that he was entirely responsible for writing and surreptitiously publishing *Eikon Basilike*.

About the text

On 30 January 1649, Charles I was beheaded by order of Parliament for 'wicked designs, wars, and evil practices … against the public interest, common right, liberty, justice, and peace of the people of this nation'.[1] *Eikon Basilike*, published ten days after the King's execution, answers these and other charges in straightforward prose that urges forgiveness for his executioners and justifies his political actions and subsequent martial exploits. Also included are private meditations in the plain style of prayers from the early English Reformation. Given its rhetorical grace and apologetic tone, Milton counter-blasted in his *Eikonoklastes* that 'the whole book might perhaps be intended a piece of poetry'.[2] Charles is portrayed both graphically on the frontispiece (see Figure 2.4) and literally in this text as a martyr and a monument to patience, guilty only of acquiescing to the execution of Thomas Wentworth, Earl of Strafford. He is presented as a man devoted to

---
[1] *The Constitutional Documents of the Puritan Revolution, 1625–1660*, ed. Samuel Rawson Gardiner (Oxford: Clarendon Press, 1899), §82, p. 374.
[2] John Milton, *Eikonoklastēs* (London: 1649; Wing M2112), I2ᵛ.

his family and the welfare of his people. The resulting image is of a faithful and authentically pious Protestant, ready for death and a martyrdom he did not seek. The lasting effect of this popular book of Royalist propaganda (thirty-six editions in 1649, and countless more thereafter), despite its being suppressed during the Protectorate and disapproved of by leaders of the Stuart Restoration,[3] was to fix in the minds of English readers an image of benevolent and sacrosanct kingship made all the more numinous by Charles's abject absence from the world stage. Our excerpt comes from 'Meditations on Death' written (according to the printer's section heading) 'after the votes of non-addresses, and his majesty's closer imprisonment in Carisbrooke Castle'.

The arts of death

While elegies were a staple for lamenting the death of monarchs and other worthies, the unprecedented execution of an English king by a provisional government that subsequently sought to contain and control public responses to the royal death called for, and generated, new kinds of textual memorializing. *Eikon Basilike* blends the tropes of the sainted martyr (Charles I is the only person 'canonized', after a fashion developed for the occasion by the Church of England, since the English Reformation) with the '*moriens*' from the *ars moriendi* patiently preparing for death. Charles's fate spelled out in *Eikon Basilike* mirrors a panel in the Dance of Death where everyone, from beggar to king, is summoned to die. King Charles thereby is humanized, which both mollifies claims of his exceptionalism and yet, at the same time, stirs up readers' deep-seated acculturated beliefs that the king somehow deserves greater sympathy. Not at all a typical 'Fall of Princes' narrative (like those found earlier in *A Mirror for Magistrates*[4]), *Eikon Basilike* presents this fallen monarch as being raised higher, going 'from a corruptible, to an incorruptible crown' (alluding to 1 Cor 15:42), as he is reported to have said on the scaffold.[5]

---

[3] See *MA* VI.19 ('Crackfart and Tony'), which satirizes the 'Act of ... Oblivion' designed to enforce the fragile civil peace after the Restoration by pardoning and protecting those indirectly involved in the execution of Charles I.
[4] Cf. entry III.4 (Churchyard).
[5] *King Charl[e]s his tryal ... also His Majesties Speech on the scaffold before his execution on Tuesday, Jan. 30* (London: 1649; Wing K556), F1r.

Textual notes

Eikon Basilike. The Portaicture of His Sacred Majesty in His Solitude and Sufferings (n.p.: 1649; Wing E299A), Q6^r–R4^v.

Eikon Basilike

As I have leisure enough, so I have cause more than enough, to meditate upon and prepare for my death. For I know, there are but few steps between the prisons and graves of princes.

It is God's indulgence which gives me the space, but man's cruelty that gives me the sad occasions for these thoughts.

For, besides the common burthen of mortality, which lies upon me, as a man; I now bear the heavy load of other men's ambitions, fears, jealousies, and cruel passions, whose envy or enmity against me, makes their own lives seem deadly to them, while I enjoy any part of mine.

I thank God, my prosperity made me not wholly a stranger to the contemplations of mortality.

Those are never unseasonable since this is always uncertain, death being an eclipse which oft happeneth as well in clear as cloudy days.

[…]

Indeed, I never did find so much the life of religion, the feast of a good conscience, and the brazen wall of a judicious integrity and constancy, as since I came to these closer conflicts with the thoughts of death.

I am not so old, as to be weary of life; nor (I hope) so bad, as to be either afraid to die, or ashamed to live: true, I am so afflicted, as might make me sometime even desire to die, if I did not consider. That it is the greatest glory of a Christian's life to die daily, in conquering by a lively faith, and patient hopes of a better life, those partial and quotidian deaths, which kill us (as it were) by piece-meals, and make us over-live our own fates; while we are deprived of health, honour, liberty, power, credit, safety, or estate, and those other comforts of dearest relations, which are as the life of our lives.

Though, as a king, I think myself to live in nothing temporal so much as in the love and good-will of my people; for which, as I have suffered many deaths, so I hope I am not in that point as yet wholly dead: notwithstanding, my enemies have used all the poison of falsity and violence of hostility to destroy, first the love and loyalty, which is in my subjects; and then all that content of life in me, which from these I chiefly enjoyed.

[…]

If I must suffer a violent death with my Saviour, it is but mortality crowned with martyrdom, where the debt of death, which I owe for sin to nature, shall be raised as a gift of faith and patience offered to God.

Which I humbly beseech him mercifully to accept; and although death be the wages of my own sin, as from God, and the effect of others' sins, as men, both against God and me; yet as I hope my own sins are so remitted, that they shall be no ingredients to embitter the cup of my death, so I desire God to pardon their sins, who are most guilty of my destruction.

The trophies of my charities will be more glorious and durable over them, than their ill managed victories over me.

Suggested further reading
Jim Daems and Holly Faith Nelson (eds.), *'Eikon Basilike' with Selections from 'Eikonoklastes'* (Peterborough, Canada: Broadview Press, 2005).
Helen Pierce, 'Text and Image: William Marshall's Frontispiece to the *Eikon Basilike* (1649)', in *Censorship Moments: Reading Texts in the History of Censorship and Freedom of Expression*, ed. Geoff Kemp (London: Bloomsbury, 2015), pp. 79–86.

11.14

FRANCIS BEAUMONT

'An Elegy on the Lady Markham' (1653)

About the author

Francis Beaumont (1584/5–6 March 1616) entered London's Inner Temple in 1600 to practise law, but instead pursued a career in theatre. He collaborated with John Fletcher on at least eight plays. His solo works were written to appeal to urbane audiences, such as his metatheatrical parody of both citizen comedy and chivalric romance, *Knight of the Burning Pestle* (1609); and, on 20 February 1613, an elaborate court masque sponsored by Inner Temple and Gray's Inn, performed in the Banqueting House at Whitehall Palace, in celebration of the marriage of Princess Elizabeth, only daughter of James I, to Frederick V, Elector Palatine of the Rhine.

About the text

Beaumont was known for his playful and at times irreverent wit, evident in this self-conscious reflection on and clever approach to sporting with the commercial elegy, a popular literary form for paying tribute to the recently deceased. Far from being considered too outré for publication owing to the grotesque imagery of the woman being thus dubiously celebrated, one such comparable piece attributed to Beaumont was selected to open Henry Fitzgeffrey's *Certain Elegies* (London: 1618), containing the tongue-in-cheek lines: 'Where if I sing your praises in my rhyme / I lose my ink, paper, and my time' (A3ᵛ). Our selection, 'An Elegy on the Lady Markham', likewise is characterized by Beaumont's signature literary parody, which would have been appreciated by the probable patron of this endeavour, Henry Hastings, given the refined aesthetic sensibilities he shared with his first cousin, Bridget Markham (a lady of Queen Anne's bedchamber), buried 19 May 1609.

The arts of death

This seemingly indecorous treatment of Lady Markham deploys in unusual ways the usual tropes associated with the *contemptus mundi* and *vanitas* traditions. The poet's saying that he never met her gives him licence in this elegy (or, more properly, this anti-elegy) to jest that in death she is incapable of putting him through the agonies as have his former mistresses. The result is a send-up of shop-worn tropes of the *carpe diem* ('seize the day') style of erotic poetry, unsettlingly coupled with the *memento mori* theme of funeral elegies. Instead of writing about etching her virtues in a mirror or eternizing her beauty through verse, he conjures up lurid images of the worms penetrating her body – especially her face and forehead – thereby transforming Petrarchan conceits used for blazoning the beloved's physical beauty into a *vanitas* image reminiscent of the 'worm-eaten maw' of Skelton's 'Upon a dead man's head'.[1] Beaumont thus recycles in verse sepulchral representations of the deceased undergoing bodily decay (see Figure 2.5); and, more specifically, vermiculation (tracks left by worms) often incised on the recumbent figures (or *gisants*) of transi-tombs. Given Lady Markham's reputed delight in such sophisticated *jeux d'esprit*, this grisly elegy seems less out of place. Further, her will

---

[1] Cf. *MA*, pp. 280–83.

FIGURE 2.5 Gisant effigy. Transi-tomb of Archbishop Henry Chichele (d.1443). Canterbury Cathedral. Photo credit, William E. Engel

(published the day before she died) calls for *memento mori* rings with death's heads to be purchased for Henry Carey,[2] Benjamin Rudyerd,[3] and a 'Mr John Gill'.

Textual notes

Poems: by Francis Beaumont, Gent. Viz. The hermaphrodite. The remedy of love. Elegies. Sonnets, with other poems (London: 1653; Wing B1602), D8ʳ–E1ʳ.

'An Elegy on the Lady Markham'

> As unthrifts[4] groan in straw for their pawned beds,
> As women weep for their lost maidenheads,
> When both are without hope or remedy,

---

[2] 1st Earl of Dover (*c.*1580–1666), MP for Sussex and later Hertfordshire
[3] (1572–31 May 1658), poet, politician, colonial investor   [4] 'spendthrifts', 'wastrels'

Such an untimely grief I have for thee.
   I never saw thy face, nor did my heart
Urge forth mine eyes unto it whilst thou wert;
But being lifted hence, that which to thee
Was death's sad dart, proved Cupid's shaft to me.[5]
   Whoever thinks me foolish that the force
Of a report can make me love a corse,[6]
Know he, that when with this I do compare
The love I do a living woman bear,
I find myself most happy: now I know
Where I can find my mistress, and can go
Unto her trimmed bed, and can lift away
Her grass-green mantle, and her sheet display,
And touch her naked; and though th' envious mould
In which she lies uncovered, moist, and cold,
Strive to corrupt her, she will not abide
With any art her blemishes to hide,
As many living do, and, know their need,
Yet cannot they in sweetness her exceed;
But make a stink with all their art and skill,
Which their physicians warrant with a bill;
Nor at her door doth heaps of coaches stay,
Footmen and midwives to bar up my way:
Nor needs she any maid or page to keep,
To knock me early from my golden sleep,
With letters that her honour all is gone,
If I not right her cause on such a one.
Her heart is not so hard to make me pay
For every kiss a supper and a play:
Nor will she ever open her pure lips
To utter oaths, enough to drown our ships,
To bring a plague, a famine, or the sword,
Upon the land, though she should keep her word;

---

[5] For additional commentary on the iconography of this motif, see *MA* 'Introduction' (esp. pp. 29–30).
[6] 'corpse'

Yet, ere an hour be past, in some new vein
 Break them, and swear them double o'er again.
Pardon me, that with thy blest memory
 I mingle mine own former misery:
Yet dare I not excuse the fate that brought
 These crosses on me; for then every thought
That tended to thy love was black and foul,
 Now all as pure as a new-baptized soul:
For I protest, for all that I can see,
 I would not lie one night in bed with thee;
Nor am I jealous, but could well abide
 My foe to lie in quiet by thy side.
  You worms[7] (my rivals), whilst she was alive,
How many thousands were there that did strive
To have your freedom? for their sake forbear
Unseemly holes in her soft skin to wear:
But if you must (as what worms can abstain
To taste her tender body?) yet refrain
With your disordered eatings to deface her,
But feed yourselves so as you most may grace her.
First, through her ear-tips see you make a pair
Of holes, which, as the moist inclosed air
Turns into water, may the clean drops take,
And in her ears a pair of jewels make.
Have ye not yet enough of that white skin,
 The touch whereof, in times past, would have been
Enough to have ransomed many a thousand soul
Captive to love? If not, then upward roll
Your little bodies, where I would you have
This epitaph upon her forehead grave:
  'Living, she was young, fair, and full of wit;
   Dead, all her faults are in her forehead writ.'

---

[7] Worms feasting on corpses has been a staple for reflecting on mortality at least since the twelfth century, with Innocent III's *De contemptu mundi* (*PL*, 217.735–37) and Bernard of Clairvaux's meditations on the human condition (*PL*, 182.241B).

Suggested further reading
Kathleen Cohen, *Metamorphosis of a Death Symbol: The Transi Tomb in the Late Middle Ages and the Renaissance* (Berkeley, CA: University of California Press, 1973).
Philip J. Finkelpearl, *Court and Country Politics in the Plays of Beaumont and Fletcher* (Princeton, NJ: Princeton University Press, 1990), pp. 20–24.

11.15

THOMAS BROOKS

A String of Pearls (1657)

About the author

Thomas Brooks (1608–1680) was a London minister, Protectorate supporter, and religious writer who wrote over a dozen treatises on Christian conduct, devotion, and comfort, several of which saw multiple editions. Brooks was a member of the dissenting sect of Independents, otherwise known as Congregationalists.

About the text

A String of Pearls, preached at the 1657 funeral of Mary Blake, a merchant's wife, conforms to the typical Protestant sermon's framework of explicating doctrine for the purposes of application. Discoursing upon the 'last thing' experienced by the elect, Brooks takes 1 Peter 1:4 as his scriptural text: 'To an inheritance incorruptible, and undefiled and that fadeth not away, reserved in Heaven for you'. The most immediate behaviour he expects from his auditors who contemplate the doctrine of Heaven could not be clearer: 'If the best things are reserved for believers till last, then let not Christians mourn immoderately' (M3^v). Consistent, too, with the structure of the period's funeral sermon, *A String of Pearls* includes a short commendation of Mary's virtues, as well as two elegies. The 'lean-to' method of separating the commendation from the explication of doctrine signals the great theological caution preachers exercised in remembering the dead. The Reformation harboured deep suspicions toward the funeral sermon on the grounds that its former ties with Catholic burial rites would perpetuate praise-mongering, belief in Purgatory, and the cult of saints among the wrong-headed. Although varying degrees of puritanical distrust lingered throughout the period, the marketplace of print affirms that Protestants of many stripes embraced this form. To deflect accusations of breeding Catholic superstitions, Protestant preachers reasoned that their homiletics aimed to stir up the living by rehearsing the deceased's moral actions and attributes. In his commendation of Mary, Brooks praises her influence upon his personal spirituality, following the late Renaissance's inclination to represent women as models of active virtue, not just passive piety.

The arts of death

As with many of this anthology's excerpts, the passage below enfolds death arts within death arts: the funeral sermon comforts mourners and fortifies them in the prospect of their own mortality by commemorating the deceased. This particular sermon spoke to the period's readers, having gone through at least ten editions over the second half of the seventeenth century. Its extraordinary popularity may have resulted from the way in which Brooks uses the language of inheritance to amplify his thoughts on the afterlife. The privilege of acceding to an estate – the basis of sustaining England's gentry and noble families – was determined by primogeniture, which thereby excluded most of society's members. The socio-legal discourses and practices of inheritance comprise an elitist death art in that they keep intact the testator's economic legacy so as to preserve his family name and heir's status; the spiritual inheritance Brooks describes thus democratizes the privilege – or at least for the chosen ones. In heralding the heavenly estate at the expense of the earthly, Brooks's sermon captures the imaginations of the dispossessed, while permitting them emotional licence to discharge their *ressentiment* toward the prosperity enjoyed by the landowning class.

Textual notes

A string of pearles: or, the best things reserved till last. Discovered, in a sermon preached in London, June 8. 1657 (London: 1657; Wing B4963), C8^r, M5^r–M6^r.

A String of Pearls

The inheritance reserved for believers till they come to heaven is[1] a pure, undefiled, and incorruptible inheritance. It is an inheritance that cannot be defiled, nor blemished with abuse one way or another; other inheritances may, and often are with oaths, cruelty, blood, deceit, etc. The Greek word (*amiantos*) signifies a precious[2] stone, which though it be never so much[3] soiled, yet it cannot be blemished, nor defiled; yea, the oftener you cast it into the fire and take it out, the more clear, bright, and shining it is; all earthly inheritances are true gardens of Adonis, where we can gather nothing but trivial flowers, surrounded with many briers,[4] thorns, and thistles. O the hands, the[5] hearts, the thoughts, the lives, that have been defiled, stained, and polluted with earthly inheritances!

[…]

Ah poor Christians, what though you have little in hand, yet you have much in hope, though you have little in possession, yet you have much in reversion;[6] he that hath but little in present possession, yet if he hath a fair estate in reversion, he comforts himself, and solaces his spirit in the thoughts of it, that there will come a day when he shall live like a man, when he shall live bravely and sweetly, and this makes him sing care and sorrow away;[7] why Christians, do you do so, you have[8] a fine, a fair estate in reversion,[9] though you have but little in possession, and therefore bear up bravely and live comfortably.

Christ who was the heir of all, yet he lived[10] poor, and died poor; as he was born in another man's house, so he was buried in another man's tomb; when Christ died he made no will, he had no crown lands, only his coat was left, and that the soldiers parted among them; if thy outward condition be conformable to his, there is no reason why thou shouldst be discouraged, for thou hast a rich and royal revenue, that will shortly come into thy hand, and

---

[1] Marginal note: 'Vide Zanchius.' [i.e., Jerome Zanchius, an Italian Protestant writer (1516–1590)]
[2] Marginal note: '1 King. 21.20.'
[3] Marginal note: '*Quam sordet mihi terra, cum Coelum intueor?* Adrian.' [i.e., 'How vile the earth seems to me, when I look at the sky?' Adrianus Turnebus, a French classical scholar (1512–1565)]
[4] Marginal note: 'Gen. 3.18.'   [5] Marginal note: 'Isa. 23.9.'
[6] 'the right of succeeding to an estate'   [7] Marginal note: 'Jam 2.5.'
[8] Marginal note: '2 Tim. 4.7,8.'   [9] Marginal note: 'Psal. 16.6.'
[10] Marginal note: 'Mat. 8.20.'

then thou shalt never know what poverty and penury means more: and for thy comfort, know, that though men may for thy poverty despise thee, yet the Lord doth highly prize thee, 'twas a good saying of Basil[11] (*placet sibi Deus abstrusum in despecto corpore margaritum conspicatus*[12]) God pleaseth himself, beholding a hidden pearl in a despised and disrespected body. The truth is, Christians, if there were any real happiness in the things of this life, you should have them, but 'tis not in all the wealth and glory of this world to make up a happiness to you, and therefore as the enjoyment of them should not swell the rich, so the want of them should not trouble the poor; the angels (and saints departed) in heaven are happy, and yet they have neither silver nor gold; they are blessed, and yet they have none of the gay things of this life; they have none of the gallantry and glory of this world. You have now your worst; your best days are to come. It will not be long before you shall have your portion in hand; therefore, live sweetly, and walk comfortably up and down this world.

[11] Marginal note: 'Basil. Seleuc, oratione 15.' [i.e., Basil of Seleucia, fifth-century Bishop. Homily 15, *On Faith*]
[12] The translation follows.

Suggested further reading
Becker, *Death*, pp. 121–24, 133–37.
Houlbrooke, *Family*, pp. 298, 386–87.

11.16

KATHERINE PHILIPS

Poems (1669)

About the author

Katherine Philips (1632–1664), poet, dramatist, and epistle writer, was married to the Welsh landowner and parliamentarian James Philips. After marriage, she lived in Cardigan, Wales, where she established a society of friendship, whose members were known by pseudonyms taken from pastoral romance (as discussed below).

About the text

Her coterie friendships dominate the motivations and subject matter of her poetic output, which at times breaks new ground by exploring intimate female relationships through the language of the courtly love lyric. Almost a third of her poetry intersects with the elegiac, not tangential to her musings on friendship, which often express the psychological pain of absence and separation. 'Lucasia', mentioned in 'Wiston Vault', is Anne Owen, one such coterie friend, to whom Philips, the 'matchless Orinda', addressed twenty-one poems. Written upon her infant son's death in 1655, the two other poems included here present contrasting faces to Philips's mourning and demonstrate the skill of her elegiac craft. The first served as the actual epitaph on Hector's monument, while the second was set to music – now lost – by the English composer Henry Lawes. All three poems are based on the texts in the authorized folio edition of her poetry published posthumously in 1667.

The arts of death

The first poem's title refers to a small parish church, which, located in Wiston, Pembrokeshire, seems to have been the burial place of the relatives of Anne Wogan, Philips's mother-in-law. The vault at once initiating and condensing the speaker's critical attitude toward conventional funeral culture might thus have triggered the thought that the speaker's own remains may very well someday find their resting place there. Tacitly abjuring the genealogical, the poem relocates the monumental from the tomb and the epitaph to Anne's heart. Although an intimate's inner feelings and thoughts will not endure the ravages of time, it will, according to Katia Fowler, allow the departed to have a continued life within her community through social obligation and commitment.

The most immediate difference between Philips's two elegies for her son Hector may be discerned in their structure. The traditional elegy unfolds according to the three divisions of the speaker's lamentation, her praise for the dead, and finally her consolation in the face of loss. The 'Epitaph' corresponds to this tripartite structure closely, starting with the feelings of betrayal and pain, then extolling the well-proportioned and full-spirited babe, and closing with the promise of the resurrection in the pun on the mourning yet rising 'sun'. The second elegy does not try to observe the first's public formality, unable to move beyond the stage of excessive lamentation and spiralling into an increasing state of privacy and isolation. The third stanza admits that her eulogy will only be 'piercing groans', while the fourth stanza signals her withdrawal from the world's comfort and the fifth announces her 'gasping numbers' to be her final poetic expression: inarticulateness, alienation, and silence dissolve the elegy's therapeutic design. The structural difference exhibits Philips's innovative engagement with a genre, which, W. Scott Howard argues, she helped to usher into modernity. He reads the two Hector poems as sustaining a contrast, played out in her other elegies, between transcendent consolation and historically situated solace. Along these lines, one can read her second elegy as possessing a purpose akin to that of 'Wiston Vault': a criticism and repudiation of the period's male-dominated death arts that allocate no place for female affect.

Textual notes

An unauthorized edition of Philips's poems appeared in 1664, but an 'official' edition of her *Poems* was published in 1667. The excerpts below come from this latter edition: *Poems by the most deservedly admired Mrs. Katherine Philips the matchless Orinda. To which is added Monsieur Corneille's Pompey & Horace, tragedies. With several other translations out of French* (London: 1667; Wing P2033), K2^v, Mm^v, Pp2^v–Qq^r.

Wiston Vault

And why this vault and tomb? alike we must
Put off distinction, and put on our dust.
Nor can the stateliest fabric help to save
From the corruptions of a common grave;[1]
Nor for the resurrection more prepare,
Than if the dust were scatter'd into air.
What then? Th' ambition's just, say some, that we
May thus perpetuate our memory.
Ah! false vain task of art! ah! poor weak man!
Whose monument does more than's[2] merit can:
Who by his friends' best care and love's abused,

---

[1] Commoners were buried in mass graves.   [2] 'than his'

And in his very epitaph accused:
For did they not suspect his name would fall,
There would not need an epitaph at all.
But after death too I would be alive,
And shall, if my Lucasia do, survive.
I quit these pomps of death, and am content,
Having her heart to be my monument:
Though ne'er stone[3] to me, 'twil stone for me prove,
By the peculiar miracles of love.
There I'll inscription have which no tomb gives,
Not, *Here Orinda lies*, but, *Here she lives*.

EPITAPH

On her Son H.P. at Syth's Church,[4] where her Body also lies Interred

What on earth deserves our trust?
Youth and beauty both are dust.
Long we gathering are with pain,
What one moment calls again.
Seven years childless, marriage past,
A son, a son is born at last:
So exactly limbed and fair,
Full of good spirits, mien, and air,
As a long life promised,
Yet, in less than six weeks dead.
Too promising, too great a mind
In so small room to be confined:
Therefore, as fit in heav'n to dwell,
He quickly broke the prison shell.
So the subtle alchemist,
Can't with Hermes' seal[5] resist
The powerful spirit's subtler flight,

---

[3] i.e., never hard-hearted toward the speaker
[4] St Sith's Church, also known as St Benet Sherehog, burned down in the Great Fire of London, 1666.
[5] a hermetic seal, named after Hermes Trismegistus, author of texts on magic and alchemy

But 'twill bid him long good night.
And so the sun if it arise
Half so glorious as his eyes,
Like this infant, takes a shroud,
Buried in a morning[6] cloud.

Orinda upon Little Hector Philips

1.
Twice forty months of wedlock[7] I did stay,
Then had my vows crowned with a lovely boy,
And yet in forty days[8] he dropped away,
O swift vicissitude of human joy!

2.
I did but see him and he disappeared,
I did but pluck the rosebud and it fell,
A sorrow unforeseen and scarcely feared,
For ill can mortals their afflictions spell.[9]

3.
And now, sweet babe, what can my trembling heart
Suggest to right my doleful fate or thee?
Tears are my muse, and sorrow all my art,
So piercing groans must be thy eulogy.

4.
Thus, whilst no eye is witness of my moan,
I grieve thy loss (ah, boy too dear to live)
And let the unconcerned world alone,
Who neither will, nor can refreshment give.

---

[6] a pun on mourning [7] Philips was married in August 1648.
[8] The subtitle of the manuscript copy of the poem indicates that he lived for ten days, from 23 April to 2 May 1655.
[9] 'discern'

5.
An off'ring too for thy sad tomb I have,
Too just a tribute to thy early hearse,
Receive these gasping numbers to thy grave,
The last of thy unhappy mother's verse.[10]

[10] This was not the last poem Philips wrote.

Suggested further reading
Katia Fowler, 'Memorial Culture and the Kinship of Friendship in Katherine Philips's "Wiston Vault"', *Women's Writing*, 24 (2017), 332–52.
W. Scott Howard, 'Katherine Philips's Elegies and Historical Figuration', *Women's Writing*, 24 (2017), 313–31.

11.17

MARY ASTELL

'An Essay upon Death' (1696)

About the author

Mary Astell (12 November 1666–11 May 1731) came from a moderately prosperous family involved with the coal industry in Newcastle, and was well tutored by her uncle, Ralph Astell, a follower of the Cambridge Platonists and one-time Anglican curate. After his death and a series of family setbacks, she moved to London and attracted influential patrons, most notably Lady Ann Coventry and Lady Elizabeth Hastings, who were impressed by her outspoken views on education, especially concerning the establishment of an all-women's college. A Tory pamphleteer and Anglican apologist, Astell also wrote original works of moral philosophy drawing on Cartesian dualism and traditional Neoplatonism. Her publications consistently champion reason over passion and virtue over material gain, especially those critical of the institution of marriage.

About the text

'An Essay upon Death', attributed to Astell, is the fourth of six *Familiar Essays* collected and published in 1696, the same year as *An Essay in Defence of the Female Sex*. Written in the mode of Seneca and Cicero, these six essays are couched as letters to friends offering moral instruction and consolation on 'marriage, crosses in love, sickness, death, loyalty and friendship' (A1r).

The arts of death

Our excerpt, addressed to 'a friend, who had buried her husband' (E4v), exhibits from the outset a tone of sincerity and promotes rational – as opposed to affective – condolence: 'The grief that is least, is soonest expressed … had I been unconcerned, my pen and thoughts had been freer; and … I might have offered some poor reasons against other women's afflicting themselves too much, which I should be ashamed to mention to you' (E5r). As such, it participates productively in the longstanding genre of the consolation.[1] Anglican doctrine underlies her treatment of how to comport oneself in the wake of the death of a beloved spouse: 'the power of God only can support you under such a separation, which I believe, was much more terrible to you than death itself, that so lately seemed to look you in the face with its severe attendants of pain and sickness' (E5r). Unlike *ars moriendi* tracts that programmatically prepare people for the ultimate farewell, this disquisition on death speaks to the mourner using impeccable logic, appealing to her higher nature and intellect, about continuing to live decorously in the world.

Textual notes

Six familiar essays (London: 1696; Wing S3912), E8v–F3r.

'An Essay upon Death'

By that acknowledging that death is an effect of God's great mercy, to all such to whom the following text may be applied, 'Blessed are the dead which die in the Lord, even so sayeth the Spirit, for they rest from their labours';[2] and if the dissolution of the righteous, is to exempt them from labours, though our own interest makes us eager to detain them longer with us; yet the sense of what they enjoy in Heaven, and the inconveniences that attends them, whilst

---

[1] For examples of other works that likewise draw on and contribute, each in their way, to this genre of the consolation, see entries I.6 (Bradford), I.7 (Fisher), and I.14 (Taylor).
[2] Rev 14:13; from the Burial Service in the Book of Common Prayer; see entry II.2 (Cranmer).

they are upon the Earth, must be a great means to silence our repinings[3] and to abate our grief [...] were it not for this blessed expectation, the servants of God would commonly be most wretched, since their cup is often empty, and as often filled with an unpleasant potion; whilst their ungodly neighbours have plenteousness of rivers to drink, but though we grieve the less for the death of an unfortunate friend, yet his misfortunes make us grieve the more for him, whilst he lives; a certain demonstration that the days of man are evil, as well as few,[4] since friendship, the most substantial pleasure in the world, only gives us the trouble of lamenting the unhappy life, or bewailing the untimely death of those we love: if our life then is constantly attended with such perplexity, why should we be so apprehensive of our death; and yet, except those few that are extraordinarily harassed, the rest of us are as zealous to hug our chains [...] true, we are told, that this aversion to death is natural, since all animals that have sense enough to foresee their danger, endeavour to avoid it; whether it is an instinct in nature which teaches them to fly from pain and oppression, or the fear of annihilation, is beyond my reach, but we know when their breath is gone, they have no further being, and if we were animals like them, we might have the like apprehensions too, but now the sting of death is taken away from us, by the blood of our redeemer, who graciously opens the door of life, to all such as patiently wait till their change shall come; and piously strive in the mean time to make their change happy; for which reason we ought neither to be discontented to live, nor unwilling to die; and though we must feel pain, sickness, and whatsoever else we term misfortunes, with the same senses that others do (for religion humbles, but does not stupefy) yet the knowledge that we have deserved much more stripes from our great judge, must make us resolve to lay our hands upon our mouths, and our mouths in the dust; not being able to offer one word in our own justification [...] let us in God's name rise up cheerfully and make our own way to Heaven, looking up to Jesus the author and finisher of our faith, and to the examples of those blessed saints that have gone before us, in which number you have reason to think, your dear husband deserves a place; and therefore give me leave to tell you, you are very much in the wrong, in permitting your tears to flow upon the reflection of his accomplishments, which he is now, (and not till now) receiving the reward of; and since he has been faithful in improving those gifts, that God indued[5] him with, and as far

---

[3] 'feelings of dejection'   [4] Eccl 7:15
[5] variant of endue; 'to invest' or 'endow' with some quality or faculty

as man could do, has answered the character, which David in the fifteenth Psalm gives of him that shall rest upon the holy hill, as you cannot envy, so I hope, you will not lament his promotion, nor grieve so excessively for his death, which exalts him to such a pitch of honour; and as you always thought it your happiness to have him easy whilst he was with you endeavour at least to show for his sake, you can submit to have him so without you. Your most flattering hopes could promise you the enjoyment of him but a very little longer, and if it were in your choice, whether you would live five years with so good an husband, or ten years with a worse, I know you would choose the former; and now since God has been so gracious, not only to give you a man that exceeded your wishes but let you pass thrice that number of years, in mutual love without the least disgust;[6] you must not spend all the remainder of your time, in thinking upon what you have lost; but consider how very few women are so blessed at all, and of those few how seldom their happiness lasts so long as yours has done.

[6] 'distastefulness'

Suggested further reading
Jacqueline Broad, *The Philosophy of Mary Astell: An Early Modern Theory of Virtue* (Oxford: Oxford University Press, 2015).
Alice Sowaal and Penny A. Weiss (eds.), *Feminist Interpretations of Mary Astell* (University Park, PA: Pennsylvania State University Press, 2016).
Patricia Springborg, *Mary Astell: Theorist of Freedom from Domination* (Cambridge: Cambridge University Press, 2005).

PART III
Knowing and Understanding Death

Though I be foul, ugly, lean, and mishape,
    Yet there is none in all this world wide,
That may my power withstand or escape;
    Therefore sage father, greatly magnified,
    Descend from your chair, set apart your pride,
Vouchsafe to lend, tho' it be to your pain,
To me, a fool, some of your wise brain.

    Thomas More, 'Death' from 'Pageant Verses' in *Works*
    (London: 1557; STC 18076), C3^r

He that liveth well shall make a good end, and in the day of death his decease shall be blessed, for he rest from his labours and his works do follow him. But to him that liveth ill, death is an ever-dying death: he lies tormented with the pangs of the dying flesh, amazed with the corrosive fires of the mind, frighted with the terror of that is to come, grieved with remorse of that which is past, stung with the gnawing of a guilty conscience, terrified with the rigour of a severe judge, vexed with approach of a loathsome sepulchre.

    Elizabeth Grymeston, *Miscellanea, Meditations, Memoratives*
    (London: 1604; STC 12407), D2^v

Desire with David (my best sister) to understand the Law of the Lord your God, live still to die, that you by death may purchase eternal life, and trust not that the tenderness of your age shall lengthen your life: for unto God, when he calleth, all hours, times and seasons are alike, and blessed are they whose lamps are furnished when he cometh, for as soon will the Lord be glorified in the young as in the old. My good sister once again more let me intreat thee to learn to die; deny the World, defy the Devil, and despise the Flesh, and delight yourself only in the Lord.

    Lady Jane Grey, *Four Principal Discourses Written with her*
    own Hands (London: 1615; STC 7281), C2^v–C3^r

The world's a bubble, and the life of man
    Less than a span:
In his conception wretched, from the womb
    So to the tomb;
Curst from his cradle, and brought up to years
    With cares and fears.
Who then to frail mortality shall trust,
But limns the water or writes in dust.

Thomas Farnaby, 'In vitam humana' in *Florilegium epigrammatum græcorum* (London: 1671; Wing F450), A4^v–A5^v

Introduction to Part III

Death played a vital role in Renaissance humanism in both concrete and abstract ways. Paul Oskar Kristeller has characterized this movement as an attitude toward learning and an approach to virtuous living 'that affected more or less deeply all aspects of the culture of the time'.[1] Much of the impetus of early Renaissance humanism stemmed from the antiquarian enterprise of rediscovering ancient texts and architectural remains, such as the Laocoön statuary group unearthed in 1506 in a vineyard near the ruins of Nero's Domus Aurea. The programme of this statue, easily reconstructed from classical texts then steadily being brought out in print,[2] vividly portrays the agonizing death throes of a Trojan priest and his sons. They are set upon by serpents sent by Athena (who favoured the Greeks in the Trojan War) to punish Laocoön for having urged the immediate burning of the Greeks' 'parting-gift' of a temple-sized wooden horse. Such archaeological discoveries sparked renewed interest in old sarcophagi, tomb sculptures and friezes, and inscriptions, consistent with the general effort to reconstruct a body of knowledge from long-dead civilizations otherwise consigned to oblivion.

Renaissance humanism was part and parcel of an educational programme championed by Petrarch[3] and Valla in Italy, and, in Northern Europe, Agricola and Erasmus (III.1). Many of these rediscovered classical statues and inscriptions, like translations of pre-Christian works, offered new perspectives on perennial themes involving virtuous living and mortal temporality (III.8 and III.16). A number of these texts, especially by Plato and Aristotle, long believed to have been lost, had in fact been preserved, annotated, and studied by Islamic and Jewish intellectuals in the academies and courts of the Levant and North Africa. Of these 'recovered texts', pan-European humanists tended to value those of moral philosophy because that discipline most congenially chimed with the reformed religious thinking then being entertained by self-proclaimed 'evangelicals'.[4]

---

[1] Paul Oskar Kristeller, 'Humanism', in *The Cambridge History of Renaissance Philosophy*, ed. C. B. Schmitt et al. (Cambridge: Cambridge University Press, 1988), pp. 111–138, 111.
[2] The *locus classicus* is found in the *Aeneid*, Virgil *EGA*, 2.282–316; the original Rhodian statue is praised by Pliny *NH*, 36.37.
[3] See entry II.8 (Sidney).
[4] Diarmaid MacCulloch, *The Reformation* (New York: Penguin, 2005), p. 353.

Like Erasmus, most Christian humanists were sceptical about monastic life and Scholasticism's capacity to provide the proper basis for learning how to 'die well' (III.1). Owing to their intensive training in Greek and Latin (and also Hebrew for some), humanists were ably equipped to translate the Bible, along with patristic commentaries as well as psalters, prayer books, and home devotional manuals (III.3). Another by-product of widespread humanist education was a bumper-crop of teachers, accounting for increased literacy in prosperous towns that could hire them and leading to more 'open and tolerant spirituality' and 'a ready audience for some of the writings or personal proselytising of the most independent-minded thinkers of the period'.[5] Along with this liberality of thought, co-mingled with ideas from the classical tradition, came a reflexive questioning about the nature of faith in the face of death (III.7, III.10, and III.16). The circulating of scholarly works that had been accorded some level of cultural cachet, previously the exclusive province of the manuscript tradition (whether in the monastery, university, or domestic sphere), was rapidly becoming the bread and butter of the print trade.

Part of this growing interest in making available the best of the ancients to an increasingly large audience of often new readers involved filtering and repackaging the pagan classics in novel ways, as with Lodge's complete works of Seneca which has a full explanatory apparatus (III.8). Furthermore, a premium was placed on presenting those ideas in as accessible a way as possible, such as Creech's much abridged translation of Lucretius (III.16). Accordingly, by the mid-seventeenth century, discourses and familiar essays were being published that showed a reinvigorated interest in the human soul or spirit, taking into account the validity and logical necessity of emotions and sense impressions (III.15 and III.17). At the same time, new didactic compilations brought together the extent of what could be known about the workings of the human body, not based on Aristotle but on a renovated materialist philosophy, empirical observation, and surgical procedures (III.11). To be sure, the old metaphors concerning the physiological workings of the body, humoral science, and the Galenic tradition still informed efforts to know and to understand the whole person while keeping death at bay (III.2 and III.5).

Consistent with the humanist impulse to extend the boundaries of what can be known and accomplished, bolstered by the strength of reason and

---

[5] Ibid., p. 371. On the itinerant preaching of Anne Askew, see entry II.4.

actualized by the force of will, was an ever-widening view of the world occasioned by mercantile voyages aimed principally at opening trade routes and maintaining outposts (III.13); and, correlatively, the ruthless enforcing of the colonial project when subduing people from other lands and cultures was deemed expedient (III.12). With greater economic prosperity, especially in the wake of the Restoration, came schemes to preserve and protect what had been acquired and insure against loss – hence the call for dispassionate ways of thinking about death, as with John Graunt's statistical method that underlies the origins of modern actuarial science (III.14). Linked to this drive to objectively apply logic to social issues was a rising concern for the legal rights, status, and education of women (III.6 and III.15).[6] Another part of the legacy of Renaissance humanism involved ingeniously reframing and reassessing flashpoints in recent history, exemplarily the fall of Cardinal Wolsey (III.4) and the Sea Battle of Lepanto (III.9). Each of the entries in Part III, then, is representative of some salient aspect of the death arts in Renaissance England's humanistically orientated publications from Tudor times to the co-regency of William III and Mary II; from the veneration of the classics, sententiously sprinkled throughout original treatises and literary exercises, to a more vitalist world view where experimental science and pragmatic philosophy would hold sway.

---

[6] See also entries II.17 (Astell) and IV.11 (Lanyer).

III.1

THOMAS PAYNELL

The Despising of the World (1532)

About the author

Thomas Paynell (d.1564?), canon of Merton Priory, Surrey, attended St Mary's, the Austin canons' college at Oxford. A prolific translator of humanist authors (most notably Juan Luis Vives and Desiderius Erasmus), as well as those having special interest to Catholics (St Bernard's *Living Well*) and to Protestants (Luther's exposition on Psalm 127), Paynell's irenic approach to Christianity – following Erasmus's lead – made it possible for him to serve as chaplain to Henry VIII, orator to Catholic Queen Mary, and then later orator to Elizabeth I.

About the text

Erasmus's *De contemptu mundi* (written 1485–1488) praises the contemplative life, but ultimately argues that traditional monastic practices and attitudes (such as contempt for things of the world and putting spiritual concerns above temporal gains) can be applied beyond the cloister. Our excerpt comes from chapter 6, 'Of the necessity of death, which suffers nothing to be durable'. Typical of Erasmus's commonplace method of exposition, a wide array of classical references set the groundwork for his original treatment of a broader issue; in this case, how to live a moral life in a world that is, by its very nature, subject to corruption and error.[1] Erasmus's works on philology, educational reform, theology, and political theory were extremely influential throughout Europe but especially in England, initially because of a close relationship with Thomas More to whom his *Praise of Folly* (1509) was dedicated and in whose house it was written.

The arts of death

There is a long tradition of spurning acquisitiveness and the allures of worldly pursuits in hope of living and dying well. It embraces scriptural wisdom

[1] Cf. I.3 (Lupset).

literature (Proverbs and Ecclesiastes), schools of ancient philosophy (Cynicism and Stoicism), classical satire (Juvenal and Horace), the Gospels (for example, Luke 18:22–30), monastic conduct books (Leander of Seville's *De institutione virginum et contemptu mundi*), and medieval devotional manuals (*De miseria humanae conditionis* of Pope Innocent III). All of these strands come together in a work of neo-Latin verse satire, *De contemptu mundi*, by the Benedictine monk, Bernard of Cluny. Owing in part to Bernard's scathing criticism of church officials and Rome, the work was not printed until 1557;[2] thereafter, it was reprinted frequently in the service of the Protestant cause. Paynell's choice to translate into vernacular English Erasmus's contribution to this genre at the dawning of Henry VIII's break with Rome testifies above all else to the durability – and flexibility – of this perennial offshoot of the *memento mori* tradition.

Textual notes

De co[n]temptu mundi the dispisyng of the worlde (London: 1532; STC 10470.8), E4r–F4r.

The Despising of the World

But touching death (because I spoke thereof), I am wont specially to marvel how this should be that seeing that nothing is so much in our sight as death, is that nothing is more farther out of our thought and remembrance. Yea and mortal folks are deducted and drawn out of this vocabulary or word *mors*, that is to say death. Wherefore we can no sooner be named *mortals*, that is to say mortal folks, but forthwith our own ears give us warning of death. What an oblivion or a forgetfulness is this? How reckless are folks' minds, yea may I not say how fond and frantic? Have we no more remembrance? Have we drunk so much forgetfulness of the River Lethe that we cannot bear those things in mind, that which show themselves and appear still to us on every side? Be we as it were stones astonied[3] at these things, the

---

[2] Matthias Flacius Illyricus, *Varia doctorum piorumque virorum de corrupto ecclesiae statu poemata* (Basel: 1557); Flacius was also a motive force behind the ardently Lutheran *Magdeburg Centuries* (Basel, 1559–1574), a survey of thirteen centuries of ecclesiastical history, dedicated to Elizabeth I on the year of her coronation.

[3] 'astonished'; 'dazed'

which we both see and hear so often times cannot move nor stir us? Can we see so much as one of the old world alive? And also we see that cruel death spareth or forbeareth no kind of folks in our time. Our forefathers of old time be dead and gone. And as Cicero sayeth: 'They have lived'.[4] And without any difference we must go the same way, and others that be to come shall follow after us. And so all we in manner of a swift river roll into the ocean,[5] that is to say we be all whirled into the pit of death. And as Horace sayeth,[6] 'One night abideth for us all and once[7] we must needs tread the trace[8] of death'. The funerals of young and old are very thick mingled together. And cruel Proserpine[9] forbeareth no man. Innumerable people of young, old, and middle age die here and there; of our fellows, of our acquaintance, of our kinfolk, friends, father, mother, and children, and we ourselves that must needs die. […] There be a thousand manner of sicknesses, a thousand chances or occasions of death, a thousand manner of murders, and a thousand sorts of snares that death layeth for us, through the which more die than by ancientness[10] and time. […] But and we would at all times consider the unsteadfastness and wavering of this deceitful life, and how that death still continually hangeth over us, we should drive into our own ears that which the prophet said unto the sick king: 'Dispose thy house, for thou shalt die'.[11] […] Look, seest thou not that death is at thy door, the which from this high estate will throw thee headlong to the ground, as it were a whirlwind, it will bear or carry away both thee and all thine? Wherefore Rodolphus Agricola[12] did not only right cunningly but also as veritably or truly indite as followeth:

> Death overthrow wealth and destroyeth all thing
> And all that is born must needs decay

---

[4] Plutarch, 'Cicero', in *Lives*, trans. Bernadotte Perrin, Loeb Classical Library (Cambridge, MA: Harvard University Press, 1919), vol. 7, 22.2–3. It is also quoted in Desiderius Erasmus, *Collected Works of Erasmus, Adages: I Vi 1 to I x 100*, trans. R. A. B. Mynors (Toronto, ON: University of Toronto Press, 1989), vol. 32, I.ix.50, '*Fuimus Troes*' ['We were Trojans'].
[5] A homiletic commonplace; see Hugh of St Victor's dialogue between Reason and the Soul, *De vanitate mundi*, which circulated steadily and widely in many forms throughout the period.
[6] Horace *OD*, 2.3.25   [7] 'sooner or later'   [8] 'beaten path'
[9] a Roman goddess of the underworld; Horace *OD*, 1.28.20   [10] 'old age'
[11] 2 Kgs 20:1   [12] (1443?–1485) progenitor of Northern Renaissance humanism

> Only virtue shall never have ending
> And good acts or deeds shall endure alway.[13]

[...]

What, I say, shall then remain of all thy worldly riches, honours, and possessions, the which to get together thou did consume all thy life days? On whom then wilt thou seek for succor and help? O miserable wretch, to whom wilt thou go? Whither wilt thou flee? To thy riches? Helas,[14] they can nothing help thee [...]. Be wise also and consider thy state and condition betimes, prepare and have in a readiness those things with which thou being fortified thou mayst careless or without dread abide the last day. Though riches, pleasure, and nobleness were both certain and profitable, which thing is far contrary yet undoubted to one that dieth, they are a heavy burden. But then virtue beginneth to be profitable. And surely if these worldly things would never leave us, yet must we needs forgo them; but virtue never forsaketh our company nor to help us.

---

[13] This is an English paraphrase in verse of an excerpt culled from classic literature by Agricola for his *De formando studio* (1484), originally a long letter that thirty years later was printed as a small booklet concerning a private educational programme which was to have an enormous impact on sixteenth-century pedagogy with respect to using *florilegia* as a moral filter for the pagan culture that humanists were transmitting in their translations and commentaries. See Peter Mack, 'Rudolph Agricola's Reading of Literature', *Journal of the Warburg and Courtauld Institutes*, 48 (1985), 23–41; and Rudolph Agricola, *Letters (MR 216)*, ed. Adrie van der Laan and Fokke Akkerman (Tempe, AZ: Arizona Center for Medieval and Renaissance Studies, 2002).

[14] 'alas'

Suggested further reading

Ross Dealy, *The Stoic Origins of Erasmus' Philosophy of Christ* (Toronto, ON: University of Toronto Press, 2017).

Gregory D. Dodds, *Exploiting Erasmus: The Erasmian Legacy and Religious Change in Early Modern England* (Toronto, ON: University of Toronto Press, 2009).

Helen Moore, 'Gathering Fruit: The "Profitable" Translations of Thomas Paynell', in *Tudor Translation*, Fred Schurink (ed.) (Basingstoke, UK: Palgrave Macmillan, 2011), pp. 39–57.

III.2

THOMAS ELYOT

A Preservative against Death (1545)

About the author

Thomas Elyot (*c*.1490–1546) may have gone to Oxford University, though the college he attended is unknown, and records indicate that he studied law at the Middle Temple, one of the Inns of Court. Under Henry VIII, he served as a senior clerk to the king's council and an ambassador to the Emperor Charles V, and, after losing favour in the court, devoted himself full-time to his scholarly pursuits, for which he has become recognized as an important English practitioner of Erasmian humanism.[1]

About the text

Although this short octavo treatise, the last of Elyot's publications, is his most overtly religious work, it very much continues his project of exploiting the printing press to promote learning among a vernacular readership. The preface, addressed to his neighbour and fellow knight Edward North, explains why Elyot concerns himself with matters better left to priests. Since every Christian man has the responsibility of supplying good counsel on God's laws and commandments, Elyot feels especially duty-bound. As a sheriff who has been compelled to punish transgressors of the realm's temporal edicts, he would like to do what he can to help men observe God's decrees, the disobedience of which will yield far worse punishments when Christ returns to deliver his final judgement. The treatise is loosely organized around scriptural refutations to the prosopopoeiae of the devil and his sisters – the flesh and the world.

The arts of death

Elyot takes his humanist perspective to the *ars moriendi* tradition by gathering out of scripture and the Church Fathers memorable instruction that shall be a preservative – a medical prophylactic – against 'death everlasting' (A3^v).

---

[1] On the influence of Erasmus on English humanist practices, see entries I.3 (Lupset) and III.1 (Paynell).

The title, echoing the subtitle of *The Castle of Health* whereby every person may know 'the preservation of health', sets up Elyot's continued recourse to the language of physic for understanding moral and spiritual fallibility. But it is his background in the judiciary,[2] not medicine, that, no doubt, orientates the treatise's beginning and conclusion, excerpted here, around God's ultimate tribunal. Anticipating Donne's meditative strategy of the tolling bell,[3] Elyot frames his text with an equally powerful auditory image: the Doomsday clarion, a stirring *memento mori* device with which readers can direct their thoughts each morning and evening as they await the Second Coming.

Textual notes

A preseruatiue agaynste deth (London: 1545; STC 7674), A5^r–A5^v, E1^v–E2^v.

A Preservative against Death

The high God commandeth, the angel calleth, the trumpet from heaven most terribly soundeth: arise ye that be dead and come to the Judgement.[4] Whither I do eat or drink (sayeth saint Hierom[5]) or whatsoever else that[6] I do, always this voice ringeth in mine ears: arise ye that be dead, and come to the Judgement. As often as the day of Judgement cometh to my mind, my heart and all my whole body trembleth and quaketh.[7] This is spoken by the blessed man Hierom, who not only in his childhood and youth spent his time virtuously, but also being come to the state of a man, excluded himself from all worldly business and living to the age of ninety years was ever continually occupied in spiritual exercise. Confer[8] his life with our lives, and let us behold,

---

[2] See *MA* III.1 on Elyot's *The Governor* conducing to his appointment as ambassador to the court of Charles V.
[3] See *MA* V.8, for more on Donne's strategic uses of mnemonic conceits in comparable sermons.
[4] Pseudo-Jerome, *Regula monachorum* (*PL*, 30.417)   [5] St Jerome (347–420)
[6] Marginal note: 'Hieronymus super Matth.'
[7] The original passage, which Chaucer translates in 'The Parson's Tale' in *Canterbury Tales*, Chaucer *WO*, X (I) 158–60, comes from the epigrammatic moral of 'The Fifteen Signs before Doomsday', erroneously attributed to Jerome. The moral exists in several variants and conflates a verse from 1 Corinthians 10:31, a sentence from one of Jerome's letters (*PL*, 22.644.10), and lines from the *Regula monachorum* (*PL*, 30.417), again erroneously attributed to Jerome. See Eugene F. Rice, Jr., *Saint Jerome in the Renaissance* (Baltimore, MD: Johns Hopkins University Press, 1985), pp. 161–62.
[8] 'compare'

if we ought any less to remember this sound of the trumpet: arise ye that be dead, and come to the Judgement. O good Lord, how should men here that be dead, and lacking life: how can a man rise on his feet, and if he cannot go? How may he then come to the Judgement? Yes, well enough, if thou considerest what thing that death is. Truly, death is none other thing than the privation of *corporal sensis*,[9] with the departing of the soul from the body.[10] For when we hear not, neither see, neither smell, nor taste, nor yet feel, then truly we be in dying, or else dead indeed. Christ calleth oftentimes to us: *Keep* (sayeth he)[11] *the commandments*;[12] *do works of repentance*;[13] *watch and pray*;[14] *give in my name, and ye shall receive an hundred times as much as ye give, and have life everlasting.*[15]

[…]

Many more spices may be found in holy scripture, to make a preservative more wholesome for man's soul than treacle[16] is for the body and will longer preserve it; but such as this is, being often times used, shall preserve the senses of the soul from corruption and then shall she[17] not die. But when the trumpet bloweth, although the body be dead, yet shall she go surely and safely to the throne of God, and claim his mercy, which he hath promised to them that believe in him and keep his laws. But if we do neglect it, and suffer the devil to prevail against us, with his subtle persuasions, the senses of the soul shall be taken from her and she shall be spiritually dead. Actually, she shall with her body, to whom she consented, arise and come to the Judgement, trembling and quaking, beholding above her Christ, who hath redeemed her, exceedingly angry, devils on every side of her, abiding her sentence, and all ready to swallow her. Under her hell, casting out flames of everlasting fire, ready to rake her, none there of her acquaintance, which shall be then able to help her. Princes being in equal jeopardy with her and riches being turned to powder. These things be no fables but matter true and confirmed by scripture. And who that hath any other suggestion or trust upon any excuses, he is not only deceived but his opinion is also erroneous. Wherefore let us have

---

[9] 'bodily sensations'
[10] Epicurus first defines death as 'a deprivation of sensation' ('Letter to Menoeceus', *Epicurus: The Extant Remains*, trans. Cyril Bailey (Oxford: Clarendon Press, 1926), p. 85), while death as the separation of the soul from the body goes back to the *Phaedo* in Plato *CD*, 64 c.
[11] Marginal note: 'Matt. 19. Luc. 3.'   [12] Matt 19:17   [13] Acts 26:20   [14] Luke 21:36
[15] Matt 19:29   [16] 'Theriac', a medicinal compound believed to be a panacea
[17] i.e., the soul

the sound of the trumpet in our ears, at the least in the morning and evening, thinking that the son of God cometh to the Judgement, we know not what hour. *Blessed* (sayeth Christ) *is[18] the servant, whom the Lord at his coming findeth waking: him shall he set in authority over his household.* This authority shall never be taken away. Therein shall be perpetual quietness and joy never ceasing. This household is of the company of most blessed spirits, abounding in charity, knowledge and gladness, in beholding continually in the most beautiful presence of God, the wonderful and unspeakable works of his majesty in heaven, earth, and in hell. Whereon if we truly do think, we shall pass little on[19] the devil and his sisters, nor yet fear the sound of the terrible trumpet, but desire with Saint Paul, to be separate and dissolved from this mortal body, and to be with Christ our Lord, who tenderly and most constantly loveth us, and fain would have us, if we do well our duties, who for that he suffered death for us, is worthy to receive power, divinity, sapience, fortitude, honour, glory,[20] and blessing in worlds everlasting. Amen.

[18] Marginal note: 'Luc. xii.' Luke 12:39; Matt 24:46–47
[19] 'not care much about'   [20] Rev 5:12

Suggested further reading
Pearl Hogrefe, *The Life and Times of Sir Thomas Elyot, Englishman* (Ames, IA: Iowa State University Press, 1967).
Robert G. Sullivan and Arthur E. Walzer (eds.), *Thomas Elyot: Critical Editions of Four Works on Counsel* (Leiden: Brill, 2018).

III.3

ELIZABETH I

A Godly Meditation (1548)

About the author

Elizabeth Tudor (7 September 1533–24 March 1603), daughter of Anne Boleyn (second wife of Henry VIII, beheaded for 'high treason' when Elizabeth was two years old), had a precarious minority. With the official annulment of her mother's marriage to the king in 1536 a week before the execution, Elizabeth was declared illegitimate and barred from the succession. Even though no longer a princess, owing to the efforts of her last stepmother, Katherine Parr,[1] she shared many of the same teachers (including the author of *The Schoolmaster*, Roger Ascham[2]) as her half-brother, the future Edward VI then Prince of Wales, and received a Renaissance Christian humanist education that included learning French, Italian, Spanish, Latin, and Greek. As can be seen in our excerpt, 'Lady Elizabeth' possessed near-native proficiency in French; the same can be said of her Latin. During the reign of her Catholic half-sister, Mary I, she was imprisoned in the Tower for two months and thereafter closely guarded owing to her perceived inclination toward the reformed Church. She survived to rule England after Mary's death in 1558, returning England to the Protestant *status quo ante* of young King Edward's reign.

About the text

As a New Year's gift for Katherine Parr in 1545, Elizabeth made a prose translation of a French poem by Marguerite de Navarre (who supported religious reform). The bound manuscript displays eleven-year-old Elizabeth's skill at embroidery, her laudable handwriting, and precocious learning. In line with the humanist tradition in which she was trained, it also demonstrates her practical application of foreign language study and, in translating the work of a pious noblewoman, indicates her subtle understanding of the decorum expected of her gender and rank. Within four years John Bale published Elizabeth's translation as 'A Godly Meditation of the Christian Soul'. Later, when she was queen, Elizabeth cannily allowed new editions to be released in 1568, 1582, and 1590. She kept up with her languages and translated (though did not publish) a number of classical authors, including Tacitus and Boethius.[3]

The arts of death

The composition of *Miroir de l'âme pécheresse* (1531) coincides with Marguerite de Navarre's mourning her infant son who died on Christmas Day 1530. Aspects of death encountered in life underpin this literary exercise in

---

[1] See entry I.4 (Parr).
[2] See *MA* III.2 for an excerpt from Ascham's pedagogical manual.
[3] John-Mark Philo, 'Elizabeth I's Translation of Tacitus', *Review of English Studies*, 71.298 (2020), 44–73; and '*The Consolation' of Queen Elizabeth I*, ed. Noel Harold Kaylor, Jr. and Philip Edward Phillips (Tempe, AZ: Arizona Center for Medieval and Renaissance Studies, 2009).

self-abasement and surrendering to God's divine plan. The passages excerpted here typify the work's preoccupation with situating human mortality in its proper Christian perspective by presenting a sustained focus on the paradox of the union of death and life. The female narrator addresses Christ, figured as her abiding and forgiving intercessor and companion, from a four-fold point of view – as mother, daughter, sister, and wife – such that each of these roles provides a topical heading for the presentation of biblical *exempla* that showcase the distressed who put their faith in God.

Textual notes

A Godly Medytacyon of the christen sowle (London: 1548; SCT 17320), D3^r–D4^r, D6^r, E2^v.

A Godly Meditation

O love, thou madest this agreement when thou didst join life and death together. But the union hath made alive death. Life dying, and life without end, have made one death a life. Death hath given unto life a quickness. Through such death I being dead, received life, and by death I am ravished with him which is alive. I live in thee, and as for me, of myself I am dead. And as concerning the bodily death, it is nothing else unto me, but a coming out of prison. Death is life unto me. For through death, I am alive. This mortal life filleth me full of care, and sorrow, and death yieldeth me content.

    O what a goodly thing it is to die, which causeth my soul to live. In delivering her[4] from this mortal death, it excepteth her from the death miserable, and matcheth her with a most mighty lover. And unless she thus dieth, she languisheth always. Is not then the soul blameless, which would fain[5] die for to have such life? Yes truly, and she ought to call death her well beloved friend. O sweet death, pleasant sorrow, mightily delivering from all wickedness. Those which trusted in thee (O lord) and in thy death, were mortified, because they did trust in thee, and in thy passion. For with a sweet sleep thou put them out of that death which causeth many to lament. O how happy is the same sleep unto him, which when he awaketh, doth find through thy death, the life everlasting. For the death is no other thing to a Christian man, but a liberty or deliverance from his mortal band.[6]

[4] 'the soul' [5] 'willingly desire' [6] 'something that constricts'

And the death which is fearful to the wicked is pleasant and acceptable to them that are good. Then is death through thy death[7] destroyed. Therefore, my God, if I were rightly taught, I should call the death life, and this life death, end of labour, and beginning of everlasting joy. For I know that the long life doth let me from thy sight. O death, come, and break the same obstacle of life. Or else love, do a miracle now, since that I cannot yet see my spouse transform me with him both body and soul, and then shall I the better tarry for the coming of death. Let me die that I may live with him. For there is none that can help me, unless it be thou only. O my saviour, through faith I am planted, and joined with thee. O what union is this, since that through faith I am sure of thee. And I may call thee, father, brother, son, and husband. O what gifts thou dost give, by the goodness of those names. […] In this world I cannot have perfectly this my desire. Which thing considered maketh me fervently and with all my heart, to desire the departing from this body of sin, not fearing the death nor yet any of her instruments. For what fear ought I to have of my God, which through love offered himself and suffered death not of debt or duty, but because he would for my only sake undo the power that mortal death had. Now is Jesus dead, in whom we are all dead, and through his death he causeth every man to live again. I mean those which through faith are partakers of his Passion. For even as the death before the great mystery of the cross was hard to everybody, and there was no man but was feared therewith, considering the copulation of the body and the soul, their order, love, and agreement, so were their sorrows extreme in the departing of the one from the other. […] O death where is thy sting and victory,[8] which are so much spoken of? Instead of death, thou death givest us life, and so dost thou contrary to thy will.

[7] i.e., Christ's death (Rom 7:4)   [8] 1 Cor 15:55

Suggested further reading
Anne Lake Prescott, 'Elizabeth's Marguerite: Mirroring Sinful Souls and Royalty through Black Letter', in *New Ways of Looking at Old Texts, VI*, ed. Arthur Marotti (Tempe, AZ: Renaissance English Text Society, 2019), pp. 117–26.
Susan Snyder, 'Guilty Sisters: Marguerite de Navarre, Elizabeth of England, and the *Miroir de l'âme Pécheresse*', *Renaissance Quarterly*, 50.2 (1997), 443–58.

III.4

THOMAS CHURCHYARD

A Mirror for Magistrates (1587)

About the author

Thomas Churchyard (*c*.1529–1604) served as a page to Henry Howard, Earl of Surrey. Military exploits took him several times to the Continent until he settled in London where he wrote poetry. His verse about 'Davy Dycar'[1] (*c*.1551), based on the medieval allegory *Piers Plowman* first printed in 1550,[2] brought him to the attention of William Baldwin and George Ferrers who were planning a second part of their *Mirror for Magistrates*. His ensuing 'Shore's Wife' (Edward IV's mistress) appeared in the 1563 edition; immediately popular, it was reprinted and much imitated.

About the text

Churchyard contributed periodically to the *Mirror* including, in 1587, the tragedy of Thomas Wolsey (1475?–1530), Archbishop of York and Lord Chancellor to Henry VIII who fell from favour for his inability to win papal annulment of the king's marriage to Catherine of Aragon.[3] Allowed some degree of artistic freedom by John Higgins (director of the publication of *Mirror* after Baldwin's death), Churchyard rewrote the prose introduction to 'Shore's Wife' (Ll3ʳ) with Mistress Shore introducing her own tragedy, and followed the same conceit for 'Wolsey', the volume's final entry. From *Mirror*'s first appearance in 1559 to its last major revision in 1610,[4] nearly a hundred lives are presented, ranging from Albanactus[5] (1085 BCE) to Elizabeth I (d.1603), most often written in alliterative rhyme royal stanzas.

---

[1] 'diker'; a ditch digger
[2] Lawrence Warner, 'Robert Crowley and the Alterations to a Manuscript of Piers Plowman C', *Studies in Bibliography* (in press).
[3] See entry II.1 (Hall and Grafton).
[4] On the 'Induction' to the 1610 edition, see *MA* VI.4.
[5] a descendant of Trojan Aeneas; Brutus's youngest son, linked to Scotland's founding by Geoffrey of Monmouth; see *History of the Kings of Britain*, trans. and ed. David W. Burchmore (Cambridge, MA: Harvard University Press, 2019), II.23–24, p. 43.

The arts of death

Mirror for Magistrates continued Lydgate's *Fall of Princes*.[6] The title alludes both to the medieval *speculum*[7] tradition and also to *de casibus*[8] literary conventions.[9] The poems take the form of pitiful, sometimes mangled, ghosts recalling their lives and recriminating themselves. This evokes an eerie parallax, or alternating perspective, that bespeaks a displacement or difference in the apparent position of the subjects narrating their own histories, viewed along two different, temporally conditioned lines of sight. The forlorn expostulations of these wraiths looking back on their mortal strivings and failings make the past at once viscerally and emotionally present – as a kind of loquaciously dramatized *memento mori*. The poets of the *Mirror* thereby imbue these figures from history (and pseudo-history) with an uncanny sense of admonitory reflection that is augmented by metatextual tropes. As both the narrating subject and the object of his own *exemplum*, Wolsey, in effect, holds himself up to readers as a mirror reflecting their own mortality. And yet, moreover, by way of an admonitory coda both to his story and those of the other ghosts, Wolsey is the only *Mirror* speaker to lament that it is all in vain: 'And worst of all, when we our tales have told, / Our open plagues,[10] will warning be to none' (Mm8^v).

Textual notes

The mirour for m[a]gistrates (London: 1587; STC 13445), Mm1^r–Mm8^v.

A Mirror for Magistrates

I thought it necessary as a kind of benevolence and courtesy of mind to bestow some credit on that person that not only hath preferred my tragedy to the printer (being of his own device and penning) but also hath enlarged, by plain and familiar verse, the matter the world desires to hear or read, and made things common among a multitude that were secret and held private among a few. Which study and pains of his own purpose procures me (as one whom

---

[6] See entry IV.3 (Lydgate).
[7] 'mirror' in Latin; the literary genre of assembling much knowledge about some topic within a single work
[8] from Latin *casus*, 'fall'; as a genre, using historical *exempla* to show the decline of the great
[9] nature (experience) and scripture (divine word) 'both as mirrors be to amend our faults' (Langland *PP*, 12.95)
[10] 'wounds'

Fortune hath flattered and afflicted) to appear unto him, for the hearing of my calamity and for the setting out both of my rising up and falling down. So to the whole world, by this help and mine own desire, I step out from the grave where long I lay in forgetfulness, and declare in the voice of a cardinal a curious discourse; yet sadly and sorrowfully told, as well unto Churchyard (the noter[11] thereof) as to the rest that pleaseth to hear any piece of my misfortune.

1–14

Shall I look on, when states[12] step on the stage,
And play their parts, before the people's face?
Some men live now, scarce four score years of age,
Who in time past, did know the Cardinal's grace.
A gamesome world, when bishops run at base,[13]
Yea, get a fall, in striving for the goal,
And body lose, and hazard seely[14] soul.

Ambitious mind, a world of wealth would have,
So scrats[15] and scraps,[16] for scorfe,[17] and scorvy[18] dross:[19]
And till the flesh, and bones, be laid in grave,
Wit never rests, to grope for muck[20] and moss.
Fie[21] on proud pomp, and gilded bridle's boss.[22]
O glorious gold, the gaping[23] after thee,
So blinds men's eyes, they can no danger see.

[...]

36–42

My chance was great, for from a poor man's son,
I rose aloft, and chopped[24] and changed degree:
In Oxford first, my famous name begun,

---

[11] one assigned to keep a written record of what is spoken in a meeting or interview for future reference
[12] 'those of high estate'; 'people of rank and privilege'
[13] 'prisoners' base'; game of chase and tag akin to 'Barley-Break'
[14] an archaic form of 'silly', denoting vulnerability
[15] 'scratches'   [16] 'fights'   [17] 'cast-off tissue'; 'scab'
[18] 'scurvy'; 'contemptible'   [19] 'scum'; 'impure remains'
[20] 'manure'; a term of contempt often used to designate corrupting worldly goods
[21] an exclamation expressing disdain   [22] a gold-plated ornament on a horse's bridle
[23] 'desire greedily'   [24] 'moved suddenly or violently'

Where many a day, the scholars honoured me.
  Then thought I how, I might a courtier be:
So came to court, and feathered there my wing,
With Henry th' Eight, who was a worthy king.

[…]

463–476

I told you how, from Cawood[25] I was led,
And so fell sick when I arrested was:[26]
What needeth now, what more words herein be said?
I knew full well, I must to prison pass,
And saw my state, as brittle as a glass:[27]
So gave up ghost,[28] and bade the world farewell,
Wherein, God wot,[29] I could no longer dwell.

  Thus unto dust, and ashes I returned,
When blaze of life, and vital breath went out,
Like glowing coal that is to cinders burned:
All flesh and blood, so end, you need not doubt.
But when the bruit[30] of this was blown about,
The world was glad, the Cardinal was in grave,
This is of world lo[31] all the hope we have.

---

[25] a North Yorkshire village, whose castle was the residence of the Archbishops of York
[26] Marginal note: 'He died of a continual flyxe [flux; dysentery] in the Abbey of Leicester, as Stowe writeth.'
[27] 'mirror'; another of the self-reflexive references to the book's title and aim
[28] 'soul'; 'spirit' (ME. *gast*)   [29] 'knows'   [30] 'report'
[31] an interjection calling attention to the main matter (namely, that all will end in the grave)

Suggested further reading
Paul Budra, '*A Mirror for Magistrates' and the 'de casibus' Tradition* (Toronto, ON: University of Toronto Press, 2000).
Scott Lucas (ed.), *A Mirror for Magistrates* (Cambridge: Cambridge University Press, 2019), pp. xv–xlii.
Matthew Woodcock, *Thomas Churchyard* (Oxford: Oxford University Press, 2016), pp. 230–35.

III.5

THOMAS COGAN

The Haven of Health (1588)

About the author

Thomas Cogan (*c*.1545–1607) was a fellow of Oriel College, Oxford, until he accepted the position of schoolmaster at a grammar school in Manchester, where he also practised medicine. In 1595, he donated Galen's works along with other medical books to Oriel's library.

About the text

Cogan's work is an English regimen, a category of medical writing identified as the largest and most popular among the 153 separate vernacular medical titles published in England between 1486 and 1604.[1] Vernacular regimens, essentially handbooks addressed to medical laity, particularly students, proposed preventative methods and routines to regulate one's eating, habits, and activities with physical well-being in mind. In his dedicatory preface, Cogan explains how his handbook, like its peers, concentrates on hygiene, the conservation of health, rather than on therapeutics, the treatment of disease. But unlike its peers, his handbook deviates slightly from the six non-naturals of the Galenic tradition (air, food and drink, rest and exercise, sleep and waking, excretions and retentions [coitus], and the mental passions), which distinguished themselves from the natural things (elements, complexions, humours, members, powers, operations, and spirits) and the things against nature (sickness, cause of sickness, and accident). For the benefit of preserving the Englishman's health, Cogan organizes his treatise according to the briefer and more memorable Hippocratic aphorism 'Labour, meat, drink, sleep, Venus all in measure' (¶¶3ᵛ). The largest portion of the book concerns recipes for preparing food, given diet's centrality to the Hippocratic and Galenic canon. In the excerpt, Cogan considers how a person's age determines what food he

---

[1] Paul Slack, 'Mirrors of Health and Treasures of Poor Men: The Uses of the Vernacular Medical Literature of Tudor England', in *Health, Medicine, and Mortality in the Sixteenth Century*, ed. Charles Webster (Cambridge: Cambridge University Press, 1979), pp. 238–39, 243.

or she should consume. Cogan's work, though popular, did not surpass the sixteen editions of Thomas Elyot's *The Castle of Health*, the period's exemplar of the vernacular regimen.

The arts of death

In the excerpt, from the beginning of chapter 213, Cogan draws upon a Galenic tradition stemming from the second book of *On Temperaments*, where Galen correlates the stages of life with the qualities of heat, cold, moisture, and dryness.[2] This tradition, which took the four humours to be derivatives of the four elements along with their qualities, regarded the body's ageing as a progression from the robust heat and moisture of youth to the enfeebling cold and dryness of senescence. As with many early modern medical writers, Cogan pictures the process of a 'natural death' by resorting to the Aristotelian and Galenic trope of a lamp's flame: when the oil (the radical moisture) is consumed by the burning (the innate heat), the light (vitality) is extinguished.

Textual notes

The hauen of health chiefly made for the comfort of students ... (London: 1588; STC 5479), AA4^r–BB1^r. This, the second edition after that of 1584, translates the first's Latin quotations.

The Haven of Health

The third thing appertaining to diet is the age of the party, which may the better be perceived, if first I define[3] what age is and what difference there is in age. Age, after Fuchsius,[4] is the race of life, wherein manifestly the state of the body of itself is changed. And in the same chapter, according to Galen, he maketh five parts or differences of age, to wit, childhood from our birth to fifteen years, hot and moist. Adolescency, from fifteen years to five and

---

[2] See entry for Levinus Lemnius, *MA* III.3.
[3] Marginal note: 'what age is and what difference in age. Inst. Lib. I Sect. 3. Cap. 5' (Leonhart Fuchs, *Institutionum medicinae ad Hippocratis, Galeni, aliorumque veterum scripta recte intelligenda mire utiles libri quinque* (Venice: 1550), bk. 1, sec. 3, ch. 5).
[4] Leonhart Fuchs (1501–1566), botanist and professor of medicine at Tübingen, Germany

twenty, of a mean and perfect temperature. Lusty *juventus*,[5] from twenty-five years to thirty-five, hot and dry. Middle age or man's age, from thirty-five years, to forty-nine, declining to cold and dry. Old age from forty-nine years until the end of life, naturally cold and dry, as touching the substance of all parts of the body though accidentally by excrements, as spittle, phlegm, and such like, it may seem to be of moist temperature. In all this course of life, there is a continual change of the body, but especially every seventh year, which of the philosophers is called *annus criticus*,[6] the year of judgement, at which time ordinarily (as they say) we are in greater danger touching life and death, than in any other years. How be it evermore the saying of Job is true,[7] *man that is born of a woman, liveth but a while, and is full of miseries, he cometh forth like a flower, and is withered, and passeth away as a shadow, and never abideth in one state*, which Hippocrates also confesseth in the very first aphorism,[8] saying, *life is short*.[9] And if we do consider well the state of mankind in this life, we may see that a man beginneth to die as soon as he is born into this world, for that the radical moisture,[10] which is the root of life, can never be restored and made up again, so good as it was at our nativity, but continually by little and little decayeth until the last end of our life.[11] Yet by that moisture which cometh of nourishment, through meat and drink, it is preserved and prolonged, so that it is not so soon wasted and consumed as otherwise it would be. Like as a lamp, by pouring oil moderately, the light is long kept burning, yet it goeth out at the last. And this is it which Hippocrates speaketh,[12] *The same heat which brought us forth consumeth us*. Yet the beginning of our age, while nature is yet strong, more of the nourishment is converted into the substance of the body than is consumed, and that while the body increaseth and groweth. Afterward so much only is restored as is wasted, and then the body is in perfect growth: at length nature waxing weaker is not able to restore and repair so much as is wasted and decayed, whereby the body

[5] 'youth'   [6] Marginal note: '*Annus Criticus*' [critical year].
[7] Marginal note: 'cap. 14' [Job 14:1–2].
[8] Marginal note: 'man beginneth to die as soon as he is born.'
[9] Hippocrates, *Aphorisms*, in *Nature of Man. Regimen in Health. Humours. Aphorisms. Regimen 1–3. Dreams.* Heracleitus, *On the Universe*, trans. W. H. S. Jones, Loeb Classical Library (Cambridge, MA: Harvard University Press, 1931), 1.1. On the currency of this aphorism in early modern England, see also entry III.8 (Lodge).
[10] Galenic medicine's concept of the moisture necessary for the continuance of the body's vitality
[11] Marginal note: 'how meat and drink do preserve life.'
[12] Marginal note: 'Ga. de mar. cap. 3. One cause of life and death in man.' (Galen, *De marcore*, in *Galeni opera omnia*, ed. C. G. Kühn, vol. 7 (Leipzig: Car. Cnoblochii, 1821–1833), ch. 3, pp. 672–77).

beginneth to decrease, and the powers and strength thereof be more and more diminished until such time as life, even[13] as the light of a lamp, be clean extinguished. And this is called natural death, which few attain unto, but are prevented by death casual, when by sickness, or otherwise, the said natural moisture is overwhelmed and suffocate.[14] Now the means to preserve this natural moisture, and consequently to preserve life, is to use meats and drinks, according to the age of the person. For the diet of youth is not convenient for old age; nor contrariwise, as Hippocrates[15] teacheth, *Natural heat aboundeth in them which are growing, wherefore they need much nourishment, for otherwise, their bodies would decay. But in old men, there is little heat; therefore, they need little food, for much overcometh them.*

---

[13] Marginal note: 'natural death, what it is.'   [14] past participle
[15] Marginal note: 'a diverse diet requisite in youth and age 1 Apho. 14'; the italicized sentence is from *Aphorisms*, in *Nature of Man*, 1.14.

Suggested further reading
Jennifer Richards, 'Useful Books: Reading Vernacular Regimens in Sixteenth-Century England', *Journal of the History of Ideas*, 73.2 (2012), 247–71.
Daniel Schäfer, 'More than a Fading Flame: The Physiology of Old Age between Speculative Analogy and Experimental Method', in *Blood, Sweat and Tears: the Changing Concepts of Physiology from Antiquity into Early Modern Europe*, ed. H. F. J. Horstmanshoff, Helen King, and Claus Zittel (Leiden: Brill, 2012), pp. 241–66.
Wear, *Medicine*.

III.6

JANE ANGER

Protection for Women (1589)

About the author

Jane Anger (*fl.* 1588), about whom we know nothing, may have been a pseudonym for the pamphlet's author, whose first dedicatory letter plays upon the choler implied by the surname. The potential pseudonym raises the further possibility that a man penned the pamphlet, although many scholars take the author to be a woman.

About the text

This short pamphlet is the first known defence of women written by an English woman in the long-standing genre known as the *querelle des femmes*, which debated the question of whether or not the feminine was the superior sex. Anger's lively and witty counter-attack upon men appears to respond to *Boke his Surfeit in Love*, no copies of which survive. Thomas Orwin, the printer of Anger's pamphlet, entered this other title in the Stationers' Register in 1588. With psychological acumen, Anger argues that male railing against the beloved's putative seductiveness or wantonness for drawing lovers into folly conceals the surfeited lover's discontent and self-loathing at having been overtaken by his own filthy lust.

The arts of death

The excerpt stands on its head the commonplace complaint in the period's poetry that the beloved, the frigid courtly lady, will precipitate the lover's death (see Beaumont's parody of this trope, entry II.14). Man's lecherous tongue actually threatens women with mortal peril. But when it comes to braving death on behalf of duty, many classical exemplars, as seen in Anger's catalogue of heroic women, can also silence the Surfeiter's[1] irrational calumny.

Textual notes

Jane Anger her protection for women (London: 1589; STC 644), C3ʳ–C4ʳ.

Protection for Women

It is a wonder to see how men can flatter themselves with their own conceits, for let us look, they will straight affirm that we love, and if then lust pricketh them, they will swear that love stingeth us. Which imagination only is sufficient to make them assay the scaling of half a dozen of us in one night, when they will not stick[2] to swear that if they should be denied of their requests, death must needs follow.[3] Is it any marvel, though, they surfeit when they are so greedy, but is it not pity that any of them should perish,

---

[1] i.e., the author of *Boke his Surfeit in Love* [2] 'continue firmly in a belief'
[3] On this literary topos, see IV.4 (Howard).

which will be so soon killed with unkindness? Yes truly. Well, the onset[4] given, if we retire for a vantage, they will straight affirm that they have got the victory. Nay, some of them are so carried away with conceit that shameless they will blaze abroad among their companions that they have obtained the love of a woman, unto whom they never spake above once, if that. Are not these froward[5] fellows? You must bear with them, because they dwell far from lying neighbours.[6] They will say *mentiri non est nostrum*,[7] and yet you shall see true tales come from them, as wild geese fly under London bridge.[8] Their fawning is but flattery, their faith falsehood, their fair words allurements to destruction, and their large promises tokens of death, or of evils worse than death. Their singing is a bait to catch us, and their playings plagues to torment us. And, therefore, take heed of them, and take this as an axiom in logic and a maxim in the law: *nulla fides hominibus*.[9] There are three accidents[10] to men, which, of all, are most inseparable: lust, deceit, and malice—their glozing[11] tongues, the preface to the execution of their vile minds and their pens the bloody executioners of their barbarous manners. A little gall maketh a great deal of sweet sour, and a slanderous tongue poisoneth all the good parts in man.

Was not the folly of Vulcan worthy of Venus's flouts, when she took him with the manner, wooing Briceris?[12] And was it not the flattery of Paris which enticed Helen to falsehood?[13] Yes truly. And the late Surfeiter[14] his remembrance in calling his pen from raging against reason showeth that he is not quite without flattery, for he putteth the fault in his pen, when it was his passion that deserved reproof. The love of Hypsicratea[15] and Pantheia,[16] the

---

[4] 'To give onset' is to begin a military assault.
[5] 'unmanageable'; 'contrary to reason'
[6] 'He dwells far from neighbours (has ill neighbours) that is fain to praise himself' (*DPE*, N117).
[7] 'we are not liars'
[8] 'London Bridge was made for wise men to go over and fools to go under' (*DPE*, L417).
[9] 'There is no truth in men'; see *DPE*, F34.   [10] non-essential properties
[11] deceitfully flattering
[12] Briceris was Vulcan's paramour, whom he gave up for Venus. See *Tell-Troth's New-Year's Gift* (London: 1593; STC 23867.5), E2ʳ.
[13] Paris's abduction of Helen from Menelaus started the Trojan War.
[14] See n.1 in this entry.
[15] the Queen of Pontus (*fl.* 63 BCE), who followed her husband into exile
[16] the Queen of Susa (*fl.* 550 BCE), who committed suicide when her husband died in battle

zeal of Artemisia[17] and Portia,[18] the affection of Sulpicia[19] and Arria,[20] the true fancy of Hipparchia[21] and Pisca,[22] the loving passions of Macrina[23] and of the wife of Paudocrus[24] (all manifested in his *Surfeit*[25]) shall condemn the indiscreetness of men's minds, whose hearts delight in naught, save that only which is contrary to good. Is it not a foolish thing to be sorry for things unrecoverable? Why then should Sigismunda's[26] answer be so descanted[27] upon, seeing her husband was dead, and she thereby free for any man. Of the abundance of the heart, the mouth speaketh, which is verified by the railing kind of man's writing. Of all kind of voluptuousness, they affirm lechery to be the chiefest, and yet some of them are not ashamed to confess publicly that they have surfeited therewith. It defileth the body, and makes it stink, and men use it. I marvel how we women can abide them but if they delude us, as (they say) we deceive them with perfumes.

[17] the ruler of Caria (d.350 BCE), who built a wonder of the ancient world, the eponymous mausoleum for her husband, and, stricken with inconsolable grief, mixed her husband's ashes into her daily drink
[18] the Roman wife (70–43 BCE) of Marcus Brutus, Julius Caesar's chief assassin, who swallowed hot coals upon learning of Brutus's death
[19] the Roman wife of Lentulus Cruscellio, who followed him into exile in 43 BCE
[20] the Roman wife (d.42 CE) of Aulus Caecina Paetus, who showed her husband how to commit suicide after the emperor condemned him to death
[21] a Greek woman (*fl.* 325 BCE), who against her family's wishes married a poor Cynic philosopher
[22] wife who committed suicide with her dying husband (Pierre de La Primaudaye, *The French Academy*, trans. T(homas) B(owes) (London: 1586; STC 15233, LL5ʳ))
[23] the wife of the consul Torquatus, who did not leave her house for the duration of her husband's year-long voyage (La Primaudaye, LL5ᵛ)
[24] probably the wife of Pandoërus in La Primaudaye (LL5ʳ), who chose suicide over marriage to the Persian king who slayed her husband
[25] Anger says this list appeared in her opponent's work *Boke his Surfeit in Love*, but the list of women can also be found in La Primaudaye, *The French Academy*, 'Of the particular duty of a wife towards her husband'.
[26] Ghismonda in Boccaccio's *Decameron* (Day 4, Tale 1), whose love for her father's squire led to his death and her suicide. See *The Decameron: Selected Tales*, trans. and ed. Donald Beecher and Massimo Ciavolella (Peterborough, Canada: Broadview, 2017), pp. 135–43.
[27] 'carped at'; Ghismonda was criticized for defending her sexual freedom.

Suggested further reading
Mark Breitenberg, *Anxious Masculinity in Early Modern England* (Cambridge: Cambridge University Press, 1996), pp. 171–74.
Lynne A. Magnusson, '"His pen with my hande": Jane Anger's revisionary rhetoric', *English Studies in Canada*, 17 (1991), 269–81.

III.7

JOHN FLORIO

Montaigne's Essays (1603)

About the author

John Florio (1553–1625), son of a Protestant Italian immigrant, like his father was a translator and teacher of foreign languages. Supported by William Cecil, Lord Burghley and favoured by Robert Dudley, Earl of Leicester, Florio published dual-language phrase books to instruct courtiers in conversational Italian as well as Continental ideas and manners. A fixture at the French embassy during the 1580s, he went on to translate new humanist works such as Montaigne's *Essays*. With James I's accession, Florio became language tutor to Prince Henry and later Queen Anne, to whom his Italian–English dictionary is dedicated.

About the text

This is the first English edition of the *Essays* by Michel de Montaigne, originally published in French (1580–1588). It is marked by the same studied nonchalance as the original, albeit freshly augmented by Florio's exuberant and accretive prose style. Drawing on classical precedents and building on the humanist commonplace book approach to composition, Montaigne in effect invented the 'essay' form. He suggestively uses the word *essai* ('trial' or 'attempt') to describe his literary exercises that combine the rigorous testing of ideas (following Pyrrhonic Scepticism[1]) with a new mode of unflinching self-exposure, self-exploration, and self-discovery.

The arts of death

This entry, typical of the earliest written parts of Montaigne's *Essays*, bristles with classical quotations and anecdotes about death in order to test the Epicurean and Stoical concept of the highest good, *ataraxia* (tranquillity achieved by indifference to fortune). By looking back to and recuperating

---

[1] See *MA* 'Introduction to Part IV' (esp. p. 187).

this materialist pagan perspective on self-control, the author is able to sidestep and tacitly criticize the religious comfort offered by the *ars moriendi*. The deathbed scene alluded to in our excerpt expresses impatience with doctors, mourners, and prelates; it rails against displays of grief. The *vanitas* genre itself is thus turned on its head, shown to be yet another instantiation of mortal vanity. Consistent with the Stoic principles of Seneca and Cicero, derived from Epicurus and promoted by Roman poets including Lucretius, Manilius, and Horace (all of whom – and many more besides – are quoted by Montaigne and translated by Florio into folksy English rhymed couplets), death should be greeted with an imperturbability befitting the *ataraxia* which one has sought to practise throughout life and not just at its end.

Textual notes

The Essayes, or Morall, Politike, and Millitarie Discourses of Lo: Michaell de Montaigne … done into English by … John Florio (London: 1603; STC 18041), D3ᵛ–E2ʳ.

Montaigne's Essays

Cicero sayeth, that to 'philosophise is no other thing, than for a man to prepare himself to death',[2] which is the reason that study and contemplation doth in some sort withdraw our soul from us and severally employ it from the body, which is a kind of apprentisage[3] and resemblance of death. Or else it is, that all the wisdom and discourse of the world, doth in the end resolve upon this point, to teach us, not to fear to die. […] Let us learn to stand and combat her[4] with a resolute mind. And begin to take the greatest advantage she hath upon us from her, let us take a clean contrary way from the common, let us remove her strangeness from her, let us converse, frequent, and acquaint ourselves with her, let us have nothing so much in mind as death, let us at all times and seasons, and in the ugliest manner that may be, yea, with all faces shapen[5] and represent the same unto our imagination. At the stumbling of a horse, at the fall of a stone, at the least prick with a pin, let us presently

---

[2] Cicero *TD*, 1.31.   [3] 'apprenticeship'; 'learning by practice'
[4] i.e., Death; *la mort* in French is feminine, hence the feminine pronoun
[5] 'given the form of'; see 'The Wife of Bath's Prologue' in *Canterbury Tales*, Chaucer *WO*, III (D) 139: 'Crist was a mayde and shapen as a man'.

ruminate and say with ourselves, what if it were death itself? And thereupon let us take heart of grace and call our wits together to confront her. […] So did the Egyptians, who in the middest[6] of their banquetings, and in the full of their greatest cheer, caused the anatomy[7] of a dead man to be brought before them, as a memorandum and warning to their guests.

> *Omnem crede diem tibi diluxisse supremum,*
> *Grata superveniet, quae non sperabitur hora.*[8]

> Think every day shines on thee as thy last,
> Welcome it will come, whereof hope was past.

It is uncertain where death looks for us; let us expect her everywhere. The premeditation of death is a forethinking of liberty. He who hath learned to die, hath unlearned to serve. […] And even as the Egyptians after their feastings and carousings caused a great image of death to be brought in and showed to the guests and bystanders, by one that cried aloud, 'Drink and be merry, for such shalt thou be when thou art dead'. So have I learned this custom or lesson, to have always death not only in my imagination but continually in my mouth.

> […]

> *Nascentes morimur, finisque ab origine pendet.*[9]

> As we are born we die; the end
> Doth of th' original depend.

All the time you live, you steal it from death: it is at her charge. The continual work of your life is to contrive death. You are in death, during the time you continue in life; for, you are after death, when you are no longer living. Or if you had rather have it so, you are dead after life; but during life, you are still dying; and death doth more rudely touch the dying, than the dead, and more lively and essentially. If you have profited by life, you have also been fed thereby, depart then satisfied.

---

[6] 'middle part'; 'midst'
[7] 'skeleton'; 'cadaver' (from the Greek, denoting 'to cut up')
[8] Marginal note: 'Horace, book 1 *Epistles*, 4.13.' English translation follows.
[9] Marginal note: 'Manilius, *Astronomica*, book 4.' English translation follows.

> *Cur non ut plenus vitæ conviva recedis?*[10]
>
> Why like a full-fed guest,
> Depart you not to rest?
>
> [...]

I verily believe, these fearful looks, and astonishing countenances wherewith we encompass it, are those that more amaze and terrify us than death: a new form of life; the outcries of mothers; the wailing of women and children; the visitation of dismayed and swooning friends; the assistance of a number of pale-looking, distracted, and whining servants; a dark chamber, tapers burning round about, our couch beset round with physicians and preachers; and to conclude, nothing but horror and astonishment on every side of us: are we not already dead and buried? The very children are afraid of their friends when they see them masked; and so are we. The mask must as well be taken from things as from men, which being removed we shall find nothing hid under it but the very same death that a silly[11] varlet[12] or a simple maidservant did latterly suffer without amazement or fear. Happy is that death which takes all leisure from the preparations of such an equipage.[13]

---

[10] Marginal note: 'Lucretius, book 3.969'; cf. entry III.16 (Creech). English translation follows.

[11] 'poor'; 'simple' (from ME. 'sely'; see 'The Nun's Priest's Tale' in *Canterbury Tales*, Chaucer *WO*, VII 3375 B²)

[12] 'male attendant'

[13] i.e., requisite equipment for some purpose, usually a journey

Suggested further reading

Alfredo Bonadeo, 'Montaigne and Death', *Romanische Forschungen*, 92.4 (1980), 359–70.

Dorothea Heisch, 'Montaigne on Health and Death', in *The Oxford Handbook of Montaigne*, ed. Philippe Desan (Oxford: Oxford University Press, 2016), pp. 765–82, esp. pp. 776–82.

Neil Rhodes, 'John Florio, *The Essays of Montaigne* (1603)', in *English Renaissance Translation Theory*, ed. Neil Rhodes, Gordon Kendal, and Louise Wilson (London: Modern Humanities Research Association, 2013), pp. 382–98.

III.8

THOMAS LODGE

The Works of Seneca (1614)

About the author

Thomas Lodge (1558?–1625) was among the first to respond to Stephen Gosson's invective, *The School of Abuse* (1579), with a defence of poets, musicians, and actors. He composed much verse, several narrative fictions (notably *Rosalynde*, a source for Shakespeare's *As You Like It*), collaborated with Robert Greene[1] on two plays, and wrote a trend-setting satire, *A Fig for Momus* (1596) that adapted Horace and Juvenal to contemporary English concerns. In addition to earning medical degrees in Avignon and later Oxford, he published works related to his profession, including *A Treatise of the Plague* (1603), and also translated Josephus, Seneca, and several Catholic devotional poems.

About the text

Lodge's translation of Seneca is based on the 1605 Latin edition by Justus Lipsius, the pre-eminent humanist scholar of Stoicism. Although completed in 1611, it was not published until three years later when his domestic affairs were resolved (against all odds, as the second son of his father's third wife, Lodge became sole heir of the family estate in Rolleston, Nottinghamshire). It went through many editions and became the standard English version of Seneca's complete works for two centuries. Presented here are excerpts first from the account of Seneca's exemplary death, and then the opening and closing sections of a moral essay on living a circumspect and virtuous life ever mindful of one's mortality ('On the shortness of life').

The arts of death

Throughout the Renaissance, Seneca's enforced suicide – a Roman analogue to that of Socrates – was the quintessential expression of noble adherence to

---

[1] See entry I.8 (Greene).

one's principles.[2] (Seneca was implicated in the Pisonian[3] conspiracy to assassinate Nero, his former pupil.) Preferring an honourable death to the abrogation of one's moral duty was a theme that resonated powerfully during the early modern period, echoed in Shakespeare's Horatio declaring, 'I am more an antique Roman than a Dane'.[4] During his exile Seneca wrote to members of his circle on the tranquillity of mind provided by Stoic principles, including several consolations encouraging fortitude in the face of the death of a loved one, and letters directing decorous acceptance of his own absence. Exile becomes for Seneca a metaphor for demystifying the vagaries of the human condition: we are alienated from ourselves all the while we live thinking that there always will be time left over for what truly matters. Lodge highlights this aspect of Jacobean Neostoicism to bring out deeper ethical implications of classical bywords concerning mortal temporality, such as *tempus fugit* [time flies] and *vita brevis, ars longa* [life is short, art long].

Textual notes

The workes of Lucius Annæus Seneca, both morrall and natural (London: 1614; STC 22213), d3^r–d5^r, Lll2^r–Lll3^r.

The Works of Seneca

Hereafter followeth the slaughter of Annaeus Seneca,[5] most pleasing to the prince,[6] not because he had manifestly found him guilty of treason, but to the end he might confound him by the sword, since his attempt in poisoning him so badly succeeded. [...] Seneca, in that his body was old and lean, by reason of his sparing diet, and that by this means his blood flowed more slowly, cut the veins of his legs and hams likewise. [...] In the meanwhile Seneca, seeing the protraction and slowness of his death, besought Statius Annaeus, a man well approved unto him, both for his faith in friendship, and skill in physic, to hasten and bring him that poison which in times past was provided, and by which they were put to death who were by public judgement condemned amongst the Athenians;[7] and having it brought unto him

---

[2] Seneca's death is depicted on Lodge's frontispiece; see *MA*, pp. 187–88.
[3] Gaius Calpurnius Piso (d.65 CE), Roman senator   [4] *Hamlet*, 5.2.299
[5] i.e., Seneca the Younger (*c*.4 BCE–65 CE)   [6] i.e., Nero, Roman emperor from 54–68 CE
[7] 'hemlock'

he drunk it, in vain, by reason that his limbs were already cold and his body shut up against the force of the venom. At last he entered into a bath of hot water, besprinkling those of his slaves that stood next about him, saying that he offered up that liquor to Jove the Deliverer.[8] Then put into the bath, and stifled with the vapour[9] thereof, he was buried without any solemnity of his funeral, for so had he set it down in his will.

[…]

The greater part of men (good friend, Paulinus[10]) complaineth of the hard dealing of nature with us, who hath brought us forth to live so short a while, and yet of the time allotted us, that the moments should so suddenly and swiftly run away, as we see they do: insomuch as besides some few amongst us, the rest are then most commonly bereft of life, when indeed they begin but newly even then to live. […] Whence springeth that especial complaint of the greatest amongst physicians,[11] that our life is short, and their art very long. […] Whereas indeed we have no scantiness or scarcity of life, but we rather lose much of our life; for long enough and large enough is life allowed us, were it spent in greatest matters, or were it all spent in good matters; but when we have by riot and negligence once lost it, when it is once spent and gone, and we cannot show any good we spent it in, at length need driving us to make an end thereof; we see that now it is spent, which we did not feel to spend, before indeed it was very well-nigh wholly spent: so that we had not given us so short a life, as we will make it, but such we made it as it is; nor had we given us so little life, but so prodigal and lavish we are. Even as a prince's ample patrimony, if it come in huckster's hands, goeth away in a moment, which if it were the hundredth part thereof, and were well husbanded,[12] would yet by good usage, increase rather than prove but scarce, even so our age if it be well employed, will prove very fair and long enough. […] What is then the reason forsooth[13] you live as if you had a warrant to live forever? You reck[14] not how little time you live to yourself. […] How late is it to begin to live then, when thou must leave to live? Or how fond forgetfulness of mortality is it to delay amendment to thy fiftieth year of age, and to

---

[8] On the aptness here of such an offering to Jupiter, see Desiderius Erasmus, *Collected Works of Erasmus, Volume 34: Adages: II Vii 1 to III Iii 100*, trans. R. A. B. Mynors (Toronto, ON: University of Toronto Press, 2000), II.viii.1.

[9] 'steam'

[10] i.e., Seneca's father-in-law, Pompeius Paulinus, superintendent of Rome's grain supply

[11] Hippocrates of Kos (c.460–c.370 BCE); see entry III.5 (Cogan).

[12] 'conserved'   [13] 'truly'   [14] 'heed'

make account that then thou wilt begin to live, when few men use to aspire to such an age. Ye shall often hear great, mighty men give out speeches in praise of rest, of leisure, and quietness, they wished it, they prefer it before all their wealth; yea they wish they might with safety come down from that high tip of their authority, and intend the same; for be all things never in such quiet from abroad, yet fortune falleth even in itself, and decayeth as all other things in this mortality.

Suggested further reading
Reid Barbour, *English Epicures and Stoics: Ancient Legacies in Early Stuart Culture* (Amherst, MA: University of Massachusetts Press, 1998).
J. H. M. Salmon, 'Stoicism and Roman Example: Seneca and Tacitus in Jacobean England', *Journal of the History of Ideas*, 50.2 (1989), 199–225.

III.9
ABRAHAM HOLLAND
Navmachia (1622)

About the author

Abraham Holland (d.18 February 1626), one of ten children of Philemon Holland (the eminent English translator of Xenophon, Pliny, Livy, Plutarch, and Camden[1]), received his BA from Trinity College, Cambridge, in 1617. He was an aspiring poet who died young.

About the text

Holland's poem about the 1571 Battle of Lepanto recalls Lucan's *Pharsalia* (specifically the naval engagement at Massilia) in both its heroic tone and depiction of anatomical violence. The introductory material is half as long as the poem, with commendatory verses by Michael Drayton among others and a dedicatory epistle quoting Martial on writing as being the only

---
[1] See *MA* IV.2 for an excerpt from his translation of Camden's *Remains Concerning Britain*.

sure bulwark against death (A2ᵛ).² *Navmachia* [*Sea-Fight*] was published by his brother, Henry, who also reprinted it after Abraham's death (*Hollandi Posthuma*, 1626) and, a decade after its first publication, included it in his father's translation of Xenophon's *Cyropaedia* (1632). Lepanto, the largest naval battle in the West since classical antiquity, checked the Ottoman advance into the Mediterranean. While providing a legitimate subject for indulging in vivid if gruesome narration, *Navmachia* also can be read as a prescient warning, insofar as England at the time of Holland's composition barely had a standing navy. Neither James nor Charles was committed to funding the build-up of a stronger fleet, leaving the Channel coast open to attack and making English merchant ships easy prey to Barbary pirates.

The arts of death

The bulk of Holland's poetic endeavours reflect a variety of ways that the death arts found literary expression in Stuart England. He wrote elegies on King James³ and Henry de Vere; verse translations of select consolatory psalms; a threnody on the 1625 pestilence in London (which incidentally claimed his own life); 'A Resolution Against Death'; and his own epitaph which in *Hollandi Posthuma* (1626) contains the lines 'This is that goal whereto the man / That lieth here interred ran, / This the race-end, to which at most, / It can be said that he rode post' (L2ᵛ). A typical example of his facility with analogies involving death can be found in his 'Meditation Against the Fear of Death':

Shall the tormented sick-man grudge if from a long and languishing disease, a speedy medicine restore him to his former perfect health? Is not our life a sea of troubles? A loathsome dungeon? A lingering sickness? Is not Death the skilful pilot that guides us to Heaven? Is not he the good judge that sets us at liberty? The skilful physician that cures our mortality, and restores us to eternal life?' (*Hollandi Posthuma*, M2ʳ)

---

² '*Sola[que] non norint haec monumenta mori*'; (Martial, *Epigrams, Volume II: Books 6–10*, trans. and ed. D. R. Shackleton Bailey, Loeb Classical Library (Cambridge, MA: Harvard University Press, 1993), 10.2).
³ See *MA* VI.5, for Holland's elegy written upon the death of James I, 'an exuberant encomiastic celebration of the late king, which "salves" the reader's misery with equally spirited acclamation of his successor, Charles I' (p. 297).

Textual notes

Naumachia, or Hollands sea-fight (London: 1622; STC 13580), B3r–D4r.

Navmachia

All to their charge with trembling boldness run,
With quaking hand one charges first his gun,
Another girds his threatening sword on's side;
Some clasps their steely helmets; shields are tied
On trembling arms apace, that one might then
Have thought th' had been all moving ironmen.
    And now the martial steely-pointed staves
Were snatched in haste: the heavy murdering glaives:[4]
Bows bent to slaughter: weighty courtelaxes:[5]
And darts, Death's harbingers;[6] the black bill,[7] axe.
And other arms which before rusting stood,
But now are brought forth to be scoured with blood.
[…]

But hark th'amazing signs of battle sound,
Making the lands remote, and rocks rebound:
The shrill-voiced trumpet and courageous drum,
In barbarous language bid the foes to come.
    Death's horrid vizard now begins t'appear,
In their pale faces; terror, and ghastly fear
In their amazed hearts doth panting rise,
And future blood baths in their fiery eyes.
[…]

    Grim Death in purple, stalks upon the hatches,
With pale and grisly looks see how he snatches
Hundreds a' once unto him, till the dreary

---

[4] a metal-tipped lance with a sharp edge on its outer curve
[5] 'curtalax'; cutlass, slightly curved sword preferred by sailors
[6] An iconographic attribute associated with death; cf. entries I.2 (*Calendar*) and IV.1 (Barclay).
[7] a pole weapon resembling a halberd but with a hooked blade

Lean-faced ill-favoured Death of death grew weary.
  See on the sea how thousand bodies float
From their great ships hasting to Charon's boat,[8]
Which crabbed[9] sculler[10] now might think it meet
His old-torn boat should be new-changed a fleet.
[…]

Ships now begin to burn, that one might see
Neptune's and Vulcan's consanguinity
Yea now these ships, which free from water stood,
Strangely begin to sink with human blood,
Which as from thence with fearful gush it ran,
Filled up the wrinkles of the ocean,
Making with purpose ghastly gored hue,
Of one red sea which was before, now two:
Which sea so full of dead, it hence might come
Well to be called, *Mare Mortuum*.[11]
[…]

  The trumpeter, with brave reviving sound
Quickening their dying hearts, is felled to th' ground,
And as in's mouth he still the brass did wield,
His dying breath made it a dead march[12] yield,
And having lent his trumpet so much breath
In's life, it turned him[13] some again at's death.
  The drummer with his nimble hand repeating
His doubled blows, without compassion beating
His harmless drum, which seemed with groaning cry
To murmur at his master's cruelty,
Suddenly two rash bullets rudely come
Tearing both skin of drummer, and the drum,
Drummer of life, of sound the drum's bereft:
So drum, and drummer both are speechless left.

---

[8] the ferryman of Hades transporting souls of newly deceased across the River Styx
[9] 'ill-humoured'
[10] one who propels a boat from the stern using a long oar
[11] 'the Dead Sea'; the name given to the Holy Land's hypersaline lake
[12] 'music for a funeral procession' [13] a response to a drill call

The gunner as with nimble haste he runs
To fire his seldom-vain-reporting guns,
His head a leaden-winged bullet hits
And his hard brainpan into pieces splits,
He of a thousand this alone might vaunt,
That of his death he was not ignorant,
And this true riddle[14] might of him abide,
He lived once by's death, by's life now died.[15]
[…]

Some fearing swords, into the sea do fly,
And so for fear of death, fear not to die.
   Some fall into the ocean stained with gore,
Which from their former wounds had gushed before,
Which killed not them, as it from them was spilled,
But entering into them again, th' are killed.
   Here's one about to strike, his foe doth fall
Into the sea, before he can recall
His erring stroke, striking the sea to stay him,
The ocean in revenge o'th blow doth slay him.
   One fearing death doth fain to die and bleed,
And while he is in faining, dies indeed.
[…]

   See a poor wretch with both arms cut asunder,
Distracted leapt into the water under
Meaning to swim, but see the woeful wretch
With how much toil he laboureth to stretch
His raw-veined stumps, which for his arms before
Gush nothing now, but streams of deadly gore:
Fain would he catch t'uphold his wavering life
Some kind remain o' th' ship,[16] but all his strife
Doth make him sooner to be out of breath,

---

[14] derived from OE. *rǣdels*, meaning 'conjecture' or 'opinion'
[15] The 'riddle' is that, as a sharpshooter, he made his living by death and by that same livelihood did he himself die.
[16] i.e., flotsam providing respite from drowning

And wanting arms he yet embraces death.
[...]
  The sun[17] no longer could endure to see
'Mongst humane men such inhumanity:
Therefore his horses, bathing in their foam,
With posting speed haste to their watery home.
Where yet a while they all amazed stood,
Finding instead of sea, a sea of blood.

[17] Helios, in Greek mythology, by day drove his chariot across the sky.

Suggested further reading
Kenneth Andrews, *Ships, Money and Politics: Seafaring and Naval Enterprise in the Reign of Charles I* (Cambridge: Cambridge University Press, 1991).
Ian Runacres, 'Bloodless Imitations: Lucan's Sea Fight in Holland's *Naumachia* and May's *Continuation*', *Translation and Literature*, 19.2 (2010), 170–89.

III.10

FRANCIS BACON

'Of Death' (1625)

About the author

Francis Bacon (1561–1626) was perhaps the most gifted of early modern England's intellectual luminaries, insofar as he played important roles in law, politics, literature, philosophy, and science. His writings in philosophy and natural philosophy, and particularly his application of empiricist, inductive reasoning, is credited with contributing to the seventeenth-century scientific revolution and inspiring the institution of the Royal Society (1660).[1]

[1] Cf. *MA* IV.3 (Bacon), esp. p. 197.

About the text

Self-described as 'the fragments of [his] conceits', Bacon's *Essays*, published in multiple and expanding versions over the course of his career, were the first sustained English attempt at essay-writing. In the first edition of 1597 – Bacon's first publication – the essays are subtitled 'Religious Meditations', and he insists in its prefatory dedication, to his brother Anthony, that there is nothing 'in them contrary or infectious to the state of religion or manners'. Bacon's *Essays* (meaning 'to attempt') follow in the classical tradition of Aristotle and Plutarch, but borrow in title and format from the *Essais* of Michel de Montaigne (1533–1592), which first appeared in 1580 (see entry III.7). Bacon's *Essays* cover a range of topics from 'Suitors' to 'Atheism' to 'Gardens', revealing a personality at once empathetic and eminently sensible.

The arts of death

Bacon's essay 'Of Death' first appears in the expanded 1612 edition; this essay is then expanded in the 1625 edition, from which we derive our copy. The essay, excerpted fully here, exemplifies Bacon's no-nonsense attitude. Death, as it will come to all, is something that should not be feared, and, indeed, fear of death is best understood as the product of superstitious prattling, a relic of Catholic belief and the traditional *ars moriendi*. Death does not change the person, even at the final moment – and Bacon introduces a gallery of famous deaths from antiquity to support this – and, all in all, he asserts, it is a thoroughly natural process. Fix your mind on 'somewhat that is good' in your final moments, he advises, and the departure from this life will be less troublesome. And, after death, your 'good fame' can live on, and no one will feel envious of you anymore.

Textual notes

The essayes or counsels, ciuill and morall, of Francis Lo. Verulam, Viscount St. Alban (London: 1625; STC 1148), B3^r–C1^r.

'Of Death'

Men fear death as children fear to go in the dark; and as that natural fear in children is increased with tales, so is the other. Certainly, the contemplation of death, as the wages of sin and passage to another world, is holy and religious.² But the fear of it, as a tribute due unto nature, is weak. Yet in religious meditations, there is sometimes mixture of vanity and of superstition. You shall read in some of the friars' books of mortification, that a man should think with himself what the pain is if he have but his finger's end pressed or tortured, and thereby imagine what the pains of death are, when the whole body is corrupted and dissolved; when many times death passeth with less pain than the torture of a limb; for the most vital parts are not the quickest of sense.³ And by him that spake only as a philosopher and natural man, it was well said, *Pompa Mortis magis terret, quam Mors ipsa*.⁴ Groans and convulsions, and a discoloured face, and friends weeping, and blacks,⁵ and obsequies, and the like, show death terrible. It is worthy the observing, that there is no passion in the mind of man so weak, but it mates and masters the fear of death; and therefore death is no such terrible enemy when a man hath so many attendants about him that can win the combat of him. Revenge triumphs over death; love slights it; honour aspireth to it; grief flyeth to it; fear pre-occupateth it; nay, we read, after Otho the emperor⁶ had slain himself, pity, which is the tenderest of affections, provoked many to die, out of mere compassion to their sovereign, and as the truest sort of followers.

Nay, Seneca adds niceness and satiety: *Cogita quam diu eadem feceris; mori velle, non tantum fortis aut miser, sed etiam fastidiosus potest*.⁷ A man would

---

² Rom 6:23: 'For the wages of sin is death: but the gift of God *is* eternal life, through Jesus Christ our Lord.' (Quotations modernized from the 1599 Geneva Bible.)

³ Bacon refers to passages included in the English Jesuit priest Robert Parsons's *The First Book of the Christian Exercise appertaining to resolution* (Rouen: printed at Parsons's press, 1582): 'This pain may partly be conceived by that, if we would drive out life, but from the least part of our body (as, for example, out of our little finger, as surgeons are wont to do when they will mortify any place to make it break), what a pain doth a man suffer before he be dead?' (F3ᵛ). Parsons had fled England for the Continent in 1581, and, basing his activities out of Rouen, an important haven for recusants where there would later be established a Jesuit college, he would self-publish a series of Catholic tracts that were then covertly distributed in England.

⁴ 'Is it the trappings of death that terrify more than death itself?' (Latin sources and translations are sourced from Francis Bacon, Viscount St Alban, 'Of Death. II', 'The Essays or Counsels, Civil and Moral: The Essays', in *The Oxford Francis Bacon*, ed. Michael Kiernan (Oxford: Clarendon Press, 1985), vol. 15.

⁵ i.e., black mourning garments

⁶ Otho (32–69 CE) was Emperor of the Roman Empire for just three months; following heavy losses to Vitellius at the Battle of Bedriacum, he took his own life.

⁷ An adaptation of 'On taking one's own life' by the Roman Stoic philosopher Seneca *EP*, 2.77.6 and translated and paraphrased in Bacon's next sentence.

die, though he were neither valiant, nor miserable, only upon a weariness to do the same thing so oft over and over. It is no less worthy to observe, how little alteration in good spirits the approaches of death make; for they appear to be the same men till the last instant. Augustus Caesar died in a compliment: *Livia, conjugij nostri memor, vive et vale.*[8] Tiberius in dissimulation; as Tacitus sayeth of him: *Jam Tiberium vires et corpus, non dissimulatio, deserebant.*[9] Vespasian in a jest, sitting upon the stool: *Ut puto deus fio.*[10] Galba with a sentence: *Feri, si ex re sit populi Romani*;[11] holding forth his neck. Septimius Severus in dispatch: *Adeste, si quid mihi restat agendum.*[12] And the like. Certainly, the Stoics bestowed too much cost upon death, and by their great preparations made it appear more fearful. Better sayeth he: *Qui finem vitae extremum inter munera ponat naturae.*[13] It is as natural to die as to be born;

---

[8] 'Live mindful of our wedlock, Livia, and farewell' (Suetonius, 'Life of Augustus', in *Lives of the Caesars*, trans. J. C. Rolfe, introduction by K. R. Bradley, Loeb Classical Library (Cambridge, MA: Harvard University Press, 1914), vol. 1, p. 99.

[9] 'Now the strength and body of Tiberius were abandoning him, but not yet his powers of dissimulation.' Paraphrase of opening of Tacitus, *Annals: Books 4–6, 11–12*, trans. John Jackson, Loeb Classical Library (Cambridge, MA: Harvard University Press, 1937), 6.50. Tiberius (42 BCE–37 CE) was the second Emperor of the Roman Emperor, ruling for some twenty-two years. On his assumed deathbed, Tiberius made a remarkable recovery. The emperor-in-waiting, Caligula, who was already being acclaimed as the new leader, was suspected to have then had him murdered by various means.

[10] 'I think I am becoming a God.' As noted by Kiernan, 'Bacon conflates Suetonius, *Life of Vespasian*, 23 (quotation) and 24 (manner of death)'. Vespasian (9–79 CE) was Roman Emperor for ten years, succeeding Vitellius and preceding his son Titus. His inglorious death was infamous: an illness that led to an incapacitating bout of diarrhoea.

[11] 'Strike, if it be for the benefit of the Roman people.' Plutarch's *Lives*, 'Galba', supplies the relevant detail about Galba holding out his neck: 'But he merely presented his neck to their swords, saying: "Do your work, if this is better for the Roman people."' Plutarch, *Lives, Volume XI: Aratus. Artaxerxes. Galba. Otho. General Index*, trans. Bernadotte Perrin, Loeb Classical Library 103 (Cambridge, MA: Harvard University Press, 1926), pp. 27, 267. Galba (3 BCE–69 CE) was the Roman Emperor for seven months, succeeding Nero and preceding Otho (cited above).

[12] 'Make haste, if there is anything more for me to do.' As noted by Kiernan, it is a paraphrase of Dio Cassius: 'In fine, he showed himself so active that even when expiring he gasped: "Come, give it here, if we have anything to do."' Dio Cassius, *Roman History, Volume IX: Books 71–80*, trans. Earnest Cary and Herbert B. Foster, Loeb Classical Library (Cambridge, MA: Harvard University Press, 1927), 57.1, p. 277. Septimius Severus (145–211 CE) was Roman Emperor for eighteen years; he died in northern Britain, at York, exhausted from a campaign against the Caledonians (modern-day Scotland).

[13] 'Who considers the end of life among the gifts of nature' (Juvenal, *Satires*, in *Juvenal and Persius*, trans. and ed. Susanna Morton Braund, Loeb Classical Library, (Cambridge, MA: Harvard University Press, 2004), 10.358–59.

and to a little infant, perhaps, the one is as painful as the other. He that dies in an earnest pursuit is like one that is wounded in hot blood; who, for the time, scarce feels the hurt; and, therefore, a mind fixed and bent upon somewhat that is good doth avert the dolours[14] of death. But, above all, believe it, the sweetest canticle is *Nunc dimittis*;[15] when a man hath obtained worthy ends and expectations. Death hath this also: that it openeth the gate to good fame, and extinguisheth envy. *Extinctus amabitur idem.*[16]

---

[14] i.e., griefs, sorrows
[15] 'Now release.' Compare, 'Lord now lettest thou thy servant depart in peace, according to thy word' (Luke 2:29–32).
[16] 'Once dead, he will be loved just the same' (Horace *EP*, 2.1.14).

Suggested further reading

Michael Kiernan (ed.), 'The Essays or Counsels, Civil and Moral' in *The Oxford Francis Bacon* (Oxford: Clarendon Press, 1985), vol. 15.

Rhodri Lewis, 'Francis Bacon and Ingenuity', *Renaissance Quarterly*, 67.1 (2014), 113–63.

Angus Vine, 'Francis Bacon's Composition Books', *Transactions of the Cambridge Bibliographical Society*, 14.1 (2008), 1–31.

III.II

HELKIAH CROOKE

Mikrokosmographia (1631)

About the author

Helkiah Crooke (1576–1648) graduated from St John's College, Cambridge, in 1596, and studied at the University of Leiden where he became a Doctor of Medicine. Upon his second application, Crooke was admitted to the Royal College of Physicians in 1613, licensing him to 'practice physic'; he was made a fellow in 1620 and anatomy reader in 1629, and was for a time appointed physician to James I. Crooke published the first comprehensive anatomy text in English for the benefit of barber-surgeons (whose activities were regulated through the guild structure).

About the text

Crooke's main sources, duly cited throughout, are *De corporis humani fabrica* (1590) by Caspar Bauhin, chair of anatomy at Basel, and *Historia anatomica humani corporis* (1600) by André Du Laurens, anatomy professor at Montpellier and physician to Henri IV; and, in the second edition ('corrected and enlarged', from which excerpts for this entry are taken), 'Three and Fifty Instruments of Chirurgery' translated from the *Oeuvres* (1575) of Ambroise Paré, who applied the anatomical ideas in *De Humani Corporis Fabrica* (1543) by the Flemish surgeon, Andreas Vesalius, physician to Charles V. *Mikrokosmographia* (1615) thus presented in English the extent of European anatomical knowledge (reprinted 1616, reissued 1618, 1631, and 1651). An epitome, principally of the illustrations, also came out in 1616 (reprinted 1634), *Somatographia anthropine, or, a description of the body of man*, to remedy the defects in works of previous authors whose 'descriptions of the parts being interposed between the figures distract the mind and defraud the storehouse of memory' (A3ᵛ). Whether in small or large format (the latter over a thousand pages), Crooke's work was designed for dispassionate and empirically minded surgeons to perform operations correctly and keep death at bay.

The arts of death

Owing to warfare, high infant mortality, and periodic pestilence, dead bodies were a common sight in the early modern world. Where the law permitted, fresh corpses regularly were opened up for investigative purposes. Notwithstanding the observational approach to experimental anatomy practised by university-trained surgeons such as Crooke, the human body remained a site of inescapable reflection on mortal temporality (see Figure 3.1 and Figure 3.2). Unlike other anatomical writers, Crooke so frequently refers to the soul as inhering in every part of the human body – as a mirror of our divine nature – that it stands out as a distinctive thematic element of his text. These references to the soul (harkening to Plato's formulation of man as the little world, or microcosm[1]) serve collectively as a defence mechanism against the desacralizing materialism inherent in the investigative enterprise of early modern surgery. Our excerpt highlights

---

[1] *Timaeus* in Plato *CD*, 29d–47e.

Crooke's revival and use of commonplace poetic analogies while describing cutting-edge approaches for disclosing the mysteries and minutiae of human anatomy.

Textual notes

Mikrokosmographia: A description of the body (London: 1631; STC 6063), B1^r–G1^v.

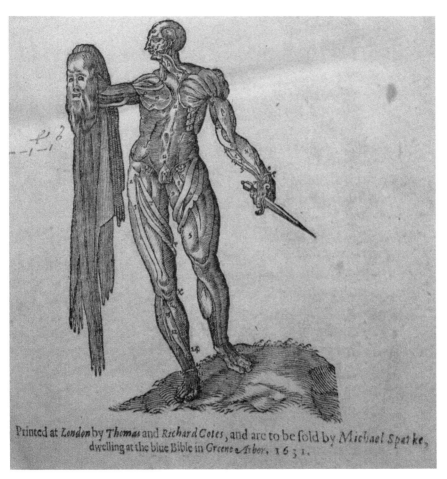

FIGURE 3.1 Anatomical cadaver presenting its skin. *Mikrokosmographia* (London: 1631; STC 6063), title page. Image used courtesy of The Huntington Library

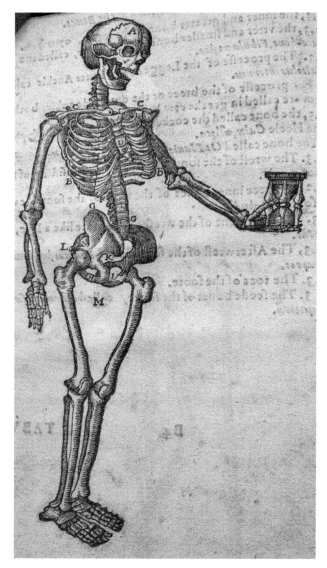

FIGURE 3.2 Animated skeleton with hourglass. *Mikrokosmographia* (London: 1631; STC 6063), B4ᵛ. Image used courtesy of The Huntington Library

Mikrokosmographia

[T]here are many arts full of secret and abstruse notions, deep mysteries and high contemplations, yet none, methinks, that can stand in competition with this we have in hand concerning the frame of man. [...] [I]n the intellectual part or power, there are two essential attributes resembling their prototype or original in God, to wit,[2] knowledge and will. As for the qualities of the soul, they are either internal or external. The internal carry the image of the creator, as St Paul interprets it, in heavenly wisdom, justice, and sanctity; the external, in majesty, dominion, and sovereignty over the creatures.[3] [...] The body also, as far as it was possible, carries the image of God. [...] [T]he admirable structure and accomplished perfection of the body, carries in it a representation of all the most glorious and perfect works of God, as being an epitome or compend[4] of the whole creation, by which he is rather signified than expressed. And hence it is that man is called a microcosm or little world, as in the following discourse will more at large appear. [...] The soul of man is wholly in the whole, and wholly in every particular part. [...] In the soul are imprinted the universal forms of things, and it hath also understanding to judge them.

As the soul of man is of all sublunary[5] forms the most noble, so his body, the house of the soul, doth so far excel, as it may well be called *metron*, the measure and rule of all other bodies. [...] The images and resemblances of which three parts, who sees not plainly expressed and, as it were, portrayed out with a curious pencil in the body of man? The head, the castle and tower of the soul, the seat of reason, the mansion-house of wisdom, the treasury of memory, judgement, and discourse,[6] wherein mankind is most like to the angels or intelligences, obtaining the loftiest and most eminent place in the body; doth it not elegantly resemble that supreme and angelical part of the world? [...] The twelve signs of the zodiac, by the astrologers elegantly depictured[7] in the body of man [see Figure 3.3], I pass over with silence for these are things ancient and

---

[2] 'let me tell you' [3] Marginal note: 'Col 3:10.' [4] 'abridgement' [5] 'under the moon'
[6] Cf. the entry on Spenser in *MA* VI.2 (esp. pp. 287–90); Crooke, in his preface to the second book of *Mikrokosmographia*, explicitly refers to and quotes a stanza from Spenser *FQ*, 2.9.22 concerning Alma's castle, an allegory of the human body submitting to the discipline of moderation; he exclaims that the body 'is put together with wonderful art, and framed according to geometrical proportion, which the English poet hath obscurely but excellently described' (G1r).
[7] 'represented'

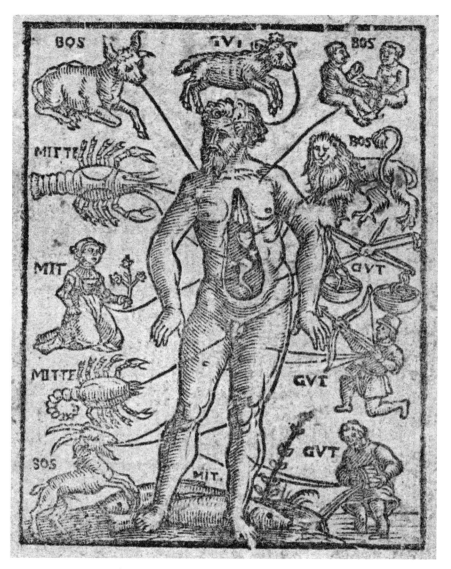

FIGURE 3.3 Zodiacal map of human body. 'Homo Signorum'. Anonymous English almanac (c.1580). The Wellcome Collection, London (Wellcome Images/ Wikimedia Commons)

commonly known as being sung in the corners of our streets.[8] We choose rather to meditate of more sublime and profound matters and to bend the eye of our mind at a higher mark. […] This little world, therefore, which we call man, is a great miracle, and his frame and composition is more to be admired and wondered at than the workmanship of the whole universe. For it is a far easier thing to depaint[9] out many things on a large and spacious table, such as is the world, than to comprehend all things in one so little and narrow, as is the compass of man's body. […] Again, it is not always or in each place easy to find and obtain such store of human carcasses, and therefore that want is well supplied by a curious draught or delineation of such observations, as are made in true dissections by cunning artists, that so both the memory of those that were present may be refricated[10] and refreshed, and such as were absent made also partakers of their labours. Yet, for all this, I do not think it fit to trust too much to these silent shadows. […] [I]t is a very vain thing to take in hand to learn anatomy by the bare inspection of figures, without practice upon the body itself. And because our art concerns the cure not of beasts but of men, we must, therefore, exercise ourselves chiefly in the anatomy of the body of man, and that not alive but dead. This body, therefore, which, indeed, is but the sepulchre of that God at first created, although to the eye it is very specious[11] and beautiful, yet it is but infirm and weakly defended […] for to death and diseases we lie open on every side. […] It shall be sufficient in this place to draw the curtain and to show you the case, rather the coffin or winding-sheet wherein nature hath wrapped this living body of death. Those are four: besides the hairs wherewith as with flowers the coffin is garnished, that is, the cuticle or scarse-skin,[12] the skin itself, the fat, and the fleshy membrane.

---

[8] the marketplace hawking of almanacs with some version of this much-circulated image; see entry I.2 (*Calendar*), and cf. Phebe Jensen, *Astrology, Almanacs, and the Early Modern English Calendar* (Oxford and New York: Routledge, 2021), pp. 76–78.
[9] 'depict'   [10] 'rubbed again'; 'polished', 'brightened'   [11] 'alluring'
[12] Glossed by Crooke as: 'void of sense itself, is ordained as a monument to defend the skin from the violence of outward injuries'.

Suggested further reading
Jillian Faith Linster, 'Books, Bodies, and the "great labor" of Helkiah Crooke's *Mikrokosmographia*', unpublished PhD thesis, University of Iowa (2017).
Jonathan Sawday, *The Body Emblazoned: Dissection and the Human Body in Renaissance Culture* (London: Routledge, 1995).

III.12

EDMUND SPENSER

'A View of the Present State of Ireland' (1633)

About the author

Edmund Spenser (1552?–1599) worked as a civil servant in Ireland in the 1580s, taking advantage, like many English colonizers, of the lands and properties to be secured there. By the late 1580s he had settled in a large estate at Kilcolman, Co. Cork, Munster. The success of his epic poem, *The Faerie Queene* (1590), helped secure Elizabeth I's patronage.

About the text

Spenser's *A View* was written *c.*1596 in the midst of the Nine Years War in Ireland. Many copies of the work survive in manuscript, and, although it would not reach print until 1633, in Sir James Ware's edition, it is likely that it was circulated widely in influential late Elizabethan circles. The work is a political treatise that advises, in the form of a dialogue, on how best to quell Irish rebellion.

The arts of death

A View is Spenser's most controversial work, more or less advocating, as our excerpt shows, for a 'scorched earth' policy, including violence and forced starvation to ensure submission and subjection. Irish laws and customs are described as evils that must be 'cut away' in the plantation process of the grand colonizing project, while 'violent means' are justified as a 'remedy' to any sustained opposition. Spenser invokes the sinister tropes of genocide: pruning away the dead wood, and cleansing and scraping away the 'foul moss'. The second, more haunting, excerpt, recounts scenes from the fall-out to the wars in Munster. The land, once bountiful, is within eighteen months left barren and the poor Irish, starving and skeletal, are like 'anatomies of death'. In the work's most controversial and unsubstantiated passage, Spenser, through Irenius, asserts that they resorted to the cannibalism of corpses. Such accusations are compounded in our third short excerpt (from earlier in the text), where Irenius offers a horrific anecdote about scenes from the execution of Murrough O'Brien, 'a notable traitor', in Limerick on 1 July 1577. The anecdote, which follows Irenius' descriptions of the Gauls' practices of blood sacrifice, shifts the practice of cannibalism from an act of starving desperation to a perverse expression of grief.

Textual notes

'A View of the State of Ireland, Written Dialogue-wise betweene Eudoxus and Irenaeus', in *Two Histories of Ireland* (Dublin, London: 1633; STC 25067), F3^{r-v}, F6^v, D4^v.

'A View of the Present State of Ireland'

EUDOXUS   How then do you think is the reformation thereof to be begun, if not by laws and ordinances?

IRENIUS   Even by the sword, for all these evils must first be cut away by a strong hand before any good can be planted, like as the corrupt branches and unwholesome boughs are first to be pruned and the foul moss cleansed and scraped away before the tree can bring forth any good fruit.

EUDOXUS   Did you blame me even now for wishing of kern,[1] horseboys,[2] and carrows[3] to be clean cut off as too violent a means, and do you yourself now prescribe the same medicine? Is not the sword the most violent redress that may be used for any evil?

IRENIUS   It is so, but where no other remedy may be devised, nor hope of recovery had, there must needs this violent means be used.

[…]

EUDOXUS   Surely of such desperate persons, as will follow the course of their own folly, there is no compassion to be had, and for others you have proposed a merciful means, much more than they have deserved, but what then shall be the conclusion of this war, for you have prefixed a short time of its continuance?

IRENIUS   The end will, I assure me, be very short and much sooner than can be in so great a trouble as it seemeth hoped for, although there should none of them fall by the sword, nor be slain by the

---

[1] 'light-armed foot soldiers'   [2] 'stable-boys' (contemptuous)   [3] 'gamblers'

soldier, yet thus being kept from manurance,[4] and their cattle from running abroad by this hard restraint they would quickly consume themselves and devour one another. The proof whereof I saw sufficiently exampled in these late wars of Munster, for notwithstanding that the same was a most rich and plentiful country, full of corn and cattle, that you would have thought they should have been able to stand long, yet ere one year and a half they were brought to such wretchedness as that any stony heart would have rued the same. Out of every corner of the woods and glens they came creeping forth upon their hands, for their legs could not bear them; they looked like anatomies of death; they spake like ghosts crying out of their graves; they did eat the dead carrions, happy were they could find them, yea, and one another soon after, insomuch as the very carcasses they spared not to scrape out of their graves; and if they found a plot of watercresses or shamrocks, there they flocked as to a feast for a time, yet not able long to continue therewithal that in a short space they were none almost left, and a most populous and plentiful country suddenly left void of man and beast, yet sure in all that war, there perished not many by the sword, but all by the extremity of famine, which they themselves had wrought.

EUDOXUS It is a wonder that you tell, and more to be wondered how it should so shortly come to pass.

[…]

[IRENIUS] […] the Gauls used to drink their enemies' blood and paint themselves therewith. So also, they write, that the old Irish were wont, and so have I seen some of the Irish do, but not their enemies' but friends' blood. As, namely, at the execution of a notable traitor at Limerick, called Murrough O'Brien, I saw an old woman, which was his foster mother, take up his head whilst he was quartered, and sucked up all the blood that run thereout, saying that the earth was not worthy to drink it, and therewith also steeped her face and breast, and tore her hair, crying out and shrieking most terribly.

EUDOXUS You have very well run thorough such customs as the Irish have derived from the first old Nations which inhabited the land [….]

---

[4] 'cultivation'

Suggested further reading

Andrew Hadfield, *Edmund Spenser's Irish Experience: Wilde Fruit and Salvage Soyl* (Oxford: Clarendon Press, 1997).

Andrew Hadfield and Willy Maley (eds.), *Edmund Spenser. A View of the State of Ireland. From the First Printed Edition (1633)* (Oxford: Blackwell, 1997).

Willy Maley, *Salvaging Spenser: Colonialism, Culture and Identity* (London: Macmillan; New York: St. Martin's Press, 1997).

Willy Maley, '*A View of the Present State of Ireland* (1596; 1633)', in *A Critical Companion to Spenser Studies*, ed. Bart van Es (London: Palgrave, 2005), 210–29.

III.13

ALEXANDER ROSS

A View of All Religions in the World (1653)

About the author

Alexander Ross (1590–1654) served as master of the Southampton grammar school and later, with the support of William Laud, became Chaplain in Ordinary to Charles I. His works regularly praise the king, denounce Parliament, defend Aristotle, and deride Catholicism. Moreover, he argues in print with leading intellectual luminaries of the day including Bacon, Browne, Copernicus (by way of attacking the geographer Nathaniel Carpenter), Harvey, and Hobbes. Drawn to the intricacies of world systems, he translated *The Alcoran of Mahomet* (1649) and continued Ralegh's *History of the World* (1652).

About the text

Ross's survey of the world's religions provides insight into what the English were likely to want to know about the customs and rituals of those beyond their shores (including Jews, who were not permitted officially to resettle in England until 1655). And yet the care Ross took with producing the first Qur'an in English (from a French version) suggests a serious effort to learn about the ways and beliefs of an alien people through their sacred text, albeit from a self-acknowledged biased perspective – the title page advertising 'a needful caveat' for those 'who desire to know what use may be made of, or if there be danger in reading the Alcoran'. With the global proliferation of English trading ports and plantations in the mid-seventeenth century, useful and reliable knowledge about other 'church governments' was held at a premium.

The arts of death

Unlike his usual eristic approach to commenting on controversial topics of the day, Ross's presentation of death rituals and related beliefs from around the world is reported as news, as useful points of information that can offer insight into the cultures in question. His carefully culled details from the most reliable sources available are arranged in a question-and-answer format. Notwithstanding his referring to sacramental practices outside the Church of England as 'heresies', he rarely belittles the various African and Asian religious observances concerning death and mourning, perhaps because he respected in principle the pious upholding of tradition and reverential adherence to received spiritual practices. Although far from being a celebration of diversity, this book is, in effect, the first English work to bring to readers' attention a range of exogenous alternatives to their familiar attitudes toward death in the West.

Textual notes

Pansebeia: or, A View of all Religions In The World (London: 1653; Wing R1971), C6^r–C7^r, H7^v–H8^r.

A View of All Religions in the World

QUESTION.   How do they [the Jews] use their dead?
ANSWER.   When the party dieth, his kindred tear off a little piece of their garments, because Jacob[1] tore his garments when he heard of Joseph's death.[2] They mourn also seven days, because Joseph did

---

[1] the third patriarch of the Israelites, later given the name of Israel (Gen 32:28); progenitor of the Twelve Tribes

[2] the preferred son whose jealous half-brothers sold him as a slave and reported he had been killed (Gen 37:12–35)

so for his father.[3] All the water in the house they pour out into the streets. They cover their face and bow his thumb, that it resembleth the Hebrew Shaddai,[4] that so they may terrify Satan from coming near the corpse. His other fingers are stretched out, to show that now he holds the world no longer, having forsaken it. They wash the body with warm water, and anoint the head with wine and the yolk of an egg, and clothe him with the white surplice he wore on the Day of Reconciliation,[5] and then they coffin him. When the corpse is carried out of the house, they cast a shell after him, signifying that all sorrow should be now cast out of that house. In the churchyard a prayer or two is said; then the corpse is buried, the next of kin casteth in the first earth. In their return, they cast grass over their heads; either to signify their frailty and mortality, 'for all flesh is grass',[6] or else their hope of the Resurrection.[7] When they enter the synagogue, they skip to and fro, and change their seat seven times. The mourners go barefoot seven days; abstaining from wine and flesh, except on sabbaths and festivals. They bathe not in thirty-three days, nor pare their nails. They burn candles for seven days together, thinking that the departed souls return to the place where they left the body, and bewail the loss thereof.

[…]

QUESTION. What rites do they [Mohumetans[8]] observe about the sick and dead?

ANSWER. Their priests and chief friends visit them, exhort them to repentance, and read psalms to them. When any dieth, the priest compasseth the corpse with a string of beads, made of

---

[3] Jacob, third patriarch of the Israelites
[4] This arrangement of fingers forms the Hebrew letter associated with one of the special talismanic names of God.
[5] the annual Day of Atonement (Yom Kippur)
[6] Isa 40:6
[7] The resurrection of the dead is not in the Torah; however, it is a point of discussion in the Babylonian Talmud (B'rakhoth 17a) and a tenet of faith listed in Maimonides's twelfth-century Mishnah Commentary.
[8] Mohammedans, by which is meant Muslims generally; Ross is aware of and elsewhere mentions the main sectarian divisions within Islam.

lignum aloes,[9] praying God to have mercy on him; then the priests carry it into the garden, wash it, and cover it with its own garments, with flowers also and perfumes, and his turban is set on his head. Women perform this office to the body of a woman. This done, the body is carried to the temple with the head forwards, and set down at the church-door, whilst the priests are performing their service; then it is carried to the burial-place without the city: the priests pray for his soul, are paid for their pains, and feasted at home. Some part of their good cheer is set on the grave, for the soul to feed on, or for alms to the poor. They believe there are two angels, who with angry looks, and flaming firebrands, examine the dead party of his former life, whom they whip with fiery torches if he be wicked; if good, they comfort him, and defend his body in the grave till the day of judgement; but the bodies of the wicked are knocked down nine fathoms underground, and tormented by their angry angels, the one knocking him with an hammer, the other tearing him with an hook, till the last day; against this torment the Turks use to pray at the graves of the dead. The women there do not accompany the dead to the grave, but stay at home weeping, and preparing good cheer for the priests and others of the departed man's friends. They believe that when the corpse hath been in the grave one quarter of an hour, that a new spirit is put into it, is set upon its knees, and is examined by the foresaid angels of his faith and works. They believe also that it is a work of charity, and conducible to the soul of the defunct, if the birds, beasts, or ants be fed with the meat which they set on the graves of the dead.

[9] i.e., agarwood; a fragrant resinous wood used in making incense

Suggested further reading

Eva Johanna Holmberg, *Jews in the Early Modern English Imagination* (Farnham, UK: Ashgate, 2011).

Nabil Matar, 'Alexander Ross and the English Translation of the Qur'an', *Journal of Islamic Studies*, 23.1 (2012), 76–84.

R. J. W. Mills, 'Alexander Ross's *Pansebeia* (1653), Religious Compendia and the Seventeenth-Century Study of Religious Diversity', *The Seventeenth Century*, 31.3 (2016), 285–310.

III.14

JOHN GRAUNT

Natural and Political Observations (1662)

About the author

John Graunt (1620–1674), apprenticed to his father, a London haberdasher, took up his freedom with the Drapers' Company. He rose to prosperity and influence, occupying important positions in the Drapers' Company, Cornhill Ward, and the city's Common Council. The Great Fire of London in 1666 destroyed his home, and rebuilding it may have led to his bankruptcy a few years before he died of jaundice.

About the text

This book's observations are based upon the compilation, tabulation, and close examination of the bills of mortality, the official records of the number of weekly deaths, classified according to cause, in 109 London parishes. Published by the Livery Company of Parish Clerks since 1592, the bills warned wealthy citizens of potential outbreaks of plague so that they could depart the city for the sanctuary of rural estates. A bill's information was collected by searchers, ancient matrons who, sworn to their office, sought out the ringing of the death knell and the freshly dug grave to locate and inspect a corpse and make inquiries about the disease or casualty from which the person died, eventually reporting their findings to the parish clerks. Even though the information was neither accurate nor thorough – clouded, as well, by 'the mist of a cup of ale, and the bribe of a two-groat fee' (D4^v) – it provided Graunt with the data for composing what has become known as the first quantitative work on demography and epidemiology. The book's success, reaching five editions by 1676, gained him election to the Royal Society and even approbation from Charles II. Because William Petty, Graunt's learned and accomplished friend and founding member of the Royal Society, vigorously advocated for the method of quantitative precision in studying demographic phenomena, he has been put forward by some as the true author of *Political Observations*; nevertheless, David Glass has soundly demonstrated Graunt's attribution.

The arts of death

With this treatise, the Renaissance death arts move toward the modern sciences founded upon mathematics. Graunt inaugurates data science by considering the city as a generator of information about death on a scale beyond the personal and beyond a single disaster. His originality comes from devising the life table, an arrangement in rows and columns of statistics calculating life expectancy according to a population's various age groups. The life table heralded the development of insurance and pension schemes, in which one could calculate how much a participating member of a group would need to pay into the common pool. Its statistical method lies at the foundation of actuarial science. In the passage excerpted below, the treatise's short preface, Graunt explains with modesty the genesis of his innovative work.

Textual notes

Natural and political observations mentioned in a following index, and made upon the bills of mortality (London: 1662; Wing G1599), B1^r–B2^r. This is the first edition.

Natural and Political Observations

[1.] Having been born and bred in the City of London, and having always observed that most of them who constantly took in the weekly bills of mortality made little other use of them than to look at the foot,[1] how the burials increased, or decreased, and, among the casualties, what had happened, rare and extraordinary, in the week current, so as they might take the same as a text to talk upon in the next company,[2] and, withal, in the plague time, how the sickness increased or decreased, that so the rich might judge of the necessity of their removal,[3] and tradesmen might conjecture what doings they were like to have in their respective dealings.

---

[1] in an account, the total of a column of numbers that is recorded below the column's final entry
[2] social gathering, assembly
[3] i.e., depart the city; a long-held practice, satirized in Ben Jonson's play, *The Alchemist* (*The Complete Plays of Ben Jonson*, ed. G. A. Wilkes (Oxford: Clarendon Press, 1982), vol. 3). See also entry II.9 (Dekker).

2. Now, I thought that the wisdom of our city had certainly designed the laudable practice of taking, and distributing these accompts,[4] for other, and greater uses than those abovementioned, or at least that some other uses might be made of them. And thereupon I, casting mine eye upon so many of the general bills as next came to hand, I found encouragement from them to look out all the bills I could, and, to be short, to furnish myself with as much matter of that kind, even as the Hall of the Parish Clerks[5] could afford me; the which, when I had reduced into tables (the copies whereof are here inserted) so as to have a view of the whole together, in order to the more ready comparing of one year, season, parish, or other division of the city, with another, in respect of all the burials, and christenings, and of all the diseases, and casualties happening in each of them respectively. I did then begin, not only to examine the conceits, opinions, and conjectures, which upon view of a few scattered bills I had taken up, but did also admit new ones, as I found reason, and occasion from my tables.

3. Moreover, finding some truths, and not commonly believed opinions, to arise from my meditations upon these neglected papers, I proceeded further to consider what benefit the knowledge of the same would bring to the world that I might not engage myself in idle and useless speculations, but like those noble *virtuosi*[6] of Gresham College,[7] who reduce their subtle[8] disquisitions upon nature into downright mechanical uses, present the world with some real fruit from those airy[9] blossoms.

4. How far I have succeeded in the premises, I now offer to the world's censure. Who, I hope, will not expect from me, not professing letters,[10] things demonstrated with the same certainty, wherewith learned men determine in their schools; but will take it well, that I should offer at a new thing, and could forbear presuming to meddle where any of the learned pens have ever touched before, and that I have taken the pains, and been at the charge, of setting out those tables, whereby all men may both correct my positions and raise others of their own, for herein I have, like a silly schoolboy, coming to say my lesson to the world (that peevish and tetchy[11] master) brought a bundle of rods wherewith to be whipt, for every mistake I have committed.

[4] accounts
[5] building where members of the livery company who administered the parish's ecclesiastical and civil affairs kept their records, including the bills
[6] i.e., esteemed members of the Royal Society
[7] An institution of higher learning that offered public lectures and whose early success fostered the establishment of the Royal Society; on the history and founding of this society, see *MA* III.7 (Sprat).
[8] 'skilful'; 'perceptive'   [9] i.e., an elevated vantage point   [10] i.e., lacking academic degrees
[11] 'irritable', 'short-tempered'

Suggested further reading

David Victor Glass et al., 'John Graunt and His Natural and Political Observations [and Discussion]', *Proceedings of the Royal Society of London. Series B, Biological Sciences*, 159.974 (1963), 2–37.

Robert Kargon, 'John Graunt, Francis Bacon, and the Royal Society: The Reception of Statistics', *Journal of the History of Medicine and Allied Sciences*, 18.4 (1963), 337–48.

III.15

MARGARET CAVENDISH

Philosophical Letters (1664)

About the author

Margaret Cavendish (*née* Lucas) (1623–1673), Duchess of Newcastle upon Tyne, gained a familiarity with contemporary issues in natural philosophy through attending meetings of the intellectual circle around her husband, William Cavendish, Duke of Newcastle upon Tyne. Mocked by some during her lifetime as an eccentric, she was a self-educated and independent thinker who published poetry, plays, stories, letters, and writings on the new science and philosophy.[1]

About the text

Through the epistolary form of the *Philosophical Letters*, Cavendish seeks to enter into a socially acceptable public dialogue with the leading philosophers of her day. Her epistles are composed to answer the metaphysical questions of the addressee, an unnamed female friend simply called 'Madam' – who, some have speculated, could have been Anne Conway. The collection falls into four sections, each of which engages with the ideas of a few thinkers, the first focusing on Hobbes and Descartes. In the second section, from which the excerpt is taken, Cavendish's letters criticize Henry More, the Cambridge Platonist, for his Cartesianism.

---

[1] For a sampling of Cavendish's poetry and excerpts from her *Sociable Letters*, with special reference to writing as a way of defeating oblivion, see *MA* VI.9.

After repudiating her earlier work's atomism, which accounts for changes in the physical world by referring to the random motions of indivisible particles, Cavendish's philosophical treatises developed her own distinctive vitalist materialism, sketched out briefly by the excerpt. This non-mechanistic theory views all animate and inanimate objects in terms of three gradations of matter that contain within themselves the principle of movement: dull matter, sensitive spirits, and rational spirits. Her materialism has been described as 'panpsychist', since, according to her reasoning, every constituent particle of the cosmos, comprised of an intermixture of the three aforementioned gradations, possesses mental properties to some degree or another. Her vitalistic materialism issues from the ferment of the period's mechanistic controversies,[2] which her husband and brother-in-law, Sir Charles Cavendish, channelled to her through their fraternization with Hobbes, Descartes, and Gassendi. Evidence suggests that these and other philosophers did not take her contributions seriously.

The arts of death

Cavendish's passage distinguishes her view of the 'natural soul' from the supernatural notion of the divine soul. But make no mistake: her view is thoroughly materialist. Cavendish adamantly argues that nothing really dies. In *The Philosophical and Physical Opinions* (London: 1655; Wing N863), she elucidates her principle without reference to the soul:

There can be no annihilation in nature: nor particular motions, and figures, because the matter remains that was the cause of those motions and figures. As for particular figures, although every part is separated that made such a figure, yet it is not annihilated; because those parts remain that made it [....] Thus the dispersing of the matter into particular figures by an alteration of motion, we call death; and the joining of parts to create a figure, we call life. Death is a separation; life is a contraction. (C3^v–C4^r)

Cavendish rejects the physical possibility of annihilation because matter is continually repurposed into new figures or shapes, which, in turn, will die to be repurposed once again. For the spiritually minded, her principle offers a

---

[2] See entry IV.17 (Behn) with reference to the philosophical materialism of the Restoration era.

sorry kind of non-annihilation, looking ahead, with other seventeenth-century materialists, to the atheistic perspective of the Enlightenment's French philosophes. And yet Cavendish tries to diplomatically smooth over her theory's negative implications for religious orthodoxy. In this regard, her vitalistic materialism buffers itself with a scepticism permitted by fideism, the belief that divine matters can be grasped only by faith not by reason.

Textual notes

Philosophical letters: or, Modest reflections upon some opinions in natural philosophy maintained by several famous and learned authors of this age, expressed by way of letters (London: 1664; Wing N866), LLL1^v–LLL2^v. The excerpt comes from letter XXX, section II.

Philosophical Letters

And thus, madam, you see the cause why I cannot give you a full description of the divine soul of man, as I mentioned already in my last, but that I do only send you my opinion of the natural soul, which I call the rational soul; not that I dare say, the supernatural soul is without natural reason, but natural reason is not the divine soul; neither can natural reason, without faith, advance the divine soul to heaven, or beget a pious zeal, without divine and supernatural grace: wherefore reason, or the rational soul is only the soul of nature, which being material, is dividable, and so becomes numerous in particular natural creatures; like as the sensitive life being also material and dividable, becomes numerous, as being in every creature, and in every part of every creature; for as there is life in every creature, so there is also a soul in every creature; nay, not only in every creature, but in every particle of every creature, by reason every creature is made of rational and sensitive matter; and as all creatures or parts of nature are but one infinite body of nature, so all their particular souls and lives make but one infinite soul and life of nature; and this natural soul hath only natural actions, not supernatural; nor has the supernatural soul natural actions; for although they subsist both together in one body, yet each works without disturbance to the other; and both are immortal; for of the supernatural soul there is no question, and of the natural soul, I have said before, that nothing is perishable or subject to annihilation in nature, and so no death, but what is called by the name of death, is only an alteration of the corporeal natural motions of such a figure to another figure; and therefore as it is impossible, that one part of matter should perish in nature, so is it impossible, that the natural or rational soul can perish, being material: the natural humane soul may alter, so as not to move in an animal way, or not to have animal motions, but this doth not prove her destruction or annihilation, but only a change of the animal figure and its motions, all remaining still in nature. Thus my faith of the divine, and my opinion of the natural soul, is, that they are both immortal; as for the immediate actions of the divine soul, I leave you to the Church, which are the ministers of God, and the faithful dispensers of the sacred mysteries of the Gospel, the true expounders of the word of God, reformers of men's lives, and tutors of the ignorant, to whom I submit myself in all that belongs to the salvation of my soul, and the regulating of the actions of my life, to the honour and glory of God. And I hope they will not take any offence at the maintaining and publishing my opinions concerning nature and natural effects, for they are as harmless, and as little prejudicial to them, as my designs; for my only and chief design is and ever hath been to understand nature rightly, obey the Church exactly, believe undoubtedly, pray zealously, live virtuously, and wish earnestly, that both Church and schools may increase and flourish in the sacred knowledge of the true word of God, and that each one may live peaceable and happily in this world, die quietly, and rise blessedly and gloriously to everlasting life and happiness. Which happiness I pray God also to confer upon your ladyship; till then, I rest,

Madam,

Your faithful and constant friend, to serve you.

Suggested further reading
Deborah Boyle, *The Well-Ordered Universe: The Philosophy of Margaret Cavendish* (Oxford: Oxford University Press, 2017).
Lisa T. Sarasohn, *The Natural Philosophy of Margaret Cavendish: Reason and Fancy During the Scientific Revolution* (Baltimore, MD: Johns Hopkins University Press, 2010).

III.16

THOMAS CREECH
Lucretius's Six Books (1683)

About the author

Thomas Creech (1659–1706) entered Oxford University as a commoner at Wadham College in 1675. He advanced to the position of scholar and then from 1680–1696 earned a string of degrees. His translations of Manilius, Horace, Theocritus, Ovid, and Juvenal were highly regarded. Creech's verse translation of Lucretius, the first complete version in English, earned him a fellowship at Oxford. He was headmaster of Sherborne School in Dorset for two years (1694–1696) before returning finally to Oxford.

About the text

Creech's 1682 translation of Lucretius's *On the Nature of Things* helped fuel the classical poetic revival in England that peaked with Dryden's *Virgil* (1697) and Pope's *Homer* (1715–1720). Mindful of his readers' preference for a more straightforward exposition of materialist philosophy (consistent with advances in scientific inquiry lately published by the Royal Society[1]), Creech excised most of Lucretius's didactic comments to Memmius. The resulting shortened poem was so well received that a second edition came out the following year with laudatory and commendatory verses by important Caroline writers including Aphra Behn (Cl^r–C4^r)[2]. Dryden refers respectfully to Creech in the preface to his own translations of classical writers. Extant catalogues of both university and private libraries of the day reveal that Creech's *Lucretius* was a much-valued volume, becoming the standard translation of the 'long' eighteenth century. The poem accrued scores of additional notes by other hands after Creech's decease, with the effect of turning Epicurean thought into a systematic philosophy compatible with Enlightenment ideas.

---

[1] See entry III.14 (Graunt).   [2] See entry IV.17 (Behn).

The arts of death

Our excerpt comes from Lucretius's third book,[3] mainly from the final section that is tagged in the margin as 'Against fear of Death'. The body is described as a carcass rather than a sacred vessel, and the soul as but another modality of atomic form rather than a divine spark of life. Such a worldview resonated sympathetically with shifting attitudes in mid-seventeenth-century England away from belief in supernatural forces and toward an empirical understanding of the nature of life and death. In much the same way as Lucretius rejects divine causation and therefore finds groundless the attendant anxieties concerning death, Creech's poem implicitly obviates centuries of Christian beliefs about the afterlife. Furthermore, his heroic couplets give a new, more easy-going and breezy inflection to Lucretius's presentation and celebration of the maxims of Epicurus[4] (originally written in dactylic hexameter, the metre of classical epic poetry): 'For when I hear thy mighty reasons prove / This world was made without the power above, / All fears and terrors waste,[5] and fly apace. / Through parted heavens I see the mighty space' (I3ʳ).

Textual notes

Titus Lucretius Carus, his six books of Epicurean philosophy (London: 1683; Wing L3449A), I3ʳ, L2ʳ–L4ᵛ, M2ᵛ–N3ʳ.

Lucretius's Six Books

Next of the mind, and of the soul I'll sing,
And chase that dread of hell, those idle fears,
That spoil our lives with jealousies and cares,
Disturb our joys with dread of pains beneath,
And sully them with the black fear of death.
For though some talk, they should less fear to die,
Than live in a disease, or infamy.
[…]

---

[3] Titus Lucretius Carus (94–54 BCE); *De rerum natura* [*On the nature of things*] is divided into six books, the section on death by design coming at the chiastic midpoint.
[4] Epicurus (341–270 BCE), Athenian philosopher possibly influenced by the Cynic school of Diogenes of Sinope
[5] 'are reduced to nothing'; 'dissipate'

    Besides, experience shows, that patients die
By piece-meal, through the toes, then legs, then thigh
Creeps treacherous death; thence through the rest it moves
By slow degrees: and this one instance proves
The soul mortal, since death doth slowly spread,
And some parts are alive at once, some dead.
[…]

    Besides, since when the mind, and soul are fled,
The carcass stinks, and rots as soon as dead,
How canst thou doubt, but that, the union broke,
The scattered soul flies through the limbs like smoke;
And therefore must the body's fabric fall,
Because the soul that did preserve thee all,
Upheld and strengthened it, is now no more,
But fled through every passage, every pore.
[…]

    Besides, were souls immortal, ne'er began,
But crept into the limbs to make up man,
Why cannot they remember what was done
In former times? Why all their memory gone?
Now if the mind's frail powers so far can waste,
As to forget those numerous actions past,
'Tis almost dead, and sure can die at last.
Well then the former soul must needs be dead,
And that now informs us, newly made.
[…]

    Well then, what's death to us, since souls can die?
For as we neither knew, nor felt those harms,
When dreadful Carthage frighted Rome with arms,
And all the world was shook with fierce alarms;
Whilst undecided yet, which part should fall,
Which nation rise to glorious lord of all;
So after death, when we shall be no more,
What though the seas forsake their usual shore,
And rise to heaven? What though stars drop from thence?

Yet how can this disturb our perished sense?
[…]

   But now if Nature should begin to speak,
And thus with loud complaint our folly check:
'Fond mortal, what's the matter thou dost sigh?
Why all these tears, because thou once must die,
And once submit to strong mortality?
For if the race though hast already run
Was pleasant, if with joy thou saw'st the sun;
If all thy pleasures did not pass thy mind
As through a sieve, but left some sweets behind:
Why dost thou not then like a thankful guest,
Rise cheerfully from life's abundant feast,
And with a quiet mind go take thy rest?'[6]
[…]

   But if a wretch, if one oppressed by fate,
Mourns coming death, and begs a larger date,
Him she[7] may fiercely chide: 'Forbear thy sighs,
 Thou wretch, cease thy complaints, and dry thine eyes'.
   If old, 'Thou hast enjoyed the mighty store
Of gay delights, and now canst taste no more;
But yet, because thou still didst strive to meet
That absent, and contemnedst the present sweet,
Death seems unwelcome, and thy race half run;
Thy course of life seems ended when begun;
And unexpected hasty death destroys;
Before thy greedy mind is full of joys.
Yet leave these toys, that not befit thine age,
New actors now come on; resign the stage'.
If thus she chides, I think 'tis well enough,
I think 'tis nothing but a just reproof;
For rising beings still the old pursue,
And take their place, old die, and frame the new.
[…]

---

[6] See entry III.7 (Florio).   [7] nature personified

> Our life must once have end, in vain we fly
> From following fate; e'en now, e'en now we die.
> Life adds no new delights to those possessed.
> But since the absent pleasures seem the best,
> With winged desire and haste those we pursue,
> But those enjoyed, we straightways call for new.
> Life, life we wish, still greedy to live on;
> And yet what fortune with the following sun
> Will rise, what chance will bring, is all unknown.
>
> What though a thousand years prolong thy breath,
> How can this shorten the long state of death?
> For though thy life may numerous ages fill,
> The state of death shall be eternal still.
> And he that dies today, shall be no more,
> As long as those that perished long before.

Suggested further reading
Jonathan Kramnick, 'Living with Lucretius', in *Vital Matters*, ed. Helen Deutsch and Mary Terrall (Toronto, ON: University of Toronto Press, 2012), pp. 13–38.
Catherine Wilson, *Epicureanism at the Origins of Modernity* (Oxford: Oxford University Press, 2008).

III.17

ANNE CONWAY

Principles of the Most Ancient and Modern Philosophy (1692)

About the author

Anne Conway (née Finch) (1631–1679), Viscountess Conway and Killultagh, born into a family noted for its legal experts, acquired a deep love of philosophy, which led to her learning Latin, Greek, and Hebrew. Afflicted with headaches that grew in frequency and severity as she got older, Anne carried out her studies in the privacy of her home, assisted by her husband's library, one of the largest private collections in England, and by her mentors – her half-brother John Finch, the Cambridge Platonist Henry More, and the Quaker alchemist and Kabbalist Francis Mercury van Helmont – all of whom introduced her to the ideas of leading philosophers in England and on the Continent.

About the text

Found among her possessions after she died, her manuscript draft of the treatise was compiled by Van Helmont, who anonymously published in Amsterdam a Latin translation (1690). Two years later an English translation was anonymously published in London. Sarah Hutton proposes that van Helmont saw Conway's two versions of her treatise through the press during the time he was publishing his own controversial work, because he wanted to muster favourable support for his unorthodox views (228–29). His similar blend of Protestant and Kabbalistic ideas, including his theory on the transmigration of souls, were not well received by the Quaker community.

Beginning with the divine attributes taken from the Kabbalah, Conway's treatise builds a metaphysical system around three distinct but related types of ontology: 'Christ' the middle being connects 'God' the highest being to his 'creatures', the lowest. The body of a creature is not different in kind from spirit, for both body and spirit are modalities of the same substance. All creatures in her view are profoundly mutable, with any single body capable of transmutation into spirit and vice versa, and any animal or inanimate thing along the full chain of being capable of transforming into a different animal or thing. Her treatise accordingly wages a vitalist campaign against the era's philosophical materialism, notably advocated by Hobbes and Spinoza. She takes issue with the mechanist orientation of Cartesian science, arguing that nature is 'not a mere organical body, like a clock, wherein there is not a vital principle of motion, but a living body, having life and sense, which body is far more sublime than a mere mechanism or mechanical motion' (L2^v). The philosophical idealism of Leibniz, the German polymath and pre-eminent mathematician and logician of the Enlightenment, may have been influenced by her treatise, of which he possessed a copy.

The arts of death

Conway's radical vitalism challenged the period's predominant view of an irrevocable third death,[1] that is, the destruction of the soul in Hell when God finally forsakes it – as, for example, expressed by St Augustine in *The City of God*, Book 13.[2] In chapter 6, she denies the doctrine of Hell's eternal punishment, laying claim to God's justice and mercy (F1^v–F5^v). Taking issue with Descartes's idea of 'dead matter',[3] Conway reasons that all creation, that is, 'the whole lump' mentioned in the excerpt below, is rehabilitated from death through Christ, the Middle Being, and possesses the potential of growing in perfection. By merging metaphysical speculation with diverse religious traditions, she seeks, in effect, to kill off the last vestiges of death in orthodox Christianity.

Textual notes

The principles of the most ancient and modern philosophy, concerning God, Christ, and the creatures, viz. of spirit and matter in general, trans. J. C. (London: 1692; Wing C5989), D5^v–D7^r. The excerpt is taken from the sixth section of chapter 5.

Principles of the Most Ancient and Modern Philosophy

§. 6. But if by time, according to the common signification of the word, we understand a succedaneous[4] increase or decrease of things, according to which they grow and increase unto a certain pitch or period, and then again fail from it, until they die or are changed into another state or condition of life; in this sense it may be positively affirmed, that neither this middle being, or any creature perfectly united with the same, are subject to time, or the laws thereof; for the laws of time reach but unto a certain period or age; and when that period is completed, then those things which are subject to time decay and are consumed, and so die and are changed into quite another species of things, according to that old saying of the poet:

---

[1] Regarding the three kinds of death each person undergoes, see Introduction.
[2] *Augustine CG*, 13.2   [3] On dead matter, see Carol Wayne White, pp. 56–59.
[4] i.e., serving in the place of another

Tempus edax rerum, tuque invidiosa vetustas
Omnia destruis.[5]

Which may be thus Englished:

Thus spiteful age, and time that eats up things,
All things consumes, and to destruction brings.

And for this reason time is divided into four parts, according to the age of a man living in this world, which is infancy, youth, manhood, and old age, even until death; so that all things which are bounded with time are subject unto death and corruption, or are changed into another species of things, as we see water changed into stones, stones into earth, and earth into trees, and trees into animals or living creatures. But in this most excellent middle being is neither decay or corruption; nor to speak properly hath death any place in him. He is a most powerful and effectual balsam,[6] which can preserve all things from death and corruption, which are joined to him or united with him; so that here all things are perpetually new, springing up fresh and green. Here is perpetual youth without old age, and here is the perfection of old age, to wit, great increase of wisdom and experience without any imperfection of age. But when Christ came in the flesh, and in that body which he b[o]re with him from Heaven (for every created spirit hath a certain vehicle, either terrestrial, aerial, or aethereal, as this was) he took upon him somewhat of our nature, and by consequence the nature of all things (because the nature of man hath in it the nature of all creatures, whence also he is called the microcosm) which nature having assumed in flesh and flood, he sanctified, that by that he might sanctify all things, and so was as that little leaven that changed the whole lump. He descended then within time, and for a certain space or period, of his own accord subjected himself to the laws of time, so as to endure great torments, even death itself. But death did not long detain him, for the third day he rose again, and this was the end of all his sufferings, even of his death and burial, viz. that he might heal, cure, and redeem his creatures from death and corruption, which came upon them by the fall, and so at length hereby put an end to times and elevate the creatures above times to himself, where he abideth, who is the same yesterday, today, henceforth, and forever, without decay, death, or corruption. In like manner, in his spiritual and internal appearance in man, whereby he purposeth to save, heal, and

---

[5] Ovid *MO*, 15.234–6 [6] i.e., a soothing or healing agent

redeem the soul, he doth as it were, after a certain manner, subject himself to a kind of death and passion; and so for a certain space submits himself to the laws of time, that he might elevate the souls of men above time, and corruptibility to himself, wherein they receive blessing, and grow from one degree of goodness and virtue unto another, *in infinitum.*

Suggested further reading
Sarah Hutton, *Anne Conway: A Woman Philosopher* (Cambridge: Cambridge University Press, 2004).
Carol Wayne White, *The Legacy of Anne Conway (1631–1679): Reverberations from a Mystical Naturalism* (Albany, NY: State University of New York Press, 2009).

PART IV

Death Arts in Literature

❧

    Since death shall dure till all the world be waste,
What meaneth man to dread death then so sore?
As man might make, that life should alway last;
Without regard, the Lord hath led before
The dance of death, which all must run on row,
Though how or when the Lord alone doth know.

    Anonymous, *Songs and Sonnets* [*Tottel's Miscellany*] (London: 1557; STC 13861), N4^r

Lady. [...]
Fain would I stay, if thou my life wilt spare,
I have a daughter beautiful and fair,
I'd live to see her wed, whom I adore.
Grant me but this, and I will ask no more.
Death. This is a slender frivolous excuse.
I have you fast, and will not let you loose.
Leave her to providence, for you must go
Along with me, whether you will or no.

    Anonymous, *A Dialogue betwixt Death and A Lady* (London: 1600; Wing G1711, broadside)

Marriage is a merri-age, and this world's paradise, where there is mutual love [...] The enjoying of this great blessing made Pericles more unwilling to part from his wife than to die for his country, and Antonius Pius to pour forth that pathetical exclamation against death for depriving him of his dearly beloved wife: 'O cruel hard-hearted death in bereaving me of her whom I esteemed more than my own life!'

    Rachel Speght, *A Mouzell for Melastomus* (London: 1616; STC 23058), D3^v–D4^r

As Smoke which springs from fire is soon
  Dispersed and gone;
Or clouds which we but now beheld,
  By winds dispelled;

The spirit which informs this clay
  So fleets away.
Nothing is after Death; and this
  Too nothing is:
The gaol, or the extremest space
  Of a swift race.

> Seneca, *Troades, or, The royal captives* ... trans. Edward
> Sherburne (London: 1679; Wing S2528), E1^v

Introduction to Part IV

Early modern readers had a vast array of printed works to turn to, depending on their needs and means. There was a time to take up an *ars moriendi* treatise (Part I); a time to look after one's soul with a devotional manual (Part II); a time to be edified and entertained by a translation from the classics (Part III); and a time to lose oneself in a romance or a playbook (Part IV). To some extent all of the entries so far have been, strictly speaking, literary in that they trade in metaphors, allegorical figures, and poetic conceits as well as make use of discernible rhetorical structures and turns of phrase. This final part of our study offers a survey and closer look at works which, in the broadest generic sense, fall under the heading of 'literature' – drama, poetry, and prose fiction.

Plays by William Shakespeare, Ben Jonson, and Thomas Middleton are not included among our five representative passages from English Renaissance drama for the reasons outlined in 'Using this anthology', even though certainly their works lend themselves to discussions of key coordinates for mapping the death arts in early modern England, such as wills (most egregiously Jonson's *Volpone*, and the dead hand of the past guiding the marriage contest in Shakespeare's *The Merchant of Venice*), unusual ways of dying (Shakespeare's *The Winter's Tale* and Middleton's *Women Beware Women*), and mourning (quintessentially *Hamlet*).[1] Rather, we have aimed at bringing renewed attention to a selection of plays that otherwise use the dramaturgical techniques and performance sensibilities associated with Tudor and Stuart tragic drama that fundamentally depend on an awareness of the death arts for understanding and appreciating the dynamics of their presentation and reception: *The Summoning of Everyman* (IV.2), Christopher Marlowe's *Edward II* and *Doctor Faustus* (IV.9), Cyril Tourneur's *The Atheist's Tragedy* (IV.12), and Elizabeth Cary's closet drama, *The Tragedy of Mariam* (IV.13).

With poetry, we offer ten examples designed to showcase the variety of verse forms and subgenres through which the death arts found expression from the first decade of the sixteenth century to the close of the seventeenth. Included is a religious poem, Aemilia Lanyer's *Salve Deus Rex Judaeorum*, that treats the passion and death of Christ by way of highlighting the

---

[1] See *MA* VI.12 (Shakespeare) and *MA* VI.13 (Webster), the entries on *Hamlet* and *The Duchess of Malfi* respectively, for further discussion on intersections between memory and death studies.

predicaments and ingenuity of women from Eve's apology for the Fall, to the lamentation of women of conquered Jerusalem, and the trials of the Virgin Mary (IV.11). Other examples of didactic poetry, specifically social and moral commentaries on death artfully conceived that build implicitly on standard Christian beliefs, are Alexander Barclay's voluminous *The Ship of Fools* (IV.1) and a work of more personal pious reflection, *Gascoigne's Goodnight*, in which the poet is both the speaker and the subject of the discourse (IV.6). Closely related to this dualistic format are samples taken from actual 'dialogue poems' which resemble set-scenes from within a closet drama played out in the mind's eye: Samuel Rowlands's *Terrible Battle between … Time and Death* (IV.10), and John Lydgate's *Dance of Death* (IV.3) where Death always – quite literally – gets the last word in each exchange and then moves on to the next person in line who is made to leave the world of the living and join the universal *danse macabre*. Speakers in *The Dance of Death* each complain in a way befitting their condition and station, but to no avail.

The lyrical complaint, quite closely involved with the death arts since antiquity, was brought back to prominence by the metrical interludes in Boethius's sixth-century *Consolation of Philosophy*. Another of the classical forms that enjoyed a revival during the English Renaissance was the pastoral tradition (discussed in the Introduction in terms of the motto '*et in Arcadia, ego*'); and, as such they are self-consciously 'literary' in their conception, design, and presentation of the death arts (IV.4 and IV.16). Another kind of a complaint poem typical of the period and featured in what follows (IV.10) involves *exempla* that emphasise the close relationship or kinship between those doing or ordering the killing and those being killed. To be sure, elegies, within the larger literary field, pertain to that branch of consolation poetry fully integrated into funereal and related commemorative arts (like those discussed in Part II), such as the 'doleful lay' by 'Clorinda', which is to say Mary Sidney (II.8), and the frisson elicited from Francis Beaumont's anti-elegy (II.14) which uses while, at the same time, subverting the familiar elegiac tropes. And so our example, in Part IV, pertains to a very specific literary form: publications geared to facilitate – and to cash in on – the public mourning of an eminent figure, in this case the heir apparent (IV.12).[2] Counterbalancing this is our poetic selection of a socio-economic critique

---

[2] Cf. Andrew Hiscock, 'The Many Labours of Mourning a Virgin Queen', in *Memory and Mortality in Renaissance England*, ed. William E. Engel, Rory Loughnane, and Grant Williams (Cambridge: Cambridge University Press, 2022), ch. 11.

based on the last will and testament, Isabella Whitney's jaunty if poignant satirical *tour de force* which indicates something of the reach and range of the death arts in Tudor England (IV.7). Satire of course cuts across all literary genres, and so our example of the same in prose, published during the Interregnum (IV.15), uses the serious legal mechanism to lampoon a traitorous nobleman by staging an ill-prepared death.

Other prose selections highlight aspects of the death arts through the English borrowings and transformations of vernacular tales from Continental Europe, specifically Marguerite de Navarre's *Heptaméron* (IV.5). The death arts are part and parcel of the adventures found in episodic novels. Accordingly, our three examples of this literary type run the gamut of mimetic verisimilitude from Margaret Tyler's chivalric romance (IV.8), to Mary Wroth's pastoral romance reprising the ethos of the Sidneys' *Arcadia* (IV.14), and Aphra Behn's captivity narrative reflecting Caroline England's own 'here and now', the slave trade in the New World (IV.17). What we find in the period is that literature has been not only caught up in and representative of the death arts but also, through its endless strategies to prompt reflection upon mortality, profoundly constitutive of them.

IV.1

ALEXANDER BARCLAY

The Ship of Fools (1509)

About the author

Alexander Barclay (*c*.1476–1552), poet and priest, was chaplain at the College of Ottery St Mary, Devon in 1509 when his *Ship of Fools* was published.[1] A Benedictine monk at Ely, and later a Franciscan friar of Canterbury, by 1546 he had conformed to Protestantism and received benefices in Essex and Somerset, ending his career as rector of All Hallows, London.

About the text

Barclay's moral satire is based largely on Jakob Locher's 1497 Latin version of Sebastian Brandt's *Das Narrenschiff* (Basel, 1494); he also made some use of a French adaptation by Pierre Rivière (Paris, 1497). His vignettes of various types of folly are written in Chaucerian 'Troilus stanzas', or rhyme royal (printed in 'black letter', or Gothic, type), and commented on in Latin verse (in Roman type), thus satisfying at once and bridging popular and scholarly tastes. Copious references flank the margins, creating an ongoing side-discourse that lends to the whole a self-consciousness well suited to the subject matter. Moreover, the recut pictures, like the specifically English proverbs in Barclay's colloquial adaptation of this international best-seller, make the work truly a ship of fools of sixteenth-century England.[2]

The arts of death

Our excerpt comes from a section entitled 'fools that despise death making no provision thereof',[3] one of the many poems with an accompanying woodcut (see Figure 4.1) designed to make readers reflect on and acknowledge their

---

[1] See entry I.2 (*Calendar*).
[2] Observed in detail by Edwin H. Zeydel, *The Ship of Fools* (New York: Columbia University Press, 1944), p. 19.
[3] i.e., obliviousness of death; associated with the pride of life, a familiar medieval motif; see Langland *PP*, 20.143–55.

FIGURE 4.1 Death summoning Fool. Alexander Barclay, *The Ship of Fools* (London: 1509; STC 3545), 177ᵛ. Image used courtesy of The Huntington Library

failings so as to amend their ways, thus recalling both the traditional *danse macabre* and *vanitas* emblems. The *stultifera navis* theme has several English precedents, including Nigel Wireker's clerical satire, *Speculum stultorum*[4] [*Mirror of Fools*] and John Lydgate's *The Order of Fools*.[5] The timeless metaphor of life being a ship requiring vigilant manoeuvring had become such a

---

[4] better known by its English title, *Daun Burnel the Asse*, mentioned in 'The Nun's Priest's Tale' in *Canterbury Tales*, Chaucer *WO*, VII 3312 B2
[5] Cf. entry IV.3 (Lydgate).

popular literary and visual trope by the fifteenth century that it was often the subject of moral and social satire.[6] There was a real-life analogue of the Ship of Fools to be found in Tudor court revellers' pleasure barges aimlessly traversing the rivers of cosmopolitan areas and along the newly built canals. Sermons were composed on the theme of the fools' ship, rehearsing the specific ways that people are too easily distracted from their Christian duties, such as by not making proper provision for death. Barclay's *Ship of Fools* likewise interweaves quotations from the Bible (especially Job, Proverbs, and Ecclesiastes), the Church Fathers, and edifying Greek and Roman authorities (most frequently Homer, Xenophon, Plutarch, Ovid, Virgil, Cicero, and Boethius).

Textual notes

the Shyp of folys of the worlde (London: 1509; STC 3545), F6^r–G3^r.

The Ship of Fools

O cruel death, O fury favourless
So fierce art thou of look and countenance
That thou naught sparest virtue nor riches,
Beauty nor birth, strength nor alliance.
Each creature thou bringest to uttrance,[7]
Thou showest none his season nor his tide,[8]
So is he unwise that will thee not provide.

O brother in Christ conjoined by belief
Our blind presumption doth us sore abuse
Trust of long life our souls oft doth grieve
We have plain warning and yet we it refuse
Unwarily we wander, and nothing we muse
On death, but despise his furor intreatable[9]
Which sure shall come, though time be variable.

---

[6] e.g., Hieronymus Bosch, *The Ship of Fools* (*c*.1490–1500) at the Musée du Louvre
[7] 'utterance' (ME. *uttraunce*); the last extremity, bitter end
[8] 'period' (OE. *tid*, meaning 'portion of time')   [9] 'inexorable'

Man die thou shalt, this thing thou knowest plain
But as for the time, how, where, and when
These are and shall be kept uncertain
From thee, and me, and almost from every man.
Thus die thou must, provide it if thou can
We all must thereto, old, young, ill and good
Our life still passeth as water of a flood.

[…]
O death, how bitter is thy remembrance,
And how cruel is it thy pains to induce
To them that in earth setteth their pleasance
On wretched riches, unstable and unsure,
And on vain pleasures, yet every creature
Must from these riches (though they be loath) depart
When death them woundeth with his mortal dart.[10]

[…]
This dreadful death of colour pale and wan
To poor and rich in favour is equal.
It spareth neither women, child, nor man
But is indifferent both to great and small
For as sayeth Flaccus,[11] poet heroical
With one foot, it striketh at the door
Of king's palaces, and of the wretched poor.

[…]
One Rodopis[12] called by such a name
Builded[13] such another vain sepulchre[14]

---

[10] See, again, Figure 0.1.
[11] Horace *OD*, 1.4; Roman lyric poet (65–8 BCE).
[12] a legendary Greek courtesan (sixth century BCE), who was entombed in a pyramid built at great expense perhaps by her lovers
[13] 'built' (the late medieval preterit ending has been retained to preserve the pentameter of the original verse)
[14] 'place of burial'

The rich Amasis[15] also did the same,
But what was this, else but a vain pleasure?
It is a great folly to any creature
To make so great expenses and travail
About vain things that are of none avail.[16]

So great expense, such foolish cost and vain
Is done on tombs and all by pomp and pride
That this my ship can it scarcely contain
But the soul's health (alas) is set aside
Which ever should live and without end abide,
And the carrion and filth is magnified
By such vain tombs that are edified.[17]

Behold a tomb and precious sepulture[18]
Though it be gay, advise what is within:
A rotten carrion viler than all ordure[19]
By this proud tomb the soul no wealth can win
But is damned if the body died in sin
So is it folly great cost and vanity
To use in tombs such curiosity.

Every ground unto God is sanctified
A right wise man that well doth live and
Shall in high heaven in soul be glorified
In whatever ground his wretched carcass lie,
But where a tomb is builded curiously
It is but cause of pride to the offering
Helping the soul right little or nothing.

---

[15] Ahmose II (in Greek, Amasis II), Egyptian pharaoh (570–526 BCE), whose tomb was desecrated by the conquering Persian King Cambyses (Herodotus, *The Persian Wars, Volume II: Books 3–4*, trans. A. D. Godley, Loeb Classical Library (Cambridge, MA: Harvard University Press, 1921), 3.16).
[16] See *MA* VI.18; Thomas Browne similarly takes to task the vainglory of tomb builders who 'grossly erred in the art of perpetuation' (p. 350).
[17] 'constructed'   [18] 'sepulchre'   [19] 'excrement'

The envoy[20] of Barclay

 Man, keep thy body from sin, excess, and crime;
And if thou fall, arise shortly again.
Be ever ready, provide thy death by time
For die thou shalt, one thing is certain.
And oft death stealeth on man by course sudden;
He warneth none, but who that dies in sin
Dies worst of all, and sure is of hell pain.
Thus is it peril long to abide therein.

 Unto an archer death may I well compare
Which with his dart striketh sometime the mark,
That is, last age delivering them from care
Of mundane thought, and pain of worldly work.
Sometime he shooteth over, as he were dark
Of sight, and sometime too short, or else aside.
But well is him that taketh thought and cark[21]
At every season his darts to provide.

---

[20] Consistent with the form of this literary device (from medieval French poetry, *l'envoi*), literally a 'farewell' to the reader, these detached verses at the end of the poem reiterate and underscore the moral of the longer work.

[21] 'concern'

Suggested further reading

Robert C. Evans, 'Forgotten Fools: Alexander Barclay's *Ship of Fools*', in *Fools and Folly*, ed. Clifford Davidson (Kalamazoo, MI: Western Michigan University, 1996), pp. 47–72.

Zita Turi, 'Vessels of Passage: Reading the Ritual of the Late-Medieval Ship of Fools', *Forum*, 17 (2013), 1–11.

IV.2

ANONYMOUS

The Summoning of Everyman (1528)

About the text

The anonymous *Everyman* is a morality play, a form of homiletic religious drama that flourished in western Europe in the late fourteenth and early fifteenth centuries. Morality plays expound a Christian ideal, where personified abstractions, which may include vice or virtue figures, (e.g., 'Mischief', 'Good Deeds'), battle microcosmically for the soul of eponymous figures such as 'Everyman' or 'Mankind'. An edifying tool for lay audiences, they also helped instruct listeners in some of the more abstract concepts of medieval Christian doctrine (e.g., the Seven Deadly Sins and Seven Heavenly Virtues appear in *The Castle of Perseverance*). *Everyman* is an adapted translation of a Dutch morality, *Elckerlijc*, written in the 1480s or 1490s. It was published in a range of early editions. Our excerpt is from the earliest preserved complete copy, produced at John Skot's printshop. Bruster and Rasmussen date the quarto to between 1521 and 1528; for convenience, we have adopted the latest date. The title page of this edition, incidentally, has the same picture of Death as that used in *The Calender of Shepherds* (entry I.2; see Figure 1.2).

The arts of death

As the play begins, Everyman encounters Death who tells him to 'make ready' because, for him, today 'is the day / That no man living may scape away'. Death departs, and Everyman, in turn, encounters 'Fellowship' (his friends), 'Kindred and Cousin' (his family), 'Goods' (his possessions), none of whom can join him on his journey towards death. Everyman, it becomes clear, is ill-prepared for his death. Later, 'Discretion', 'Strength', 'Five Wits' (the five senses),[1] and 'Beauty' must also depart from him. He comes to realize that only 'Good Deeds' and her counterpart, 'Knowledge' will support him as he dies, and it is only 'Good Deeds' who will pass with him into the afterlife

---

[1] Cf. *MA* VI.14, a decidedly more light-hearted and comical allegorization of the five senses by Thomas Tomkis.

where he will be judged.[2] Our excerpt, from the end of the play, shows Everyman making his final, fearful preparations to enter with Good Deeds into his grave. Thereafter, no mercy or pity will be found from God, and all will depend upon whether the balance of his 'reckoning' (his figurative account book of good deeds) sends him to Heaven or Hell. All depends upon what he did in this life, soon to be departed, for, as the Doctor notes, 'after death amends may no man make'.

Textual notes

Here begynneth a treatise how ye hye fader of heuen sendeth dethe to somon euery creature to come and gyue a counte of theyr lyues in this worlde and is in maner of a morall play (London: 1521–1528; STC 10606), C3[r]–C4[r].

The Summoning of Everyman

EVERYMAN	O Jesu, help, all hath forsaken me!
GOOD DEEDS	Nay, Everyman, I will bide with thee.
	I will not forsake thee indeed;
	Thou shalt find me a good friend at need.
EVERYMAN	Gramercy,[3] Good Deeds. Now may I true friends see.
	They have forsaken me every each one;
	I loved them better than my Good Deeds alone.
	Knowledge, will ye forsake me also?
KNOWLEDGE	Yea, Everyman, when ye to death shall go,
	But not yet, for no manner of danger.
EVERYMAN	Gramercy, Knowledge, with all my heart.
KNOWLEDGE	Nay, yet I will not from hence depart
	Till I see where ye shall be come.
EVERYMAN	Methink, alas, that I must be gone,

---

[2] See *MA* VI.20 on John Bunyan's seventeenth-century adaptation of this same *homo viator* motif, where every person is considered a wayfarer, consonant with Augustine's metaphor concerning life being a journey – and more particularly, if seen aright, a pilgrimage (*peregrinus*) in Augustine *CG*, 14.28 and Augustine, *On Christian Doctrine*, trans. D. W. Robertson (Indianapolis, IN: Bobbs-Merrill; Liberal Arts Press, 1958), 1.4.

[3] 'thank you'

	To make my reckoning and my debts pay
	For I see my time is nigh[4] spent away.
	Take example, all ye that this do hear or see,
	How they that I love best do forsake me,
	Except my Good Deeds that bideth truly.
GOOD DEEDS	All earthly things is but vanity
	Beauty, Strength, and Discretion do man forsake,
	Foolish friends and kinsmen that fair spake;
	All fleeth save Good Deeds, and that am I.
EVERYMAN	Have mercy on me, God most mighty,
	And stand by me, thou mother and maid, holy Mary.
GOOD DEEDS	Fear not, I will speak for thee.
EVERYMAN	Here I cry God mercy.
GOOD DEEDS	Short our end and minish[5] our pain;
	Let us go and never come again.
EVERYMAN	Into thy hands, Lord, my soul I commend;
	Receive it, Lord, that it be not lost.
	As thou me boughtest, so me defend
	And save me from the fiend's boast,
	That I may appear with that blessed host
	That shall be saved at the day of doom
	In manus tuas, of mights most
	Forever, *commendo spiritum meum*.[6]

[EVERYMAN *enters his grave with* GOOD DEEDS.]

KNOWLEDGE	Now hath he suffered that we all shall endure.
	The Good Deeds shall make all sure.
	Now hath he made ending.
	Methinketh that I hear angels sing
	And make great joy and melody
	Where Everyman's soul received shall be.

---

[4] 'near', 'nearly'   [5] 'diminish', 'reduce'
[6] 'Father into thy hands I commend my spirit.' Jesus Christ's last words on the cross (Luke 23:46); Everyman begins this speech with an alternative English translation. Everyman's good death might be usefully compared with our excerpt from the ending of Marlowe's *Doctor Faustus* (entry IV.9).

THE ANGEL	Come, excellent elect spouse,[7] to Jesu!
	Here above thou shalt go
	Because of thy singular virtue.
	Now the soul is taken the body fro,
	Thy reckoning is crystal clear.
	Now shalt thou into the heavenly sphere,
	Unto the which all ye shall come
	That liveth well before the day of doom.

[*Exeunt the* ANGEL *and* KNOWLEDGE.]

[*Enter* DOCTOR, *for the epilogue.*]

Doctor	This moral[8] men may have in mind.
	Ye hearers, take it of worth, old and young,
	And forsake Pride, for he deceiveth you in the end,
	And remember Beauty, Five Wits, Strength, and Discretion:
	They all at the last do every man forsake,
	Save his Good Deeds there doth he take.
	But beware an[9] they be small,
	Before God he hath no help at all;
	None excuse may be there for Everyman.
	Alas, how shall he do then?
	For after death amends may no man make,
	For then mercy and pity doth him forsake.
	If his reckoning be not clear when he doth come
	God will say, '*Ite maledicti in ignem eternum*'.[10]
	And he that hath his account whole and sound,

---

[7] Everyman is elected into salvation; Jesus is here figured as a spouse to those achieving everlasting life in Heaven. The notion of God's saving grace bestowed on the elect according to sovereign decree originally was popularized by Augustine of Hippo in the fourth century in the context of his debates with Pelagius, which is of a different order from later Calvinist dogma concerning 'unconditional election'. See especially his 'Tractates on the Gospel According to St. John', trans. John Gibb, in *Nicene and Post-Nicene Fathers, First Series*, ed. Philip Schaff, rev. and ed. Kevin Knight (Buffalo, NY: Christian Literature Publishing Co., 1888), vol. 7, www.newadvent.org/fathers/1701.htm. Cf. entry I.9 (Perkins); and, for other references to the Augustinian understanding of election, as it is being used here in *Everyman*, see entries I.2 (*Calendar*), I.4 (Parr), I.17 (Smith), II.2 (Cranmer), II.15 (Brooks).

[8] An early version of the play, only preserved partially, reads 'memorial' rather than 'moral', which makes what the listeners must store 'in mind' more emphatic.

[9] 'if'   [10] 'Depart from me, ye cursed, into eternal fire' (Matt 25:41).

High in heaven he shall be crowned;
Unto which place God bring us all thither,
That we may live body and soul together.
Thereto help the Trinity!
Amen, say ye, for saint charity!

Suggested further reading
Douglas Bruster and Eric Rasmussen (eds.), *Everyman and Mankind*, Arden Early Modern Drama (London: Methuen Drama, 2009).
Donald F. Duclow, '*Everyman* and the *ars moriendi*: Fifteenth-Century Ceremonies of Dying', *Fifteenth-Century Studies*, 6 (1983), 93–113.
Merle Fifield, 'Methods and Modes: The Application of Genre Theory to Descriptions of Moral Plays', in *Everyman & Company*, ed. Donald Gilman (New York: AMS Press, 1989), pp. 7–74, esp. pp. 10–26.

IV.3

JOHN LYDGATE

The Dance of Death (1554)

About the author

John Lydgate (*c*.1370–*c*.1449/50), a Benedictine monk of Bury St Edmunds, wrote scholastically enriched texts such as *Aesop's Fables* which provided entrée to the courts of Henry IV, Henry V, and Henry VI. He also found patronage with the mayor and aldermen of London, the chapter of St Paul's (site of his *Dance of Death* commission), and, starting in 1422, Humphrey, Duke of Gloucester, which enabled him to travel, translate, and versify. In addition to writing poems on Chaucerian themes, Lydgate reworked earlier romances and moral texts, including his *Troy Book* and *Fall of Princes*.

About the text

Lydgate's *Dance of Death* circulated in manuscript during the 1470s, greatly influencing ideas about the personification of death in England.[1] While a number of devotional books showing scenes from the *danse*

---

[1] Nigel Mortimer, *John Lydgate's 'Fall of Princes'* (Oxford: Oxford University Press, 2005), p. 47.

macabre as well as ballads and broadsides addressing this perennial theme came out during the first decades of printing,[2] Lydgate's verse dialogue was not published until 1554. Richard Tottel appended it to Lydgate's 1430s translation of Boccaccio's *De Casibus Virorum Illustrium* (1355–1374), by way of a French version by Laurent de Premierfait (*c*.1400), which contained over fifty biographical vignettes 'showing and declaring', as the subtitle relates, 'in manner of tragedy, the falls of sundry most notable princes and princesses with other nobles'. Although other printed versions of this work exist (most notably by Richard Pynson in 1494), Tottel's is the first to include *The Dance of Death* with accompanying illustrations (see Figure 4.2). A century later, serving an antiquarian recovery agenda, a composite text of the two main extant versions of Lydgate's poem was appended to William Dugdale's *History of St. Paul's Cathedral* (1658) (see Figure 4.3).[3]

The arts of death

Lydgate's poem combines several Continental literary forms including the complaint poem, estates satire, the *memento mori* subgenre of 'the three dead and the three living',[4] and of course the 'dance of death' in which people of all stations are halted, summoned, and mocked by an animated cadaver. Notwithstanding the dialogue format, Death always gets the last word, symbolically and existentially reducing each respondent to silence. Typical of the genre, men and women of all social degrees and conditions are made to join the *danse macabre*. In the manuscript preface Lydgate recounts he saw a mural at St Innocents churchyard in Paris and translated 'out of the French *Macabrees daunce*' so that the proud 'as in a mirror' their 'ugly sin may clearly there behold / By example that they amend their life', stressing that 'this world is but a pilgrimage'. John Stowe repeats this account in his *Survey of London* (London: 1598; STC 23341), leading later authorities to assume that on the 'cloister of the north side' of St Paul's, from the reign of Henry VI until 1549, 'was artificially and richly painted the dance of Machabray, or dance of death'

---

[2] See entry I.2 (*Calendar*).
[3] See *MA* IV.10, which helps to situate Dugdale's St Paul's project in the context of his larger antiquarian project.
[4] as described in the 'Introduction'

FIGURE 4.2 Message from the tomb. John Lydgate, 'The Daunce of Machabree' appended to *The Fall of Princes* (London: 1554, STC 3177), fol. CCxx5^r. Image used courtesy of The Newberry Library

of Lydgate, with 'the picture of Death leading all estates painted about the cloister'.[5] The image accompanying Tottel's printing of the poem bears the motto '*Cunctis mortalibus mors debetur*' ['Everyone is subject to death'] (see Figure 4.4).

Textual note

the falles of sondry most notable princes and princesses (London: 1554; STC 3177), CC2^r–CC6^v.

---

[5] John Stowe, *Survey of London* (London: 1598; STC 23341), pp. 264–65.

FIGURE 4.3 Dance of Death. William Dugdale, *History of St. Paul's Cathedral* (London: 1658; STC 23341), Uuu1v. Image used courtesy of The Newberry Library

The Dance of Death

Death speaks to the Emperor.

Sir Emperor, lord of all the ground,
[Most] sovereign prince, surmounting of nobles,
You must forsake of gold your apple round,[6]
Sceptre and sword, and all your high prowess;
Behind you leave your treasure and riches,
And with other to my dance obey:

---

[6] 'orb', an emblem of temporal power

The Dance of Death (1554)

FIGURE 4.4 Dance of Death. John Lydgate, 'The Daunce of Machabree' appended to *The Fall of Princes* (London: 1554; STC 3177), fol. CCxxv. Image used courtesy of The Newberry Library

Against my might is worth none hardiness,
Adam's children all they must die.

The Emperor answers.

I [know not] to whom that I may appeal
Touching death, which doth me so constrain;
There is no gin[7] to help my quarrel,
But spade and pickaxe my grave to attain,
A simple sheet, there is no more to say,
To wrap in my body and visage:
And thereupon I may me sore complain,
That lords great have little advantage.

---

7 'engine'; 'device', 'means'

Death speaks to the Physician.

(See Figure 4.5)

Master of Physic, which on your urine
So look and gaze and stare against the sun,
For all your craft[8] and study of medicine,
[And] all the practice and science[9] that you cunne,[10]
Your life's course so far forth is run,
Against my might your craft may not endure,
For all the gold that you thereby have won:[11]
Good leech[12] is he that can himself recure.[13]

The Physician answers.

Full long ago that I unto physic
Set my wit and eke[14] my diligence,
In speculative and also in practical,
To get a name through mine excellence,
To find out against pestilence
Preservatives to staunch it and to fine:[15]
But I dare [say] shortly in sentence,[16]
Against Death is worth no medicine.[17]

Death speaks to the Gentlewoman.

Come forth, mistresses, of years young and green,
Which hold yourself of beauty souverain,
As fair as you was whilom[18] Pollixene,[19]
Penelope[20] and the queen Helen.[21]

---

[8] i.e., trade skill obtained through experience   [9] 'knowledge'   [10] 'learned by study'
[11] a jocular parallel of monetary gain ('all the gold') to the golden hue of urine inspected by physicians as part of their diagnostic process; a late medieval joke featured as well in 'General Prologue', *Canterbury Tales*, Chaucer *WO*, I (A) 444–45.
[12] 'doctor'; associated with this parasite used to draw out 'bad blood'
[13] an ancient proverb; cf. Luke 4:23, 'Physician heal thyself'.   [14] 'also'
[15] 'make an end of it'   [16] 'to wrap up in an adage'
[17] a variant of the proverb, 'there is no remedy for death'; cf. *The Greek Anthology, Volume II: Book 7: Sepulchral Epigrams. Book 8: The Epigrams of St. Gregory the Theologian*, trans. W. R. Paton, Loeb Classical Library (Cambridge, MA: Harvard University Press, 1917), 7.8.
[18] 'once', 'formerly'   [19] Polyxena, daughter of Priam of Troy, betrothed to Achilles
[20] Odysseus's wife, who held off numerous suitors during the Trojan War
[21] wife of Menelaus abducted by Paris, the *casus belli* of the Trojan War

The Dance of Death (1554)

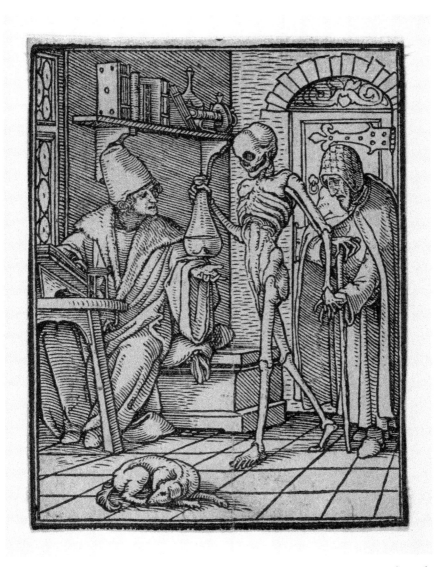

FIGURE 4.5 Death summons the Physician. Hans Holbein, *The Dance of Death* (Lyons: 1538). Image used courtesy of the New York Metropolitan Museum of Art (Creative Commons)

Yet on this dance they went both twain,
And so shall you, for all your strangeness;[22]
Though danger[23] long in love hath led your rein,
Arrested is your change[24] of doubleness.

The Gentlewoman answers.

O cruel Death, that spares none of estate,[25]
To old and young thou art indifferent;
To my beauty thou hast said checkmate,[26]
So hasty is thy mortal judgement.
For in my youth this was mine intent,
To my service many man to have lured;
But she is a fool, shortly in sentment,[27]
That in her beauty is too much assured.

Death speaks to the Child.

Little infant, that were but late born,
Shape[28] in this world to have no pleasance,
You must with others that gone here before,
Be led in haste by fatal ordinance.
Learn of new to go on my dance:
There may none age escape in sooth there from.
Let every wight[29] have this in remembrance:
Who longest lives most shall suffer woe.

The Child answers.

A, a, a,[30] a word I cannot speak;
I am so young;[31] I was born yesterday.

---

[22] 'aloofness' [23] 'reluctance' [24] 'inconstancy' [25] 'high social rank'; 'nobility'
[26] a conventional trope associated with death; cf. Skelton, 'Upon a Dead Man's Head', l.30 (see *MA* VI.1).
[27] 'sentiment'; 'summary view' [28] 'person' [29] 'prepare'; 'set yourself'
[30] phonetic imitation of the pre-linguistic sounds an infant might make, conducing thence to its articulate complaint
[31] Cf. Jer 1:6: 'Oh Lorde God, I canne not speake, for I am yet but younge' (Great Bible, 1539).

Death is so hasty on me to be wreke,[32]
And list[33] no longer to make no delay.
I come but now, and now I go my way;
Of me no more tale shall be told.
The will of God no man withstand may;
As sooner die a young man as an old.

[32] 'lay claim to'; with reference to the recovery of property, including people previously bound to a master
[33] 'desires'

Suggested further reading
Megan L. Cook and Elizaveta Strakhov (eds.), *John Lydgate's 'Dance of Death'* (Kalamazoo, MI: Medieval Institute Publications, 2019).
Elina Gertsman, *The Dance of Death in the Middle Ages* (Turnhout, BE: Brepols, 2010).

IV.4

HENRY HOWARD

'Complaint of a Dying Lover' (1557)

About the author

Henry Howard, Earl of Surrey (?1517–1547), soldier, courtier, and poet, was of high noble ancestry (descended from Edward I on his father's side and Edward III on his mother's). He unwisely – and treasonably – quartered the royal arms with his own, resulting in imprisonment and execution by Henry VIII. His literary legacy includes a translation of Virgil's *Aeneid* (books 2 and 4) which models the suppleness of heroic blank verse (unrhymed iambic pentameter) that subsequently became the preferred metre for English dramatic and epic poetry.

About the text

Richard Tottel's *Miscellany* (going through nine editions between 1557 and 1587) was the first printed anthology of English poetry. It consisted originally of 271 poems written in the 1530s, most of which had not previously been published. Although more poems in it are attributed to Wyatt, Surrey is given pride of place on the title page. Our excerpt, 'Complaint of a Dying Lover, refused upon his lady's unjust misunderstanding of his writing', combines pastoral imagery with epic conventions, and is written in poulter's measure[1] (couplets having first an alexandrine line, in iambic hexameter or with twelve syllables, followed by a 'fourteener' in iambic heptameter).

The arts of death

Renaissance poets tirelessly rehearsed the courtly ideal of service to one's beloved even unto death, a relationship mirrored in the fealty pledged to one's liege lord. A range of related poetic conceits popularized in Italy by Petrarch (1304–1374), such as the hyperbolic expression of agonies experienced by a suffering lover owing to the indifference or refusal of his mistress, found their way into English love poetry principally because of the efforts of Wyatt and Surrey. 'Complaint of a Dying Lover' is a dialogically narrated frame poem (allowing the poet to avoid direct address to his intended) that borrows from the *ars moriendi* by depicting on-the-scene death throes and the final confession of a martyr to love. The burial of the 'dying lover' beside Troilus's tomb fixes in the mind's eye a contemporary if co-opted and hence double monument of love *in extremis*, offered here as a parting argument to the intended of the courtier-poet taking on the identity of a shepherd within the frame of this poem so that she might, unlike the beloved of the now dead lover, deign to be merciful toward him and relent before it is too late.

Textual notes

Songes and sonettes, written by the right honorable lorde henry haward late earle of surrey, and other (London: 1557; STC 13862), B4^v–C1^v.

---

[1] Poulterers traditionally gave an extra couple of eggs when selling by the dozen.

'Complaint of a Dying Lover'

In winter's just return, when Boreas[2] 'gan[3] his reign,
And every tree unclothed fast, as nature taught them plain:[4]
   In misty morning dark, as sheep are then in hold,
I hied[5] me fast, it sat me on, my sheep for to unfold.
   And as it is a thing that lovers have by fits,   5
Under a palm[6] I heard one cry as he had lost his wits.
   Whose voice did ring so shrill in uttering of his plaint,[7]
That I amazed was to hear how love could him attaint.[8]
   'Ah! wretched man', quoth he; 'come, death, and rid this woe;
A just reward, a happy end, if it may chance thee so.   10
   Thy pleasures past have wrought[9] thy woe without redress;
If thou hadst never felt no joy, thy smart had been the less'.
   And reckless of his life, he 'gan both sigh and groan
A rueful thing me thought it was, to hear him make such moan.
[…]
   'What woeful wight[10] art thou, that in such heavy case
Torments thyself with such despite, here in this desert[11] place?'   30
   Wherewith as all aghast, fulfilled with ire and dread,
He cast on me a staring look, with colour pale and dead:
   'Nay, what art thou', quoth he, 'that in this heavy plight
Dost find me here, most woeful wretch, that life hath in despite?'
   'I am', quoth I, 'but poor, and simple in degree;   35
A shepherd's charge I have in hand, unworthy though I be'.
   With that he gave a sigh, as though the sky should fall,
And loud, alas! he shrieked oft, and, 'shepherd,' 'gan he call,
   'Come, hie thee fast at once, and print it in thy heart,
So thou shalt know, and I shall tell thee, guiltless how I smart'.   40

---

[2] i.e., the north-wind, harsh and cold   [3] 'began'
[4] a line quoted as exemplary in *The Art of English Poesy by George Puttenham: A Critical Edition*, ed. Frank Whigham and Wayne A. Rebhorn (Ithaca, NY: Cornell University Press, 2007), bk. 3, ch. 18, regarding *periphrasis*
[5] 'go quickly'
[6] colloquially a willow, fronds of which were used in ceremonies in lieu of palm; also a florilogical emblem of the victory achieved through martyrdom
[7] 'complaint'; presenting one's case seeking redress for an injury
[8] 'affect'; a legal term associated with charges carrying a death sentence   [9] 'made'
[10] 'person', typically an unfortunate one   [11] 'isolated', 'remote'

  His back against the tree sore feebled[12] all with faint,
With weary sprite he stretched him up, and thus he told his plaint:
  'Once in my heart', quoth he, 'it chanced me to love
Such one, in whom hath nature wrought, her cunning for to prove.
  And sure I cannot say, but many years were spent,   45
With such good will so recompensed, as both we were content.
  Whereto then I me bound, and she likewise also,
The sun should run his course awry, ere we this faith forego.
  Who joyed then but I? who had this world's bliss?
Who might compare a life to mine, that never thought on this?   50
  But dwelling in this truth, amid my greatest joy,
Is me befallen a greater loss than Priam[13] had of Troy.[14]
  She is reversed clean, and beareth me in hand,[15]
That my deserts have given cause to break this faithful band:
  And for my just excuse availeth no defence.   55
Now knowest thou all; I can no more; but, shepherd, hie thee hence,
  And give him leave to die, that may no longer live
Whose record, lo! I claim to have, my death I do forgive.
  And eke when I am gone, be bold to speak it plain,
Thou hast seen die the truest man that ever love did pain'.   60
  Wherewith he turned him round, and gasping oft for breath,
Into his arms a tree he raught,[16] and said: 'Welcome my death!
  Welcome a thousand-fold, now dearer unto me
Than should, without her love to live, an emperor to be'.
  Thus in this woeful state he yielded up the ghost;   65
And little knoweth his lady, what a lover she hath lost.
[…]
  Then as I could devise, to seek I thought it best   75
Where I might find some worthy place for such a corse[17] to rest.
  And in my mind it came, from thence not far away,
Where Cressid's love, King Priam's son, the worthy Troilus[18] lay.
  By him I made his tomb,[19] in token he was true,

---

[12] 'weak'   [13] i.e., the last king of Troy
[14] i.e., the capital city razed by Greeks ending the decade-long siege
[15] 'keep in expectation'   [16] 'reached for'   [17] 'corpse'
[18] In medieval romance and epic poetry, Troilus embodies the faithful courtly lover, and Criseyde represents faithlessness and inconstancy (for taking up with Diomede).
[19] an excavation in earth or rock for burial of a corpse

And as to him belonged well, I covered it with blue.[20] 80
Whose soul by angels' power departed not so soon,
But to the heavens, lo! it fled, for to receive his doom.[21]

[20] the colour symbolizing fidelity
[21] 'judgement' (OE. *dōm*, situate in proper place)

Suggested further reading
Jonathan Crewe, *Trials of Authorship: Anterior Forms and Poetic Reconstruction from Wyatt to Shakespeare* (Berkeley, CA: University of California Press, 1990), ch. 2.
Andrew Hiscock, *Reading Memory in Early Modern Literature* (Cambridge: Cambridge University Press, 2011), ch. 1.

IV.5

WILLIAM PAINTER

'A Strange Punishment' (1566)

About the author

William Painter (1540?–1595), who likely came from a Kentish family, was a translator and clerk of the ordnance at the Tower of London. One of many Elizabethan civil servants accused of corruption, he bolstered his office's meagre income by siphoning off monies from the funds that he managed over his career.

About the text

'The Strange Punishment' is the fifty-sixth tale in Painter's *The Palace of Pleasure*, a collection of novellas he compiled and translated from Continental sources. This volume, in addition to the second tome of thirty-four tales published a year later, would become one of the staple vade-mecums that English dramatists (most notably Shakespeare with *Romeo and Juliet* and Webster with *The Duchess of Malfi*) plundered for plot and character ideas. In the dedicatory epistle to his master at the Tower's armoury, Ambrose Dudley, the Earl of Warwick, Painter explains that the genesis of his collection started with selecting stories out of Livy that he deemed worthy to be disseminated 'in our noble tongue' (*2ᵛ) and then turned his attention to 'sundry proper and commendable histories' (*3ʳ) found in Boccaccio, Bandello, and other French and Italian authors. These tales, intermingled with diverting jests and devices, run the gamut from the heroic exploits and noble deeds of princes to the cruelties and despicable excesses of tyrants: 'All which may render good example for all sorts to follow the best and embrace the virtuous, contrariwise to reject the worst and contemplate the vicious' (*3ᵛ). Painter's preliminary comments, however, give readers little guidance through the moral landscape of 'The Strange Punishment', which recounts the extraordinary mental torture a German gentleman subjects his adulteress wife to: Painter appropriates the narrative from the thirty-second story on the fourth day of Marguerite de Navarre's *Heptaméron*, but, consistent with his practice in *The Palace of Pleasure*, neglects to translate the original frame narrative wherein a courtly audience debates and thus questions the justness of the wife's enforced penance.

The arts of death

In the tale, the emissary Bernage travels to Germany on behalf of Charles VIII of France and late one evening seeks lodging at a gentleman's castle. When Bernage and his host sit down to eat, a beautiful woman, dressed in black and with shorn hair, joins the table, but throughout the meal she remains silent, drinking from 'a strange cup', namely, the 'head of a dead man trimmed with silver' (KKKK4ᵛ). Sensing that Bernage is disturbed by the sight – the conception of which would make Spenser proud – the host explains in the passage below the events that have led to this weird spectacle. The tale provides readers with a different kind of gloss on *Hamlet*'s graveyard scene[1] and casts an instructive light on Ferdinand's cruel torment of his sister in *The Duchess of Malfi*[2] insofar as the host recruits the instruments of *memento mori*, both the skull and the corpse, as the means of punishment, a worldly punishment that seems to feed an outrageous *Schadenfreude* rather than satisfying any notion of justice. Opening up the tale's verbal complexity for the death arts, Richard Sugg takes its use of 'anatomy', instead of 'skeleton', and 'head'-cup, instead of 'skull'-cup, to imply that Painter wants to startle his readers with an *écorché*, the flayed body just recently introduced by

---

[1] See *MA* VI.12 (Shakespeare).   [2] See *MA* VI.13 (Webster).

Vesalius's *De Fabrica* and its imitators, thereby preferring the visceral sense of corporeal violence to the familiar iconography embedded in the *memento mori* tradition.

Textual notes

The palace of pleasure beautified, adorned and well furnished, with pleasaunt histories and excellent nouelles (London: 1566; STC 19121), KKKK4ᵛ–LLLL1ᵛ.

'A Strange Punishment'

'But in a journey which I made, which to attempt[3] mine honour forced me, she forgot[4] both herself, her conscience, and the love which she bear towards me, and fell in love with a gentleman, that I brought up in this house, which upon my return I perceived to be true. Notwithstanding the love that I bear her was so great, that I had no mistrust in her, til such time as experience did open mine eyes and saw the thing that I feared more than death. For which cause love was turned into fury and despair, in such wise that I watched her so near that upon a day feigning myself to go abroad, I hid myself in the chamber where now she remaineth. Into the which soon after my departure she repaired and caused the gentleman to come thither, whom I did behold to do that thing, which was altogether unmeet for any man to do to her, but myself. But when I saw him get up, upon the bed after her, I stepped forth and took him between her arms, and with my dagger immediately did kill him. And because the offence of my wife seemed to be so great, that like death was not sufficient to punish her. I devised a torment which in mine opinion is worse unto her than death. I do lock her up in the chamber wherein she accustomed to use her delights, and in the company of him that she loved far better than me. In which chamber I have placed the anatomy[5] of her friend, reserving the same in a little closet as a precious jewel. And to the end she may not forget him at meals, at the table before my face, she useth the head[6] of that varlet instead of a cup to drink, to the intent she may behold him alive, in the presence of him whom through her own fault she hath made her mortal enemy, and him dead and slain for her sake, whose love she preferred before mine. And so beholdeth those two things at dinner and supper which ought to displease her most, her enemy living, and her friend dead, and all through her own wickedness

---

[3] 'to essay' [4] 'to forget … herself': to behave unethically
[5] 'preserved corpse', 'skeleton' [6] 'skull'

howbeit I do use her no worse than myself, although she goeth thus shaven, for the ornament of the hair doth not appertain to an adulteress, nor the veil or other furniture of the head to an unchaste woman.[7] Wherefore she goeth so shaven, in token she hath lost her honesty. If it please you sir to take the pain to see her, I will bring you to her.' Whereunto Bernage willingly assented. And descending into her chamber which was very richly furnished, they found her sitting alone before the fire. And the gentleman drawing a curtain, which was before the closet, he saw the anatomy of the dead man hanging.

[7] Cf. 1 Cor 11:5–6; a shaved head stigmatized a woman, no longer married or faithful to her husband, as a prostitute.

Suggested further reading
Abigail Shinn, 'Managing Copiousness for Pleasure and Profit: William Painter's "Palace of Pleasure"', *Renaissance Studies: Journal of the Society for Renaissance Studies*, 28.2 (2014), 205–24.
Richard Sugg, *Murder after Death: Literature and Anatomy in Early Modern England* (Ithaca, NY and London: Cornell University Press, 2007), pp. 13–17.

IV.6

GEORGE GASCOIGNE

'Gascoigne's Goodnight' (1573)

About the author

George Gascoigne (*c*.1534–1577) left Cambridge University to enter Gray's Inn in 1555, although was never admitted to the Bar. He served in Parliament for Bedford from 1557 to 1559 and, after being detained in Bedford Gaol for debt around 1570, sought his fortune as a soldier in the Low Countries supporting William I of Orange-Nassau against the Spanish (for which he received bonus pay from the stadtholder for his role in the Siege of Middleburg) and was briefly a prisoner of the Spanish. His collected works appeared anonymously in 1573, thus spurring him to publish *The Poesies of George Gascoigne* (1575). A literary innovator (and recognized as such by Elizabethan literati[1]) as

[1] See, for example, Thomas Nashe's preface to Robert Greene's *Menaphon* (London: 1589; STC 12272): 'Master Gascoigne … who first beat the path to that perfection which our best poets have aspired to since' (**4ᵛ).

well as a deft translator (most notably of Ariosto's *Supposes* and Euripides's *Phoinissae (as Jocasta)*), Gascoigne blazed a trail for others to follow his lead in English drama, prose fiction, lyric poetry, and criticism.

About the text

'Gascoigne's Goodnight' is featured in *A Hundred Sundry Flowers*, a veritable grab-bag of verse and prose. His corrected and carefully organized revised edition (which clarifies various connections between pairs, triads, and sometimes groups of poems) appeared in 1575 with the significant addition of 'Certain Notes of Instruction', the first treatise on English prosody. 'Gascoigne's Goodnight' (written in fourteeners with both medial and end rhymes) is a companion poem to 'Gascoigne's Goodmorrow', each with its own special chiastic elements as well as thematic and structural links between the two. The title, 'Gascoigne's Goodnight', in addition to completing the cyclic diurnal-nocturnal conceit,[2] not only refers to a salutation but also announces its participation in that literary genre concerned with the final words of people about to die[3] typically set later in ballad form and known as 'farewell songs' and 'dirges'.[4]

The arts of death

This poem offers an intensely focused and highly self-conscious *memento mori* meditation in which things encountered in everyday life – brought starkly to prominence through night-time reflection – are figured as a microcosm that corresponds to, and thereby prepares us for, our ultimate end. Gascoigne here plays upon the commonplace Renaissance trope of sleep being like or a rehearsal for death, and death being a kind of necessary sleep

---

[2] a similar structure marks Henry Vaughan's 'Morning-watch' and 'Evening-watch' in *Silex Scintillans* (London: 1650; WING V125), C5ᵛ–C7ʳ.
[3] See, for example, the single-sheet broadside 'On the lamentable death of the Earl of Essex' which, by 1700, gives the tune as 'Essex last Goodnight' (Wing L266A), most probably the earlier popular tune 'Welladay' as is given on most earlier versions of the same ballad (London: 1603: STC 6791). Cf. entry I.12 ('The Unnatural Wife').
[4] Cf. Shakespeare, *2 Henry IV* (3.2.260–61); Falstaff derides Justice Shallow for hearing tunes whistled by carriage drivers and swearing they are his own 'fancies or his good-nights'.

prior to the soul awakening to find its portion in the afterlife.[5] Neatly divided into two equal parts, the first half pointedly refers seven times to 'thou' (ll. 1–18) and then shifts, in the latter part, to the first person, using 'I' eleven times (ll. 19–38). Such an arrangement suggests a deliberate evocation of medieval dialogue-poems staged between the body and the soul. The poem also gives a nod to *ars moriendi* treatises such as Thomas Becon's *The Sick Man's Salve* (1561), a long deathbed scene in which four companions prepare their dying friend for his death, insofar as Gascoigne's poem embodies both sides of this divide, embracing the monitors and the *moriens* alike. As such, and especially when taken together with 'Gascoigne's Goodmorrow', it raises the stakes on English devotional poetics by presenting a pattern for meditation in the form of a spiritual conduct manual that step-by-step explains how to interpret and 'try thy daily deeds' (l.11) in anticipation of death.

Textual notes

A hundreth sundrie flowres bounde vp in one small poesie (London: 1573; STC 11635), Y2[r-v].

'Gascoigne's Goodnight'

When thou hast spent the lingering day in pleasure and delight,
Or after toil and weary way, dost seek to rest at night:
Unto thy pains or pleasures past, add this one labour yet,
Ere sleep close up thine eye too fast, do not thy God forget,
But search within thy secret thoughts, what deeds did thee befall: 5
And if thou find amiss in aught,[6] to God for mercy call.[7]
Yea though thou find nothing amiss, which thou canst call to mind,
Yet ever more remember this, there is the more behind:
And think how well so ever it be, that thou hast spent the day,
It came of God, and not of thee, so to direct thy way.   10

---

[5] e.g., the penultimate line of Donne's Holy Sonnet 'Death be not proud': 'One short sleep past, we live eternally' (Donne *PO*, p. 139, l. 13); and the 'To be, or not to be' soliloquy in which Shakespeare's Hamlet contemplates: 'to die, to sleep— / To sleep, perchance to dream, ay, there's the rub. / For in that sleep of death what dreams may come' (*Hamlet*, 3.1.65–67).
[6] 'anything at all'   [7] 1 John 1:8

Thus if thou try thy daily deeds, and pleasure in this pain,
Thy life shall cleanse thy corn from weeds,[8] and thine shall be the gain:
But if thy sinful sluggish[9] eye, will venter[10] for to wink,[11]
Before thy wading will may try, how far thy soul may sink,
Beware and wake, for else thy bed, which soft and smooth is made,   15
May heap more harm upon thy head, than blows of enemies' blade.
Thus if this pain procure thine ease, in bed as thou dost lie,
Perhaps it shall not God displease, to sing thus soberly:
I see that sleep is lent me here, to ease my weary bones,
As death at last shall eke[12] appear, to ease my grievous groans.   20
My daily sports, my paunch full fed, have caused my drowsy eye,
As careless life in quiet led, might cause my soul to die:
The stretching arms, the yawning breath, which I to bedward use,
Are patterns of the pangs of death, when life will me refuse:
And of my bed each sundry part in shadows doth resemble,   25
The sundry shapes of death, whose dart[13] shall make my flesh to tremble.
My bed itself is like the grave, my sheets the winding sheet,
My clothes the mould[14] which I must have, to cover me most meet:
The hungry fleas which frisk so fresh, to worms I can compare,
Which greedily shall gnaw my flesh, and leave the bones full bare: 30
The waking cock that early crows to wear the night away,
Puts in my mind the trump that blows before the latter[15] day.[16]
And as I rise up lustily, when sluggish sleep is past,
So hope I to rise joyfully, to Judgement at the last.
Thus will I wake,[17] thus will I sleep, thus will I hope to rise,   35
Thus will I neither wail nor weep, but sing in godly wise.

---

[8] *Eclogues* in Virgil *EGA*, 1.47–48; cf. Desiderius Erasmus, *Collected Works of Erasmus, Volume 34: Adages: II Vii 1 to III Iii 100*, trans. R. A. B. Mynors (Toronto, ON: University of Toronto Press, 2000), II.ix.81.
[9] 'indolent'   [10] 'venture'; 'undertake'
[11] 'close for sleep'; figuratively, disregarding some fault or irregularity   [12] 'also'
[13] This is one of the principal iconographic attributes assigned to death personified in the West (see Figure 0.1); for example, see *MA* VI.10 (esp. p. 318, n3) on Milton's use of Death's 'dreadful dart' in *Paradise Lost*.
[14] 'earth' (usually in reference to the soil of hallowed burial ground)   [15] 'last'
[16] 'In a moment, in the twinkling of an eye, at the last trump. For the trump shall blow, and the dead shall rise incorruptible, and we shall be changed' (1 Cor 15:52; Bishops' Bible). See entry III.2 (Elyot).
[17] Ps 130:6

My bones shall in this bed remain, my soul in God shall trust,
By whom I hope to rise again from death and earthly dust.
Haud ictus sapio.[18]

---

[18] 'Having been struck, I still am not wise'; a signature motto (used by Gascoigne at the end of select poems) suggesting that wisdom will come in its own time; also an obvious play upon the proverb *Piscator ictus sapiet* ['Once stung, the fisherman will be wiser']. See Desiderius Erasmus, *Collected Works of Erasmus, Volume 32: Adages: I Vi 1 to I x 100*, trans. R. A. B. Mynors (Toronto, ON: University of Toronto Press, 1989), I.i.29.

Suggested further reading
Gillian Austen, *George Gascoigne* (Cambridge: D. S. Brewer, 2008), pp. 84–133.
Roy T. Eriksen, '"Two into One": The Unity of George Gascoigne's Companion Poems', *Studies in Philology*, 81.3 (1984), 275–98.
G. W. Pigman III, 'Introduction', *A Hundreth Sundrie Flowres* (Oxford: Clarendon Press, 2000), pp. iii–lxv.

IV.7

ISABELLA WHITNEY

'The Manner of her Will' (1573)

About the author

Isabella Whitney (*fl.* 1566–1573) apparently served from an early age in a London household. To make her way further in the world she wrote verse, attracting the notice of the printer Richard Jones who also specialized in publishing ballads and pamphlets. While only two major collections definitively are attributed to Whitney, other works published by Jones are conjectured to have been written by her on the basis of similarity of tone (social satire), style (written from a woman's point of view), and theme (censuring economic disparities and legal inequities of the day). She is the first Englishwoman to publish secular poetry under her own name.

About the text

The poem entitled 'The Manner of her Will and what she left to London, and to all those in it, at her departing' is the last section of Whitney's *A Sweet Nosegay*. Her episodic book clearly draws on the age-old anthological metaphor[1] and successful textual formula of Hugh Plat's *Flowers of Philosophy* (1572)[2] and George Gascoigne's *Hundred Sundry Flowers* (1573).[3] Its middle section consists of verse epistles to friends and family with their responses, after the imaginative autobiographical fashion of Ovid's *Heroides* but concerning mundane rather than heroic matters. 'The Manner of her Will' follows thematically from her complaints voiced earlier in the longer work regarding the allures and unfulfilled promises of urban life. Whitney's quatrains recount scenes from the trials of an unattached woman quitting an inconstant lover. Owing to the epigrammatic wit displayed in her vivid caricatures of London mercers and widowers among other recognizable urban types, this poem anticipates later dramatized vignettes of English Renaissance citizen comedy, satirical adaptations of Theophrastean character sketches,[4] and the 'speaking pictures' of emblem books.

The arts of death

Although couched as a jaunty survey of the harsh yet enticing realities of cosmopolitan life that Whitney says she is leaving behind, the poem is suffused with both an abiding sense of the vanity of mortal striving and admonitory contempt for things of this world. The main textual model for this lively romp through a city full of merchandise just out of reach for someone of her station is the last will and testament, a legal document, drawn up when one's departure is imminent, bequeathing what one has acquired in this vale of tears.[5] Whitney's clever use of the mock-testament as a literary pretence predates by two decades Thomas Nashe's socially relevant 'pleasant comedy' about the farewell of Will Summers, jester of Henry VIII.

Textual notes

A Sweet nosgay, or pleasant posye: contayning a hundred and ten phylosophicall flowers (London: 1573; STC 25440), E3ʳ–E8ᵛ.

---

[1] from the Greek *anthos* ('flower') and *logia* ('collection', from *legein*, 'to gather')
[2] On Plat's miscellaneous writings, see *MA* I.5.   [3] See entry IV.6 (Gascoigne).
[4] See *MA* VI.16, on John Earle's satirical micro-essays that likewise describe various public personae *in situ*.
[5] For another parodic will, see entry IV.15.

'The Manner of her Will'

I whole in body, and in mind,
    but very weak in purse,
Do make, and write my testament
    for fear it will be worse.
And first I wholly do commend
    my soul and body eke,[6]
To God the Father and the Son,
    so long as I can speak.
And after speech, my soul to him,
    and body to the grave,
Till time that all shall rise again,
    their Judgement for to have,
And then I hope they both shall meet,
    to dwell for aye[7] in joy;
Whereas I trust to see my friends
    released from all annoy.
Thus have you heard touching my soul,
    and body what I mean:
I trust you all will witness bear,
    I have a steadfast brain.
And now let me dispose such things,
    as I shall leave behind,
That those which shall receive the same,
    may know my willing mind.
I first of all to London leave,
    because I there was bred,
Brave buildings rare, of churches store,
    and Paul's to the head.
Between the same, fair streets there be,
    and people goodly store;
Because their keeping craveth cost,
    I yet will leave him more.
[…]

---

[6] 'each'; a shopworn phrase from medieval English theological legalist disputation. See 'The Friar's Tale' in *Canterbury Tales*, Chaucer *WO*, III (D) 1492–93: 'And somtyme han we myght of bothe two– / This is to seyn, of soule and body eke.'

[7] 'ever after', 'eternally'

And those which are of calling such,
    that costlier they require,
I mercers leave, with silk so rich,
    as any would desire.
In Cheap[8] of them, they store shall find,
    and likewise in that street,
I goldsmiths leave, with jewels such,
    as are for ladies meet.
[…]
For nets[9] of every kind of sort,
    I leave within the pawn:
French ruffs, high purls,[10] gorgets[11] and sleeves
    of any kind of lawn[12]
For purse or knives, for comb or glass,
    or any needful knack
I by the stocks have left a boy,
    will ask you what you lack.
I hose do leave in Birchin Lane
    of any kind of size:
For women stitched, for men both trunks
    and those of Gascoyne guise.[13]
Boots, shoes or pantables[14] good store,
    Saint Martin's hath for you.
In Cornwall[15], there I leave you beds,
    and all that long[16] thereto.
[…]
Now when thy folk are fed and clad
    with such as I have named,
For dainty mouths, and stomachs weak
    some junckets[17] must be framed.

---

[8] literally 'marketplace' (OE. *ceap*, 'bargaining'), indicating here a specific shopping area
[9] 'woven goods', 'fabrics'
[10] 'the raised stitch ridge made from precious metal wire often used on lace collars'
[11] 'the band of linen wrapped around a woman's neck as part of chaperon hood'
[12] 'fine plain-weave textile'   [13] 'wide breeches' (in the latest fashion)   [14] 'slippers'
[15] linen shopping side street, east of the Tower of London   [16] 'belong'
[17] 'sweetmeats' (custard-like flavoured curds of milk from the stomach of an unweaned calf)

Wherefore I potecaries[18] leave,
   with banquets in their shop,
Physicians also for the sick,
   diseases for to stop.
Some roysters[19] still must bide in thee,
   and such as cut it out;
That with the guiltless quarrel will,
   to let their blood about.
For them I cunning surgeons leave,
   some plasters to apply,
That ruffians may not still be hanged,
   nor quiet persons die.
[…]
To all the bookbinders by Paul's,[20]
   because I like their art:
They every week shall money have,
   when they from books depart.
Among them all, my printer must
   have somewhat to his share;
I will my friends these books to buy
   of him, with other ware.
For maidens poor, I widowers rich
   do leave, that oft shall dote:
And by that means shall marry them,
   to set the girls afloat.
And wealthy widows will I leave
   to help young gentlemen;
Which when you have, in any case,
   be courteous to them then:
And see their plate and jewels eke
   may not be marred with rust;
Nor let their bags too long be full,
   for fear that they do burst.
[…]

---

[18] 'apothecaries' (storekeepers who prepared medicines and sold herbs and spices)
[19] 'swaggerers', 'revellers'
[20] i.e., St Paul's Churchyard, a primary site for stationers in London

This twenty of October, I,
    in ANNO DOMINI,
A thousand, five hundred seventy-three,
    as almanacs descry,
Did write this will with mine own hand,
    and it to London gave;
In witness of the standers-by,
    whose names, if you will have,
Paper, pen and standish[21] were,
    at that same present by,
With Time, who promised to reveal
    so fast as she could buy
The same, lest of my nearer kin
    For anything should vary;
So finally I make an end
    no longer can I tarry.

[21] 'tray for holding an inkpot and other writing equipment'

Suggested further reading

Laurie Ellinghausen, 'Literary Property and the Single Woman in Isabella Whitney's *A Sweet Nosegay*', *Studies in English Literature*, 45.1 (2005), 1–22.

Dana E. Lawrence, 'Isabella Whitney's "Slips"', *A History of Early Modern Women's Writing*, ed. Patricia Phillippy (Cambridge: Cambridge University Press, 2018), pp. 119–36.

Kirk Melnikoff, 'Isabella Whitney amongst the Stalls of Richard Jones', in *Women's Labour and the History of the Book in Early Modern England*, ed. Valerie Wayne (London and New York: Bloomsbury, The Arden Shakespeare, 2020), pp. 145–61.

Betty Travitsky, 'The "Wyll and Testament" of Isabella Whitney', *English Literary Renaissance*, 10.1 (1980), 76–94.

IV.8

MARGARET TYLER

The Mirror of Princely Deeds and Knighthood (1578)

About the author

Margaret Tyler (*c.*1540–*c.*1590) was attached to the household of Thomas Howard, Viscount Howard of Bindon, to whom *Mirror of Princely Deeds* is dedicated. It remains uncertain when she learned Spanish, unless, as has been conjectured, she was born in Spain and came to England with the retinue of Philip II's ambassador, staying on with the Howard family well known for their Catholic sympathies. This is the first romance published in England by a woman, and the first to be translated from Spanish. It therefore offers insight into Spanish–English literary relations and the development of romance, especially as regards women's reading habits and writing practices.

About the text

Mirror of Princely Deeds, a translation of the first part of Diego Ortúñez de Calahorra's *Espejo de Príncipes y Cavalleros* (1555), anticipates the coming revival of English romance prose fiction with Philip Sidney's *Arcadia*[1] and John Lyly's *Euphues*; in fact, in the latter, Euphues mentions by name the enchanter from *Mirror*. Tyler's prefatory address is the first published English defence of female writers and translators. In it she asserts intellectual equality of the sexes and refutes the criticism that women should confine themselves solely to conduct books and works of piety. *Mirror* sold well, being republished in 1580 and 1599, and a translation of the Second Part was commissioned. The story follows the fortunes of Trebatio and his descendants across three continents. Our excerpt comes from chapter 5, which inaugurates the main plot-arc: Prince Edward, en route to his fiancée, the chaste Princess Briana, is killed by his rival, Emperor Trebatio, who then impersonates Edward, schemes to marry Briana and, in short order, sires 'two noble children, the Knight of the Sun and Rosicleer' (cap.7).

---

[1] See entry II.8 (Mary Herbert Sidney).

The arts of death

As a genre, romance fantastically depicts the human condition; it is driven by separation, delay, death, and loss – and attempts to redeem something from what has been lost. The word 'mirror' in the book's title refers only obliquely to *speculum* literature,[2] implying more simply here a reflection of the exaggerated interactions and serendipitous encounters of chivalric figures. Chivalric romance, more particularly, has its own operating procedures and decorum, namely the impenetrability of disguise, sensationally violent mortal combat, supernatural occurrences, and extraordinary situational dilemmas. As such, it played into the blood lust typically associated with and fostered by print romance. The redemptive element of such extreme vignettes of chivalric doom (somewhat reminiscent of Greek tragedy, which is allusively recalled throughout this novel) comes into focus through readers observing how the noble characters, pledged to uphold various high-minded ideals, adapt to and bear up under the setbacks – death included – that they encounter in a world recognized as being manifestly treacherous and, as often as not, morally ambiguous. Our excerpt begins with a narrative rumination on hazarding one's life (and the lives of others swept up in the carnage) to attain a goal.

Textual notes

The mirrour of princely deedes and knighthood (London: 1578; STC 18859), cap. 5 [pages incorrectly signed and misnumbered].

The Mirror of Princely Deeds and Knighthood

O what a common thing is it to die. And how many ever saw happy end in it? How joyful and pleasant was to Paris that desired match of Helena,[3] and how sorrowful and lamentable was the end, not only to him but to his parents and brethren and the greatest part of all Asia? For not only in Greece, but in all the out islands thereabouts was bewept his bitter bridal. With how great care and diligence do men hasten on the causes of their care, occasions of their heaviness, means of their pains, and matter for their grief, and do not content themselves with the continual affliction wherein fortune schooleth

---

[2] See entry III.4 (Churchyard).
[3] Trojan prince who abducted Helen, wife of Menelaus; *casus belli* of the Trojan War

them? But by new means they invent new matters of danger which crosseth them at every step. They frame new causes and, as it were, forge unto themselves sharp spurs to prick forward this woeful life. Where they think to find pleasure and rest, there they find for their loss travail, and trouble for the death which they would fly from.

[…]

The prince hit the emperor in the middest[4] of the shield, and piercing farther left the head remaining in the fine and well steeled armour, whereby the staff broken in many shivers[5] made a great whistling in the air. But the emperor's stroke was much more fell, for he levelled it with such force that it entered not only into the shield and strong armour of the prince, but passed through unto his amorous heart all bedewed with blood a whole arm's length.

Then the prince fell dead executing the sentence which he had given in these words: 'that that love should be very dear and bitter'. When his people saw him stretched upon the ground, there might no sorrow be compared unto theirs, and as raging mad they ran altogether upon the emperor thinking to put in practice their deadly anger upon his carcass. Some with spears and other with swords strake[6] him on all parts with great rage and haste, so that if his armour had not been very good, in short space they had hewed it in pieces. But that most valiant Greek, no less strong than any of his ancestors, bearing his fine and sharp sword, turned himself among them in such manner, that he sheathed it in their bodies. The first whom he met he cleaved unto the eyes, the second's arm he cut off by the elbow, and being sore wounded he overthrew the third at another blow, neither stayed he here, but in his rage, he dealt blows and wounded many, which for fear accounting him rather a devil of hell than a knight, put themselves to flight. […] [T]he emperor […] ruing the loss of so great a prince slain out of his own country in the beauty of his age, when also yielding a great sigh which sigh seemed to have come from the bottom of his heart, he said with a troubled and low voice in this wise:

'O unhappy and unfortunate prince, God knoweth how sorrowful and grievous thy death is to me, and how fain[7] I would have given remedy in some other manner to that I most desired, and although thou wast mine enemy and come in favour of the King Tiberio to take from me my land and high estate, yet would I not have been so cruel an enemy unto thee, but the entire love of the Princess Briana drave[8] me more thereto, than mine own enmity. Now I

---

[4] 'middle'   [5] 'small pieces' (of a shattered object)   [6] 'struck'   [7] 'well-pleased', 'glad'
[8] 'drove'; 'propel forward'

wish that by some other means I might have been relieved and not to have bought my life by thy loss. But as love is tyrannous, so marvel not though he want pity towards thee, which could not otherwise purchase it to himself. Pardon me therefore, O mighty and worthy prince, and judge if thou wert alive what thou wouldst do if by my death thou mightest find remedy of thy love'.

Suggested further reading
Victoria Muñoz, '"[C]arried away with *The Myrrour of Knighthood*": Hispanophobia and the Rhetorical Feminization of Romance Literature', in *New Ways of Looking at Old Texts, VI*, ed. Arthur Marotti (Tempe, AZ: Renaissance English Text Society, 2019), pp. 269–96.

Margaret Tyler, *Mirror of Princely Deeds and Knighthood*, ed. Joyce Boro (London: Modern Humanities Research Association, 2014), pp. 1–42.

IV.9

CHRISTOPHER MARLOWE
Selected Works (1594, 1604)

About the Author

Christopher Marlowe (1564–1593) was a poet and dramatist, educated at the King's School, Canterbury, and Corpus Christi, Cambridge, renowned for his 'over-reaching' tragic heroes and bombastic blank verse (Ben Jonson acclaimed 'Marlowe's mighty line'). He died at the age of twenty-nine, fatally stabbed in a disagreement over the payment of a 'recknyng' (or bill), leaving behind a legacy of influential works such as *1* and *2 Tamburlaine*, *The Jew of Malta*, and *Hero and Leander*. He may have worked in espionage for Elizabeth I's government, and was later, notoriously, accused of being an atheist and homosexual. His early death was rued by fellow poets but interpreted by puritanical writers as 'a manifest sign of God's judgement' (Thomas Beard, *Theatre of God's Judgments* (London: 1597; STC 1659), K6ʳ).

About the text

Edward II is a historical tragedy that analyses the perils of weak or distracted leadership and the power dynamic between the crown and peerage. The play begins soon after Edward II has ascended to the throne. Edward I had exiled a low-born nobleman, Piers Gaveston, because of his intimate relationship with, and influence over, his son. Edward II now recalls Gaveston to the court and lavishes him with gifts, titles, and attention, much to the displeasure of his wife, Isabella of France, and the leading members of the peerage. The others plot against Gaveston, and, to Edward's horror, find ways to banish and then kill him. In the power struggle that ensues, Edward ends up captured, is imprisoned, and is murdered in his cell in a brutal manner.

The arts of death

Marlowe's primary source for Edward II's infamous death at Berkeley Castle was Holinshed's *Chronicles*, which describes how his murderers came into the cell while Edward was sleeping, kept him held down with a heavy featherbed or table, and:

> withal put into his fundament [i.e., anus] an horn, and through the same they thrust up into his body an hot spit, or (as other[s] have) through the pipe of a trumpet a plumber's instrument of iron made very hot, the which passing up into his entrails, and being rolled to and fro, burnt the same, but so as no appearance of any wound or hurt outwardly might be once perceived [...] [Edward's screams] did move many within the castle and town of Berkeley to compassion, plainly hearing him utter a wailful noise.[1]

Marlowe's dramatic portrayal of Edward's final moments draws upon Holinshed's gossipy and unhistorical account but introduces the character of Lightborn (English for 'Lucifer') as a highly skilled and charismatic assassin, whose 'looks ... harbour nought but death'. The method of murder has been frequently interpreted as a form of *contrapasso*, depicted vividly in Dante's *Inferno*, whereby the sinner is punished by the means by which they have sinned. Yet this interpretation of the murder, as a form of judgement upon and punishment for the Christian sin of 'sodomy', is nuanced and complicated by the introduction of the Devil-assassin as punisher and how Marlowe directs audience sympathy towards the fallen king.

---

[1] Raphael Holinshed, *The First and Second Volumes of Chronicles* (London: 1587; STC 13569), KK1r.

Textual notes

The troublesome raigne and lamentable death of Edward the second, King of England (London: 1594; STC 17437), L4ʳ–M1ʳ.

Edward II

EDWARD	Who's there? What light is that? Wherefore comes thou?
LIGHTBORNE	To comfort you, and bring you joyful news.
EDWARD	Small comfort finds poor Edward in thy looks.
	Villain, I know thou com'st to murder me.
LIGHTBORNE	To murder you, my most gracious lord?
	Far is it from my heart to do you harm,
	The queen sent me to see how you were used,
	For she relents at this your misery.
	And what eyes can refrain from shedding tears,
	To see a king in this most piteous state?
EDWARD	Weep'st thou already? List a while to me,
	And then thy heart, were it as Gurney's is,
	Or as Matrevis', hewn from the Caucasus,[2]
	Yet will it melt ere I have done my tale.
	This dungeon where they keep me is the sink
	Wherein the filth of all the castle falls.
LIGHTBORNE	O, villains!
EDWARD	And there in mire and puddle have I stood
	This ten day's space, and, lest that I should sleep,
	One plays continually upon a drum.
	They give me bread and water, being a king;
	So that, for want of sleep and sustenance,
	My mind's distempered and my body's numbed,
	And whether I have limbs or no I know not.
	O, would my blood dropped out from every vein
	As doth this water from my tattered robes!
	Tell Isabel, the queen, I looked not thus,
	When for her sake I ran at tilt[3] in France,
	And there unhorsed the Duke of Clermont.

[2] i.e., the Caucasus mountains, a byword for hardness (and therefore unfeeling)
[3] tournament jousting

LIGHTBORNE	O, speak no more, my lord! This breaks my heart.
	Lie on this bed, and rest yourself awhile.
EDWARD	These looks of thine can harbour naught but death:
	I see my tragedy written in thy brows.
	Yet stay a while; forbear thy bloody hand,
	And let me see the stroke before it comes,
	That and even then when I shall lose my life,
	My mind may be more steadfast on my God.
LIGHTBORNE	What means your highness to mistrust me thus?
EDWARD	What means thou to dissemble with me thus?
LIGHTBORNE	These hands were never stained with innocent blood,
	Nor shall they now be tainted with a king's.
EDWARD	Forgive my thought for having such a thought,
	One jewel have I left; receive thou this.
	[*He gives* LIGHTBORNE *a jewel.*]
	Still fear I, and I know not what's the cause,
	But every joint shakes as I give it thee.
	O if thou harbour'st murder in thy heart,
	Let this gift change thy mind, and save thy soul.
	Know that I am a king. O, at that name
	I feel a hell of grief! Where is my crown?
	Gone, gone, and do I remain alive?
LIGHTBORNE	You're overwatched, my lord. Lie down and rest.
EDWARD	But that grief keeps me waking, I should sleep;
	For not these ten days have these eye-lids closed.
	Now as I speak they fall, and yet with fear
	Open again. O, wherefore sits thou here?
LIGHTBORNE	If you mistrust me, I'll be gone, my lord.
EDWARD	No, no, for if thou mean'st to murder me,
	Thou wilt return again, and therefore stay. [*Sleeps.*]
LIGHTBORNE	He sleeps.
EDWARD	[*waking*] O, let me not die yet! Stay, O, stay a while!
LIGHTBORNE	How now, my lord?
EDWARD	Something still buzzeth in mine ears,
	And tells me if I sleep I never wake;
	This fear is that which makes me tremble thus.
	And therefore tell me, wherefore art thou come?

LIGHTBORNE	To rid thee of thy life. Matrevis, come!
	[*Enter* MATREVIS *and* GURNEY.]
EDWARD	I am too weak and feeble to resist.
	Assist me, sweet God, and receive my soul!
LIGHTBORNE	Run for the table!
EDWARD	O, spare me, or dispatch me in a trice!
	[MATREVIS and GURNEY bring in a table and a red-hot spit.[4]]
LIGHTBORNE	So, lay the table down, and stamp on it.
	But not too hard, lest that you bruise his body.
	[EDWARD *dies.*]
MATREVIS	I fear me that this cry will raise the town,
	And therefore let us take horse and away.
LIGHTBORNE	Tell me sirs, was it not bravely done?
GURNEY	Excellent well; take this for thy reward,
	Then GURNEY *stabs* LIGHTBORNE.

Suggested further reading

Jonathan Crewe, 'Disorderly Love: Sodomy Revisited in Marlowe's *Edward II*', *Criticism*, 51.3 (2009), 385–99.

David Stymeist, 'Status, Sodomy, and the Theater in Marlowe's *Edward II*', *Studies in English Literature, 1500–1900*, 44.2 (2004), 233–53.

About the text

Doctor Faustus is Marlowe's best-known work today; the first English dramatization of the Faust legend, it tells the story of an extraordinarily learned man who seeks to command even greater knowledge. A would-be necromancer, Faustus summons a devil, and via Mephistopheles, makes a pact with Lucifer to exchange his body and soul at death (to be damned eternally) for twenty-four more years of life to 'live in all voluptuousness' and to be attended by Mephistopheles. The play is preserved in two substantive versions, both published posthumously (an A-Text, 1604 and B-Text 1616); the passage excerpted here, drawn from the A-Text, is substantively similar

---

[4] Notably, the first quarto text does not include any stage directions for the murder; earlier Lightborne had instructed Matrevis and Gurney to prepare a 'red hot' spit, so it is implied that this is the instrument that kills Edward rather than the table that presses him down.

in the B-text, though in the later printed text there is a hellmouth on stage throughout this sequence and Faustus's damnation seems assured. The ending in the A-Text, as given below, has been interpreted by some scholars as leaving open the possibility that Faustus's soul can still be saved.

The arts of death

His pact with Lucifer sealed, a countdown begins until the end of Faustus's life. In the play proper's final scene, as the clock strikes on its way to midnight, a terrified and humbled Faustus contemplates his imminent damnation. Looking to the heavens, he fantasizes about time standing still. He says he cannot appeal for God's mercy because the Devil threatened to tear him to pieces if he did, and, even when he attempts to speak or gesture to God, his tongue is stayed and his arms are held. But Faustus's reluctance to appeal to God creates an interpretative crux: what would happen if he repented and was able to call for God's mercy? Left alone, Faustus instead appeals to the Devil – 'oh spare me, Lucifer' – to no avail, before fully recognizing his folly and renouncing his learning. Faustus refers to the Pythagorean theory of the transmigration of the soul, metempsychosis, wishing it were true so that he could become a beast and achieve finality with death. Rather, he 'must be damned perpetually'. This scene embodies the period's worst kind of death according to the Protestant *ars moriendi*; in his last speech, Faustus even prays for a bastardized form of Purgatory ('Let Faustus live in hell a thousand years / A hundred thousand, and at last be saved!').

Textual notes

The tragicall history of D. Faustus (London: 1604; STC 17429), F2^v–F3^r.

Doctor Faustus

The clock strikes eleven.

FAUSTUS   Ah, Faustus,
                Now hast thou but one bare hour to live,
                And then thou must be damned perpetually.
                Stand still, you ever-moving spheres of heaven,
                That time may cease and midnight never come!

Fair nature's eye,[5] rise, rise again, and make
Perpetual day, or let this hour be but
A year, a month, a week, a natural day,
That Faustus may repent and save his soul!
O lente, lente currite noctis equi![6]
The stars move still, time runs, the clock will strike,
The devil will come, and Faustus must be damned.
O, I'll leap up to my God! Who pulls me down?
See, see, where Christ's blood streams in the firmament!
One drop would save my soul, half a drop. Ah, my Christ!
Ah, rend not my heart for naming of my Christ,
Yet will I call on him. O, spare me, Lucifer!
Where is it now? 'Tis gone: and see, where God
Stretcheth out his arm and bend his ireful brows!
Mountains and hills, come, come, and fall on me,
And hide me from the heavy wrath of God!
No, no!
Then will I headlong run into the earth.
Earth, gape! O, no, it will not harbour me.
You stars that reigned at my nativity,[7]
Whose influence hath allotted death and hell,
Now draw up Faustus like a foggy mist,
In the entrails of yon labouring cloud,
That when you vomit forth into the air,
My limbs may issue from the smoky mouths,
So that my soul may ascend to heaven.

The watch strikes.

Ah, half the hour is past: 'twill all be past anon.
O God,
If thou wilt not have mercy on my soul,
Yet for Christ's sake, whose blood hath ransomed me,
Impose some end to my incessant pain.
Let Faustus live in hell a thousand years,

---

[5] i.e., the sun
[6] 'O run slowly, slowly, horses of the night' from Ovid's love poems *Amores* (which Marlowe translated), referring to the slowing of Time's chariot to permit more time between lovers (Ovid, *Heroides, Amores*, trans. Grant Showerman, rev. and ed. G. P. Goold, Loeb Classical Library (Cambridge, MA: Harvard University Press, 1914), 1.13.40).
[7] Faustus refers to the astrological position of the stars at his birth.

A hundred thousand, and at last be saved!
Oh, no end is limited to damnèd souls.
Why wert thou not a creature wanting soul?
Or, why is this immortal that thou hast?
Ah, Pythagoras' metempsychosis,[8] were that true,
This soul should fly from me and I be changed
Unto some brutish beast.
All beasts are happy, for, when they die,
Their souls are soon dissolved in elements;
But mine must live still to be plagued in hell.
Curst be the parents that engendered me!
No, Faustus, curse thyself. Curse Lucifer,
That hath deprived thee of the joys of heaven.

The clock striketh twelve.

Oh, it strikes, it strikes, now body turn to air,
Or Lucifer will bear thee quick[9] to hell.

Thunder and lightning.

O soul, be changed into little water drops,
And fall into the ocean, ne'er be found:
My God, my God, look not so fierce on me!

Enter devils.

Adders and serpents, let me breathe awhile!
Ugly hell gape not! Come not, Lucifer!
I'll burn my books – ah, Mephistopheles!

[*The devils*] *exeunt with him.*

---

[8] In Pythagoras' (*c.*570–*c.*495 BCE) theory of metempsychosis, he argued that upon death the soul transmigrated to another living being.
[9] 'alive'

Suggested further reading

Jonathan Dollimore, 'Subversion through Transgression: Doctor Faustus', in *Staging the Renaissance: Reinterpretations of Elizabethan and Jacobean Drama*, ed. David Scott Kastan and Peter Stallybrass (New York and London: Routledge, 1991), pp. 122–32.

Neill, *Issues*, pp. 207–11.

Vinter, *Acts*, ch. 1.

IV.10

SAMUEL ROWLANDS

Selected Works (1606, 1614)

About the author

Samuel Rowlands (*fl.* 1598–1628) was a prolific satirist, of obscure origin, whose works found a significant readership in the Jacobean period.

About the text

A Terrible Battle between … Time and Death features a dialogue between the allegorical personages of Time and Death. Time interrupts Death on his ceaseless journey around the world, asking him to confer 'to understand how matters thrive'. Death agrees to speak with him for as long as the sands run halfway through Time's hourglass. In their ensuing conversation, they discuss the relationship between time and death, and observe man's foolishness in not preparing for death. Death describes how several sinful persons (stock character types such as a 'lawyer' or 'poet') have met their fate. Despite the work's title, no 'terrible battle' ever occurs, and, following a minor disagreement, the two figures part ways on good terms.

The arts of death

Rowlands's work draws on the rich allegorical heritage of depicting Death in dialogue with interlocutors. In the first excerpt we read how Rowlands establishes the interdependence between the twin concepts enlivened by the allegorical personages. Their polite exchange, at once lightly comic and gravely serious, alerts the reader to heed their own mortality and to learn from the sins of others. Later Death says that 'A happy soul' is 'one that had learned to die, / And rightly understood his earthly state' (C3^r). In the final excerpt – where, notably, Death has the final say – Death laments that they have conversed too long and have urgent business to attend to. Time, urged along by Death at the tolling of the funeral bells, must wait for no man.

Textual notes

A terrible battell betweene the two consumers of the whole world: time, and death (London: 1606; STC 21407), A3^{r-v}; F2^{r-v}; F4^v.

A Terrible Battle between ... Time and Death

TIME. Dread potent monster, mighty from thy birth,
Giant of strength against all mortal power,
God's great earl marshal over all the earth,
Taking account of each man's dying hour,
Landlord of graves and tombs of marble stones,
Lord Treasurer of rotten dead-men's bones.

Victorious consort, slaughtering cavalier,
Mated with me, to combat all alive,
Know, worthy champion, I have met thee here
Only to understand how matters thrive:
As our affairs alike in nature be,
So let us love, confer, and kind agree.

Great register of all things under sun,
God's speedy post that ever runs and flies,
Ender of all that ever was begun,
That hast the map of life before thine eyes:
And of all creatures since the world's creation,
Hast seen the final dusty consummation.

DEATH. Let me entreat thee pardon me a while,
Because my business now is very great,
I must go travel many a thousand mile
To look with care that worms do lack no meat:
There's many crawling feeders I maintain;
I may not let those cannibals complain.

I must send murderers with speed to hell,
That there with horror they may make abode;
I must show atheists where the devils dwell,
To let them feel there is a powerful God;
I must invite the glutton and the liar,
Unto a banquet made of flames of fire.

I must bring Pride where fashions are invented—
You idle-headed women, quake and fear,
Your toyish fooleries will be prevented,
A suit of crawling serpents you shall wear:
You that endeavour only to go brave,[1]
What hell affords you shall be sure to have.

I have the swag'ring ruffian to dispatch,
That moth and canker of the commonwealth,
The graceless thief that on the prey doth watch,
The drunkard a carousing of his health:
And of all sinners such a damned rout,
As full of work as Death can stir about.

TIME. This lawful bus'ness I do well allow,
But in my absence how wilt thou proceed?
I must be present too as well as thou,
Before Time come thou canst not do the deed;
My scythe cuts down; upon thy dart they die;
Thou hast an hourglass, and so have I.
[…]

TIME. Where goest thou now? Marry, hark in thine ear.
DEATH. I have a lady presently to kill:
One that's at dice, and doth no danger fear.
But have at all,[2] she says, come set me still,
She is at passage,[3] passing sound and well
And little thinketh on the passing bell.

And then I go to bail an honest man,
Lies in the counter[4] for a little debt,
Whom's creditor in most extremes he can
Doth deal withal, now he is in the net;
He swears he'll keep him there this dozen year,
Yet the knave lies, this night I'll set him clear.

And then I go to see two fellows fight,
(With whom there is no reason to be had)

---

[1] 'finely-dressed' (*OED*)
[2] 'the action or an act of risking all of one's money in a gamble' (*OED*)
[3] 'a gambling game for two people played with three dice' (*OED*)
[4] 'prison attached to … a city court; the name of certain prisons for debtors in London, Southwark etc' (*OED*)

About a cup of wine they drank last night,
One swore 'twas good, and t'other vowed 'twas bad;
I'll give one that no surgeon's like to heal,
And with the t'other, let the hangman deal.

And hundreds more; come, Time, with speed along,
About our business we have stood here now:
Till priest, and clerk and sexton have the wrong,
More dead work for their profit let's allow.
My dart is dry, there's no fresh blood thereon,
We suffer sick to lie too long and groan.
[…]
No more, away, look here my glass is out,
Thou art too tedious, Time, in telling tales,
Our bloody business let us go about,
Thousands are now at point of death, breath fails;
To work, to work, and lay about thee man,
Let's kill as fast as for our lives we can.

Hark, listen, Time, I pray give ear,
What bell is that a tolling there?

Suggested further reading
Sandra Clark, *The Elizabethan Pamphleteers: Popular Moralistic Pamphlets, 1580–1640* (Rutherford, NJ: Fairleigh Dickinson University Press, 1983).
Joad Raymond, *Pamphlets and Pamphleteering in Early Modern Britain* (Cambridge: Cambridge University Press, 2003).

About the text

Thomas Overbury was a trusted confidant of Robert Carr, a favourite in the court of James I and VI. When Carr began an affair with Frances Howard, who was then married to the third Earl of Essex, Robert Devereaux, Overbury strongly opposed his friend's relationship. The affair continued regardless, and Overbury fell into disfavour with the King when he declined a foreign assignment so that he could remain close to his friend, and, he hoped, put an end to Carr's relationship with Howard. James sent Overbury to the Tower of London in April 1613. In September that year Overbury died while imprisoned. Soon thereafter rumours began to circulate that foul play was the cause, and that he had been poisoned. Two years later, the full details of the crime were revealed. The fallout to the Overbury murder was to be the greatest scandal of the Jacobean age. Carr and Howard, who had married in the meantime following an annulment of Howard's marriage to Devereaux, were tried, along with four others, for their alleged role in the crime. All six were found guilty, with Carr and Howard imprisoned for several years and their four convicted accomplices hanged. Rowlands's pamphlet, spoken from Overbury's perspective, opportunistically capitalizes on the rumours first circulating about this infamous murder.

The arts of death

The 'complaint', published here in full, is remarkable for how Rowlands works to situate Overbury's murder within a panoply of famous biblical and historical deaths, ranging from Cain's killing of Abel to Edward II's infamous murder. Notably, he includes two other famous murderous acts that took place in the Tower of London. Rowlands's selected *exempla* largely emphasize the close relationship or kinship between those killing (or ordering the murder) and the killed. Rowlands, thus, seems to implicate someone close to Overbury as the killer, with the *exempla* of deaths recruited to augment the injustice around Overbury's murder. The poem calls for justice through revenge, and, in the voice of Overbury, begs 'Let not a murderer remain concealed'. We also print here (see Figure 4.6) a copy of the print pamphlet, with its woodcut image of the coffined Overbury, skeletal remains, and the figures of Time (holding the hourglass) and Justice (calling for revenge, and holding the scales) surrounding Overbury's family crest.

Textual notes

Sir Thomas Overbury, or, The poysoned knights complaint (London: 1616(?); STC 21406, broadside).

Sir Thomas Overbury, or the Poisoned Knight's Complaint

> Within this house of death, a dead man lies,
> Whose blood like Abel's up for vengeance cries;
> Time hath revealed what to truth belongs,
> And Justice's sword is drawn to right my wrongs.
> You poisoned minds did me with poison kill,
> Let true repentance purge you from that ill.
>
> Great powerful God, whom all are bound to love,
> How graceless bad, doth man, thy creature, prove?
> Thy supreme creature over all the rest,
> In number numberless to be expressed,

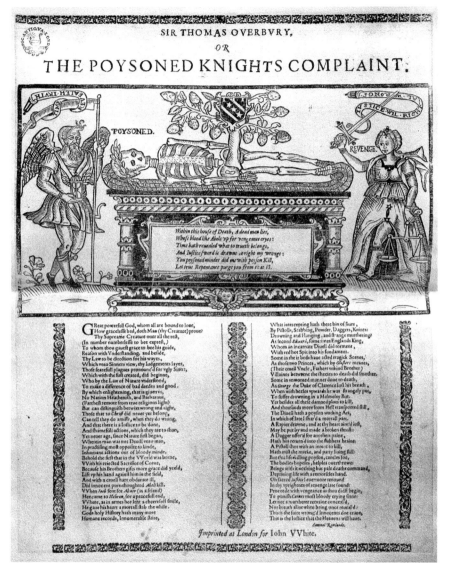

FIGURE 4.6 Coffined Overbury. Broadside of *Sir Thomas Overbury or The Poysoned Knights Complaint* (London: 1616(?); STC 21406). © of the Society of Antiquaries of London

To whom thou gavest grace to be his guide,
Reason with understanding, and beside,
Thy law to be direction for his ways,
Which unto sinners view thy judgements lays,

Those fearful plagues pronounced for ugly sin,
Which with the first created did begin,
Who by the law of nature understood,
To make a difference of bad deeds and good,
By which enlightening, that is given us,
No nation heathenish, and barbarous,
Farthest remote from true religion's light
But can distinguish betwixt wrong and right,
Those that to Christ did never yet belong,
Can tell they do amiss, when they do wrong,
And that there is a justice to be done,
And shameful actions, which they are to shun,
Yet never age since nature first began,
Wherein man was not devil unto man,
In practising most opposite to kind,
Inhumane actions out of bloody mind.
Behold the first that in the world was born,[1]
With his rejected sacrifice of corn,
Because his brother's gifts more grace did yield,
Lift up his hand against him in the field,
And, with a cruel heart obdurate ill,
Did innocent pure-thoughted Abel kill.
When Joab sent for Abner, as a friend,
He came to Hebron, for a peaceful end,
Where, as in arms he lent a cheerful smile,
He gave his heart a mortal stab the while.[2]
God's holy history hath many more
Human records, innumerable store,
What intercepting hath there been of lives,
By pistols, stabbing, powder, daggers, knives.
Drowning and hanging, and strange murdering?
As second Edward, sometimes England's king,
Whom an incarnate devil did torment
With red hot spit into his fundament.[3]

---

[1] Cain's murder of Abel is described in Genesis 4:8.
[2] Joab killed Abner in revenge for Abner's earlier killing of his brother, Asahel, in combat (2 Sam 3:30).
[3] Marlowe dramatizes the murder in *Edward II* (1592); see entry IV.9.

Some in their beds have acted tragic scenes,
As those two princes, which by Gloucester's means,
Their cruel uncle, father's unkind brother,
Villains, between the sheets to death, did smother.[4]
Some in unwonted manner done to death,
As George the Duke of Clarence lost his breath,
When with heels upwards he was strangely put,
To suffer drowning in a Malmsey butt.[5]
Yet besides all these damned plots to kill,
And thousands more from Hell transported still,
The devil hath a poison working art,
In which of late I shared a mortal part.
A rapier drawn, and at thy heart aimed just,
May be put by and made a broken thrust:
A dagger offered for another's pain,
Hath been returned into the stabber's brain:
A pistol shot with an intent to kill,
Hath missed the mark, and party living still:
But this life-killing poison, cureless foe,
The bodies hopeless, helpless overthrow:
Brings with it nothing but pale death's command,
Depriving life with a remorseless hand.
O sacred justice! Evermore renowned
In thy uprightness of revenge late found:
Proceed with vengeance as thou didst begin,
To punish Cain's most bloody crying sin:
Let not a murderer remain concealed,
Nor breath alive when being once revealed:
This is the suit wronged innocents do crave,
This is the justice that the Heavens will have.

---

[4] Edward IV's two sons, Edward and Richard, were staying at the Tower of London, under the protection of Richard, Duke of Gloucester, at the time of their disappearance and likely murder. Gloucester, suspected of ordering their killing, would ascend to the throne as Richard III. Shakespeare's *Richard III* dramatizes this sequence of events.

[5] Clarence, brother to Edward IV, was prosecuted and convicted for treason by the King. He was killed at the Tower of London in 1478, rumoured to have drowned, as the poem suggests, in a cask ('butt') of Malmsey wine (Madeira). Shakespeare's *Richard III* also includes this sequence of events.

Suggested further reading
Alastair Bellany, *The Politics of Court Scandal in Early Modern England: News Culture and the Overbury Affair, 1603–1660* (Cambridge: Cambridge University Press, 2002).
David Lindley, *The Trials of Frances Howard: Fact and Fiction at the Court of King James* (London and New York: Routledge, 1993).

IV.11

AEMILIA LANYER

Salve Deus Rex Judaeorum (1611)

About the author

Aemilia Lanyer (*c.*1569–1645), of Jewish–Italian descent, was baptized in Bishopsgate, London. She was the daughter of court musicians and also married one, later becoming the mistress of Henry Carey, Baron Hunsdon (Elizabeth I's first cousin and Lord Chamberlain, and patron of Shakespeare's acting company). Lanyer was therefore familiar with the dynamics of royal preferment and cultivated patronage relations among influential women. Lanyer is the first Englishwoman to be considered a professional poet.

About the text

Lanyer's literary reputation rests on a single book consisting of eleven poems and letters. The main poem, 230 ottava rima stanzas in iambic pentameter on the passion and death of Christ, presents the predicaments and ingenuity of women – starting with Eve. The judicious reader (exemplarily Queen Anne, to whom the first section is dedicated) is asked by Lanyer to judge whether her interpretation agrees with scripture: 'And if it do, why are poor women blamed, / Or by more faulty men so much defamed' (A4^r). The title, *Salve Deus Rex Judaeorum* ('Hail, God, King of the Jews') refers to words spoken by Pilate's wife (Matt 27:19), her only appearance in the gospels. Midway through the poem, her voice merges with and takes over the narrative. This novel way of presenting Christ's story, from a woman's point of view, moves on then to Eve's apology, to 'famous women' in 'elder times' who defied arbitrary patriarchal rule (notably Judith, Esther, and Susanna), to the lamentation of 'the Daughters of Jerusalem', and finally to the sorrow of Mary with a coda on Christ's sacrifice that is mirrored in sainted martyrs since 'His sweetness sweet'ned all the sour of death' (G4^r).

The arts of death

The death and resurrection of Christ are necessary preconditions for the redemption of humankind from eternal death: 'For the wages of sin is death: but the gift of God is eternal life, through Jesus Christ our Lord' (Rom 6:23). This theme drives the seemingly digressive narrative, and Lanyer's compelling approach to retelling the story of Christ's sacrifice, 'Whose death killed Death, and took away his sting' (E1^r), highlights the pious virtues and compassion of women in contrast to the vindictive cruelty of men who abuse their positions of power. Howsoever one interprets the social agenda of this religious poem, the work clearly partakes of an earlier tradition of female pity popularized by Jacobus de Voragine's portrayal of the tribulations and martyrdom of virgins and saints in *The Golden Legend* (the first English version was printed in 1483–1484[1]). It also draws on the spiritual exercise of meditating on the scourged and dead body of Christ which, although recalling a Catholic contemplative practice systematized in the sixteenth century by Ignatius of Loyola, is wholly consistent with the decorum of Protestant devotional poetics.[2] The excerpted section here begins with one of several stories about exemplary women who chose death over dishonour, thus setting up a favourable parallel to those who die a good death in Christ.

Textual notes

Salue Deus Rex Iudaeorum (London: 1611; STC 15227.5), A4^v, B2^r, E1^r, E4^r.

Salve Deus Rex Judaeorum

Holy Matilda[3] in a hapless hour
Was born to sorrow and to discontent,
Beauty the cause that turned her sweet to sour,
While chastity sought folly to prevent.

---

[1] See entry I.1 (Caxton).
[2] On the *Christus Mortuus* tradition in England, see entry I.4 (Parr).
[3] a daughter of Robert FitzWalter, a baron who supported the Magna Carta to limit powers of King John (1167–1216).

Lustful King John refused, did use his power,
By fire and sword, to compass his content:
    But friend's disgrace, nor father's banishment,
    Nor death itself, could purchase her consent.

Here beauty in the height of all perfection,
Crowned this fair creature's everlasting fame,
Whose noble mind did scorn the base subjection
Of fears, or favours, to impair her name:
By heavenly grace, she had such true direction,
To die with honour, not to live in shame;
    And drink that poison with a cheerful heart,
    That could all heavenly grace to her impart.

This grace, great lady,[4] doth possess thy soul,
And makes thee pleasing in thy maker's sight;
This grace doth all imperfect thoughts control,
Directing thee to serve thy God aright;
Still reckoning him, the husband of thy soul,
Which is most precious in his glorious sight:
    Because the world's delights she doth deny
    For him, who for her sake vouchsafed to die.

And dying made her dowager[5] of all;
Nay more, co-heir of that eternal bliss
That angels lost, and we by Adam's fall;
Mere castaways, raised by a Judas kiss,[6]
Christ's bloody sweat, the vinegar and gall,[7]
The spear, sponge, nails, his buffeting[8] with fists,
    His bitter passion, agony, and death,
    Did gain us heaven when he did lose his breath.
[…]

---

[4] Margaret Clifford (*née* Russell), Countess of Cumberland (1560–1616), designated as the addressee in a marginal note
[5] 'a widow with title and property'
[6] Matt 26:47–50; sign of betrayal identifying Jesus to the Roman soldiers in the Garden of Gethsemane precipitating his arrest and crucifixion, presented here as a vital part of the divine salvific plan
[7] Matt 27:34   [8] 'repeated beating'

A matter far beyond my barren skill,
To show with any life this map of death,
This story, that whole worlds with books would fill,
In these few lines, will put me out of breath,
To run so swiftly up this mighty hill,
I may behold it with the eye of faith;
    But to present this pure unspotted lamb,[9]
    I must confess, I far unworthy am.

Yet if he pleaseth t'illuminate my spirit,
And give me wisdom from his holy hill,
That I may write part of his glorious merit,
If he vouchsafe to guide my hand and quill,
To show his death, by which we do inherit
Those endless joys that all our hearts do fill;
    Then will I tell of that sad black-faced night,
    Whose mourning mantle covered heavenly light.
[…]

Her tears did wash away his precious blood,
That sinners might not tread it under feet
To worship him, and that it did her good
Upon her knees, although in open street,
Knowing he was the Jesse flower and bud,[10]
That must be gath'red when it smelled most sweet:
    Her son, her husband, father, saviour, king,
    Whose death killed Death, and took away his sting.[11]
[…]

Being dead, he killed Death, and did survive
That proud insulting tyrant: in whose place
He sends bright immortality to revive
Those whom his iron arms did long embrace;
Who from their loathsome graves brings them alive

---

[9] John 1:29; Jesus as the metonymic substitution for Old Testament sacrificial system
[10] the father of David, the messiah predicted as coming from this family tree (Isa 11:1)
[11] 1 Cor 15:55

>   In glory to behold their saviour's face,
>   Who took the keys of all death's power away,
>   Opening to those that would his name obey.
>
>   O wonder, more than man can comprehend,
>   Our joy and grief both at one instant framed,
>   Compounded; contrarieties contend
>   Each to exceed, yet neither to be blamed.
>   Our grief to see our saviour's wretched end,
>   Our joy to know both death and hell he tamed:
>   That we may say, O death, where is thy sting?
>   Hell, yield thy victory to thy conq'ring king.

Suggested further reading

John Rogers, 'The Passion of a Female Literary Tradition: Aemilia Lanyer's *Salve Deus Rex Judaeorum*', *Huntington Library Quarterly*, 63.4 (2000), 435–46.

Audrey E. Tinkham, '"Owning" in Aemilia Lanyer's *Salve Deus Rex Judæorum* ("Hail God King of the Jews")', *Studies in Philology*, 106.1 (2009), 52–75.

IV.12

CYRIL TOURNEUR

Selected Works (1611, 1613)

About the author

Cyril Tourneur (*fl.* 1600–d.1626) was a poet, dramatist, and soldier, of uncertain origins. His preserved works include an obscure allegory, *The Transformed Metamorphosis* (1600), and a series of rich elegiac writings on the deaths of Sir Francis Vere (1609) and Prince Henry (1613). Closely connected with two of the most important political families, the Veres and Cecils, Tourneur appears to have foregone a literary career to pursue a military life.

About the text

The Atheist's Tragedy, or The Honest Man's Revenge belongs to the final period of Tourneur's literary career. The play is an anti-revenge tragedy, representing the culmination of a generation of English dramatic writing about acts of vengeance. Tourneur upends generic convention, producing a thoughtful exposition about what happens when victims choose to avert vengeful action and place their trust in divine providence. Our excerpt derives from the churchyard scene in the play. Similar to events in *Hamlet*, Charlemont has recently learned from the ghost of his father, Montferrers, that his uncle, D'Amville, was responsible for his father's death. Charlemont is followed closely by D'Amville's henchman, Borachio. A murder attempt fails and Charlemont instead fells Borachio. Languebeau Snuffe, a hypocritical Puritan figure, then enters with a serving girl, Soquette, whom he attempts to seduce, during a tryst, in this macabre setting.

The arts of death

This excerpt includes several well-worn *memento mori* tropes deployed in the revenge tradition: the striking of clock-bells; meditations upon mortality, with death seen as a great equalizer; the hero's readiness for, if not anticipation of, death; macabre humour among the graves; ghosts; and, of course, skulls. Later still, D'Amville enters and stares upon a skull, à la Hamlet in Shakespeare's tragedy and Vindice in Middleton's *Revenger's Tragedy*. Tourneur therefore plays upon playgoer expectations, inviting recognition of such generic norms and conventions. But, at the same time, he insists moralistically that we should learn to place our faith in God's unseen providential design and reject the popular genre's routine mode of satisfaction via blood revenge. For Charlemont's patient course of action, Tourneur draws from Paul's Epistle to the Romans: 'Dearly beloved, avenge not yourselves, but give place for wrath: for it is written, Vengeance is mine: I will repay, sayeth the Lord' (12:19), which borrows from the Song of Moses (Deut 32:35). The churchyard scene, where disguise and surprise collapse the distance between the living and the dead, reminds playgoers vividly of the ever-nearness of death. Charlemont stumbling over the death's head as he enters the charnel house, where further heaps of unidentified skeletal remains await, exaggerates and intensifies the play's *memento mori* theme.

Textual notes

The atheist's tragedie: or The honest man's reuenge (London: 1611; STC 24146), H3^v–H4^v.

The Atheist's Tragedy, or The Honest Man's Revenge

Enter CHARLEMONT, BORACHIO *dogging him in the churchyard. The clock strikes twelve.*

CHARLEMONT. Twelve.
BORACHIO. [*aside*] 'Tis a good hour; 'twill strike one anon.
CHARLEMONT. How fit a place for contemplation
Is this dead of night, among the dwellings
Of the dead. This grave—perhaps th'inhabitant
Was in his lifetime the possessor of
His own desires. Yet in the midst of all
His greatness and his wealth, he was less rich
And less contented than in this poor piece
Of earth, lower and lesser than a cottage,
For here he neither wants nor cares. Now that
His body savours of corruption,
He enjoys a sweeter rest than e'er he did
Amongst the sweetest pleasures of this life,
For here there's nothing troubles him. And there—
In that grave lies another. He, perhaps,
Was in his life as full of misery
As this of happiness; and here's an end
Of both. Now both their states are equal. O,
That man with so much labour should aspire
To worldly height, when in the humble earth
The world's condition's at the best! Or scorn
Inferior men, since to be lower than
A worm is to be higher than a king.
BORACHIO. [*aloud*] Then fall and rise.
        Discharges [the pistol, which] gives false fire.
CHARLEMONT. What villain's hand was that?
Save thee or thou shalt perish.
        They fight.
BORACHIO. Zounds![1] Unsaved, I think.
        Fall[s].

---

[1] an oath meaning 'by Christ's wounds'

CHARLEMONT. What? Have I killed him? Whatsoe'er thou beest,
 I would thy hand had prospered, for I was
 Unfit to live and well prepared to die.
 What shall I do? Accuse myself, submit
 Me to the law, and that will quickly end
 This violent increase of misery?
 But 'tis a murder to be accessory
 To mine own death. I will not. I will take
 This opportunity to 'scape. It may
 Be Heaven reserves me to some better end.
 Exit CHARLEMONT.

Enter [LANGUEBEAU] SNUFFE *and* SOQUETTE *into the churchyard.*

SOQUETTE. Nay, good sir, I dare not. In good sooth I come of a generation both by father and mother that were all as fruitful as costermongers'[2] wives.

SNUFFE. Tush, then a tympany[3] is the greatest danger can be feared. Their fruitfulness turns but to a certain kind of phlegmatic windy disease.

SOQUETTE. I must put my understanding to your trust, sir. I would be loath to be deceived.

SNUFFE. No, conceive thou shalt not. Yet thou shalt profit by my instruction too. My body is not every day drawn dry, wench.

SOQUETTE. Yet methinks, sir, your want of use should rather make your body like a well: the lesser 'tis drawn, the sooner it grows dry.

SNUFFE. Thou shalt try that instantly.

SOQUETTE. But we want place and opportunity.

SNUFFE. We have both. This is the back side of the house which the superstitious[4] call Saint Winifred's church[5], and is verily a

---

[2] 'street-sellers'   [3] 'an abdominal swelling or tumour' (here a bawdy joke)
[4] that is, those of the Catholic faith
[5] The beautiful St Winifred, *c.* seventh century CE, chose a life of faith and celibacy as a nun; her spurned suitor, Caradoc, beheaded her, but she was restored to life by St Beuno. Beuno invoked the heavens and, in divine retribution, the ground opened up and swallowed Caradoc. The allusion to St Winifred, with her story of unwanted male advances and divine providence, is therefore ironic in the context of this passage (where Soquette is far from unwilling) and the wider play.

	convenient unfrequented place, where under the close curtains of the night—
SOQUETTE.	You purpose i' the dark to make me light.[6]

[LANGUEBEAU SNUFFE] *pulls out a sheet, a hair,[7] and a beard.*

	But what ha' you there?
SNUFFE.	This disguise is for security sake, wench. There's a talk, thou know'st, that the ghost of old Montferrers walks. In this church he was buried. Now if any stranger fall upon us before our business be ended, in this disguise I shall be taken for that ghost and never be called to examination, I warrant thee. Thus we shall 'scape both prevention and discovery. How do I look in this habit, wench?
SOQUETTE.	So like a ghost that, notwithstanding I have some foreknowledge of you, you make my hair stand almost an end.
SNUFFE.	I will try how I can kiss in this beard. —O fie, fie, fie. I will put it off, and then kiss, and then put it on. I can do the rest without kissing.

Enter CHARLEMONT *doubtfully, with his sword drawn. [He] is upon them before they are aware. They run out divers ways and leave the disguise.*

CHARLEMONT.	What ha' we here? A sheet, a hair, a beard? What end was this disguise intended for? No matter what. I'll not expostulate The purpose of a friendly accident. Perhaps it may accommodate my 'scape; I fear I am pursued. For more assurance, I'll hide me here i'th' charnel house, This convocation-house of dead men's skulls.

To get into the charnel house he takes hold of a death's head; it slips and staggers him.

	Death's head, deceiv'st my hold? Such is the trust to all mortality.

Hides himself in the charnel house.

---

[6] 'have sexual intercourse with'   [7] 'a wig'

Suggested further reading
Huston Diehl, '"Reduce Thy Understanding to Thine Eye": Seeing and Interpreting in *The Atheist's Tragedy*', *Studies in Philology*, 78.1 (1981), 47–60.
Andrew Griffin, *Untimely Deaths in Renaissance Drama* (Toronto, ON; University of Toronto Press, 2020), esp. ch. 4.
Rory Loughnane, 'The Enigma of Divine Revelation in Tourneur's *The Atheist's Tragedy*', in *Enigma and Revelation in Renaissance English Literature*, ed. Mark Sweetnam and Helen Cooney (Dublin: Four Courts Press, 2012), pp. 136–151.

About the text

The sudden death of Henry Stuart, the eldest son of James I and Queen Anne, and heir apparent to the crown, led to an unprecedented public outpouring of grief. Henry's death at eighteen, from typhoid fever, occasioned and inspired elegiac writing from both major and hack writers of the period. Our excerpt is drawn from a collection of three elegies, written by Tourneur, John Webster, and Thomas Heywood. Published with an eye-catching, and expensively-inked, all black title-page (each verso page within is also blacked out), the collection exemplifies the best and worst tendencies of such elegiac writing, as these three fine poets try to find original ways to sensibly express grief. In Tourneur's prefatory dedication, he notes that Henry's death made it 'a season for elegies of this kind' (A4^r).

The arts of death

Tourneur's 'broken elegy'[8] develops along three conceits: that virtue is in mourning at the loss of the prince; that although the prince only lived until he was eighteen, his 'good hours' mean he lived to more than eighty; and, third, that his death is an insurmountable loss to artists, whom the prince patronized along with soldiers (a combination of occupations that is Tourneur's calling card). Our excerpt comes from the third and final part of the elegy, with Tourneur encouraging artists and writers to endlessly preserve the Prince's memory. We have kept some of the elegy's distinctive orthography, including capitalized pronouns for Henry, which works to intensify the expression of loss.

---

[8] For other examples of the elegy as a death art, see entries II.14 (Beaumont) and II.16 (Philips).

Textual notes

Three elegies on the most lamented death of Prince Henrie (London: 1613; STC 24151), C1^r–C2^r.

Three Elegies

[…]
But I would have their studies never die,
For preservation of HIS memory.
How can that perish? That will ever keep;
Because th'impression of it is so deep.
When any painter to the life that saw
HIS presence fully takes in hand to draw
An Alexander or a Caesar; his best
Imaginations will be so possessed
With HIS remembrance that as HE does limn,
He'll make that worthy's picture like to HIM.
And then 'twill be a piece of such a grace
For height and sweetness, as that only face
Will make another painter, that ne'er knew
HIM living, follow as the other drew.
How great a character deserves HE then
Whose memory shall but expire with men?
When a divine or poet sets down right
What other princes should be, he shall write
What THIS was, that's HIS character, which bears
My sorrow inward, to go forth in tears.
Yet some of joy too, mixed with those of grief;
That flow from apprehension of relief.
I see HIS spirit turned into a star,
Whose influence makes that HIS own virtues are
Succeeded justly; otherwise, the worst,
As at HIS funeral should proceed the first.
HIS native goodness, follows in HIS room;
Else good men would be buried in HIS tomb.
O, suffer this to be a faithful verse,
To live forever, weeping o'er HIS hearse.

Suggested further reading
C. A. Patrides, '"The Greatest of the Kingly Race": The Death of Henry Stuart', *The Historian*, 47.3 (1985), 402–08.
Adrian Streete, 'Elegy, Prophecy, and Politics: Literary Responses to the Death of Prince Henry Stuart, 1612–1614', *Renaissance Studies*, 31.1 (2017), 87–106.

IV.13

ELIZABETH CARY

The Tragedy of Mariam (1613)

About the author

Elizabeth Cary (1585–1639), poet and translator, was the first female dramatist to write and publish original plays in English. A prodigious talent with fluency in multiple languages, she produced major works such as a translation of Abraham Ortelius's *Le mirroir du monde* ('The mirror of the world') and her neo-Senecan closet drama, *The Tragedy of Mariam*, while in her teens and early twenties. Cary later gained notoriety in the Caroline court for publicly converting to Catholicism.

About the text

Cary's play was not written for performance on London's commercial public stages, but rather for an elite readership. Copies of the play would have first circulated in manuscript, read aloud in an intimate group or private setting. Written in a classical style, complete with choric commentators and long, meditative speeches, Cary's play also borrows elements from the popular genre of neo-Senecan revenge tragedies performed in London's playhouses. The play tells the tale of Mariam, Queen of Judaea, the beautiful and outspoken second wife of Herod the Great, who is sentenced to die by her tyrant husband on the grounds of her supposed adultery and attempted treason. Mariam is innocent however, a victim of lies spread by Herod's sister, Salome.

The arts of death

In keeping with the classical tradition, any violence in Cary's play takes place off-stage and is reported. In our excerpt, from the play's final act, Herod is informed of Mariam's death by a messenger, Nuntio. Herod, already regretting ordering Mariam's death, is entirely overcome with remorse upon hearing of her 'good death'. Cary's passage about Mariam's stoic martyrdom is replete with Christological overtones, in the *imitatio Christi*[1] tradition of hagiography, including her prediction that her resurrection would be wished for by Herod 'three days hence' (Jesus was resurrected after three days). Mariam's fearless death, as she places her trust in God and ignores the baying of the hostile crowd (including her mother, Alexandra), supplies an exemplar of female Christian faith, virtue, and heroism. All-powerful Herod, distraught at what he has brought about, is forced to humbly confront death's irreversible finality.

Textual notes

The tragedie of Mariam, the faire queene of Iewry (London: 1613; STC 4613), H2r–H3r.

The Tragedy of Mariam

Enter HEROD.

[NUNTIO]	Your Mariam greets you well.
HEROD	What? Lives my Mariam? Joy, exceeding joy!
	She shall not die.
NUNTIO	Heaven doth your will repel.
HEROD	Oh, do not with thy words my life destroy,
	I prithee tell no dying-tale: thine eye
	Without thy tongue doth tell but too, too much:
	Yet let thy tongue's addition make me die,
	Death welcome comes to him whose grief is such.
NUNTIO	I went amongst the curious gazing troop,
	To see the last of her that was the best:
	To see if death had heart to make her stoop,
	To see the sun-admiring phoenix'[2] nest.

---

[1] See entry I.4 (Parr) on the presence early on and favourable reception of this tradition in English court circles.

[2] The phoenix, a bird from Greek mythology that cyclically regenerates every five hundred years after immolating itself on its own funeral pyre or nest, has strong Christological implications of resurrection. On another deployment of this trope, see entry II.12 (Heywood).

	When there I came, upon the way I saw
	The stately Mariam not debased by fear:
	Her look did seem to keep the world in awe,
	Yet mildly did her face this fortune bear.
HEROD	Thou dost usurp my right, my tongue was framed
	To be the instrument of Mariam's praise:
	Yet speak: she cannot be too often famed:
	All tongues suffice not her sweet name to raise.
NUNTIO	But as she came she Alexandra met,
	Who did her death (sweet queen) no whit bewail,
	But as if nature she did quite forget,
	She did upon her daughter loudly rail.
HEROD	Why stopped you not her mouth? Where had she words
	To darken that, that Heaven made so bright?
	Our sacred tongue no epithet affords
	To call her other than the world's delight.
NUNTIO	She told her that her death was too, too good,
	And that already she had lived too long:
	She said, she shamed to have a part in blood
	Of her that did the princely Herod wrong.
HEROD	Base pickthank[3] devil. Shame, 'twas all her glory,
	That she to noble Mariam was the mother:
	But never shall it live in any story
	Her name, except to infamy, I'll smother.
	What answer did her princely daughter make?
NUNTIO	She made no answer, but she looked the while,
	As if thereof she scarce did notice take,
	Yet smiled, a dutiful, though scornful, smile.
HEROD	Sweet creature, I that look to mind do call;
	Full oft hath Herod been amazed withal.
	[Go on.]
NUNTIO	She came unmoved, with pleasant grace,
	As if to triumph her arrival were:
	In stately habit, and with cheerful face:
	Yet every eye was moist but Mariam's there.
	When justly opposite to me she came,

---

[3] 'obsequious', 'sycophantic'

	She picked me out from all the crew:
	She beckoned to me, called me by my name,
	For she my name, my birth, and fortune knew.
HEROD	What, did she name thee? Happy, happy man,
	Wilt thou not ever love that name the better?
	But what sweet tune did this fair dying swan[4]
	Afford thine ear? Tell all, omit no letter.
NUNTIO	'Tell thou my lord', said she—
HEROD	Me, meant she me?
	Is't true, the more my shame: I was her lord,
	Were I not mad, her Lord I still should be:
	But now her name must be by me adored.
	Oh say, what said she more? Each word she said
	Shall be the food whereon my heart is fed.
NUNTIO	'Tell thou my Lord thou saw'st me lose my breath'.
HEROD	Oh that I could that sentence now control.
NUNTIO	'If guiltily, eternal be my death'.
HEROD	I hold her chaste even in my inmost soul.
NUNTIO	'By three days hence, if wishes could revive,
	I know himself would make me oft alive'.
HEROD	Three days: three hours, three minutes, not so much,
	A minute in a thousand parts divided;
	My penitency for her death is such,
	As in the first I wished she had not died.
	But forward in thy tale.
NUNTIO	Why, on she went,
	And after she some silent prayer had said,
	She did as if to die she were content,
	And thus to heaven her heavenly soul is fled.
HEROD	But art thou sure there doth no life remain?
	Is't possible my Mariam should be dead?
	Is there no trick to make her breathe again?
NUNTIO	Her body is divided from her head.
HEROD	Why, yet methinks there might be found by art,
	Strange ways of cure; 'tis sure rare things are done

---

[4] In Greek mythology a swan sings a beautifully harmonious song before its death (hence 'swansong').

	By an inventive head, and willing heart.
NUNTIO	Let not, my lord, your fancies idly run.
	It is as possible it should be seen,
	That we should make the holy Abraham live,
	Though he entombed two thousand years had been,
	As breath again to slaughtered Mariam give.

Suggested further reading

Nandra Perry, 'The Sound of Silence: Elizabeth Cary and the Christian Hero', *English Literary Renaissance*, 38.1 (2008), 106–41

Wray Ramona, 'Performing *The Tragedy of Mariam* and Constructing Stage History', *Early Theatre*, 18.2 (2015), 149–66.

IV.14

MARY WROTH

Urania (1621)

About the author

Mary Wroth (1587–1653?) was the eldest daughter of Robert Sidney, brother of the courtier and poet Philip Sidney,[1] and of the translator and pre-eminent literary patron Mary Sidney Herbert,[2] for whom she was named and with whom she resided during some of her childhood. Briefly part of Queen Anne's inner circle, she had to contend with the deaths of her husband in 1614 and, two years later, her young son, James, which led to her brother-in-law claiming the Wroth estate. Little else is known about her other than that she lived thereafter in dire financial straits. Wroth is the first Englishwoman to have published a complete sonnet cycle (*Pamphilia to Amphilanthus*) and an original work of prose fiction (*Urania*).

About the text

Urania is dedicated to Wroth's close friend and relative, Susan (*née* de Vere) Herbert, the countess of Montgomery. Edward Denny, Baron of Waltham, complained to King James that Wroth's work contained slanderous allusions

---

[1] See entry II.6 (Philips). [2] See entry II.8 (Mary Sidney).

to his private affairs as well as defamatory portraits of others at court. The main plot of this romance involves the relationship of faithful Pamphilia and inconstant Amphilanthus, with many digressions and subsidiary episodes set in a pastoral counterpart of Continental Europe. Our excerpt comes from Book One,[3] when Perissus confides in Urania the history of his unhappy love for Limena who was killed (or so he thinks) by her jealous and abusive husband, Philargus. Urania counsels against despair, urging Perissus to regain his passion and discover Limena's fate and, if she actually is dead, to avenge her death and mourn her properly.

The arts of death

Urania finds Perissus in a cave, utterly disconsolate.[4] She entreats him to relate his tale of woe so she might be convinced to lament with him. The pathos expressed in this passage turns upon the heart-wrenching grief over the death of one's beloved. It is no less powerful when readers later discover that Perissus has been labouring under a misapprehension. For, when Perissus finds Limena alive, the overarching literary and emotional response is that of release and relief, augmented by a symbolic resurrection conducing to a supercharged union of lovers, body and soul. Such episodes, where characters come near death or are believed to be dead, mirror the aesthetic principles underlying popular tragicomedies and romance dramas of the period.[5] Wroth's gift of death to her readers is wrapped up in the renewed pleasure and vicarious sense of rejuvenation one can experience from this literary genre, the sprawling pastoral romance, then in full flower, which a generation earlier her influential aunt and uncle had cultivated in *Arcadia*.

Textual notes

The Countesse of Mountgomeries Urania. Written by the right honorable the Lady Mary Wroath (London: 1621; STC 26051), C1^v–C3^r.

---

[3] Cf. *MA* VI.15 on 'the rich emblematics of the remembering heart' critically explored in *Urania*, Book Four.
[4] The cave is modelled on the 'Cave of Despair' in Spenser *FQ*, 1.9, with an earlier analogue of 'Pit of Wanhope' in Langland *PP*, 2.98–101, 5.279–82.
[5] For example, in a representative and telling use of the *deus ex machina* convention, Jupiter descends and explains: 'Whom best I love I cross, to make my gift, / The more delayed, delighted' (*Cymbeline* 5.4.195–96).

Urania

'O God', cried out Philargus, 'what do I hear? Or what can you style virtuous and religious, since it is to one besides your husband? Hath shame possessed you? And excellent modesty abandoned you? You have in part satisfied me indeed, but thus to see that I have just occasion to seek satisfaction for this injury. Wherefore, resolve instantly to die, or obey me. Write a letter straight before mine eyes unto him. Conjure him with those sweet charms which have undone mine honour and content to come unto you. Let me truly know his answer, and be secret, or I vow thou shalt not many minutes outlive the refusal'.

She, sweetest soul, brought into this danger (like one being between a flaming fire and a swallowing gulf must venture into one or, standing still, perish by one), stood a while not amazed, for her spirit scorned so low a passion; but judiciously considering with herself what might be good in so much ill, she with modest constancy and constant determination made this answer.

'This wretched and unfortunate body is, I confess, in your hands to dispose of to death if you will. But yet it is not unblessed with such a mind as will suffer to end with any such stain as so wicked a plot and miserable consent might purchase [...] Wherefore, my lord, pardon me. For I will with more willingness die than execute your mind. And more happily shall I end, saving him innocent from ill, delivering my soul pure and I unspotted of the crime you tax me of'. [...] With floods of tears, and storms of sighs he concluded: 'And by this, is the rarest piece of womankind destroyed'. [...] 'Despair having left me no more ground for hope but this, that ere long I shall ease them all, death proving merciful unto me in delivering this grieffull body to the rest of a desired grave'.

'My lord Perissus', said Urania, 'how idle and unprofitable indeed are these courses since if she be dead, what good can they bring to her? And not being certain of her death, how unfit are they for so brave a prince who will, as it were, by will without reason wilfully lose himself. Will not any, till the contrary be known, as properly hope as vainly despair? And can it be imagined her husband (who passion of love did in his fury so much temper) should have so cruel a hand, guided by so savage a heart, or seen by so pitiless eyes, as to be able to murder so sweet a beauty? No, my lord, I cannot believe but she is living and that you shall find it so, if unreasonable stubborn resolution bar you not and hinder you from the eternal happiness you might enjoy'.

'Only rare shepherdess', said the love-killed Perissus [...] 'she is dead, and with her is all virtue and bounteous constancy gone. She is dead, for how can goodness of pity be expected from him who knew nothing more than desire of ill or cruelty? Thou art dead, and with thee all my joys departed. All faith, love and worth are dead. To enjoy some part of which in short time I will be with thee that, though in life we were kept asunder, in death we may be joined together, till which happy hour I will thus still lament thy loss'.

'If you be resolved', said the dainty Urania [...] 'like a brave prince, if you know she be dead, revenge her death on her murderers and after, if you will celebrate her funerals with your own life-giving, that will be a famous act. So may you gain perpetuate glory and repay the honour to her dead, which could not be but touched by her untimely end'. [...] Then thus said he [...] 'I vow before heaven and you that I will never leave off my arms until I have [...] revenged my lady's death, and then to her love and memory offer up my afflicted life'.

Suggested further reading
Margaret P. Hannay, *Mary Sidney, Lady Wroth* (Farnham, UK: Ashgate, 2010).
Mary Ellen Lamb, 'The Biopolitics of Romance in Mary Wroth's "The Countess of Montgomery's Urania"', *English Literary Renaissance*, 31.1 (2001), 107–30.
Mary Wroth, *The First Part of The Countess of Montgomery's 'Urania'*, ed. Josephine Roberts (Binghamton, NY: Medieval and Renaissance Texts and Studies, 1995), pp. xvi–cxxi.

IV.15

ANONYMOUS

'The Last Will and Testament of Philip Herbert' (1650)

About the text

This short pamphlet satirically parodies the will of Philip Herbert, first earl of Montgomery and fourth earl of Pembroke (1584–1650), the younger son of Henry Herbert, second earl of Pembroke, and his third wife, Mary Herbert (née Sidney). The pamphlet's full title ridicules Pembroke's demotion from a peer to a member of the House of Commons, when he joined the Rump

Parliament after the regicide. The parodic will drives the title's point home under item eleven, where Pembroke bequeaths his coat of arms to noblemen's sons who 'claim their honour downwards' by descending to the rank of burgess (A3r).

Handsome and athletic, Herbert had risen to prominence as a favourite in James I's court, receiving under Charles I in 1626 the appointment of Lord Chamberlain (one of the three principal officers of the Royal Household). His moderate Protestant politics clashed with Charles I's Catholicism, however, and eventually he was relieved of the office in 1641 when his assault on Lord Maltravers with his staff gave the king the occasion to dismiss him. Pembroke had been notorious throughout his life for a choleric disposition, a foul mouth, and violent outbursts.

This pamphlet is just one of a dozen royalist satires penned at Pembroke's expense, some ridiculing his ineptitude as chancellor of the University of Oxford, others exposing his blundering and blustering opportunism in parliament, and most decrying his betrayal of England's monarchy and nobles. The excerpt below derides Pembroke's preoccupation with hunting, falconry, and sports as well as his unrefined oratory. Though not known to be a lover of books, he was a patron of many literary authors, with Shakespeare's 'First Folio' (1623) being dedicated to him and his brother. Among England's peers, he owned the most magnificent collection of paintings, the unscrupulous augmentation of which the excerpt alludes to repeatedly.

The arts of death

At least two other pamphlets[1] that target Pembroke take the mock form of a last will and testament. This particular one has eighteen clauses that distribute Pembroke's property among his beneficiaries. In the final and longest clause, excerpted here, the testator begins with bequeathing his hawks but immediately loses his train of thought, slipping into a delirious monologue as he passes away. The form of the will allows the satirist to imagine the testator's final words on his deathbed – words steeped in earthbound, materialistic desires. The reader knows where Pembroke's heart, after Matthew 6:21, is located, given the place of where his treasure is laid up. Much of the humour

---

[1] 'The first part of the last wil & testament of Philip Earle of Pembrooke' (Wing F978A) and 'The last will and testament of the Earl of Pembroke' (Wing L531A). All three are entirely different works.

also depends upon the lack of decorum characterizing Pembroke's inept and even blasphemous enactment of the *ars moriendi*. Echoes may even be heard of Richard III's guilty conscience and vision of his royal victims' ghosts. Appended to the will, but not included here, is a mock elegy on Pembroke, attributed in jest to his secretary, Michael Oldisworth. The entire pamphlet, will and elegy, constitutes a counter-memorial to one of the highest-ranking treasonous peers during the Civil Wars.

Textual notes

The last will and testament of Philip Herbert, Burgess for Barkshire, vulgarly called Earl of Pembroke and Montgomery who died of fool age, Jan. 23. 1650 with his life and death, and several legacies to the parliament and council of state, also his elegy, taken verbatim, in time of his sicknesse, and published to prevent false copies, by Michael Oldisworth (Nod-Nol [i.e., London]: 1650; Wing L524), A3^v–A4^r.

'The Last Will and Testament of Philip Herbert'

Lastly, I give all my hawks to Sir Thomas,[2] provided he hath the wit to know a hawk from a buzzard, and that he let them fly at nothing but game-royal. Damn me, I am very sick, and my memory fails me much. Refuse me,[3] if I can remember what I have else to give, but something I have, which I leave to the discretion of my executors, to be disposed as they shall think fit. Sink me, I have troubled my mind too much with things belonging to this world already, and yet judge me, nothing grieves me, but that a pox on't, now they may call me a rotten Lord indeed. Who the devil thought death had been so near? And yet by God 'tis better to die in one's bed than live to be hanged and who do you think (being a Member of Parliament) will scape that death, if the late king's son should prevail over us? Judge me, it troubles my conscience that I had a hand in his father's death; but it is a little comfort to me to die and cozen him of his revenge—Michael,[4] where a pox art thou now? 'Sblood,[5] I am well hope up to have such a comforter at my death. Ha, ha, ha, what's that? Now 'tis at my bed's feet; oh, oh, oh, all bloody too. Murder, murder,

---

[2] Sir Thomas Fairfax, English Parliamentary General
[3] '(God) refuse me' was an oath. Oaths with the same formula follow.
[4] Michael Oldisworth, secretary to Pembroke [5] an oath, literally 'God's blood'

call up my men, Ralph, Robin, Dick,[6] with a pox, there 'tis. Now 'tis like a cat, a pox mew[7] ye. Do ye take a nobleman to be a mouse? Oh, oh, it bites, it bites, it bites, the devil, the devil, the devil. Oh, my conscience. 'Sblood, give me some sack.[8] I'll drink a confusion to death.[9] Grass and hay,[10] a fool must die as well as a knave. Michael, remember me to all my friends at Whitehall.[11] Bid them have a care. Damn me, there 'tis again, a man without a head, beckoning me with his hand, and bending his fist at me.[12] What a pox art thou? Speak, if thou art a man, speak, speak, speak. 'Sblood, canst thou not speak without a head? Soho,[13] soho, that dog spends[14] well. Tat,[15] tat, Ring-wood,[16] a plague confound that cur, take him and couple him to Jowler;[17] tell 'im I'll to Guildhall[18] presently—a pox of honour, what need a dying man care for switching?[19] Oh Mistress May,[20] come to bed sweetheart come, my duck, my bird's-nye.[21] 'Sblood, I must go to Salisbury[22] tomorrow. Bring me my boots quickly. Damn me this park troubles me. I'll have it right or wrong. Zounds,[23] will not the rogues bring me more money? 'Sblood, that cock's worth a king's ransom, a[24] runs, a runs, a thousand pound to a hobby-horse.[25] Rub,[26] rub, rub—a pox rub—a whole hundred rubs. Zounds, I think my bowl's[27] bewitched, it has no more bias[28] than a bagpudding.[29] Michael, tell them I'll restore those pictures and models I had from St. James's.[30] The ceiling[31] of the banquet house at Whitehall, tell them, is as fit for my parlor in Ramsbury

---

[6] Pembroke's servants Ralph King, Robert May, and Richard Bridges
[7] 'to utter a mew'; 'to shut away, to confine'   [8] 'white wine from Spain and the Canaries'
[9] 'drink a confusion': an imprecation or exclamation
[10] echoing the saying 'Grass and hay, we are all mortal!' (*DPE*, G 413)
[11] 'palace, where the House of Commons sat'   [12] i.e., Charles I's ghost. See entry II.13.
[13] hunter's call   [14] 'leaps', 'springs', 'dashes'   [15] 'to touch lightly', 'pat', 'tap'
[16] 'wood used to make the rims of wheels and in this instance the name of the hound'
[17] 'a heavy-jawed dog'; also 'name for dog as in this case'
[18] 'the hall of the Corporation of the City of London'   [19] 'beating', 'flogging'
[20] Pembroke's concubine, the allusion to whom fans the flames of scandal since he was married at the time to his second wife, Lady Anne Clifford, Countess of Pembroke
[21] a term of endearment   [22] 'cathedral city near Wilton House', Pembroke's country seat
[23] an oath, literally 'God's wounds'   [24] 'they'; but here perhaps 'he'   [25] 'a kind of horse'
[26] i.e., uneven ground which impedes or diverts a wooden ball in the game of bowls
[27] 'a wooden ball'
[28] the bowl's construction that gives it an oblique motion; the oblique line in which the bowl runs; the spin put on the bowl to make it roll obliquely
[29] 'a pudding boiled in a bag'
[30] the London palace where Charles spent his final night before his execution
[31] a massive oil painting by Peter Paul Rubens that adorns the hall's ceiling

Manor[32] as can be. A plague, must I build a house for another to make a bawdy house of?[33] Who can make me a skeleton?[34] Commend me to Mr. Speaker. Tell him I'll have Woodstock-Bower,[35] and bid him remember the hangings[36] that came from Hampton Court. I'll come to the house tomorrow and remove the obstructions in the sale of the King's goods.[37] 'Sblood, I'll have the university reformed as I list.[38] Goodwin[39] is too scholarish.[40] I'll have a beetle-head[41] for that blockish college. Ralph, tie up Jewel[42] from her puppies; they'll suck her as bare as a bird's arse. Oh, the fiends, the fiends—

I come, I come, good devil lead the way,
When rebels die, hell makes a holiday.[43]

His Lordship having no sooner ended this his last speech, but he stared very wistfully on Mistress May (his honour's concubine), and swore damn me, sink me, and confound me, some nine times over, and so yielded up the ghost, and his soul was conveyed away in a hideous storm.[44]

Michael Oldisworth
Witness[45] Ralph King
Richard Bridges
Robert May

---

[32] a family house located in Wiltshire
[33] Pembroke was rebuilding Wilton House, unfinished at the time of his death.
[34] a request for new furnishings or a desire to have himself turned into an anatomical exhibit
[35] The bower that Henry II built to house his mistress Rosamund was located at Woodstock Palace, mostly destroyed during the English Civil War.
[36] tapestries from the King's palace   [37] 'movable property'
[38] Pembroke served as Oxford University's Chancellor from 1648 to his death.
[39] Thomas Goodwin, who authored fifteen different titles, had been supported to be the head of an Oxford College.
[40] 'scholarly'   [41] a contemptuous epithet on par with 'block-head' or 'bottle-head'
[42] his hunting dog   [43] also 'a holy day' or 'feast day'   [44] as opposed to a peaceful death
[45] Herbert's servants who attested to the execution of the will

Suggested further reading
David L. Smith, 'Herbert, Philip, First Earl of Montgomery and Fourth Earl of Pembroke (1584–1650), Courtier and Politician', *Oxford Dictionary of National Biography* (Oxford: Oxford University Press, 2004).
A. H. Tricomi, 'Philip, Earl of Pembroke, and the Analogical Way of Reading Political Tragedy', *The Journal of English and Germanic Philology*, 85.3 (1986), pp. 332–45.

IV.16

ANDREW MARVELL

'The Nymph Complaining for the Death of her Fawn' (1681)

About the author

Andrew Marvell (1621–1678), son of a Yorkshire divine, was educated at Trinity College, Cambridge, and was eventually appointed Latin Secretary to the Council of State, after holding the position of tutor – first to Thomas Fairfax's daughter and then to Oliver Cromwell's ward. Marvell politically survived the Restoration, serving as MP for Hull from 1559 to his death. During his lifetime, he was known chiefly for his satires on the corruption of the Stuart court.

About the text

Marvell's *Miscellaneous Poems* were published posthumously. A prefatory note signed by Mary Marvell, his housekeeper and, after his death, alleged spouse, vouched for their authenticity, certifying that all the texts were printed from exact copies written in his own hand. The volume is comprised of erotic verse, religious lyrics, Latin epigrams and epitaphs, pastoral monologues and dialogues, and garden poetry, including his major work 'Upon Appleton House', a country house poem. Marvell has been traditionally read as a metaphysical poet, a questionable designation applied to seventeenth-century versifiers the likes of John Donne, George Herbert,[1] and Henry Vaughan, whose work is said to display a tangle of far-fetched conceit, intellectual matter, and witty logic.

'The Nymph Complaining for the Death of her Fawn', excerpted in its entirety, superimposes a funeral ode on a lover's complaint, the former genre not quite fitting the text. Because the poem laments the young deer in its death throes, it does not fully qualify as a burial song per se. In the case of the complaint, its generic affiliation, though decorously complementing the poem's pastoral setting, is a little more complicated. The lover's complaint,

---

[1] See *MA* VI.6 for examples of Herbert's incarnational poetics in *The Temple*.

usually a poem that grieves over unreciprocated love, applies to the nymph's rejection by Sylvio, whose shadow looms above the scene, but the nymph's primary regret concerns the dying fawn, not her male paramour. But because Sylvio gifted the deer to the nymph, we are left to conjecture whether or not she grieves over its metonymic significance – the loss of a lover.

Marvell may have also had in mind Greek and Latin poems dedicated to animal companions, most notably Ovid's treatment of the myth of Cyparissus, a fair youth who, accidentally slaying his pet stag, begs Phoebus to let him mourn his loss forever and finds himself transformed into a cyprus, the tree whose resin, like tears, beads on its bark.[2] Nigel Smith claims that the poem 'has generated more interpretative difficulties in twentieth-century criticism than any of Marvell's lyrics' and much of this scholarship grapples with the question of whether or not it is allegorical (68). Graham Parry raises the fascinating possibility that Marvell's poem may be a 'veiled memorial to the death of King Charles, his own curious *Eikon Basilike*',[3] given that the dead king had no tomb during the Interregnum (250).

The arts of death

A prosopopeia of distempered grief, the poem demonstrates the extent to which death can be lavishly aestheticized in the period. Marvell practises his funereal art through having his Nymph's complaint conjure up Ovidian narratives of embalmed lamentation. Marvell handles the myths of Cyparissus, the Heliades, and Niobe as classical antetypes for the Nymph's predicament and response to that predicament. These mourners are all preserved through a transfiguration into a vegetable or lapidary memorial. What should be emphasized is that their metamorphoses create everlasting monuments of mourning in contradistinction to the expired defunct over whom they grieve. In Marvell's poem, the cemetery statuary of the nymph with the deer at her feet narrows the distance between mourned and mourner, freezing in time the scene of the deer's expiration. As much as it stimulates allegorical readings with its baroque imagery, the poem imbues the death of a favourite pet with spiritual value, during a time when non-human creatures were believed to have no souls. The nymph imagines the deer enjoying paradise with other animals and is worthy of not only burial but a monument, which enshrines the idea of never-ending human attachment.

[2] Ovid *MO*, 10.106–42   [3] Cf. entry II.13 (Charles I).

Miscellaneous Poems (London: 1681; Wing M872), D3ᵛ–E1ʳ.

'The Nymph Complaining for the Death of her Fawn'

The wanton troopers riding by
Have shot my fawn and it will die.
Ungentle men! They cannot thrive
To kill thee. Thou ne'er didst alive
Them any harm: alas nor could
Thy death yet do them any good.
I'm sure I never wisht them ill;
Nor do I for all this; nor will:
But, if my simple[4] prayers may yet
Prevail with heaven to forget
Thy murder, I will join my tears
Rather than fail. But, O my fears!
It cannot die so. Heaven's king
Keeps register of everything:
And nothing may we use in vain.[5]
Ev'n beasts must be with justice slain;
Else men are made their deodands.[6]
Though they should wash their guilty hands
In this warm life blood, which doth part
From thine, and wound me to the heart,
Yet could they not be clean: their stain
Is dyed in such a purple grain.[7]
There is not such another in
The world, to offer for their sin.
    Unconstant Sylvio, when yet
I had not found him counterfeit,
One morning (I remember well)

---

[4] 'homely', 'honest', 'innocent' [5] i.e., treat with contempt
[6] in English law, personal property which, having caused the death of a human being, is forfeited to the Crown
[7] 'a scarlet or crimson colour', 'dye'

Tied in this silver chain and bell,
Gave it to me: nay and I know
What he said then; I'm sure I do.
Said he, 'Look how your huntsman here
Hath taught a fawn to hunt his dear.'[8]
But Sylvio soon had me beguiled.
This waxed tame; while he grew wild,
And quite regardless of my smart,
Left me his fawn, but took his heart.

   Thenceforth I set myself to play
My solitary time away,
With this: and very well content,
Could so mine idle life have spent.
For it was full of sport; and light
Of foot, and heart; and did invite,
Me to its game: it seemed to bless
Itself in me. How could I less
Than love it? O I cannot be
Unkind, t'a beast that loveth me.

   Had it lived long, I do not know
Whether it too might have done so
As Sylvio did: his gifts might be
Perhaps as false or more than he.
But I am sure, for ought that I
Could in so short a time espy,
Thy love was far more better than
The love of false and cruel men.

   With sweetest milk, and sugar, first
I it at mine own fingers nurst.
And as it grew, so every day
It waxed more white and sweet than they.
It had so sweet a breath! And oft
I blusht to see its foot more soft,
And white (shall I say then my hand?

---

[8] a popular pun in literature; see, for example, Thomas Wyatt, 'Whoso List to Hunt, I Know where is an Hind', in *The Complete Poems*, ed. R. A. Rebholz (Harmondsworth, UK: Penguin, 1978), p. 77.

Nay any ladies of the land).
    It is a wondrous thing, how fleet
'Twas on those little silver feet.
With what a pretty skipping grace,
It oft would challenge me the race:
And when 't had left me far away,
'Twould stay, and run again, and stay.
For it was nimbler much than hinds;[9]
And trod, as on the four winds.
    I have a garden of my own,
But so with roses overgrown,
And lilies, that you would it guess
To be a little wilderness.
And all the springtime of the year
It only loved to be there.
Among the beds of lilies, I
Have sought it oft, where it should lie;
Yet could not, till itself would rise,
Find it, although before mine eyes.
For, in the flaxen[10] lilies shade,
It like a bank of lilies laid.
Upon the roses it would feed,
Until its lips e'en seemed to bleed:
And then to me 'twould boldly trip,[11]
And print those roses on my lip.
But all its chief delight was still
On roses thus itself to fill:
And its pure virgin limbs to fold
In whitest sheets[12] of lilies cold.
Had it lived long, it would have been
Lilies without, roses within.
    O help! O help! I see it faint:
And die as calmly as a saint.
See how it weeps. The tears do come

---

[9] literally 'female deer'; but likely 'farm labourers' in the context
[10] 'yellow' (or, more likely, white in context)   [11] 'to move nimbly, skip, caper'
[12] 'burial shroud'

Sad, slowly dropping like a gum.[13]
So weeps the wounded balsam:[14] so
The holy frankincense[15] doth flow.
The brotherless Heliades[16]
Melt in such amber tears as these.
 I in a golden vial[17] will
Keep these two crystal tears; and fill
It till it do o'erflow with mine;
Then place it in Diana's shrine.
 Now my sweet fawn is vanished to
Whither the swans and turtles go:
In fair Elysium[18] to endure,
With milk-white lambs, and ermines pure.
O do not run too fast: for I
Will but bespeak[19] thy grave, and die.
 First my unhappy statue shall
Be cut in marble; and withal,
Let it be weeping too: but there
Th' engraver sure his art may spare;
For I so truly thee bemoan,
That I shall weep though I be stone:[20]
Until my tears, still dropping, wear
My breast, themselves engraving there.
There at my feet shalt thou be laid,
Of purest alabaster[21] made:
For I would have thine image be
White as I can, though not as thee.

---

[13] 'resin-like secretion from tree'
[14] This tree's sap was believed to have medicinal properties.
[15] 'aromatic resin used for burning as incense'
[16] daughters of the Sun, who in mourning their dead brother Phaeton were transformed into poplars and their tears into amber (Ovid *MO*, 2.340–66)
[17] 'a lachrymatory' [18] Greek afterlife paradise for blessed mortals and heroes
[19] 'make arrangements for'
[20] alluding to Niobe, a proud mother whom the gods punished by slaying her children and turning her into a weeping statue (Ovid *MO*, 6.286–312)
[21] a white stone used in the period for tombs and religious statues

Suggested further reading

Graham Parry, 'What is Marvell's Nymph Complaining About?', *Critical Survey*, 5.3 (1993), 244–51.

Nigel Smith (ed.), *The Poems of Andrew Marvell* (London, New York, and Toronto: Pearson Longman, 2003), pp. 65–71.

IV.17

APHRA BEHN

Oroonoko (1688)

About the author

Aphra Behn (1640?–1689), playwright, poet, and novelist, was the first English woman to earn a livelihood as a writer. Her works are known for giving voice to a curious mixture of authorial personae from a forerunner of feminism and abolitionism to a propagandist for the monarchy and an exponent of libertinism and philosophical materialism.

About the text

An early form of the novel that mixes travel literature with romance and epic conventions, *Oroonoko* recounts the exploits of a West African prince, who is tricked into captivity by a slave trader and sold to a plantation in the British colony of Surinam, South America. Behn writes from her experiences as a visitor to Surinam in 1663–1664 before the colony had been taken over by the Dutch. She, along with her mother and sister, stayed on a plantation and apparently embroiled herself in political quarrels with the colonial administrators.

Behn was disappointed by the book's paltry sales, but in 1695 Thomas Southerne adapted the novel into a tragedy, which met with such success on the stage that it revived interest in the novel. Eventually the popular narrative became a standard bearer for abolitionists during the eighteenth and nineteenth centuries. The passage here begins at the point when Oroonoko – whom the colonialists call Caesar – is abducted by Banister, the henchman of the governor who wants to make an example of the spirited slave. Incidentally, Southerne completely rewrote Behn's grisly death scene by having Oroonoko commit suicide after he stabs his enemy, the lieutenant governor.

The arts of death

What Behn praises in Caesar are European ideals, as though his greatness has little to do with his own culture and racial identity (as discussed in the Introduction):

> His nose was rising and Roman, instead of African and flat. His mouth, was the finest shaped that could be seen; far from those great turned lips, which are so natural to the rest of the Negroes. The whole proportion and air of his face was so noble, and exactly formed, that, bating his colour, there could be nothing in nature more beautiful, agreeable and handsome. (C3^r)

Behn witnesses similarly exaggerated Western values at Caesar's execution, which perplexingly knots together some prominent premodern discourses around discipline and punishment. Critics have traditionally characterized the scene as one of martyrdom, in which Caesar, following in the footsteps of saints, endures great pain and suffering to resist a godless state power. The trouble with settling on this interpretation alone is, as Cynthia Richards highlights, that the silent Caesar does not resemble a Protestant or Catholic martyr who calls upon divine authority for strength and comfort, inspiring others to take up his or her spiritual cause (652–54). Caesar also invokes, as Catherine Gallagher observes, the seventeenth-century abstraction of kingship (73) by partially reminding us of the recent Stuart executions – Charles I as well as Charles II's illegitimate son, who tried to usurp the throne from James II. Melanie Griffin, however, underscores the interpretive conundrum of resolving his sovereignty with a punishment reserved for regicides or high traitors, particularly noted by his castration and the scattering of his limbs (110). British nobles would have been beheaded, not subjected to the brutal corporeal degradation of dismemberment and quartering. At no point does Caesar betray any recognition of the ignoble treatment in store for him and instead conducts himself according to an altogether different honour-code. He passionately prefers death over whipping, whose import his sadistic captors fail to understand, believing that they will inflict upon him greater harm. His superhuman impassivity towards dismemberment allows them no sadistic pleasure and recalls the South American aboriginals who earlier in the narrative cut off pieces of their faces to prove their fitness for military leadership. Before the executioner works his cruel knife, Caesar's boast that he will 'endure death so as should encourage them to die' suggests his intention to teach his captors a kind of stoic *ars moriendi* – a lesson apparently lost on the spectating mob. Raising more questions than it answers, Caesar's execution shows Behn's difficulty of knowing how to apply the Eurocentric death arts to the royal African in the colonial New World.

Textual notes

Oroonoko: or, The royal slave. A true history (London: 1688; Wing B1749), Q6^v–Q8^r.

Oroonoko

He [Bannister] came up to Parham and forcibly took Caesar and had him carried to the same post where he was whipped; and causing him to be tied to it and a great fire made before him, he told him, he should die like a dog as he was. Caesar replied this was the first piece of bravery that ever Banister did; and he never spoke sense till he pronounced that word; and, if he would keep it, he would declare, in the other World, that he was the only man of all the whites that ever he heard speak truth. And turning to the men that bound him, he said, 'My friends, am I to die, or to be whipped?' And they cried, 'Whipped! no, you shall not escape so well'. And then he replied, smiling, 'A blessing on thee'; and assured them, they need not tie him, for he would stand fixed like a rock and endure death so as should encourage them to die. 'But if you whip me', said he, 'be sure you tie me fast'.

 He had learned to take tobacco; and when he was assured he should die, he desired they would give him a pipe in his mouth, ready lighted, which they did; and the executioner came, and first cut off his members, and threw them into the fire; after that, with an ill-favoured knife, they cut his ears, and his nose, and burned them; he still smoked on, as if nothing had touched him; then they hacked off one of his arms, and still he bore up, and held his pipe; but at the cutting off the other arm, his head sunk, and his pipe dropped; and he gave up the ghost, without a groan, or a reproach. My mother and sister were by him all the while, but not suffered to save him, so rude and wild were the rabble, and so inhumane were the justices, who stood by to see the execution, who after paid dearly enough for their insolence. They cut Caesar in quarters and sent them to several of the chief plantations: one quarter was sent to Colonel Martin, who refused it and swore he had rather see the quarters of Banister and the Governor himself than those of Caesar on his plantations, and that he could govern his negroes without terrifying and grieving them with frightful spectacles of a mangled king.

Suggested further reading

Catherine Gallagher, *Nobody's Story: The Vanishing Acts of Women Writers in the Marketplace, 1670–1820* (Berkeley, CA: University of California Press, 1995).

Megan Griffin, 'Dismembering the Sovereign in Aphra Behn's *Oroonoko*', *ELH*, 86.1 (2019), 107–33.

Cynthia Richards, 'Interrogating *Oroonoko*: Torture in a New World and a New Fiction of Power', *Eighteenth-Century Fiction*, 25.4 (2013), 647–76.

All men must die, yet most men live as if they thought they should never die. Wherein men are very injurious to themselves; the sad and settled remembrance of death being a notable furtherance of repentance, and a profitable mean to keep us from eternal death. For, I pray you, why should man lift up himself against his Maker who ere long must fall into the earth? Why should we be proud and insolent, who are but dust? Why should we insult over any man because we surpass him in wit, wealth, strength, honour, beauty? Are we not all food for the worms? Will not death knock all our bones together? Is not our life a breath, a bubble?

> Thomas Tuke, *A Discourse of Death* (London: 1613, STC 24307), A4^r

INDEX

à Kempis, Thomas, 69
Adelman, Janet, 42
Adler, Mortimer J., 5
Adlington, Hugh, 29
Aesop, 55
Agricola, Rodolphus, 207, 213, 214
Akkerman, Fokke, 214
Alexander, Gavin, 164
allegory, 14, 15, 17, 21, 22, 45, 64, 222, 253, 273, 281, 291, 331, 343, 363
Allen, William, 150, 151
   The Glorious Martyrdom of Twelve Priests, 150–53
anatomy, 22, 235, 249, 250, 251, 255, 309, 310
Anderson, Miranda, 103
Andreadis, Harriette, 35
Andrewes, Lancelot, xiii, 178, 179, 181
   'A Sermon … the 5ᵗʰ of November, 1606', 178–81
Andrews, Kenneth, 245
Anger, Jane, 32, 229
   Protection for Women, 229–33
Angier, Tom, 7
Anne of Cleves, 133
Anne of Denmark, 178, 189, 233, 339, 348, 354
Anselm of Canterbury, 70
Apollo, 169
Appleford, Amy, 8, 58, 66, 68
Ariès, Philippe, 8, 30, 35
Ariosto, Ludovico, 311
Aristotle, 7, 51, 57, 207, 208, 227, 246, 259
ars moriendi, 5, 7, 9, 11, 12, 28, 52, 53, 55, 56, 91, 104, 113, 117, 121, 123, 182, 186, 202, 234, 281, 295, 304, 312, 328, 359, 369, *see also* moriens; deathbed
art of memory, 17, 22, 70
Ascham, Roger, 219
Askew, Anne, 69, 133, 145, 146, 147, 208
Astell, Mary, 201, 209
   'An Essay upon Death', 201–04

Astell, Ralph, 201
ataraxia, 233, 234
Athena (Minerva), 102
Atherton, John, 34
Atkinson, David W., 5, 89
Aubrey, John, 93
Augustine, St, 13, 131, 276, 292, 294
Austen, Gillian, 314

Babbitt, Frank Cole, 16
Bacon, Francis, 44, 245, 259
   'Of Death', 245–51
Bailey, Cyril, 217
Baker-Smith, Dominic, 158
Baldo, Jonathan, 85
Baldwin, William, 222
Bale, John, 145, 146, 219
Bandello, Matteo, 308
Barbier, Frédéric, 26
Barbieri Giovanni Francesco (Guercino), 19
Barbour, Reid, 240
Barclay, Alexander, 21, 58, 242, 282, 285, 286
   The Ship of Fools, 285–90
Barker, Peter, v
Bartels, Emily C., 38
Barthelemy, Anthony Gerard, 39
Basil of Seleucia, 196
Batchiler, John, 27, 116
   The Virgin's Pattern, 116–19
Bath, Michael, 20
Beard, Thomas, 323
Beaty, Nancy Lee, 6, 9, 58, 66, 68
Beaufort, Margaret, 80
Beaumont, Francis, 2, 188, 230, 282
   'An Elegy on the Lady Markham', 188–93
Becker, Lucinda, 30, 196
Becon, Thomas, v, 12, 46, 312
Bedford Gaol, 310
Beecher, Donald, 232

Behn, Aphra, 27, 40, 41, 44, 267, 270, 283, 368
   Oroonoko, 368–71
Bellany, Alastair, 339
Bellarmine, Robert, 109
Belsey, Catherine, 10
Benjamin, Walter, 14
Bernard of Clairvaux, 70, 192
Bernard of Cluny, 212
Bernard, Nicholas, 34
Bernard, St, 211
Berthelet, Thomas, 66
Best, George, 41
Beuno, St, 346
Bèze, Theodore, 87
Bill, Anna, 175, 176
Bill, John, 175
Birrell, Jean, 26
Black Death, the, 37
Blades, William, 58
Blair, R. L., 31
Blake, Mary, 193, 194
blazon, 34, 59, 189
Boase, Roger, 31
Boccaccio, 232, 296, 308
Bodenham, John, 163
Boethius, 45, 47, 219, 282, 287
Boleyn, Anne, 133, 218
Boleyn, Thomas, 66
Bonadeo, Alfredo, 236
Book of Common Prayer, 137, 141, 142
Boorde, Andrew, 42
Boro, Joyce, 323
Bos, Sander, 158
Bosch, Hieronymus, 11, 22, 287
Boulton, Jeremy, 3
Boyle, Deborah, 270
Bradford, John, 2, 76, 80, 81, 107, 202
   A Fruitful Treatise ... against the Fear of Death, 76–80
Bradley, K. R., 248
Brandt, Sebastian, 285
brasses, 10, 130
Braund, Susanna Morton, 248
Bray, Alan, 34
Breitenberg, Mark, 233
Brewer, Thomas, 182
Broad, Jacqueline, 204

Broce, Gerald, 80
Bromley, James M., 34
Brooks, Thomas, 193, 294
   A String of Pearls, 193–96
Browne, Thomas, 259, 289
Brundage, James A., 31
Brunson, James E., 39
Bruster, Douglas, 291, 295
Buccola, Regina, 41
Budra, Paul, 225
Bullinger, Heinrich, 87
Bunny, Edmund, 84, 86
Bunyan, John, 292
Burchell, Graham, 131
Burchmore, David W., 222
Burgess, Clive, 129
Burton, Jonathan, 36
Burton, Robert, 31
Burton, William, 121
Buxton, John, 158
Byman, Seymour, 80

Calabritto, Monica, 14, 20, 103
Calamy, Edmund, 117, 120
Caligula, 66, 248
Calvin, Jean, 52, 72, 84, 87
Camden, William, 240
Canius, 66
Carey, Henry, 190, 339
Carlen, Georg, 38
carpe diem, 189
Carpenter, Nathaniel, 259
Carr, Robert, 334
Cary, Elizabeth, 188, 281, 350
   The Tragedy of Mariam, 281, 350–54
Catherine of Aragon, 80, 133, 222
Cavendish, Charles, 267
Cavendish, Margaret, 44, 46, 266
   Philosophical Letters, 266–70
Cavendish, William, 266
Caxton, William, 6, 7, 13, 15, 42, 51, 54, 55, 87, 340
   To Know Well To Die, 54–58
Cecil, William, 233
Chaghafi, Elisabeth, 167
Chalmers, David, 10
Chandler, Wayne B., 39
Charles the Bold, Duke of Burgundy, 55

INDEX

Charles V, Holy Roman Emperor, 215, 250
Charles VIII of France, 308
Charles IX of France, 159
Charlton, Kenneth, 29
Chaucer, Geoffrey, 15, 31, 55, 216, 234, 236, 285, 286, 300, 316
    'Friar's Tale, The', 316
    'General Prologue, The', 300
    'Knight's Tale, The', 31
    'Nun's Priest's Tale, The', 236
    'Pardoner's Tale, The', 15
    'Parson's Tale, The', 216
    'Wife of Bath's Prologue, The', 234
    Troilus and Criseyde, 285
Chess, Simone, 108
Chettle, Henry, 83, 127
chiastic, 19, 47, 271, 311
Chichele, Henry, 19, 190
Christus mortuus, 70
Churchyard, Thomas, 133, 155, 186, 222, 321
    A Mirror for Magistrates, 222–25
Ciavolella, Massimo, 31, 232
Cicero, 51, 57, 201, 213, 234, 287
Clark, Andy, 10
Clark, Sandra, 334
Classen, Albrecht, 32
Clegg, Cyndia Susan, 25
Clifford, Anne, 360
Clifford, Margaret, 341
Clymer, Lorna, 130
Cogan, Thomas, 45, 226, 239
    The Haven of Health, 225–29
Cohen, Kathleen, 193
Cohn, Samuel K., 36
Coles, Kimberly Anne, 72
Colet, John, 65
College of Arms, The, 130
Collier, Edward, 99
Collinson, Patrick, 76
Conklin, Suzanne, 38
contemptus mundi, 2, 13, 77, 81, 113, 189
contrapasso, 324
Conway, Anne, 45, 266, 274
    Principles of the Most Ancient and Modern Philosophy, 274–78
Cook, Daniel, 119
Cook, Megan L., 303

Cooke, Anne, 28
Copernicus, Nicolaus, 259
Copland, Robert, 58
Coren, Pamela, 167
Cottam, Thomas, 150, 151, 152, 153
Coventry, Ann, 201
Cowhig, Ruth, 39
Cowley, Abraham, 60
Cox III, Gerard H., 116
Cranmer, Thomas, 86, 136, 141, 202, 294
    'The Order for the Burial of the Dead', 136–40
Crashaw, Richard, 33
Creech, Thomas, 208, 236, 270
    Lucretius's Six Books, 270–74
Cressy, David, 8, 29, 30, 130
Crewe, Jonathan, 307, 327
Cromwell, Oliver, 362
Cromwell, Thomas, 133, 134
Crooke, Helkiah, 22, 46, 249
    Mikrokosmographia, 249–56
crucifixion, 11, 24, 70, 341
Culley, Amy, 119
Cummings, Brian, 9
Cummins, Neil, 4

Dabydeen, David, 39
Daems, Jim, 188
Daly, Peter, 14, 20, 103
Dance of Death, 35, 38, 59, 186, 282, 295, 296, *see also* danse macabre
Daniel, Samuel, 31
danse macabre, 9, 15, 30, 58, 282, 286, 296, *see also* Dance of Death
Dante, 324
David, Jean, 98
Davidson, Clifford, 290
Davis, Alice, 103
Day, Alexandra, 28
Day, John, 20, 145
Day, Martin, 45, 173, 174
    'A Mirror of Modesty', 173–77
Day, Richard, 21
de Calahorra, Diego Ortúñez, 320
de casibus, 223, 296
de Coligny, Gaspard, 160, 162
de Falco, Vittorio, 47

de La Primaudaye, Pierre, 232
de Navarre, Henri, 159, 161
de Navarre, Marguerite, 32, 46, 219, 283, 308
de Premierfait, Laurent, 296
de Serres, Jean, 159
de Valois, Marguerite, 159
de Vere, Henry, 241
de Voragine, Jacobus, 340
de Worde, Wynken, 58, 62, 63
de' Medici, Catherine, 159, 160, 161
Dealy, Ross, 215
death's head, 10, 20, 24, 25, 98, 100, 190, 347, *see also memento mori*; skull
deathbed, 11, 12, 35, 56, 91, 110, 112, 121, 184, 234, 248, 358, *see also ars moriendi; moriens*
Dekker, Thomas, 94, 131, 168, 170, 264
  News from Gravesend, 171–74
  The Wonderful Year, 171
Denham, John, 93
Derrida, Jacques, 6
Desan, Philippe, 236
Descartes, René, 10, 266, 267, 276
Devereaux, Robert (The 2nd Earl of Essex), 90, 155, 334, 335
Dio Cassius, 248
Dobson, Mary J., 3
Dodds, Gregory D., 214
Doerksen, Daniel W., 177
Dollimore, Jonathan, 330
Donne, John, 13, 22, 32, 35, 44, 216, 312, 362
Dowd, Michelle M., 29
Dowriche, Anne, 28, 159, 160
  The French History, 159–63
Drayton, Michael, 240
Driver, Martha W., 65
Dryden, John, 270
Du Laurens, André, 31, 250
Dubrow, Heather, 72
Duclow, Donald F., 295
Dudley, Ambrose, 307
Dudley, Robert, 233
Duffy, Eamon, 2, 8, 129, 130, 145
Dugdale, William, 130, 296, 298
Durston, Christopher, 5
Dutton, Richard, 35
Dymond, David, 33

Eales, Jacqueline, 5
Earle, John, 315
Earle, T. F., 36, 65
Eden, Richard, 41, 42
Edgcombe, Pearse, 159
Edward I, 303
Edward III, 303
Edward IV, 55
Ellinghausen, Laurie, 319
Elton, G. R., 136
Elyot, Thomas, 44, 215, 216, 227, 313
  A Preservative against Death, 215–18
Empedocles, 45
Engel, William E., 20, 22, 37, 60, 85, 282
Epicurus, 217, 271
Erasmus, Desiderius, 11, 65, 66, 207, 208, 211, 213, 215, 239, 313, 314
Erickson, Peter, 36
Eriksen, Roy T., 314
Euclid, 47
eudaimonia, 51
Euripides, 311
Evans, Robert C., 290
exempla, 120, 134, 209, 220, 223, 230, 237, 282, 335, 340, 351
Ezell, Margaret J. M., 28

Fairfax, Edward, 43
Fairfax, Thomas, 362
Farnaby, Thomas, 206
Faulkner, T. C., 31
Fawkes, Guy, 178
Featley, Daniel, 40
Felch, Susan M., 145
Fell, Margaret, 29
Ferguson, Moira, 40
Ferrand, Jacques, 31
Ferrell, Lori Anne, 181
Ferrers, George, 222
Fifield, Merle, 295
Finch, John, 275
Finkelpearl, Philip J., 193
Finlay, Roger, 3
Fischer, Klaus P., 37
Fisher, John, 69, 80
  A Spiritual Consolation, 80–83
Fitzgeffrey, Henry, 189

FitzWalter, Robert, 340
Flacius Illyricus, Matthias, 212
Fletcher, Anthony, 122
Fletcher, John, 188
Florio, John, 233, 273
   Montaigne's Essays, 233–37
Forrest, Benjamin K., 87
Foucault, Michel, 8, 131
Fowler, Katia, 197, 201
Foxe, John, 76, 145, 146
   Acts and Monuments (*Book of Martyrs*), 145–50
Frederick V, Elector Palatine of the Rhine, 188
Freeman, Thomas S., 149
Fritz, Paul S., 30
Fuchs, Barbara, 31
Fuchs, Leonhart, 227
Fuller, Thomas, 70
Fumerton, Patricia, 108

Galba, 248
Galen, 208, 226, 227, 228
Gallagher, Catherine, 369, 371
Gardiner, Stephen, 133
Garnier, Robert, 163
Garrison, John S., 34
Gascoigne, George, 12, 21, 59, 310, 314, 315
   'Gascoigne's Goodnight', 310–14
Gassendi, Pierre, 267
Gauden, John, 185
Gentillet, Innocent, 159, 161
Geoffrey of Monmouth, 222
Gertsman, Elina, 15, 303
Gibb, John, 294
Gieskes, Edward, 86
Gill, John, 190
Gilman, Donald, 295
Gilman, Ernest B., 173
Gittings, Clare, 2, 8, 130
Glass, David, 263, 266
Godley, A. D., 289
Goeglein, Tamara A., 20
Goldberg, Jonathan, 34
Goodwin, Thomas, 361
Goold, G. P., 329
Gordon, Bruce, 2

Gosson, Stephen, 237
Gower, John, 59
Grafton, Richard, 133, 145, 222
Graunt, John, 30, 131, 209, 263
   Natural and Political Observations, 263–66
graveyard, 33, 308, *see also* monument; tomb
Gray's Inn, 188, 310
Great Fire of London, the, 199, 263
Greenblatt, Stephen, 112
Greene, Robert, 83, 86, 237, 310
   The Repentance of Robert Greene, 83–86
Gregory XIII, Pope, 159
Gregory, St, 300
Greville, Fulke, 155
Grey, Jane, 136, 205
Griffin, Megan, 372
Griffin, Melanie, 369
Gritzner, Karoline, 32
Grymeston, Elizabeth, 205
Guerrini, Anita, 108
Guthke, Karl S., 30, 35
Guyer, Benjamin, 116
Gwara, Joseph J., 58

Habib, Imtiaz, 36
Hackett, Helen, 164
Hadfield, Andrew, 259
Hall, Edward, 133, 145, 222
Hall, Edward and Richard Grafton
   Chronicles, 133–36
Hall, Joseph, 94
Hall, Kim F., 36, 39
Hampton Court, 361
Hannay, Margaret P., 164, 357
Harding, Vanessa, 3, 14
Harlan, Susan, 158
Harvey, Gabriel, 259
Hastings, Elizabeth, 201
Hastings, Henry, 189
Heaven, 2, 3, 22, 46, 75, 81, 83, 95, 113, 193, 202, 241, 277, 294, 346, 351, 352, 364, *see also* Hell; Purgatory
Hefling, Charles, 140
Heisch, Dorothea, 236
Helen of Troy, 39, 40
Helfer, Rebeca, 22

Hell, v, 2, 9, 52, 71, 76, 84, 85, 86, 120, 126, 127, 140, 143, 144, 217, 218, 271, 276, 290, 292, 322, 326, 328, 329, 330, 332, 333, 343, 361, *see also* Heaven; Purgatory
Heller, Jennifer Louise, 93
Heng, Geraldine, 36
Heninger, S. K., 45
Henri IV of France, 250
Henrietta Maria, 94, 95
Henry IV, 295
Henry V, 295
Henry VI, 295, 296
Henry VIII, 52, 69, 80, 133, 136, 141, 146, 211, 212, 215, 218, 222, 303, 315
Heraclitus, 45
Herbert, George, 33, 362
Herbert, Henry, 163, 357
Herbert, Philip, 357, 358
Herbert, Susan, 354
Hesiod, 22, 45
Heywood, Thomas, 43, 181, 183, 348, 351
  The Phoenix of these Late Times, 181–84
Hickock, Thomas, 42
Higgins, John, 222
Hill, Robert, 6
Hippocrates, 226, 228, 239
Hiscock, Andrew, 282, 307
Hobbes, Thomas, 259, 266, 267, 275
Hobby, Elaine, 29
Hogrefe, Pearl, 218
Holbein, Hans, 11, 20, 35, 301
Holinshed, Raphael, 324
Holland, Abraham, 21, 38, 240
  Navmachia, 240–45
Holland, Philemon, 240
Hollingdale, R. J., 9
Holmberg, Eva Johanna, 262
Homer, 45, 270, 287
Hopkins, Lisa, 41
Hopman, Frederik Jan, 8
Horace, 16, 212, 213, 234, 235, 237, 249, 270, 288
Horrox, Rosemary, 37
Horstmanshoff, H. F. J., 229
Hotman, François, 159
Houlbrooke, Ralph, 5, 8, 122, 196
hourglass, 22, 23, 24, 111, 252, 331, 333, 335
Hourihane, Colum, 14

House of Lords, the, 178
Howard, Catherine, 133
Howard, Frances, 334
Howard, Henry, 31, 73, 222, 303
  'Complaint of a Dying Lover', 303–7
Howard, Jean E., 35
Howard, Thomas, 133, 320
Howard, W. Scott, 198, 201
Hugh of St Victor, 213
Hughes, Merritt Y., 22
Huizinga, Johan, 8, 9
Humphrey, Duke of Gloucester, 295
Husken, Wim, 60
Hussey, Stephen, 122
Hutton, Sarah, 275, 278
Hyde, Edward, 185

Iamblichus, 47
Imhof, Arthur, 8
imitatio Christi, 351
Inner Temple, 188
Innocent III, Pope, 192, 212
Islam, 37, 207, 261

Jackson, John, 248
Jackson, MacDonald P., 34
James II, 125, 369
James, Felicity, 119
Janeway, James, 27, 120
  A Token for Children, 120–22
Janofsky, Klaus P., 83
Jeanes, Gordon, 140
Jensen, Phebe, 65, 255
Jerome, St, 20, 24, 216
Jerome, Stephen, 4, 50
Jews or Judaism, 37, 180, 207, 259, 260, 323, 339
Johanyak, Debra, 37
John of England, 340
Jones, Eldred, 39
Jones, P. E., 3
Jones, Richard, 314
Jones, W. H. S., 228
Jonson, Ben, 168, 264, 281, 323
  The Alchemist, 264
  Volpone, 281
Josephus, 237
Jowett, John, 83, 86

Judges, A. V., 3
Jupiter, 169
Jussen, Bernhard, 33
Juvenal, 212, 237, 248, 270

Kane, Stuart A., 104, 108
Kargon, Robert, 266
Kastan, David Scott, 330
Kay, Dennis, 130
Kaylor, Jr., Noel Harold, 219
Kelly, Morgan, 4
Kemp, Geoff, 188
Kempe, Robert, 90
Kempe, William, 90
Kendal, Gordon, 236
Kennedy, Kathleen E., 65
Kiernan, Michael, 247, 248, 249
Kiessling, N. K., 31
King, Helen, 229
King, John N., 150
King, Kevin L., 87
King's Bench Prison, 76
Kinney, Arthur F., 24, 158
Kishi, Tetsuo, 39
Knight, Kevin, 294
Knutson, Roslyn L., 39
Kramnick, Jonathan, 274
Kreider, Alan, 129
Kristeller, Paul Oskar, 207
Kühn, C. G., 228

Lacan, Jacques, 10
Lamb, Mary Ellen, 357
Landsberg, Paul L., 8
Lange, Marianne, 158
Langland, William, 223, 285, 355
Lant, Thomas, 156
Lanyer, Aemilia, 27, 209, 339
    Salve Deus Rex Judaeorum, 281, 339–43
Laqueur, Thomas W., 8
Latz, Dorothy L., 112
Laud, William, 112, 259
Lavagnino, John, 34
Lawes, Henry, 197
Lawrence, Dana E., 319
Le Duff, Pierre, 103
Leander of Seville, 212
Leibniz, Gottfried, 275

Leigh, Dorothy, 27, 90
    The Mother's Blessing, 90–93
Leigh, Ralph, 90
Leigh, William, 127
Lemnius, Levinus, 227
Levett, William, 185
Levin, Carole, 27
Lewis, Rhodri, 251
Liew, Warren M., 33
life expectancy, 3
Lily, William, 65
Lim, Walter S. H., 37
Lindely, David, 339
Linebaugh, Peter, 126
Linster, Jillian Faith, 256
Lipsius, Justus, 237
Livy, 240
Llewellyn, Kathleen M., 32
Llewellyn, Nigel, 14
Locher, Jakob, 285
Locke, Anne, 72, 76, 145
    'A Meditation of a Penitent Sinner', 72–76
Lodge, Thomas, 208, 237
    The Works of Seneca, 237–40
Loewenstein, David, 29
London Bridge, 134, 150
Loomba, Ania, 36, 39
Loughnane, Rory, 1, 22, 85, 282
Lowe, K. J. P., 36, 65
Lucan, 240
Lucas, Scott, 225
Lucretius, 208, 234, 236, 270, 271
Ludgate Prison, 133
Lupset, Thomas, 11, 12, 51, 55, 65
    The Way of Dying Well, 65–68
Luther, Martin, 70, 211, 212
Lydgate, John, 15, 42, 223, 286, 295, 297
    The Dance of Death, 295–303
Lyly, John, 320

MacCulloch, Diarmaid, 136, 140, 207, 208
MacDonald, Michael, 33
Mack, Peter, 214
Maddicott, J. R., 36
Magnusson, Lynne A., 232
Malcolm, Noel, 38
Mâle, Emile, 14, 24
Maley, Willy, 155, 259

INDEX

Mallory, Thomas, 55
Manilius, 234, 235, 270
Manning, John, 20
Marchant, Guyot, 58
Margaret of York, 55
Markham, Bridget, 189
Marlowe, Christopher, 34, 44, 142, 160, 323
   Doctor Faustus, 142, 281, 293, 327–30
   Edward II, 281, 323–27, 337
   Hero and Leander, 323
   Tamburlaine, 323
   The Jew of Malta, 323
   The Massacre at Paris, 160
Marotti, Arthur, 222, 323
Marshall, Peter, 2, 8, 129, 130, 153
Marston, John, 32, 104
Martial, 240
Martin, Jessica, 145
Martin, Randall, 163
martyrdom, xiii, 70, 76, 80, 184, 185, 186, 304, 369
Marvell, Andrew, 45, 362
   'The Nymph Complaining for the Death of her Fawn', 362–68
Marvell, Mary, 362
Mary II, 209
Maslen, Robert, 173
Massing, Jean Michel, 40
Matar, Nabil, 262
Matchinske, Megan, 163
McCullough, Peter, 29, 181
McDonald, Joyce Green, 39
McKenzie, Andrea, 126
McPherson, Kathryn R., 27
McQuade, Paula, 29
McRae, Andrew, 98
Melchiori, Giorgio, 104
Mellor, Anne K., 28
Melnikoff, Kirk, 25, 86, 319
memento mori, 1, 4, 7, 10, 11, 15, 19, 20, 28, 38, 50, 51, 59, 70, 113, 175, 189, 212, 216, 223, 296, 308, 309, 311, 344, *see also* death's head; *vanitas*
Middle Temple, 215
Middleton, Thomas, 33, 168, 171, 281
   The Revenger's Tragedy, 344
   Women Beware Women, 281

Milioni, Dwayne, 87
Miller, Kathleen, 174
Miller, Naomi J., 27
Miller, Walter, 57
Mills, R. J. W., 262
Milton, John, 22, 44, 185
   Paradise Lost, 313
Mnemosyne, 169
Montaigne, Michel de, 12, 233, 234, 246
monument, 10, 19, 45, 175, 177, 185, 197, 198, 199, 255, 304, 363, *see also* graveyard; tomb
Moore, Helen, 214
More, Henry, 266, 275
More, John, 51
More, Thomas, 11, 66, 133, 205, 211
moriens, 11, 55, 56, 186, 312, *see also* ars *moriendi*; deathbed
Morin-Parsons, Kel, 76
Mortimer, Nigel, 295
Most, Glenn W., 22
Mountford, Thomas, 175
Mueller, Janel, 29, 72
Muñoz, Victoria, 323
Murphy, Terence R., 33
Murray, A. T., 13
Mynors, R. A. B., 213, 239, 313, 314

Nashe, Thomas, 310, 315
Neill, Michael, 9, 36, 39, 330
Nelson, Holly Faith, 188
Neoplatonism, 47, 201
Nero, 207, 238
New Science, 22, 266
Newcomb, Lori Humphrey, 84
Newgate Prison, 107, 123, 124, 150
Newman, Kira L. S., 98
Nietzsche, Friedrich Wilhelm, 9
Nine Years War, the, 256
North, Edward, 215
Notary, Julian, 58

Ó Gráda, Cormac, 4
O'Brien, Murrough, 257
O'Connor, Mary Catharine, 42
Oberman, Heiko, 37
Oldisworth, Michael, 359

Ortelius, Abraham, 350
Orvis, David L., 35
Orwin, Thomas, 230
Ostovich, Helen, 76
Otes, Samuel, 13
Ottoman Empire, 37, 38, 241
Overbury, Thomas, 334, 335
Ovid, 34, 45, 55, 181, 270, 277, 287, 315, 329, 363, 367
   Ars Amatoria, 181
   Heroides, 315
   Metamorphoses, 34, 55, 363
Owen, Anne, 197
Owen, George, 109
Owen, Jane, 12, 46, 109
   An Antidote against Purgatory, 109–12

Pacheco, Anita, 29
Painter, William, 32, 307
   'A Strange Punishment', 307–10
Panek, Jennifer, 32
Panofsky, Erwin, 14, 23
Paré, Ambroise, 250
Parker, Patricia, 39
Parr, Katherine, v, 69, 72, 146, 219, 294, 351
   The Lamentation of a Sinner, 69–72
Parry, Graham, 368
Parsons, Robert, 84, 247
Paster, Gail Kern, 10
Patericke, Simon, 159
Paton, W. R., 300
Patrides, C. A., 350
Patterson, W. B., 29, 89
Paul, Ryan Singh, 35
Paul, St, 13, 71, 253
Paulinus, Pompeius, 239
Paynell, Thomas, 211
   The Despising of the World, 211–15
Peacham, Henry, 24, 25
Pender, Patricia, 28, 149
Perkins, William, 29, 57, 86, 294
   A Salve For A Sick Man, 86–89
Perrin, Bernadotte, 213
Perry, Nandra, 354
Pervo, Richard I., 151
Perwich, Robert, 117
Perwich, Susanna, 117, 118

Petrarch, Francesco, 163, 189, 207, 304
Pettegree, Andrew, 25
Petty, William, 263
Philip II of Spain, 320
Philip, Francis, 66
Philips, James, 196
Philips, John, 153, 354
   The Life and Death of Sir Philip Sidney, 153–58
Philips, Katherine, 27, 34, 196, 201
   Poems, 196–201
Phillippy, Patricia, 30, 35, 39
Phillips, Philip Edward, 219
Philo, John-Mark, 219
Pickering, Danby, 34
Pierce, Helen, 188
Pigman III, G. W., 314
Plat, Hugh, 315
Plato, 51, 57, 207, 217, 250
Pliny, 183, 240
Plotinus, 47
Plutarch, 16, 213, 240, 246, 248, 287
Pole, Reginald, 65, 66, 68
Poliakov, Léon, 37
Pope, Alexander, 270
Postlewate, Laurie, 60
Poussin, Nicholas, 19
Prescott, Anne Lake, 222
Pringle, Roger, 39
Purgatory, 2, 9, 52, 82, 109, 110, 111, 126, 129, 137, 141, 142, 194, 328, *see also* Heaven; Hell
Purim, 180
Pynson, Richard, 58, 296
Pythagoras, 45, 328, 330

Quarles, Francis, 98

Ralegh, Walter, 259
Ramona, Wray, 354
Rand, E. K., 45
Rashidi, Runoko, 39
Rasmussen, Eric, 291, 295
Raymond, Joad, 334
Razzell, Peter, 3
Rebholz, R. A., 365
Rebhorn, Wayne A., 305

Rhatigan, Emma, 29
Rhodes, Neil, 236
Rice, Eugene F., 216
Richard III, 359
Richards, Cynthia, 369, 371
Richards, Jennifer, 229
Richardson, Laurence, 150, 152, 153
Riehl, Anna, 39
Rivière, Pierre, 285
Roberts, Josephine, 357
Robertson, D. W., 292
Robisheaux, Thomas, 8
Roche Dasent, John, 41
Roebuck, Graham, 76
Rogers, John, 343
Rolfe, J. C., 248
Rollenhagen, Gabriel, 98, 99
Ross, Alexander, 37, 259
   A View of All Religions in the World, 259–62
Ross, Sarah, 72
Rowlands, Samuel, 22, 43, 44, 282, 331, 335
   A Terrible Battle, 331–34
   Sir Thomas Overbury, 334–39
Royal Society, the, 245, 263, 265, 270
Rubens, Peter Paul, 22
Rudyerd, Benjamin, 190
Runacres, Ian, 245
Rylands, W. Harry, 11
Ryrie, Alec, 145
Rywiková, Daniela, 14

Salmon, J. H. M., 240
Sarasohn, Lisa T., 269
Sawday, Jonathan, 255
Schäfer, Daniel, 229
Schaff, Philip, 294
Schmitt, C. B., 207
Schofield, R. S., 3
Schurink, Fred, 214
Scobie, Edward, 41
Seneca, 51, 52, 66, 201, 208, 234, 237, 238, 247, 280, 350
Senellart, Michel, 131
Sessions, Barbara, 14
Seven Deadly Sins, the, 11, 14, 17, 291
Seven Heavenly Virtues, the, 291

Severus, Septimius, 248
Seznec, Jean, 14
Shackleton Bailey, D. R., 241
Shakespeare, William, 4, 39, 44, 237, 281, 308, 358
   2 Henry IV, 311
   A Midsummer Night's Dream, 41
   As You Like It, 237
   Cymbeline, 2, 355
   Hamlet, 142, 238, 281, 312, 344
   Measure for Measure, 1, 35
   Othello, 39
   Richard III, 121, 338
   Romeo and Juliet, 33, 35, 307
   Sonnets, 35
   The Comedy of Errors, 38
   The Merchant of Venice, 2, 281
   The Winter's Tale, 281
Shami, Jeanne, 29
Shattuck, Cynthia, 140
Sherburne, Edward, 280
Sheridan Smith, A. M., 8
Shinn, Abigail, 310
Shohet, Lauren, 28
Shore, Jane, 222
Shoulson, Jeffrey, 37
Showerman, Grant, 329
Shyllon, F. O., 41
Sidney, Mary, 27, 28, 155, 163, 282, 320, 354, 357
   'Doleful Lay of Clorinda', 163–67
Sidney, Philip, 31, 155, 156, 163, 164, 283, 320
Sidney, Robert, 354
Silcox, Mary V., 76
Simonides of Keos, 16
Six, Jeanine, 158
Skelton, Anne, 28, 50
Skelton, John, 24, 64, 189, 302
skull, 10, 19, 20, 21, 24, 33, 99, 102, 170, 308, 309, 344, 347, *see also* death's head; *memento mori*
Slack, Paul, 4
Smith, Bruce R., 35
Smith, David L., 362
Smith, Ian, 39
Smith, Nigel, 368

Smith, Rosalind, 72
Smith, Samuel, 107, 123, 126, 294
    'A True Account of … Last Dying Speeches', 123–26
Smithfield, 76, 105, 107
Snook, Edith, 93
Snyder, Susan, 221
Socrates, 51, 237
Solomon, 57
Souden, David, 184
Southerne, Thomas, 368
Southwark, 76
Sowaal, Alice, 204
speculum, 223, 321
Speght, Rachel, 279
Spence, Christine, 3
Spencer, Theodore, 33
Spenser, Edmund, 14, 21, 31, 45, 163, 164, 253, 256, 355
    'A View of the Present State of Ireland', 256–59
    Colin Clout's Come Home Again, 163
    The Faerie Queene, 14, 21, 45, 253, 256, 355
Spinoza, Baruch, 275
Spinrad, Phoebe S., 42
Spivak, Gayatri Chakravorty, 6
Sprat, Thomas, 265
Springborg, Patricia, 204
Spufford, Margaret, 29
St Bartholomew's Day Massacre, the, 159
Stallybrass, Peter, 330
Stanivukovic, Goran, 34
Stanwood, P. G., 116
Stegemeier, Henri, 38
Stein, Arnold, 22
Stewart, H. F., 45
Stockton, Will, 34
Stoicism, 41, 51, 212, 233, 234, 237, 238, 248, 351, 369
Stowe, John, 296
Strakhov, Elizaveta, 303
Strauss, Paul, 83
Streete, Adrian, 350
Strickland, Ronald, 46, 157, 158
Strier, Richard, 72
Strode, George, 13, 51

Stuart, Charles (Charles I), 94, 95, 112, 146, 168, 185, 241, 259, 358, 360, 363, 369
    Eikon Basilike, 185–88
Stuart, Charles (Charles II), 263, 369
Stuart, Henry, 178, 233, 343, 348
Stuart, James (James VI and I), 168, 173, 178, 188, 233, 241, 249, 334, 348, 354, 358
Stuart, Mary, 125
Stymeist, David, 327
Suetonius, 248
Sugg, Richard, 308, 310
Sullivan, Robert G., 218
Summers, Will, 315
Sutton, Christopher, 12

Tacitus, 219
Targoff, Ramie, 33, 35
Tasso, Torquato, 43
Taylor, Gary, 34
Taylor, Jeremy, 2, 51, 55, 87, 112, 114, 116, 202
    Holy Dying, 112–16
Taylor, John, 182
Tester, S. J., 45
Teter, Magda, 37
Theocritus, 270
Theophrastus, 315
Thomas, Keith, 27
Thompson, Ayanna, 36
Tiberius, 248
Tinkham, Audrey E., 343
Tittler, Robert, 130
Titus, 248
Tomaini, Thea, 14
tomb, 19, 33, 35, 130, 195, 197, 198, 199, 201, 206, 207, 288, 289, 304, 306, 332, 349, 354, 363, 367, *see also* graveyard; monument
Tomeo, Niccolò Leonico, 65
Tomkis, Thomas, 291
Topcliffe, Richard, 151, 152
Totaro, Rebecca, 98, 173
Tottel, Richard, 279, 296, 297, 299, 303
Tourneur, Cyril, 343
    'A Grief on the Death of Prince Henry', 348–50
    The Atheist's Tragedy, 281, 343–48

Tower of London, the, 80, 134, 135, 150, 307, 317, 334, 335
transi-tomb, 10, 19, 20, 189
Traub, Valerie, 30, 34, 35
Travitsky, Betty, 164, 319
Trechsel, Gaspar, 20
Trechsel, Melchior, 20
Tricomi, A. H., 361
Trismegistus, Hermes, 199
Tromly, Frederic B., 130
Tudor, Edward (Edward VI), 52, 136, 141, 219
Tudor, Elizabeth (Elizabeth I), 28, 35, 39, 46, 141, 142, 150, 151, 168, 212, 218, 219, 222
  A Godly Meditation, 218–22
Tudor, Mary (Mary I), 52, 136, 145, 150, 211, 219
Tuke, Thomas, 13, 372
Turi, Zita, 290
Turnebus, Adrianus, 195
Tyburn, 66, 85, 123, 124, 150
Tyler, Margaret, 28, 31, 44, 283, 320, 323
  The Mirror of Princely Deeds and Knighthood, 320–23
Tymme, Thomas, 159
Tyrwhit, Elizabeth, 145

ut pictura poesis, 24

Valla, Lorenzo, 207
van de Passe, Crispijn, 98
van der Laan, Adrie, 214
Van Dorsten, Jan, 158
van Helmont, Francis Mercury, 275
Van Sertima, Ivan, 39
vanitas, 13, 19, 99, 113, 189, 234, 286, *see also* death's head; *memento mori*
Vaughan, Henry, 311, 362
Vaughan, Richard, 112, 113
Vaughan, William, 32
Venn, Anne, 127
Vérard, Antoine, 58
Vere, Francis, 343
Vesalius, Andreas, 250, 309
Vespasian, 248
Vine, Angus, 249
Vinter, Maggie, 7, 330
Virgil, 270, 287, 303, 313

Viswanathan, S., 13
Vitellius, 248
Vitkus, Daniel J., 38
Vives, Juan Luis, 211
Vovelle, Michel, 8

Walker, John, 66, 68
Wall, Sarah E., 149
Wall, Wendy, 28
Waller, G. F., 164
Walløe, Lars, 36
Walvin, James, 41
Walzer, Arthur E., 218
Ware, James, 256
Wayne, Valerie, 26, 319
Wear, Andrew, 29, 229
Weaver, Helen, 8
Webster, Charles, 226
Webster, John, 32, 281, 308, 348
  The Duchess of Malfi, 281, 307, 308
Weever, John, 137
Weisman, Karen, 28, 130
Weiss, Penny A., 204
Welby, Henry, 181, 182, 183
Welch, Christina, 14
Wells, Stanley, 39
Wentworth, Thomas, 185
West-Pavlov, Russell, 177
Wheathill, Anne, 127
Whigham, Frank, 305
Whitchurch, Edward, 133
White, Carol Wayne, 276, 278
White, Micheline, 72, 145
Whitehall Palace, 188
Whitford, Richard, 7, 11, 13
Whitney, Geoffrey, 19, 21, 102
Whitney, Isabella, 43, 49, 283, 314
  'The Manner of her Will', 314–19
Wilcox, Helen, 164
William I of Orange-Nassau, 310
William III of Orange, 125, 209
Williams, Grant, 20, 22, 85, 282
Willis, John, 43
wills, 7, 10, 281
Wilson, Catherine, 274
Wilson, Louise, 236
winding sheet, 30
Winifred, St, 346

Winkler, Amanda Eubanks, 119
Wireker, Nigel, 286
Wither, George, 24, 46, 93, 101, 103, 168
   A Collection of Emblems, 98–103
   Britain's Remembrancer, 93–98
Wogan, Anne, 197
Wolsey, Thomas, 133, 209, 222
Wong, Alexander T., 33
Wood, Andy, 27
Woodcock, Matthew, 225
Wooding, Lucy E. C., 153
Woodstock Palace, 361
Wright, Louis B., 89
Wrigley, E. A., 3
Wriothesley, Thomas, 149

Wroth, Mary, 31, 45, 283, 354, 357
   Urania, 354–57
Wunderli, Richard, 80
Wyatt, Thomas, 73, 304, 365
Wyatt, William E., 13

Xenophon, 240, 241, 287
   Cyropaedia, 241

Yavneh, Naomi, 27
Young, Alan R., 20

Zanchius, Jerome, 195
Zeydel, Edwin H., 285
Zittel, Claus, 229